Shojo Beat

The Cain Saga

kafka

Earl Cain Series 3

Story & Art by Kaori Yuki

Read Kaori Yuki's entire
Earl Cain Series

Series 1:
The Cain Saga: Forgotten Juliet

Series 2:
The Cain Saga: The Sound of a Boy Hatching

Series 3:
The Cain Saga: Kafka

Series 4:
The Cain Saga: The Seal of the Red Ram, Parts 1 & 2

Series 5:
Godchild, Volumes 1-8

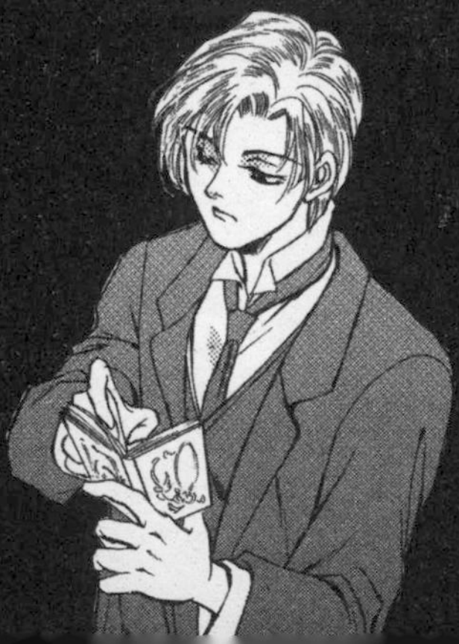

Y ou don't need to know the title to get that this third volume in
The Cain Saga is Kaori Yuki's ode to the style of Franz Kafka, the
German literary master of surreal paranoid delusion. You could
even argue that the entire *Earl Cain Series* begs at least thematic
comparison to that other Kafka classic of convolution, *The Trial*.
Here we meet the mysterious Justine, referenced later in *Godchild*, for the
first time. Jizabel fills in a horrid hole in Cain's family tree. And, in true
Kafkaesque fashion, we are treated to the mind-bending tale of a very confused young girl in the one-off, "Ellie in Summer Clothes."

Enjoy,
Joel Enos
Editor
Earl Cain Series

Contents

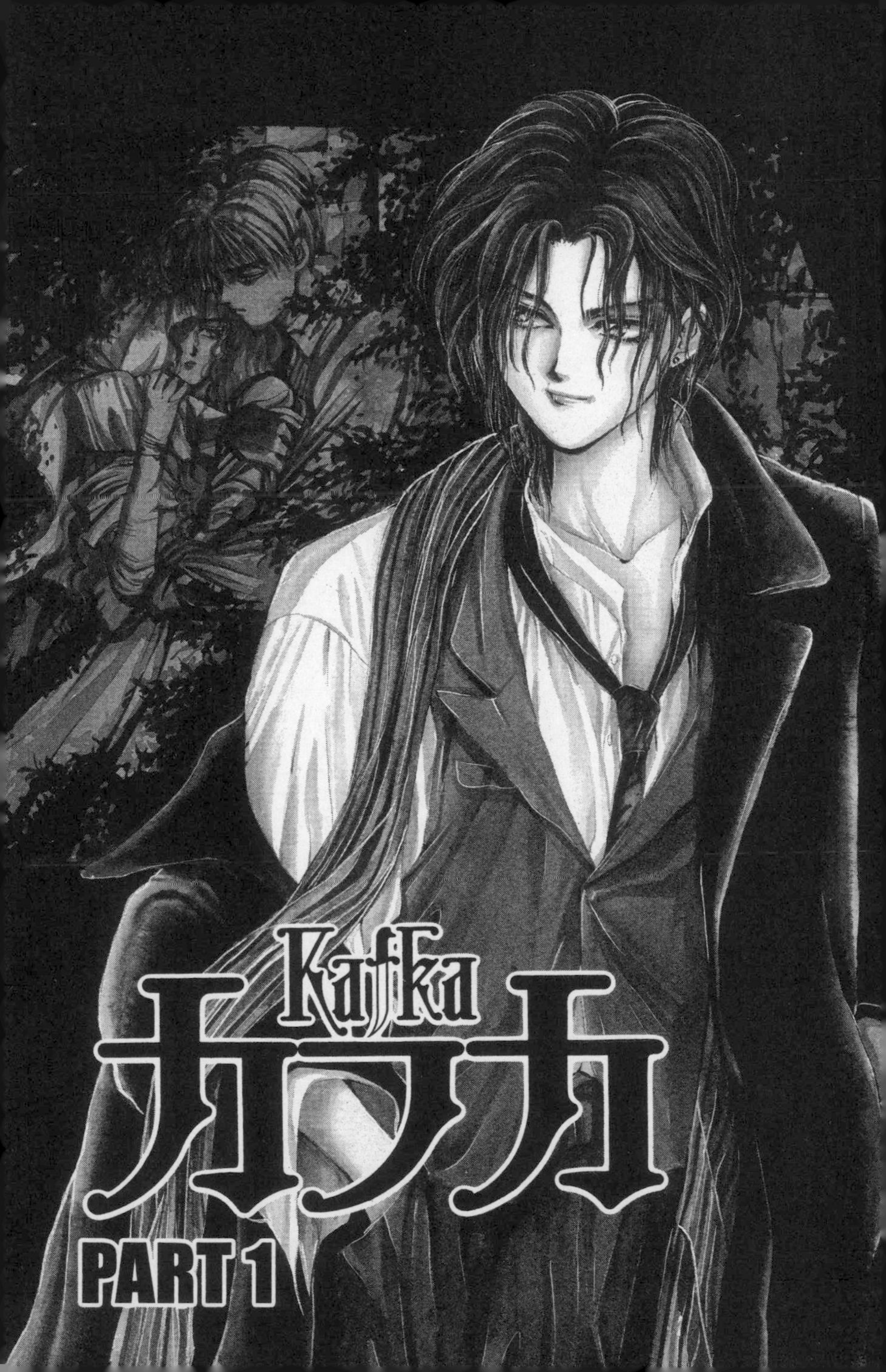

Kafka
カフカ
PART 1

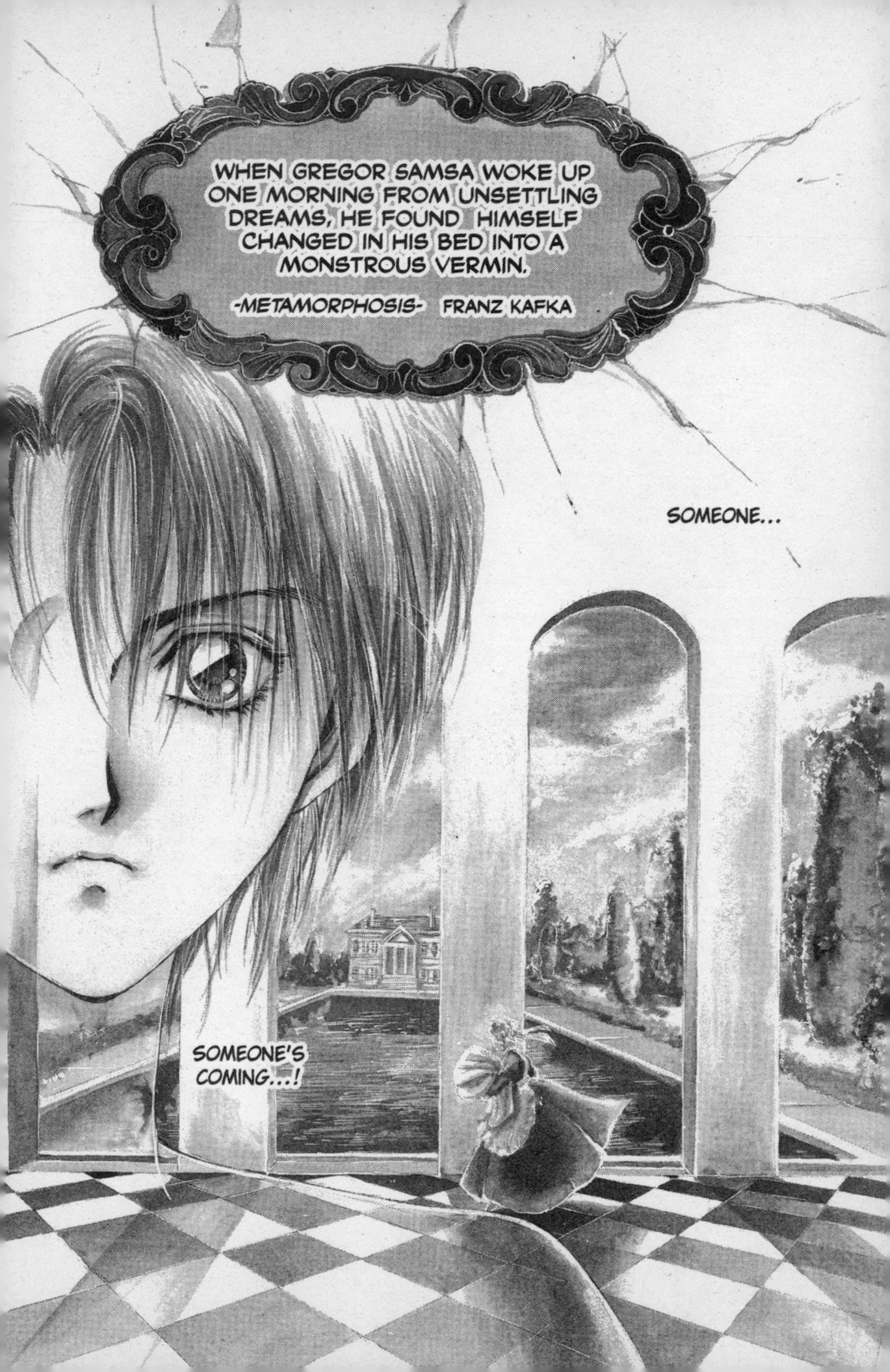
WHEN GREGOR SAMSA WOKE UP ONE MORNING FROM UNSETTLING DREAMS, HE FOUND HIMSELF CHANGED IN HIS BED INTO A MONSTROUS VERMIN.
-METAMORPHOSIS- FRANZ KAFKA
SOMEONE...
SOMEONE'S COMING...!

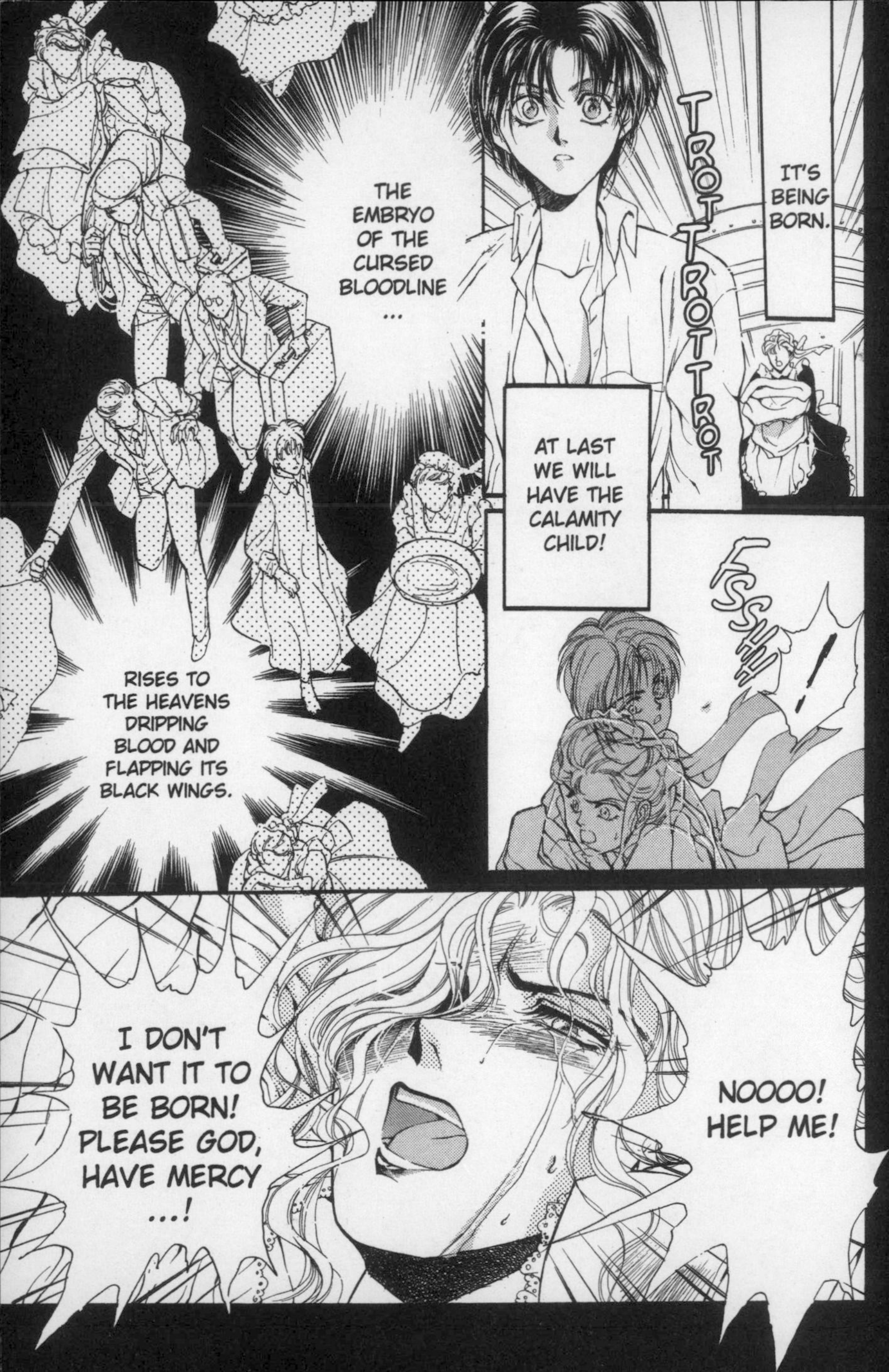

IT'S BEING BORN.
TROT TROT TROT TROT
AT LAST WE WILL HAVE THE CALAMITY CHILD!
FSSH!!
!
THE EMBRYO OF THE CURSED BLOODLINE ...
RISES TO THE HEAVENS DRIPPING BLOOD AND FLAPPING ITS BLACK WINGS.
NOOOO! HELP ME!
I DON'T WANT IT TO BE BORN! PLEASE GOD, HAVE MERCY ...!

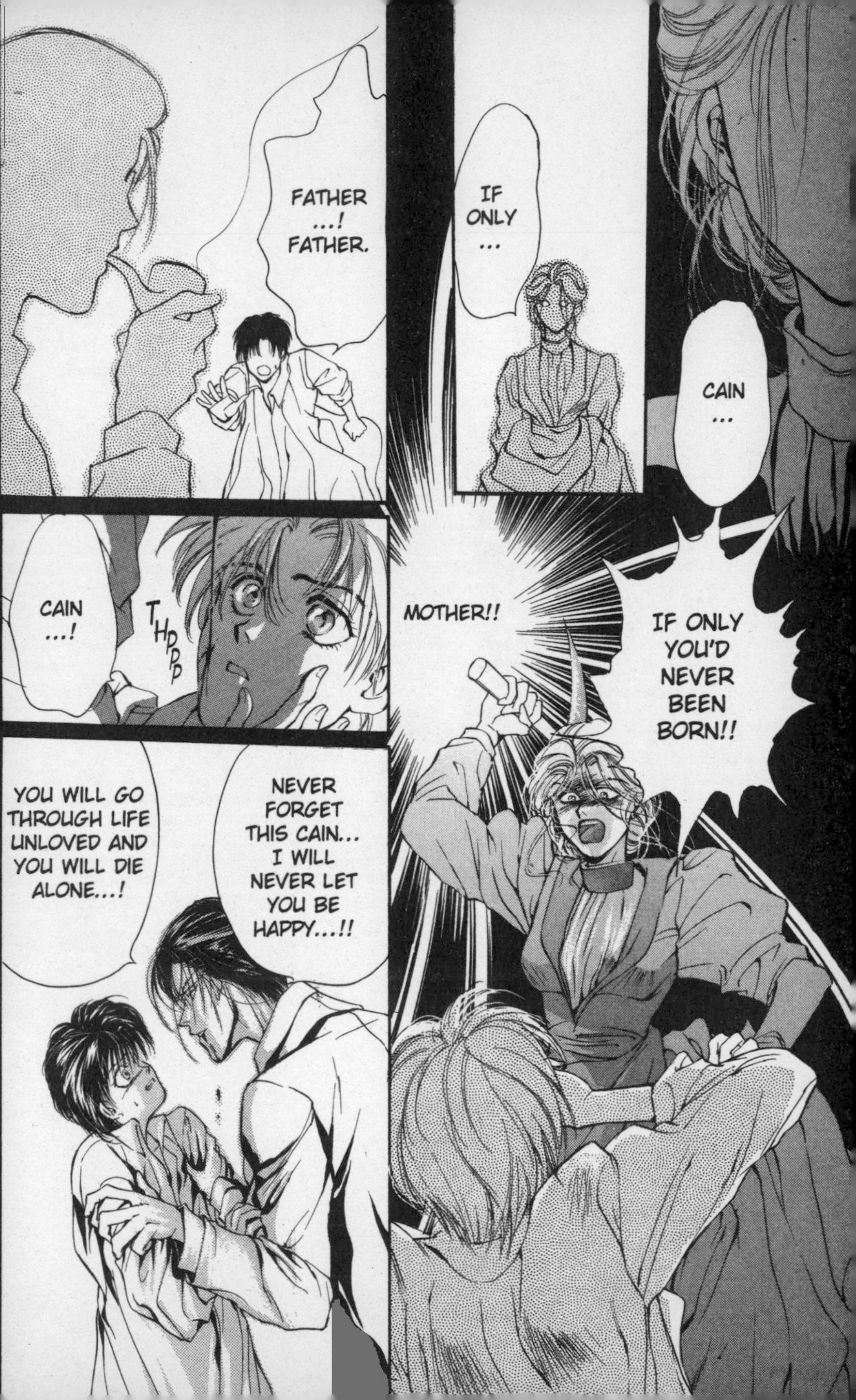
CAIN ...
IF ONLY ...
IF ONLY YOU'D NEVER BEEN BORN!!
MOTHER!!
FATHER ...! FATHER.
CAIN ...!
THPPP
NEVER FORGET THIS CAIN... I WILL NEVER LET YOU BE HAPPY...!!
YOU WILL GO THROUGH LIFE UNLOVED AND YOU WILL DIE ALONE...!

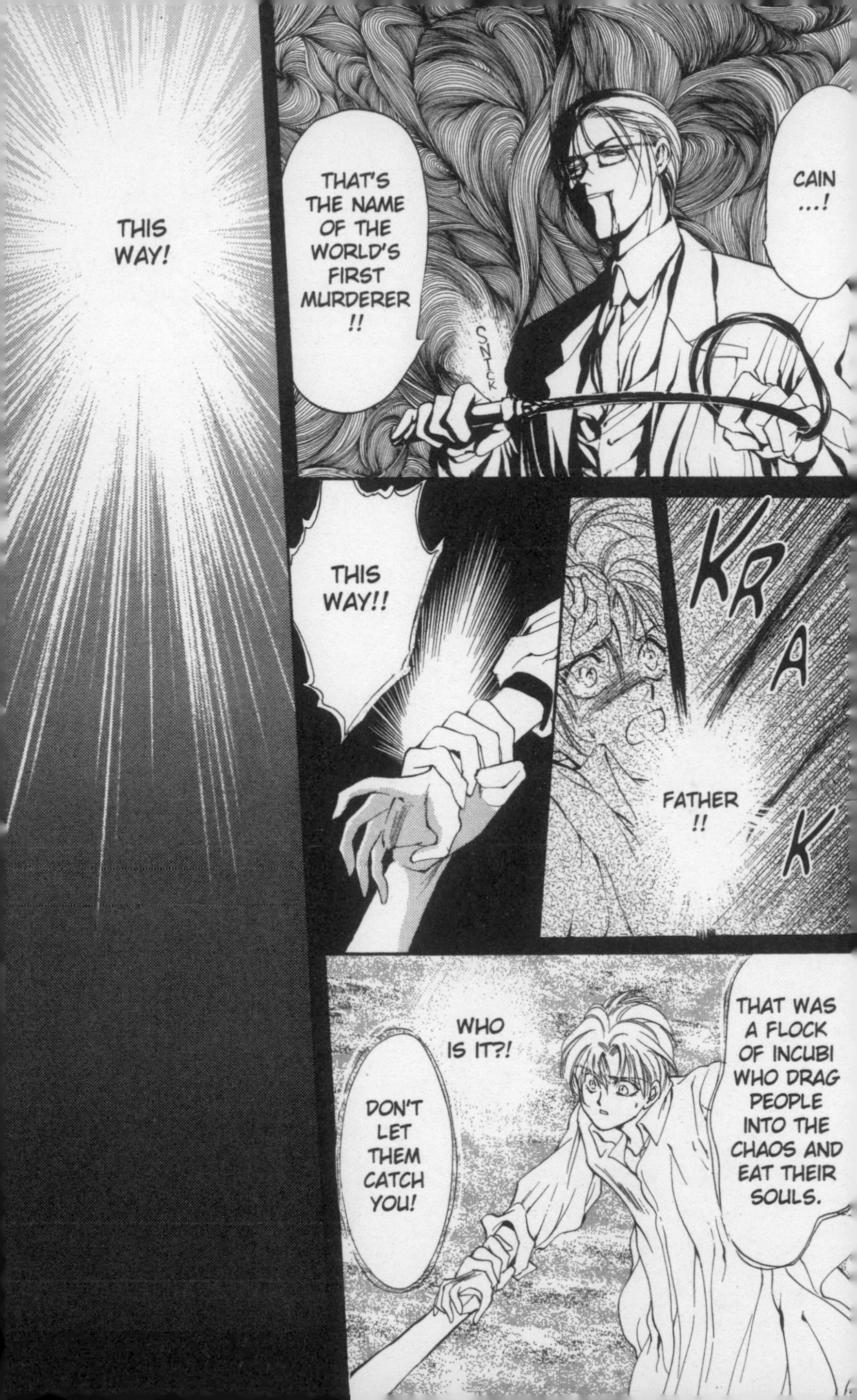
CAIN ...!
THAT'S THE NAME OF THE WORLD'S FIRST MURDERER !!
SNICK
KRAK
FATHER !!
THIS WAY!!
THAT WAS A FLOCK OF INCUBI WHO DRAG PEOPLE INTO THE CHAOS AND EAT THEIR SOULS.
WHO IS IT?!
DON'T LET THEM CATCH YOU!
THIS WAY!

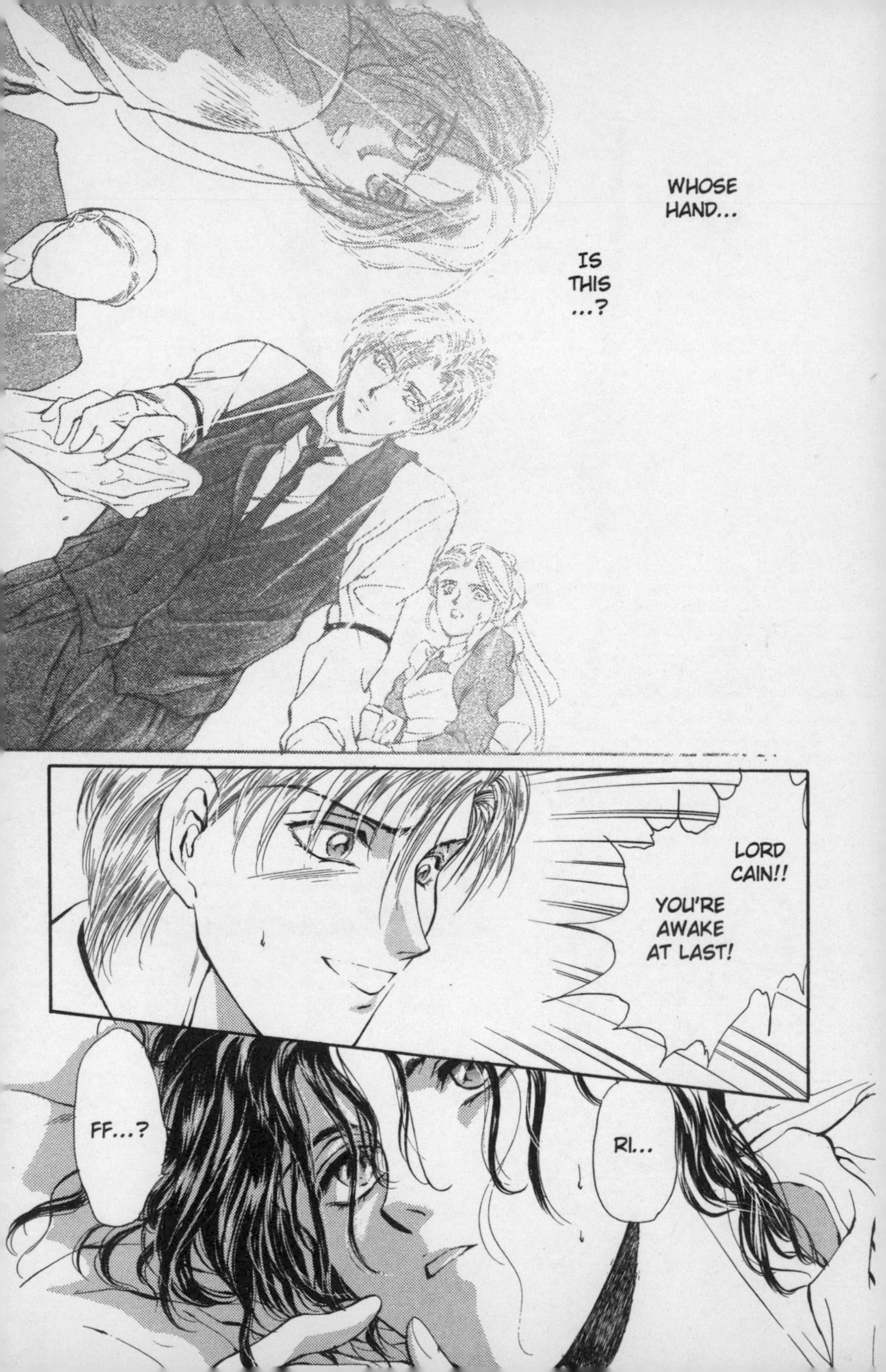
WHOSE HAND...
IS THIS ...?
LORD CAIN!!
YOU'RE AWAKE AT LAST!
RI...
FF...?

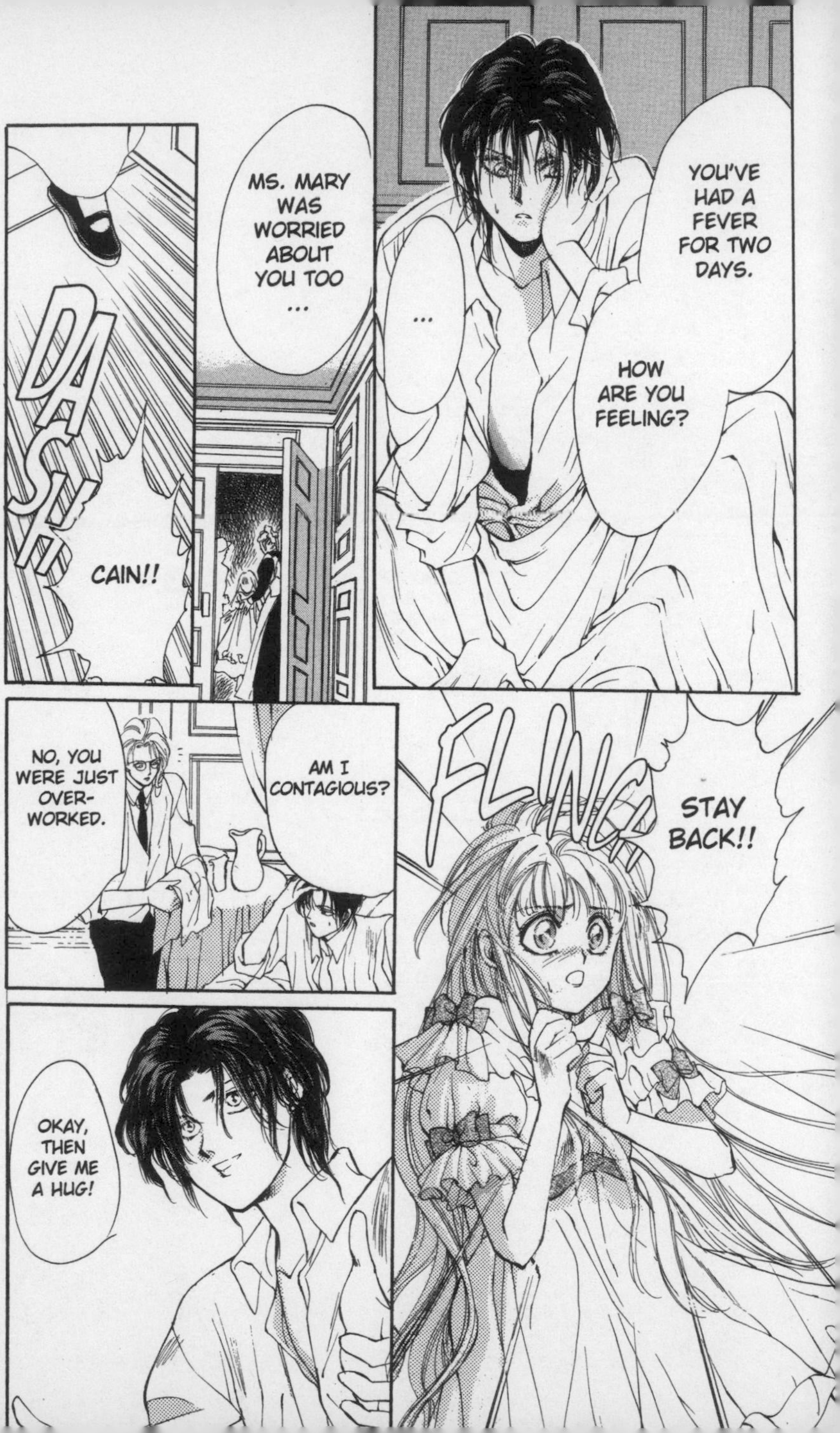
YOU'VE HAD A FEVER FOR TWO DAYS.
...
HOW ARE YOU FEELING?
MS. MARY WAS WORRIED ABOUT YOU TOO ...
DASH
CAIN!!
FLING
STAY BACK!!
AM I CONTAGIOUS?
NO, YOU WERE JUST OVER-WORKED.
OKAY, THEN GIVE ME A HUG!

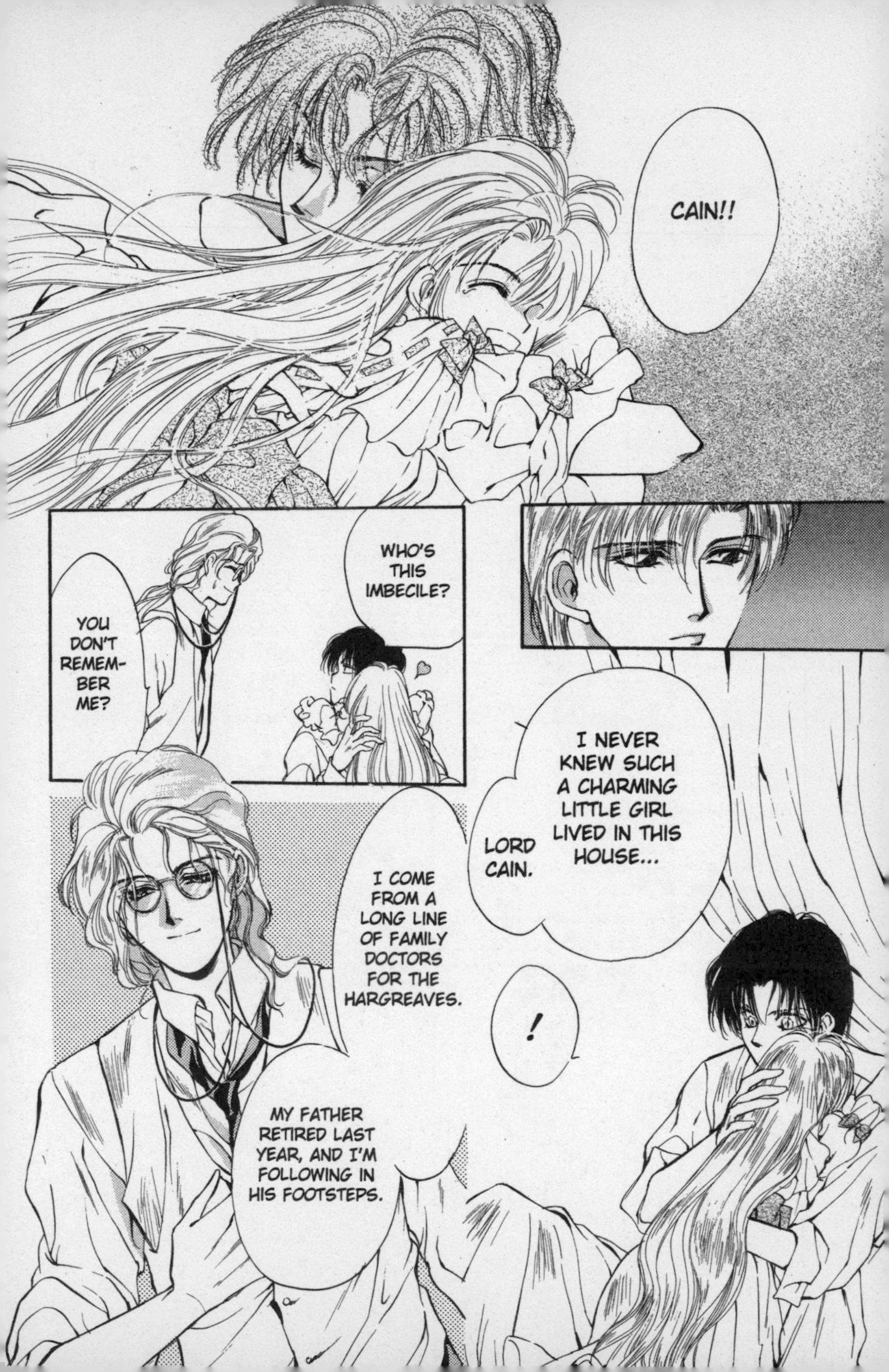
CAIN!!
WHO'S THIS IMBECILE?
YOU DON'T REMEM-BER ME?
I NEVER KNEW SUCH A CHARMING LITTLE GIRL LIVED IN THIS HOUSE...
LORD CAIN.
I COME FROM A LONG LINE OF FAMILY DOCTORS FOR THE HARGREAVES.
!
MY FATHER RETIRED LAST YEAR, AND I'M FOLLOWING IN HIS FOOTSTEPS.

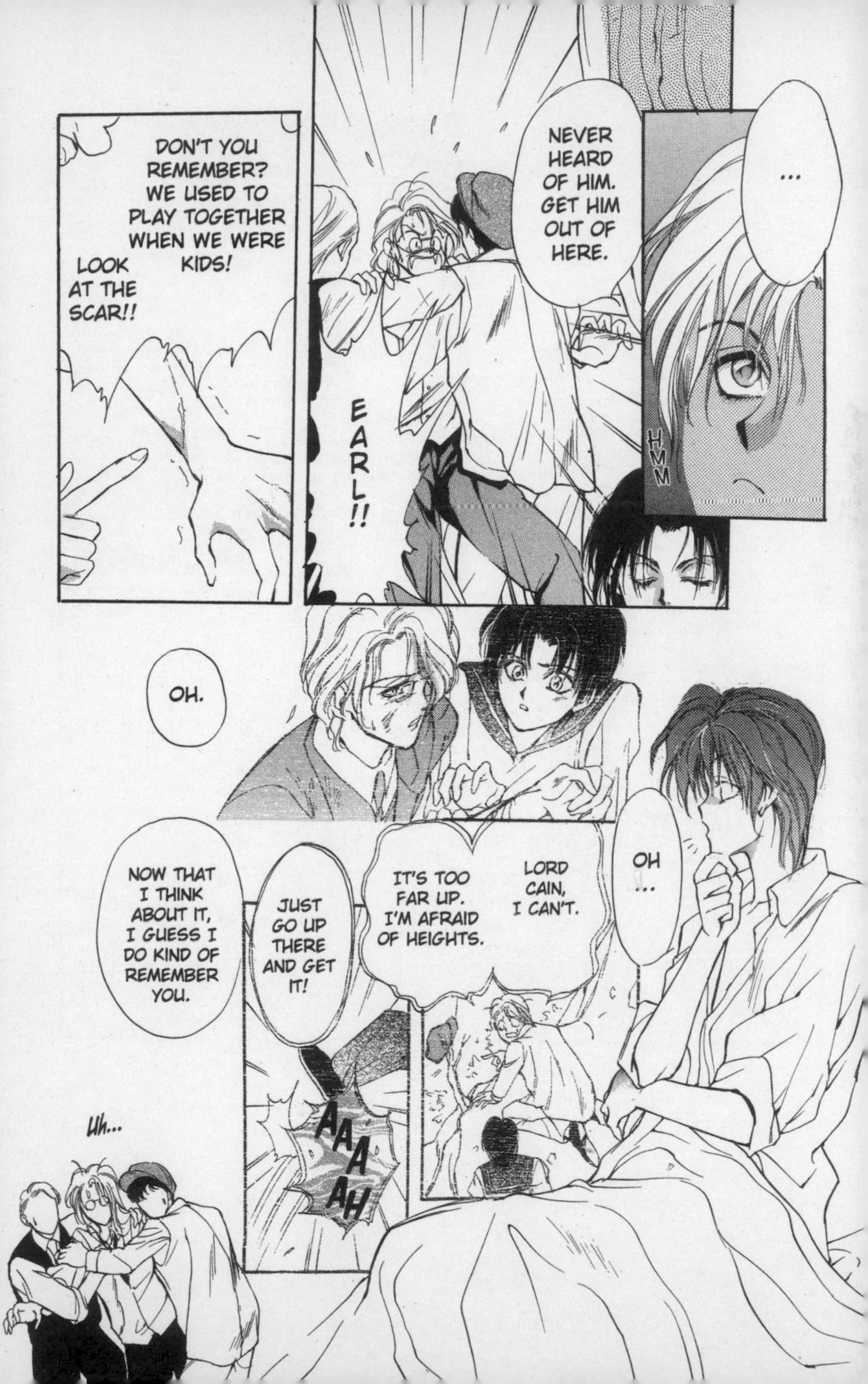
...
HMM
NEVER HEARD OF HIM. GET HIM OUT OF HERE.
EARL!!
DON'T YOU REMEMBER? WE USED TO PLAY TOGETHER WHEN WE WERE KIDS!
LOOK AT THE SCAR!!
OH.
OH...
LORD CAIN, I CAN'T.
IT'S TOO FAR UP. I'M AFRAID OF HEIGHTS.
JUST GO UP THERE AND GET IT!
AAAAH
NOW THAT I THINK ABOUT IT, I GUESS I DO KIND OF REMEMBER YOU.
Uh...

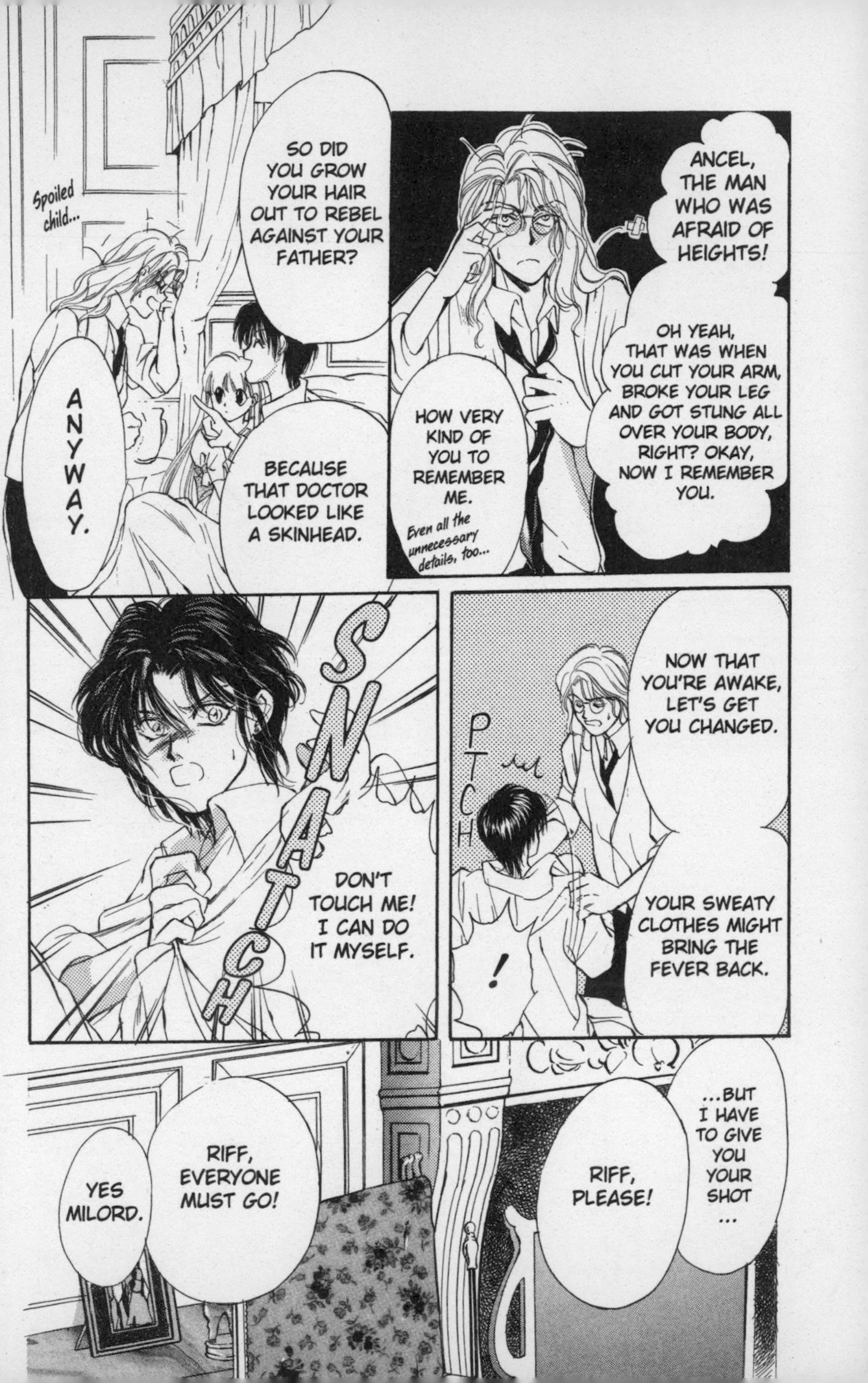
ANCEL, THE MAN WHO WAS AFRAID OF HEIGHTS!
OH YEAH, THAT WAS WHEN YOU CUT YOUR ARM, BROKE YOUR LEG AND GOT STUNG ALL OVER YOUR BODY, RIGHT? OKAY, NOW I REMEMBER YOU.
HOW VERY KIND OF YOU TO REMEMBER ME.
Even all the unnecessary details, too...
SO DID YOU GROW YOUR HAIR OUT TO REBEL AGAINST YOUR FATHER?
Spoiled child...
BECAUSE THAT DOCTOR LOOKED LIKE A SKINHEAD.
ANYWAY.
NOW THAT YOU'RE AWAKE, LET'S GET YOU CHANGED.
PTCH
YOUR SWEATY CLOTHES MIGHT BRING THE FEVER BACK.
!
SNATCH
DON'T TOUCH ME! I CAN DO IT MYSELF.
...BUT I HAVE TO GIVE YOU YOUR SHOT ...
RIFF, PLEASE!
RIFF, EVERYONE MUST GO!
YES MILORD.

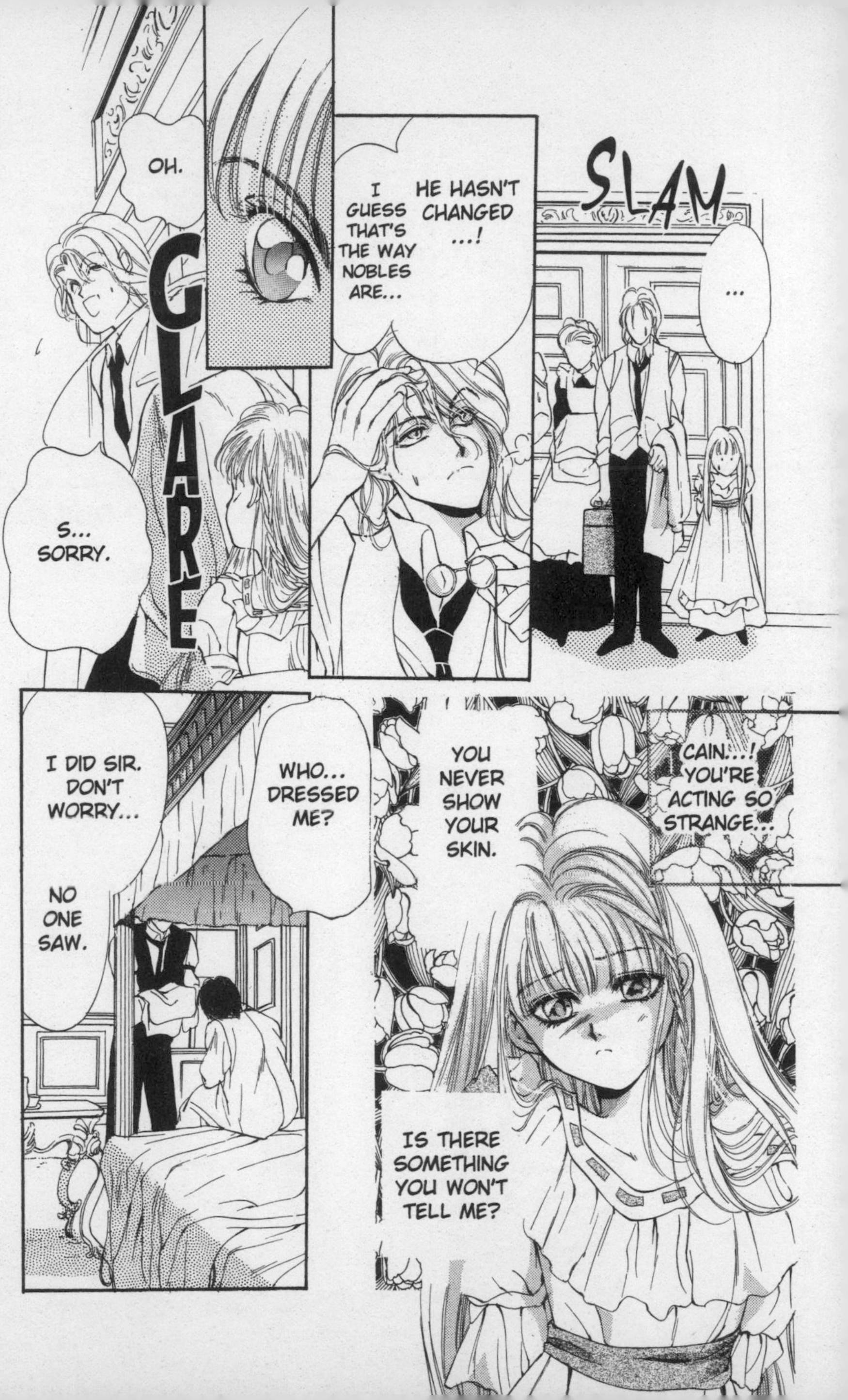
SLAM
...
HE HASN'T CHANGED ...!
I GUESS THAT'S THE WAY NOBLES ARE...
OH.
GLARE
S... SORRY.
CAIN...! YOU'RE ACTING SO STRANGE...
YOU NEVER SHOW YOUR SKIN.
IS THERE SOMETHING YOU WON'T TELL ME?
WHO... DRESSED ME?
I DID SIR. DON'T WORRY...
NO ONE SAW.

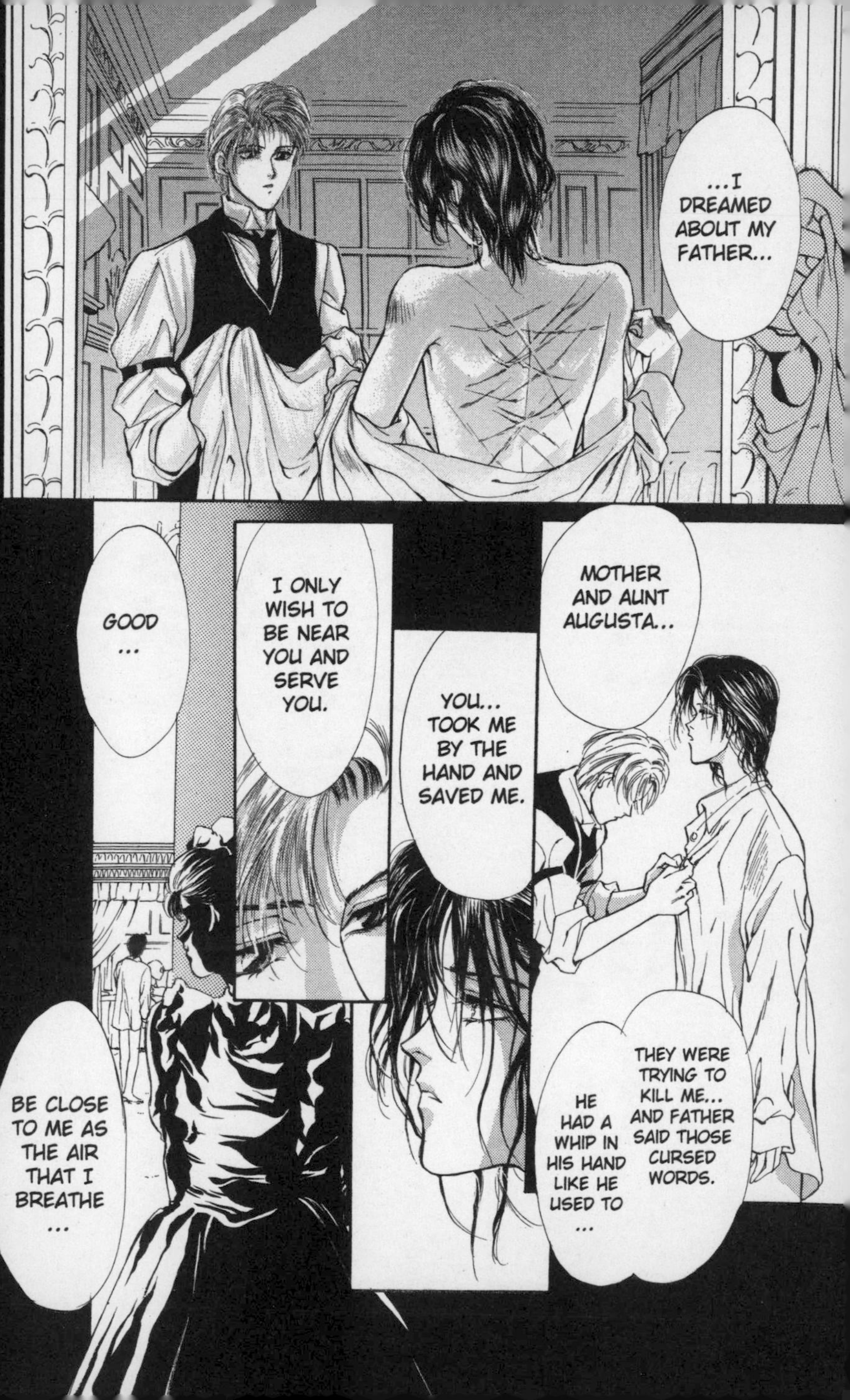
...I DREAMED ABOUT MY FATHER...
MOTHER AND AUNT AUGUSTA...
THEY WERE TRYING TO KILL ME... AND FATHER SAID THOSE CURSED WORDS.
HE HAD A WHIP IN HIS HAND LIKE HE USED TO ...
YOU... TOOK ME BY THE HAND AND SAVED ME.
I ONLY WISH TO BE NEAR YOU AND SERVE YOU.
GOOD ...
BE CLOSE TO ME AS THE AIR THAT I BREATHE ...

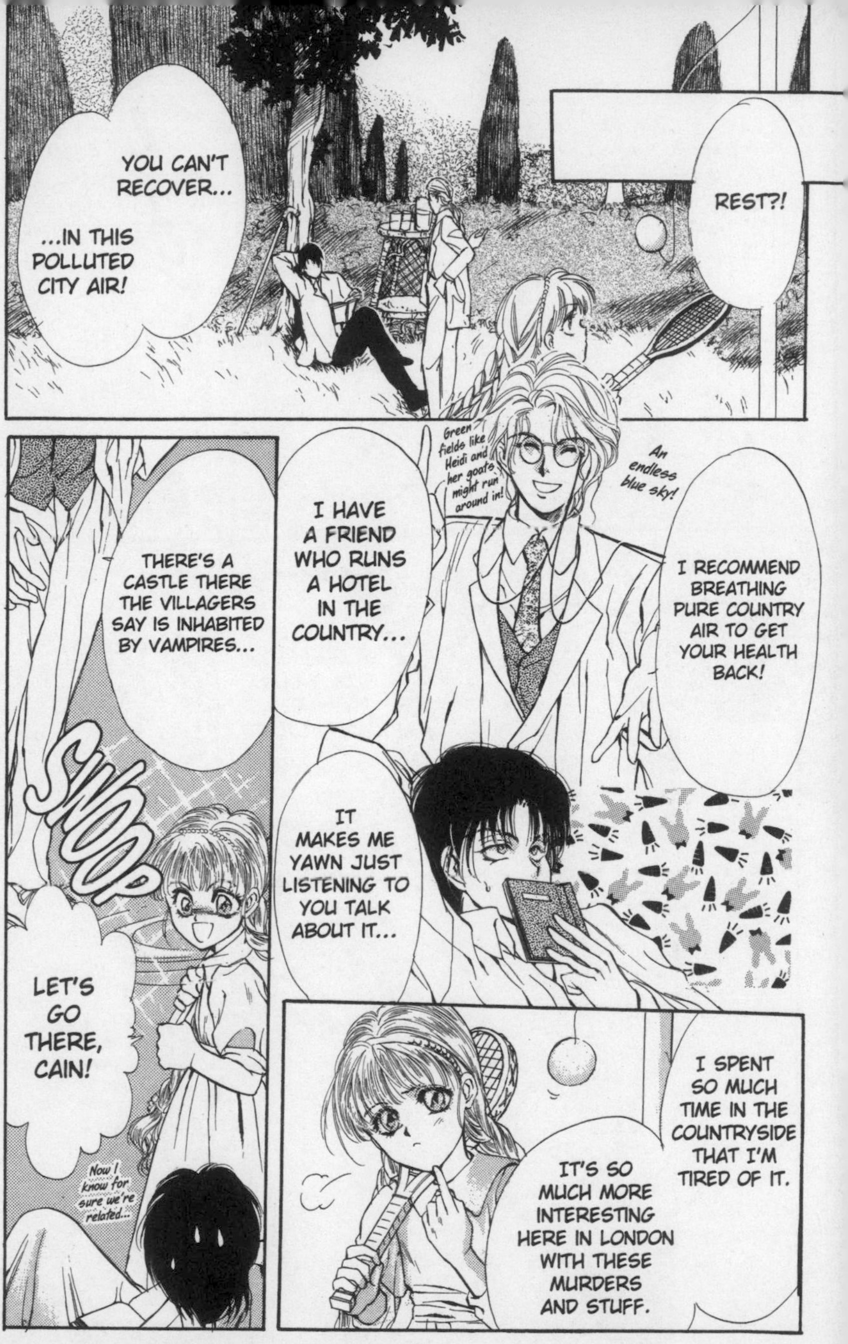
REST?!
YOU CAN'T RECOVER...
...IN THIS POLLUTED CITY AIR!
I RECOMMEND BREATHING PURE COUNTRY AIR TO GET YOUR HEALTH BACK!
An endless blue sky!
I HAVE A FRIEND WHO RUNS A HOTEL IN THE COUNTRY...
Green fields like Heidi and her goats might run around in!
IT MAKES ME YAWN JUST LISTENING TO YOU TALK ABOUT IT...
I SPENT SO MUCH TIME IN THE COUNTRYSIDE THAT I'M TIRED OF IT.
IT'S SO MUCH MORE INTERESTING HERE IN LONDON WITH THESE MURDERS AND STUFF.
THERE'S A CASTLE THERE THE VILLAGERS SAY IS INHABITED BY VAMPIRES...
SNOOP
LET'S GO THERE, CAIN!
Now I know for sure we're related...

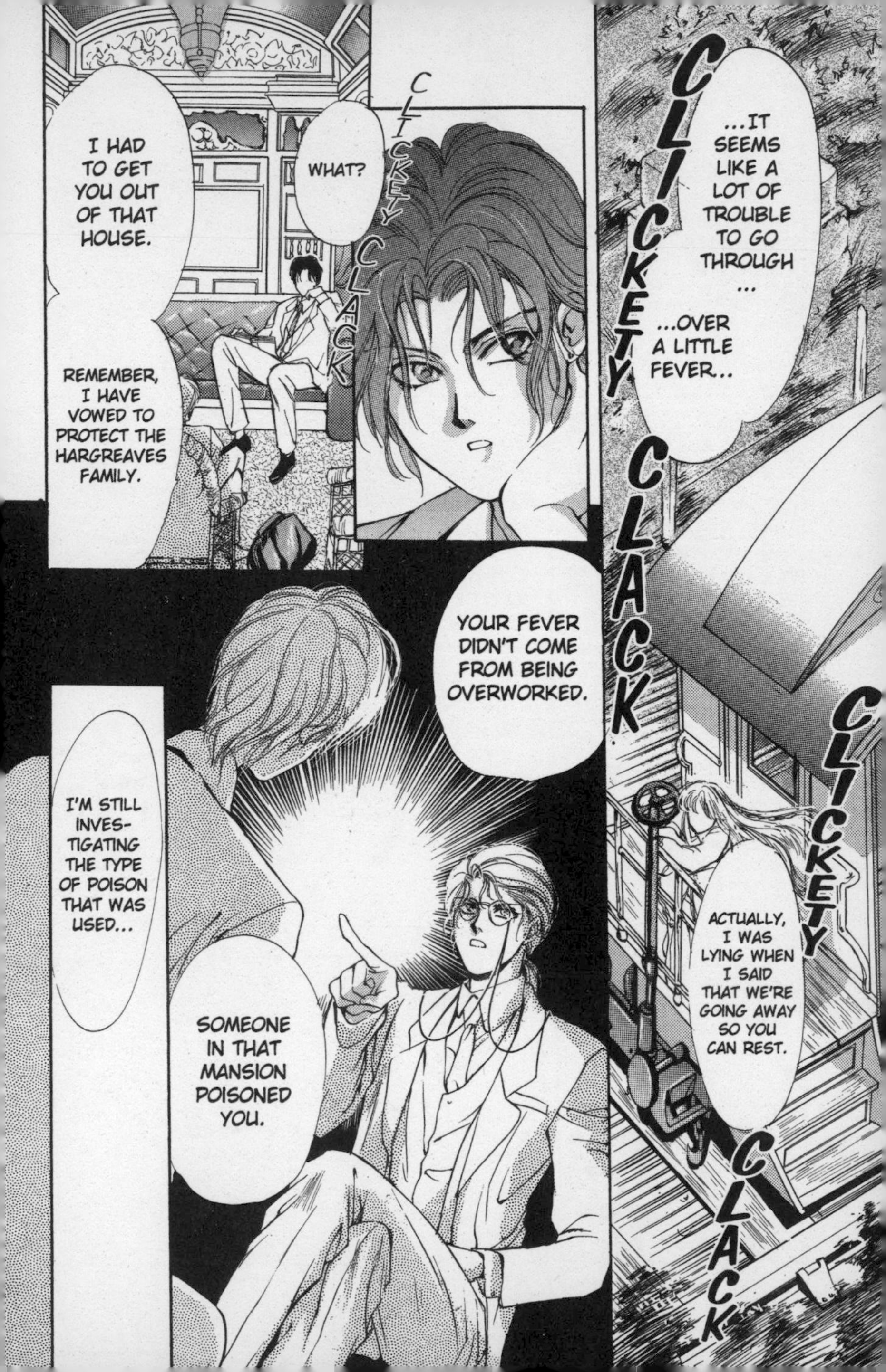
CLICKETY CLACK
...IT SEEMS LIKE A LOT OF TROUBLE TO GO THROUGH ...
...OVER A LITTLE FEVER...
CLICKETY CLACK
ACTUALLY, I WAS LYING WHEN I SAID THAT WE'RE GOING AWAY SO YOU CAN REST.
CLICKETY CLACK
WHAT?
I HAD TO GET YOU OUT OF THAT HOUSE.
REMEMBER, I HAVE VOWED TO PROTECT THE HARGREAVES FAMILY.
YOUR FEVER DIDN'T COME FROM BEING OVERWORKED.
SOMEONE IN THAT MANSION POISONED YOU.
I'M STILL INVES-TIGATING THE TYPE OF POISON THAT WAS USED...

WILD ♦ TALK

Hi, we meet again! This is Sister Yuki here, who's been writing some pretty wild comics lately with a twist. I'm actually still in my mid twenties so please don't ever again write me letters that say "You must be in your thirties." You there! Yes you! Okay? (I've been getting a lot of those letters.♪) All kidding aside, Cain Series vol. 3 is the real start of the Cain series. In other words, it's the start of the main part. There was so much that I wanted to write about that it might seem kind of cluttered in certain sections (especially the last episode...♪) but please read it. And I'm sure you know this already but Kafka is the name of the novelist, Franz Kafka. Why, you ask? I'm not sure...

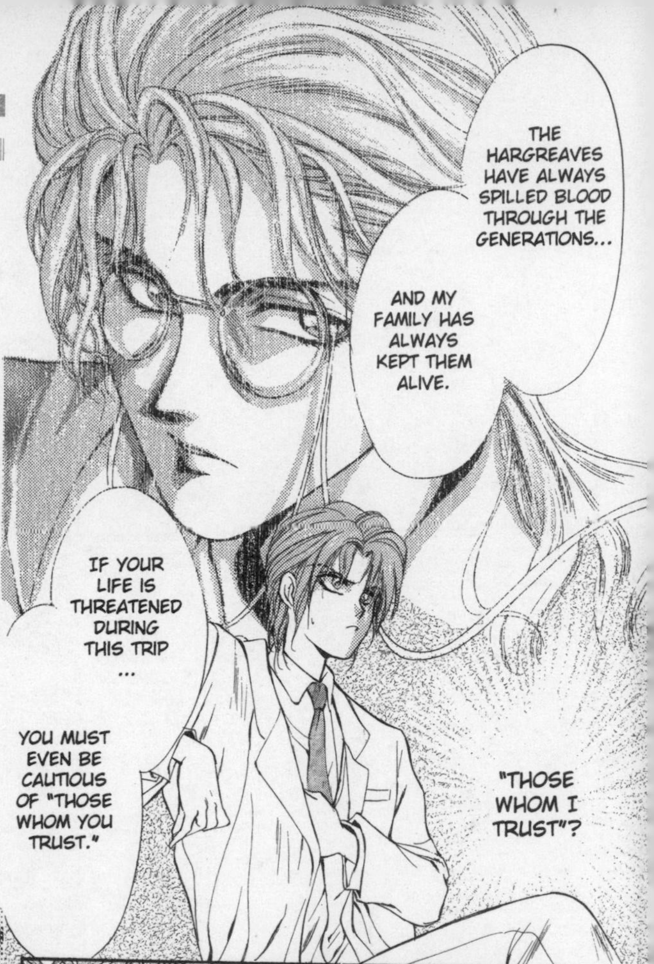
THE HARGREAVES HAVE ALWAYS SPILLED BLOOD THROUGH THE GENERATIONS...
AND MY FAMILY HAS ALWAYS KEPT THEM ALIVE.
IF YOUR LIFE IS THREATENED DURING THIS TRIP ...
YOU MUST EVEN BE CAUTIOUS OF "THOSE WHOM YOU TRUST."
"THOSE WHOM I TRUST"?

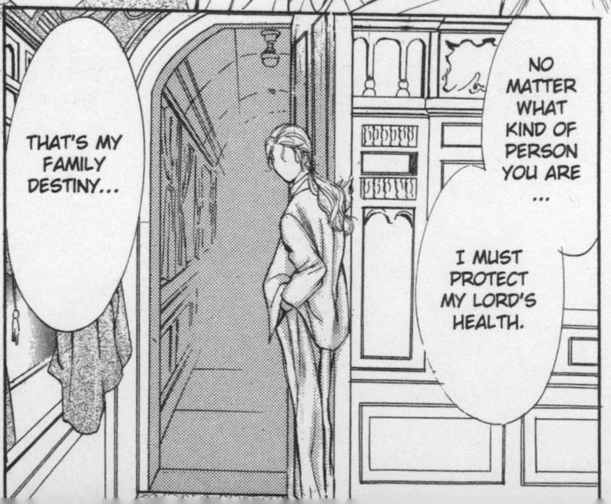
NO MATTER WHAT KIND OF PERSON YOU ARE ...
I MUST PROTECT MY LORD'S HEALTH.
THAT'S MY FAMILY DESTINY...

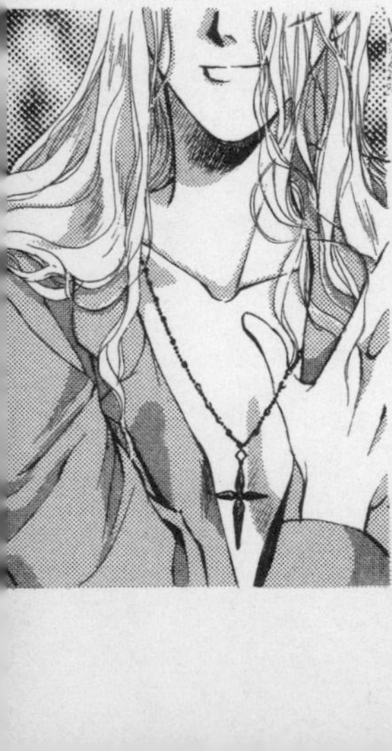

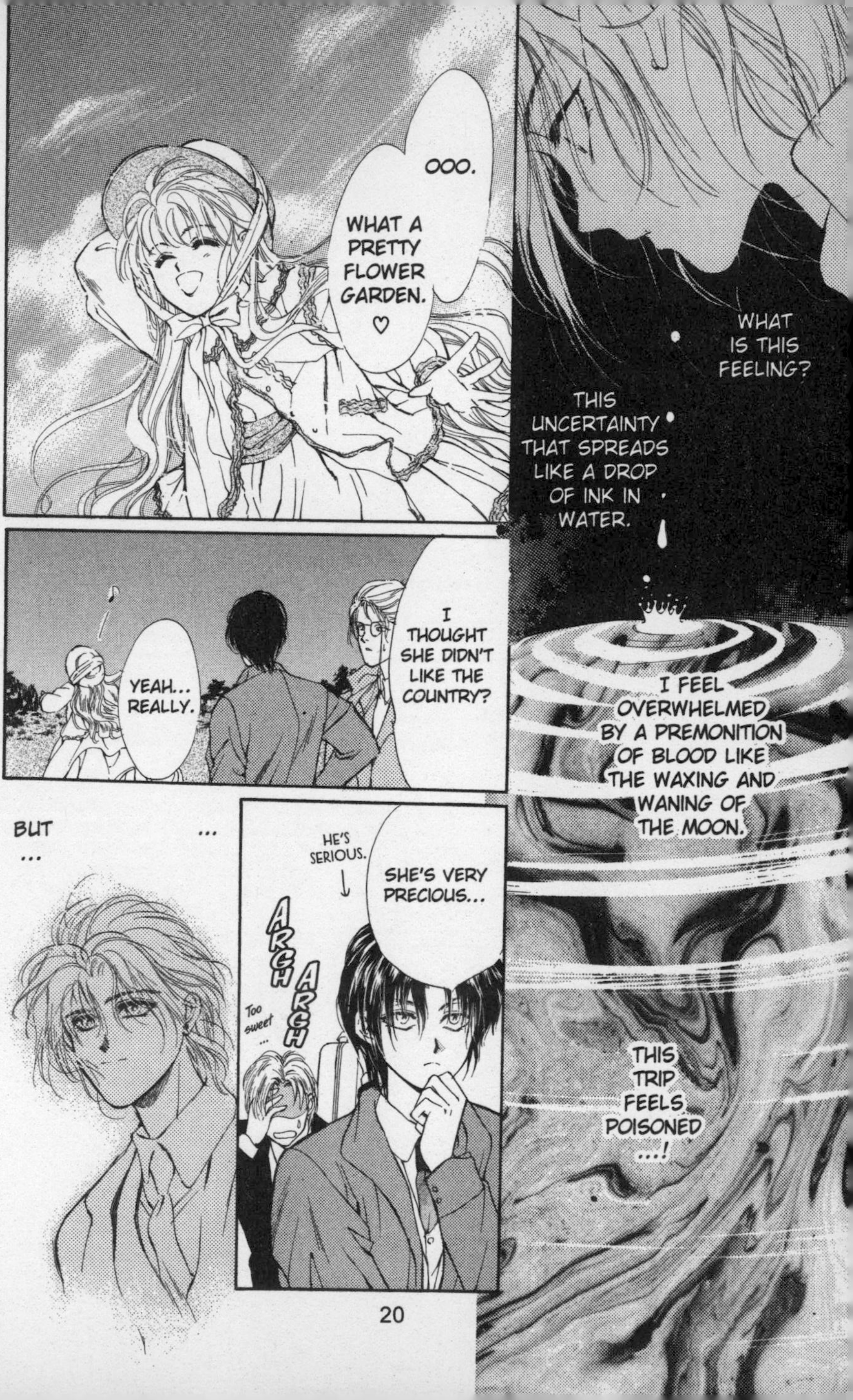
WHAT IS THIS FEELING?
THIS UNCERTAINTY THAT SPREADS LIKE A DROP OF INK IN WATER.
I FEEL OVERWHELMED BY A PREMONITION OF BLOOD LIKE THE WAXING AND WANING OF THE MOON.
THIS TRIP FEELS POISONED ...!
OOO.
WHAT A PRETTY FLOWER GARDEN. ♡
I THOUGHT SHE DIDN'T LIKE THE COUNTRY?
YEAH... REALLY.
SHE'S VERY PRECIOUS...
HE'S SERIOUS.
ARGH ARGH
Too sweet ...
BUT ... ...

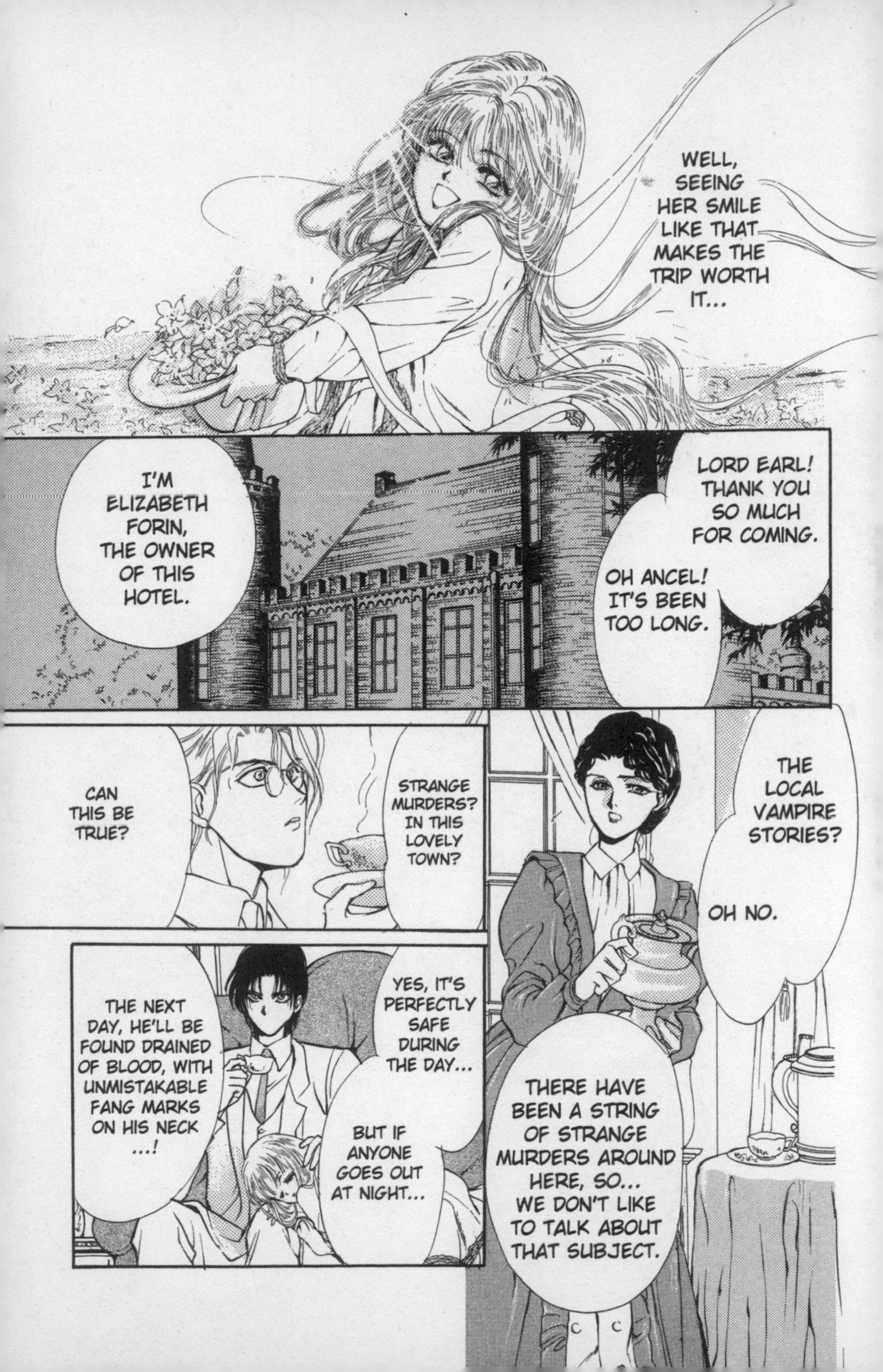
WELL, SEEING HER SMILE LIKE THAT MAKES THE TRIP WORTH IT...
LORD EARL! THANK YOU SO MUCH FOR COMING.
OH ANCEL! IT'S BEEN TOO LONG.
I'M ELIZABETH FORIN, THE OWNER OF THIS HOTEL.
THE LOCAL VAMPIRE STORIES?
OH NO.
THERE HAVE BEEN A STRING OF STRANGE MURDERS AROUND HERE, SO... WE DON'T LIKE TO TALK ABOUT THAT SUBJECT.
STRANGE MURDERS? IN THIS LOVELY TOWN?
CAN THIS BE TRUE?
YES, IT'S PERFECTLY SAFE DURING THE DAY...
BUT IF ANYONE GOES OUT AT NIGHT...
THE NEXT DAY, HE'LL BE FOUND DRAINED OF BLOOD, WITH UNMISTAKABLE FANG MARKS ON HIS NECK ...!

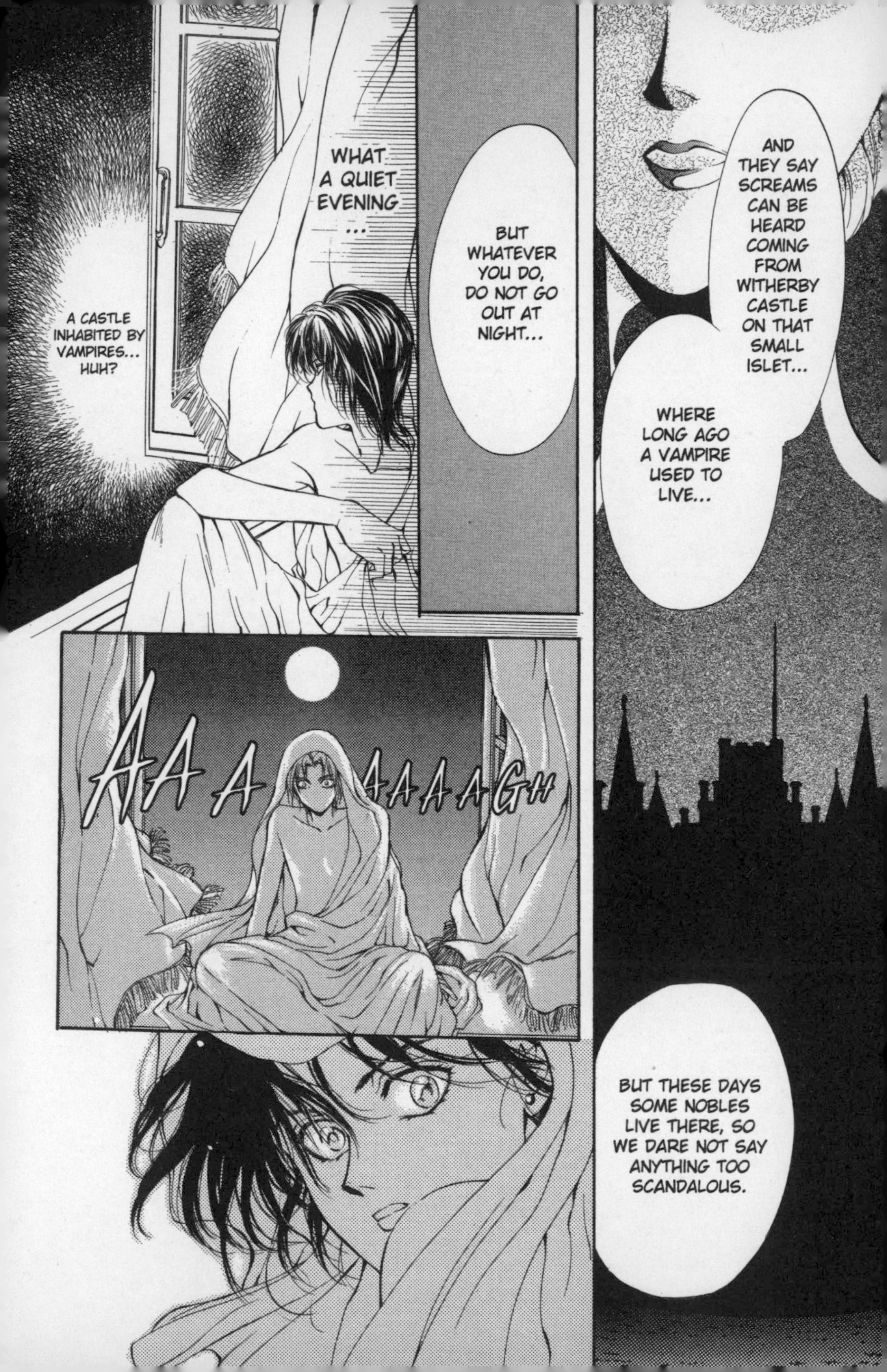
AND THEY SAY SCREAMS CAN BE HEARD COMING FROM WITHERBY CASTLE ON THAT SMALL ISLET...
WHERE LONG AGO A VAMPIRE USED TO LIVE...
BUT THESE DAYS SOME NOBLES LIVE THERE, SO WE DARE NOT SAY ANYTHING TOO SCANDALOUS.
BUT WHATEVER YOU DO, DO NOT GO OUT AT NIGHT...
WHAT A QUIET EVENING...
A CASTLE INHABITED BY VAMPIRES... HUH?
AAAAAAAAGH

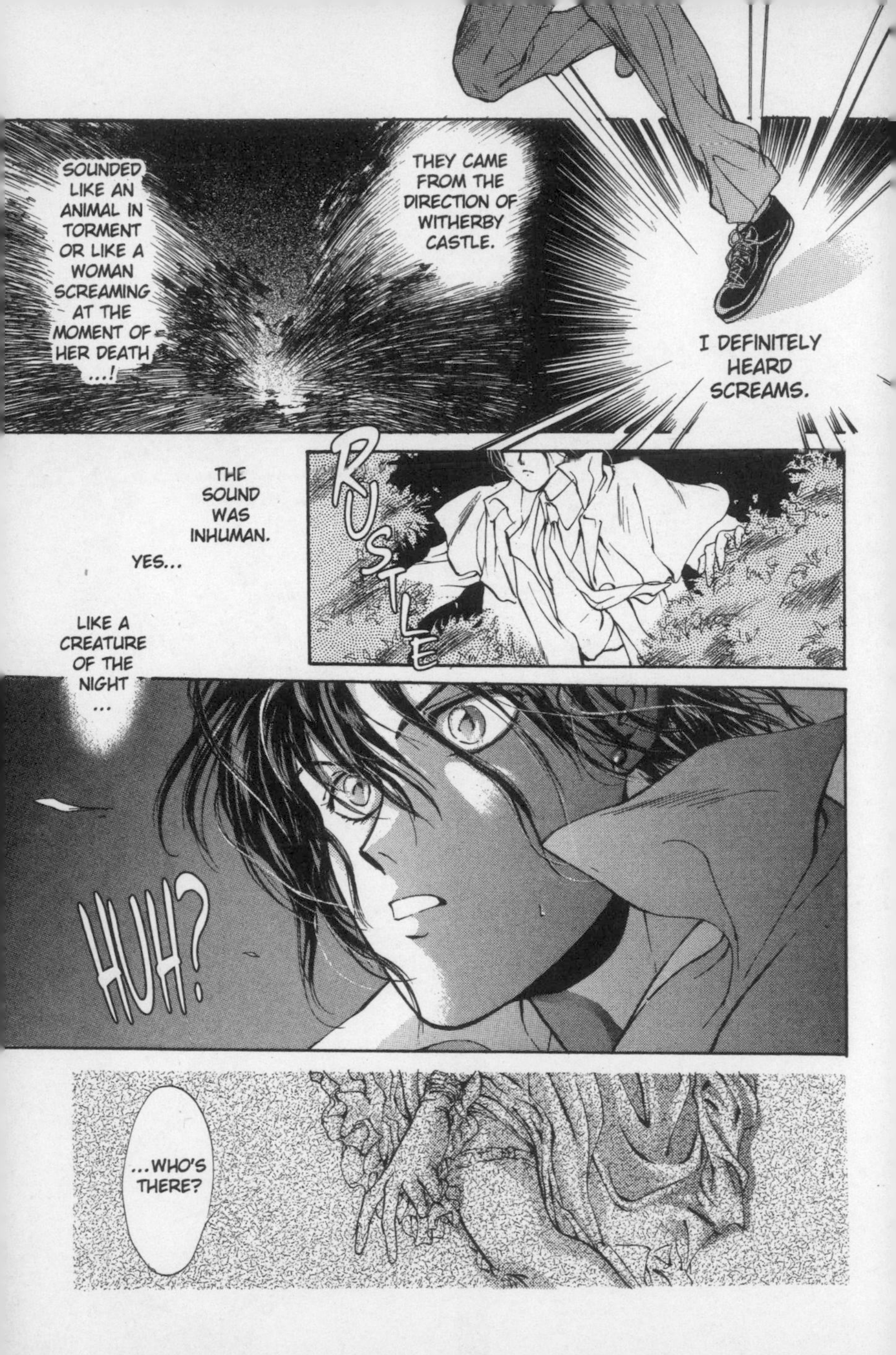
I DEFINITELY HEARD SCREAMS.
THEY CAME FROM THE DIRECTION OF WITHERBY CASTLE.
SOUNDED LIKE AN ANIMAL IN TORMENT OR LIKE A WOMAN SCREAMING AT THE MOMENT OF HER DEATH ...!
RUSTLE
THE SOUND WAS INHUMAN.
YES...
LIKE A CREATURE OF THE NIGHT ...
HUH?
...WHO'S THERE?

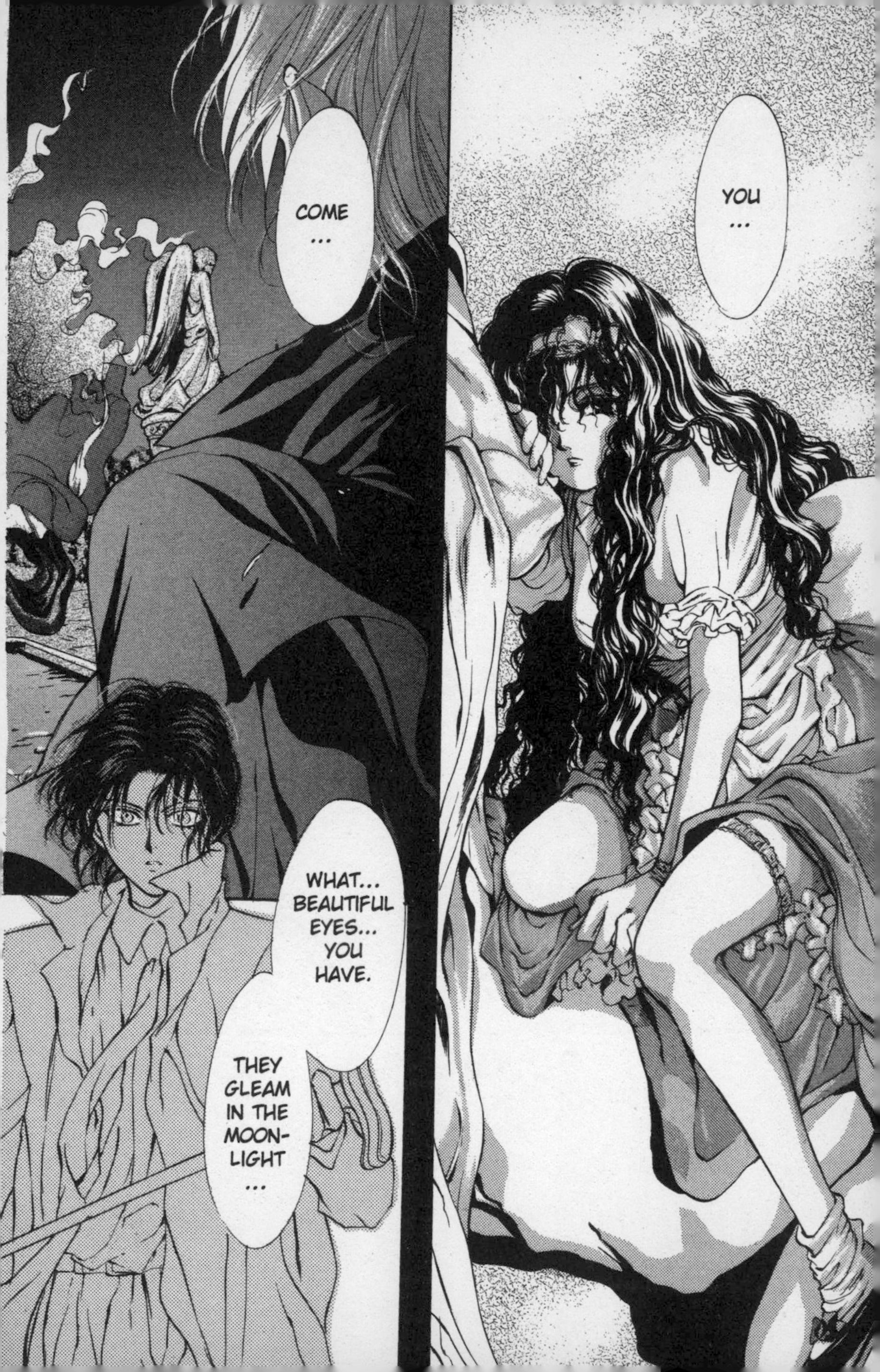
YOU ...
COME ...
WHAT... BEAUTIFUL EYES... YOU HAVE.
THEY GLEAM IN THE MOON-LIGHT ...

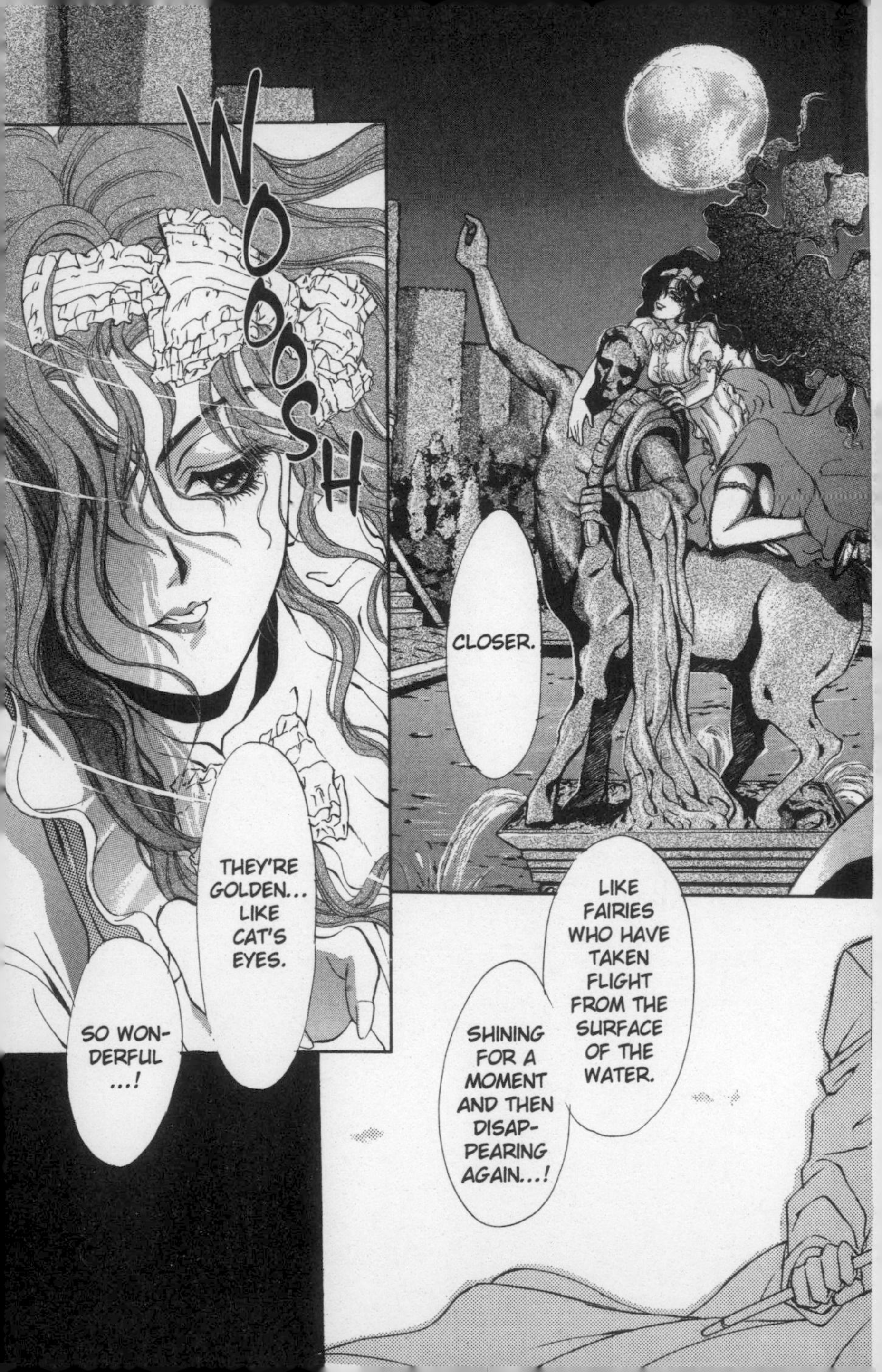
CLOSER.
LIKE FAIRIES WHO HAVE TAKEN FLIGHT FROM THE SURFACE OF THE WATER.
SHINING FOR A MOMENT AND THEN DISAP-PEARING AGAIN...!
WOOSH
THEY'RE GOLDEN... LIKE CAT'S EYES.
SO WON-DERFUL ...!

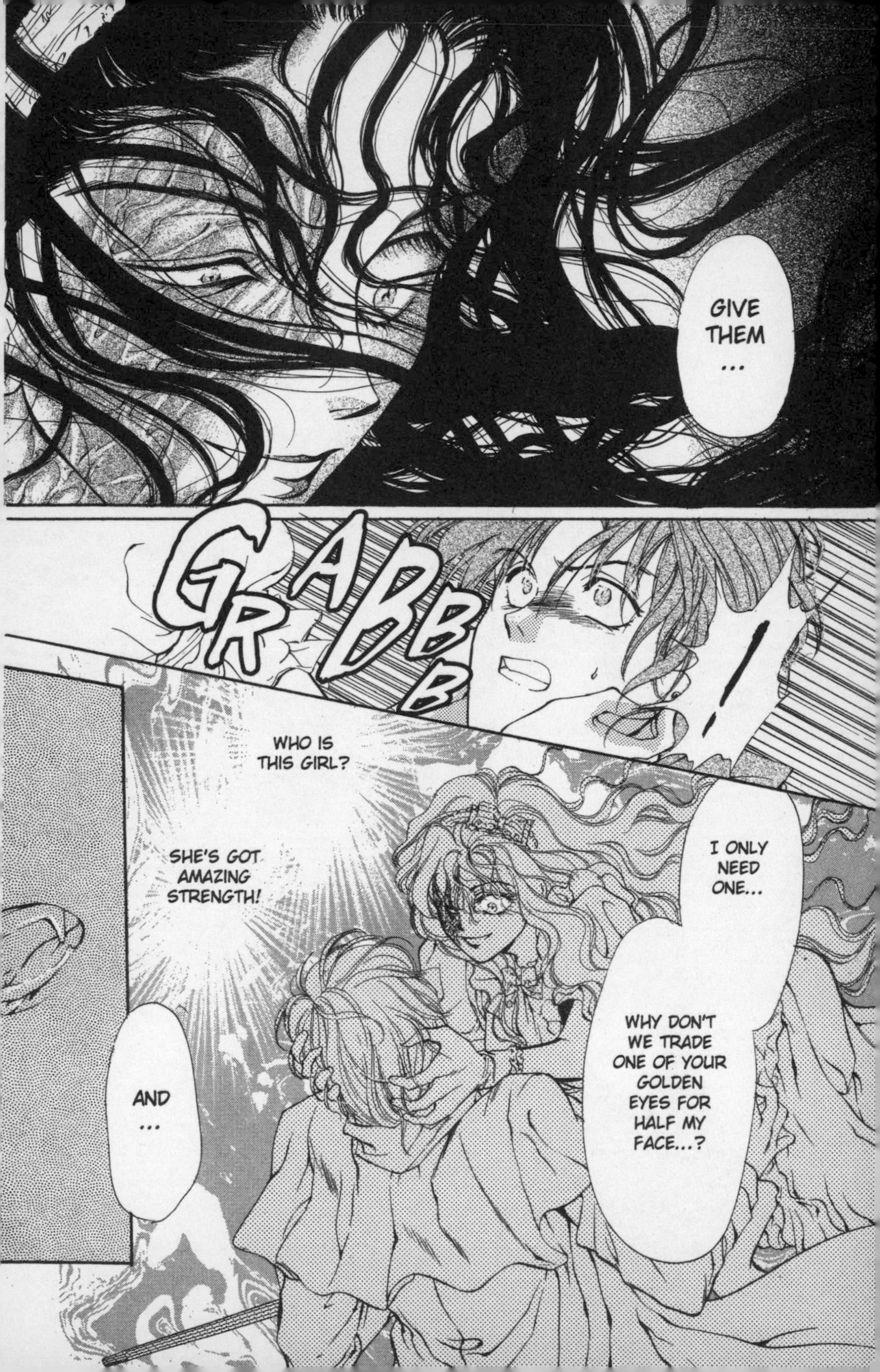
GIVE THEM ...
GRABBB
!
I ONLY NEED ONE...
WHO IS THIS GIRL?
SHE'S GOT AMAZING STRENGTH!
WHY DON'T WE TRADE ONE OF YOUR GOLDEN EYES FOR HALF MY FACE...?
AND ...

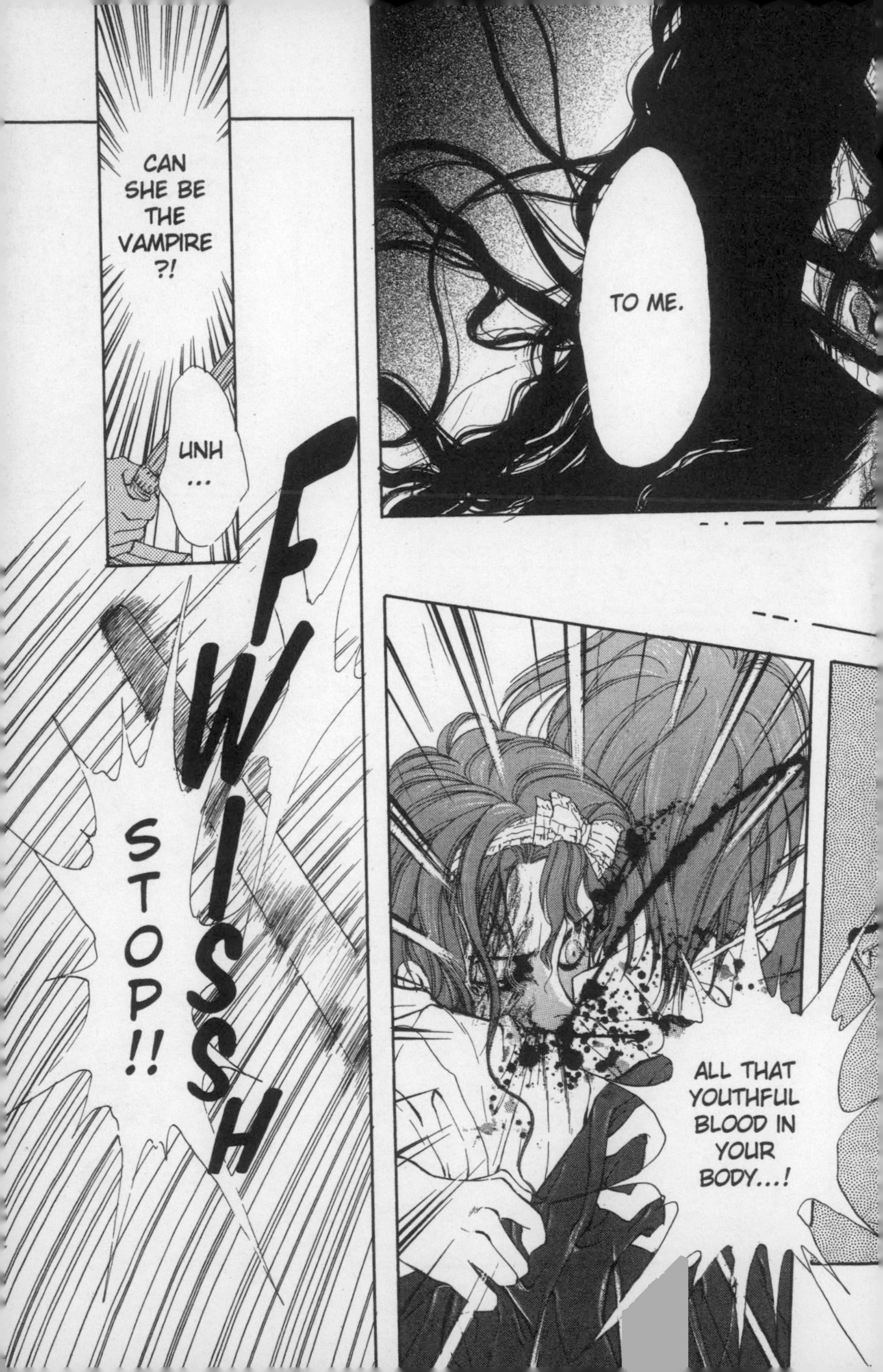
TO ME.
ALL THAT YOUTHFUL BLOOD IN YOUR BODY...!
CAN SHE BE THE VAMPIRE?!
UNH...
FWISSH
STOP!!

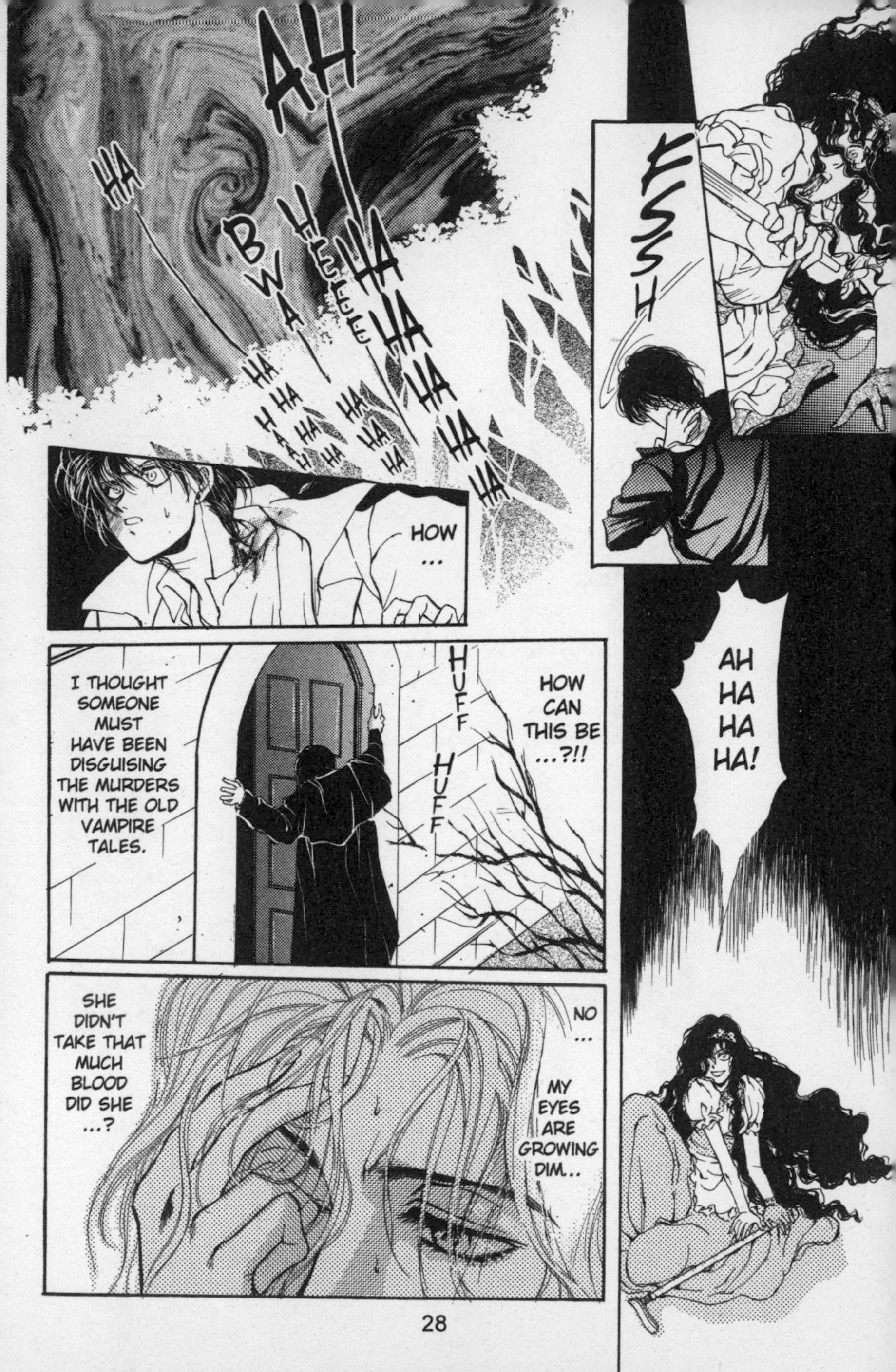
ESSH
AH HA HA HA!
AH HA HA HA HA HA HA
HA
BWA
HEEEE
HA HA HA HA HA HA HA HA HA HA HA HA HA HA HA
HOW ...
HOW CAN THIS BE ...?!!
HUFF HUFF
I THOUGHT SOMEONE MUST HAVE BEEN DISGUISING THE MURDERS WITH THE OLD VAMPIRE TALES.
NO ...
MY EYES ARE GROWING DIM..
SHE DIDN'T TAKE THAT MUCH BLOOD DID SHE ...?

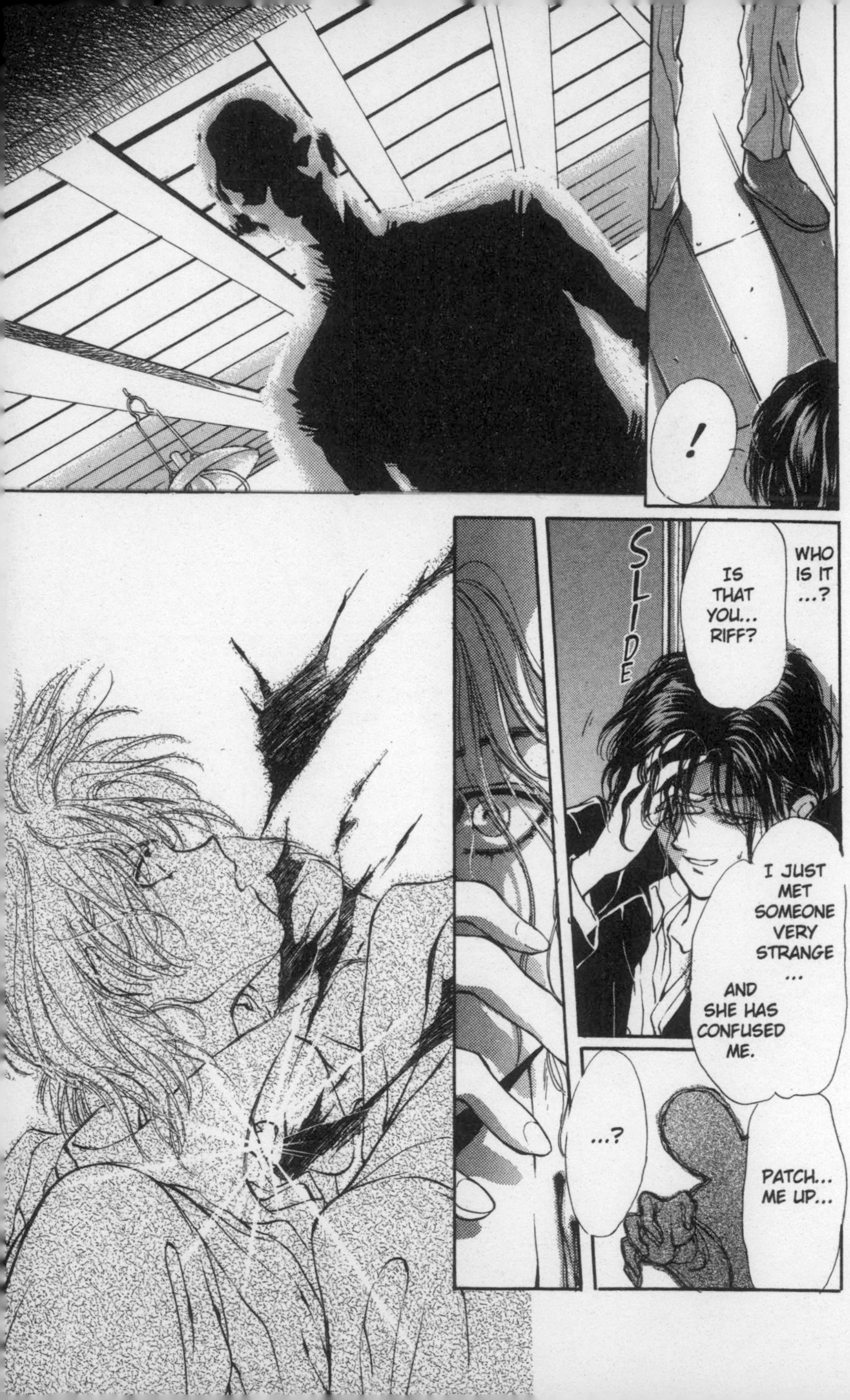
!
WHO IS IT ...?
IS THAT YOU... RIFF?
SLIDE
I JUST MET SOMEONE VERY STRANGE ...
AND SHE HAS CONFUSED ME.
PATCH... ME UP...
...?

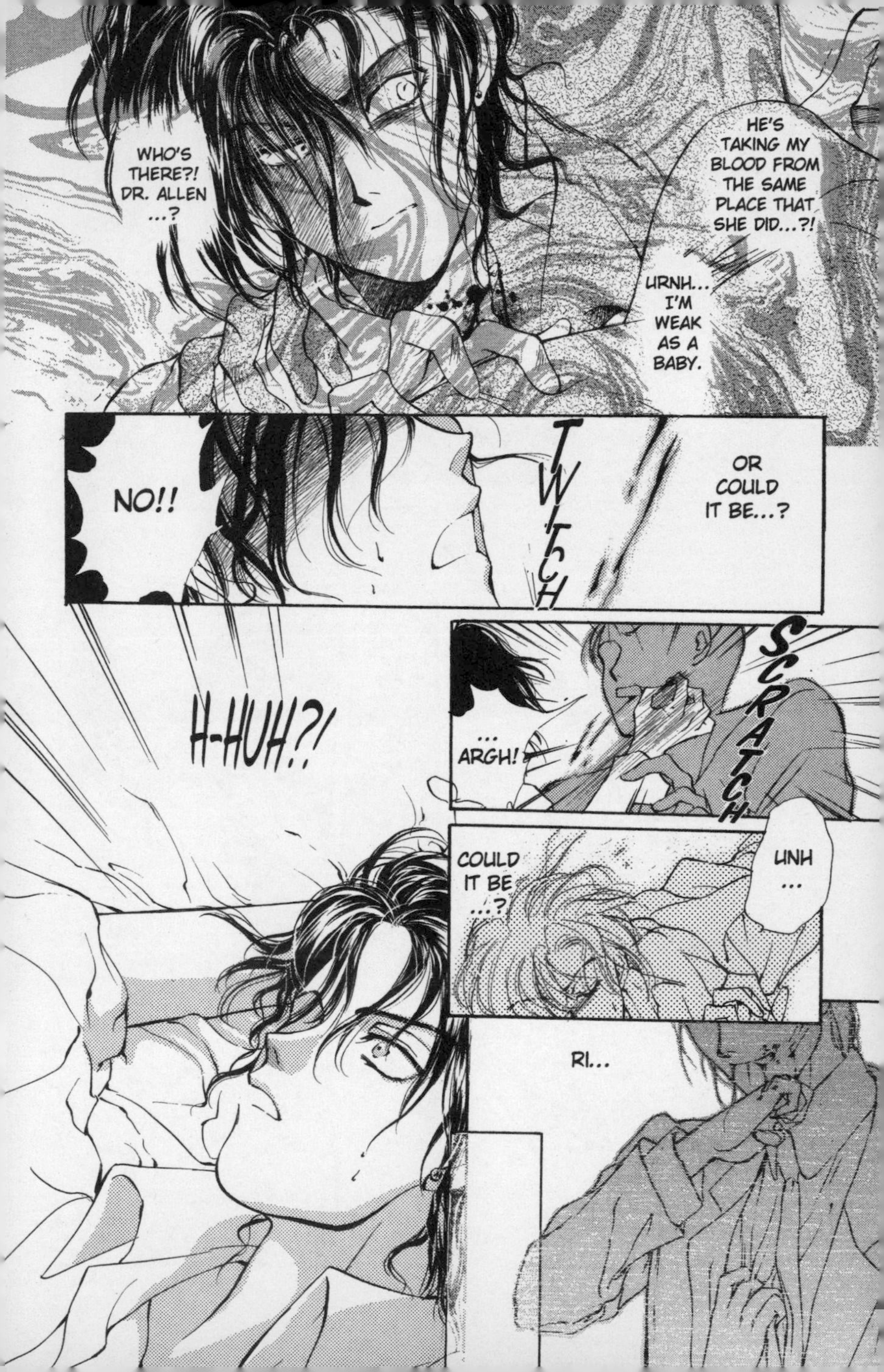
HE'S TAKING MY BLOOD FROM THE SAME PLACE THAT SHE DID...?!
URNH... I'M WEAK AS A BABY.
WHO'S THERE?! DR. ALLEN ...?
OR COULD IT BE...?
TWITCH
NO!!
SCRATCH
... ARGH!
UNH ...
COULD IT BE ...?
RI...
H-HUH?!

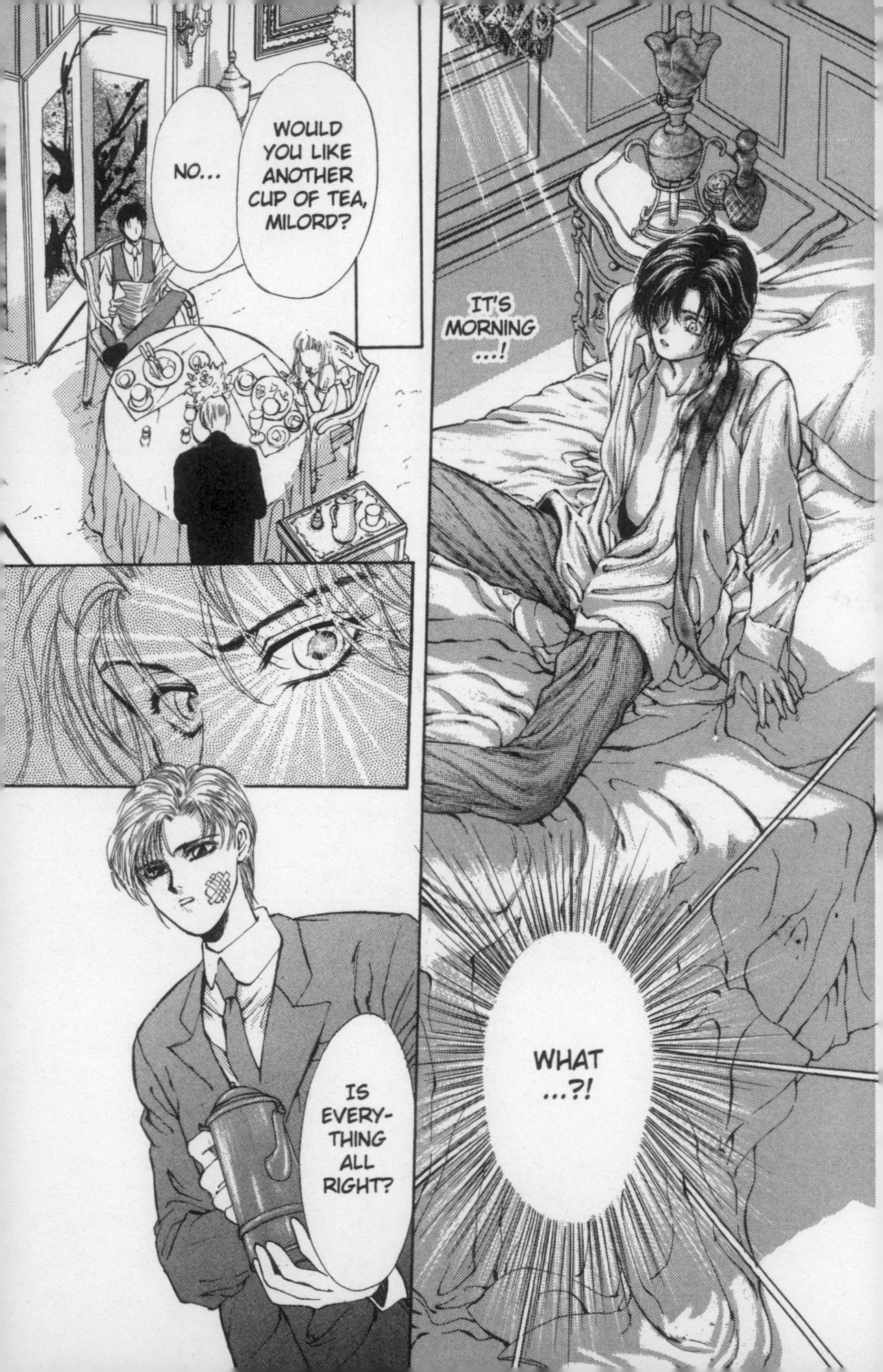
IT'S MORNING ...!
WHAT ...?!
WOULD YOU LIKE ANOTHER CUP OF TEA, MILORD?
NO...
IS EVERY-THING ALL RIGHT?

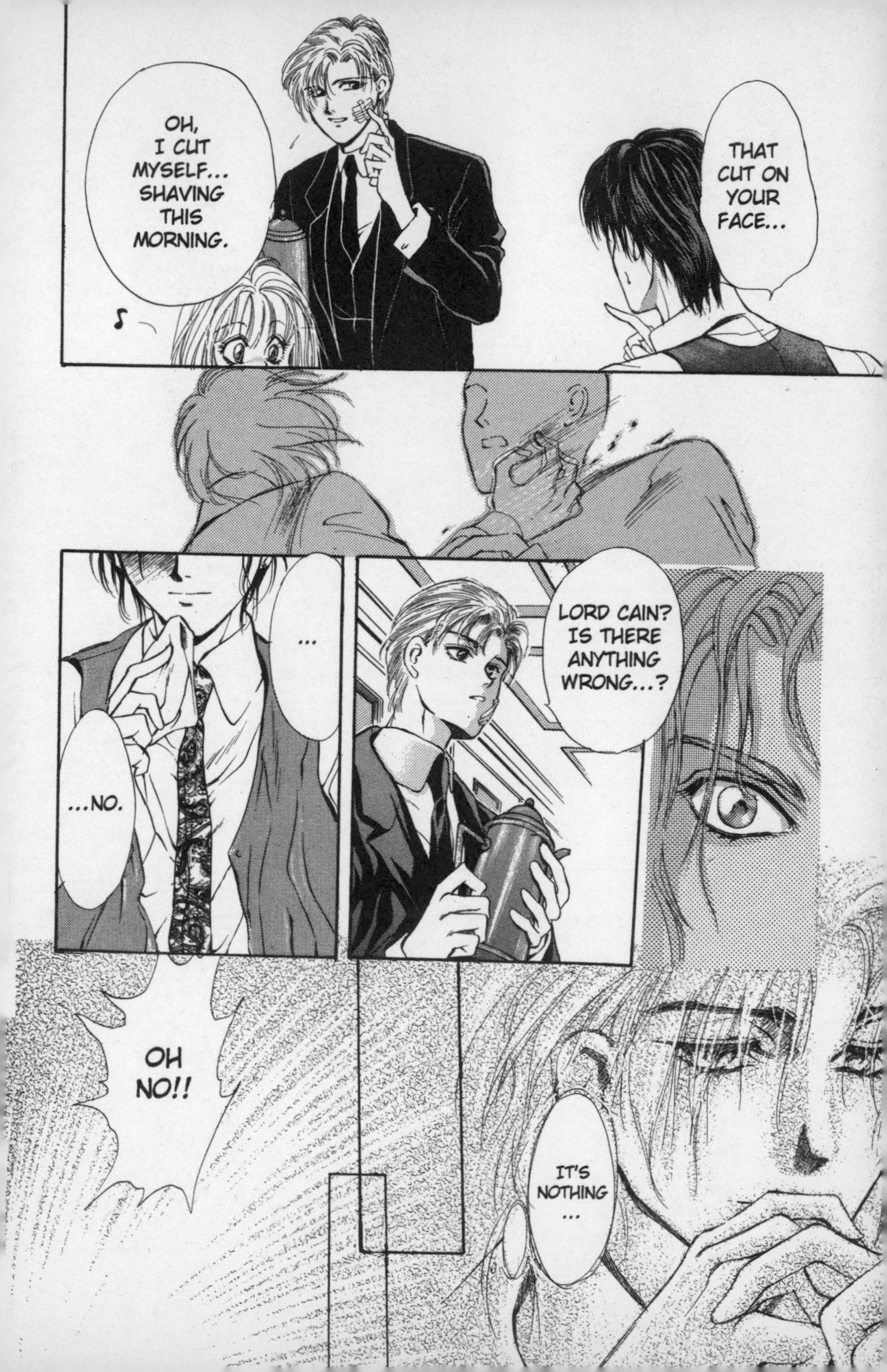
THAT CUT ON YOUR FACE...
OH, I CUT MYSELF... SHAVING THIS MORNING.
LORD CAIN? IS THERE ANYTHING WRONG...?
...
...NO.
IT'S NOTHING ...
OH NO!!

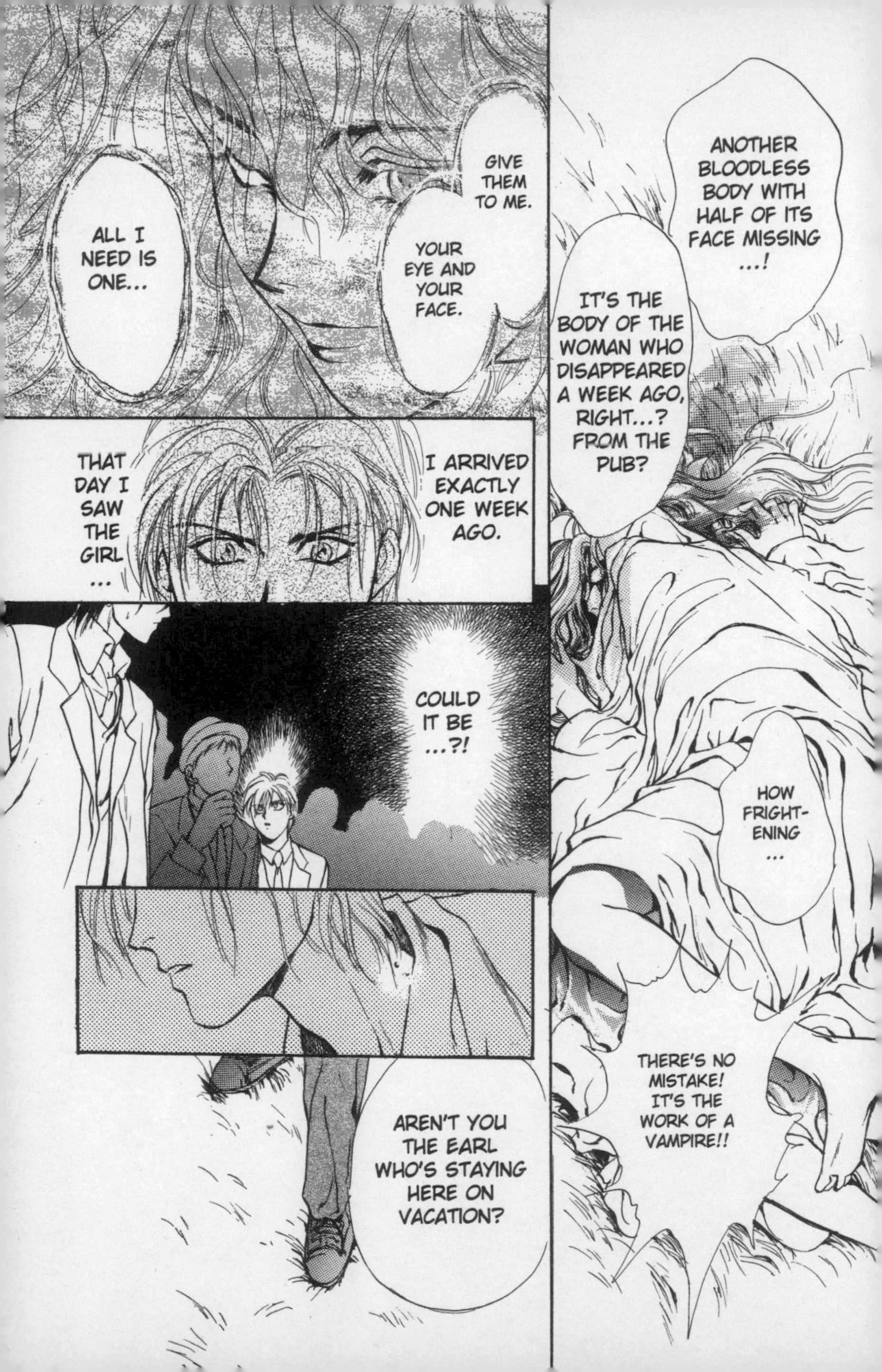
ANOTHER BLOODLESS BODY WITH HALF OF ITS FACE MISSING ...!
IT'S THE BODY OF THE WOMAN WHO DISAPPEARED A WEEK AGO, RIGHT...? FROM THE PUB?
HOW FRIGHT-ENING ...
THERE'S NO MISTAKE! IT'S THE WORK OF A VAMPIRE!!
GIVE THEM TO ME.
YOUR EYE AND YOUR FACE.
ALL I NEED IS ONE...
I ARRIVED EXACTLY ONE WEEK AGO.
THAT DAY I SAW THE GIRL ...
COULD IT BE ...?!
AREN'T YOU THE EARL WHO'S STAYING HERE ON VACATION?

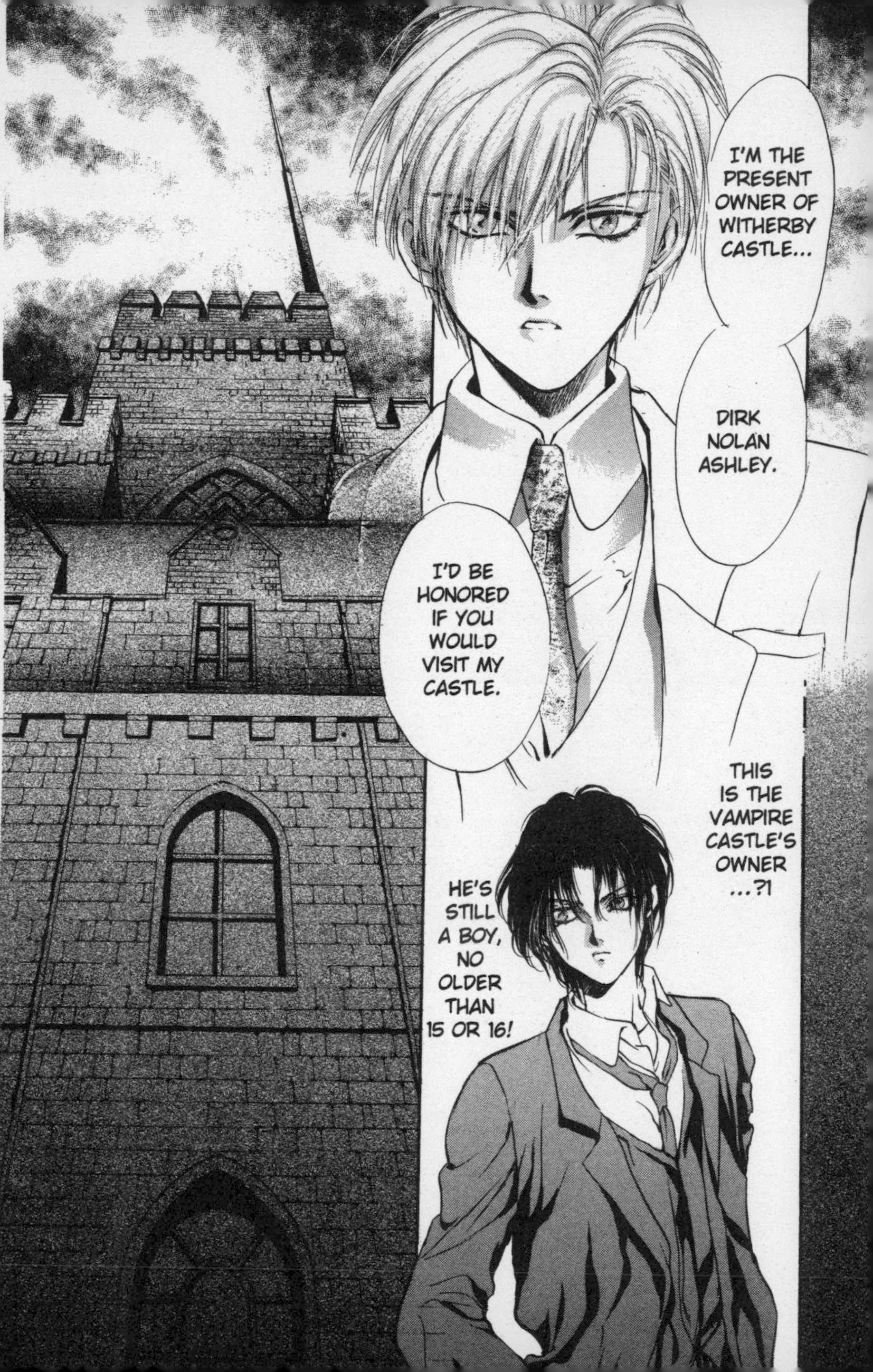
I'M THE PRESENT OWNER OF WITHERBY CASTLE...
DIRK NOLAN ASHLEY.
I'D BE HONORED IF YOU WOULD VISIT MY CASTLE.
THIS IS THE VAMPIRE CASTLE'S OWNER ...?!
HE'S STILL A BOY, NO OLDER THAN 15 OR 16!

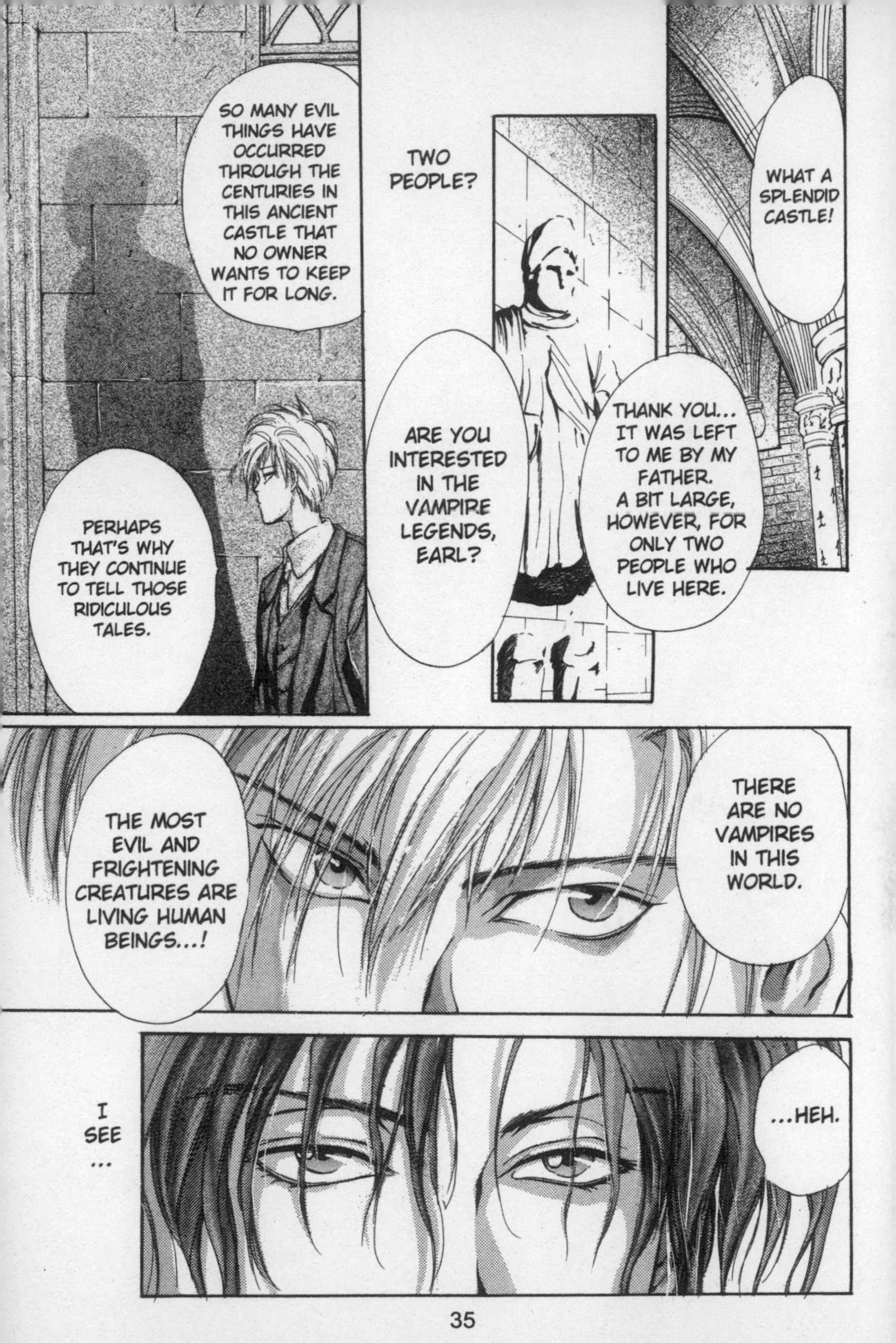
WHAT A SPLENDID CASTLE!
THANK YOU... IT WAS LEFT TO ME BY MY FATHER. A BIT LARGE, HOWEVER, FOR ONLY TWO PEOPLE WHO LIVE HERE.
TWO PEOPLE?
ARE YOU INTERESTED IN THE VAMPIRE LEGENDS, EARL?
SO MANY EVIL THINGS HAVE OCCURRED THROUGH THE CENTURIES IN THIS ANCIENT CASTLE THAT NO OWNER WANTS TO KEEP IT FOR LONG.
PERHAPS THAT'S WHY THEY CONTINUE TO TELL THOSE RIDICULOUS TALES.
THERE ARE NO VAMPIRES IN THIS WORLD.
THE MOST EVIL AND FRIGHTENING CREATURES ARE LIVING HUMAN BEINGS...!
...HEH.
I SEE ...

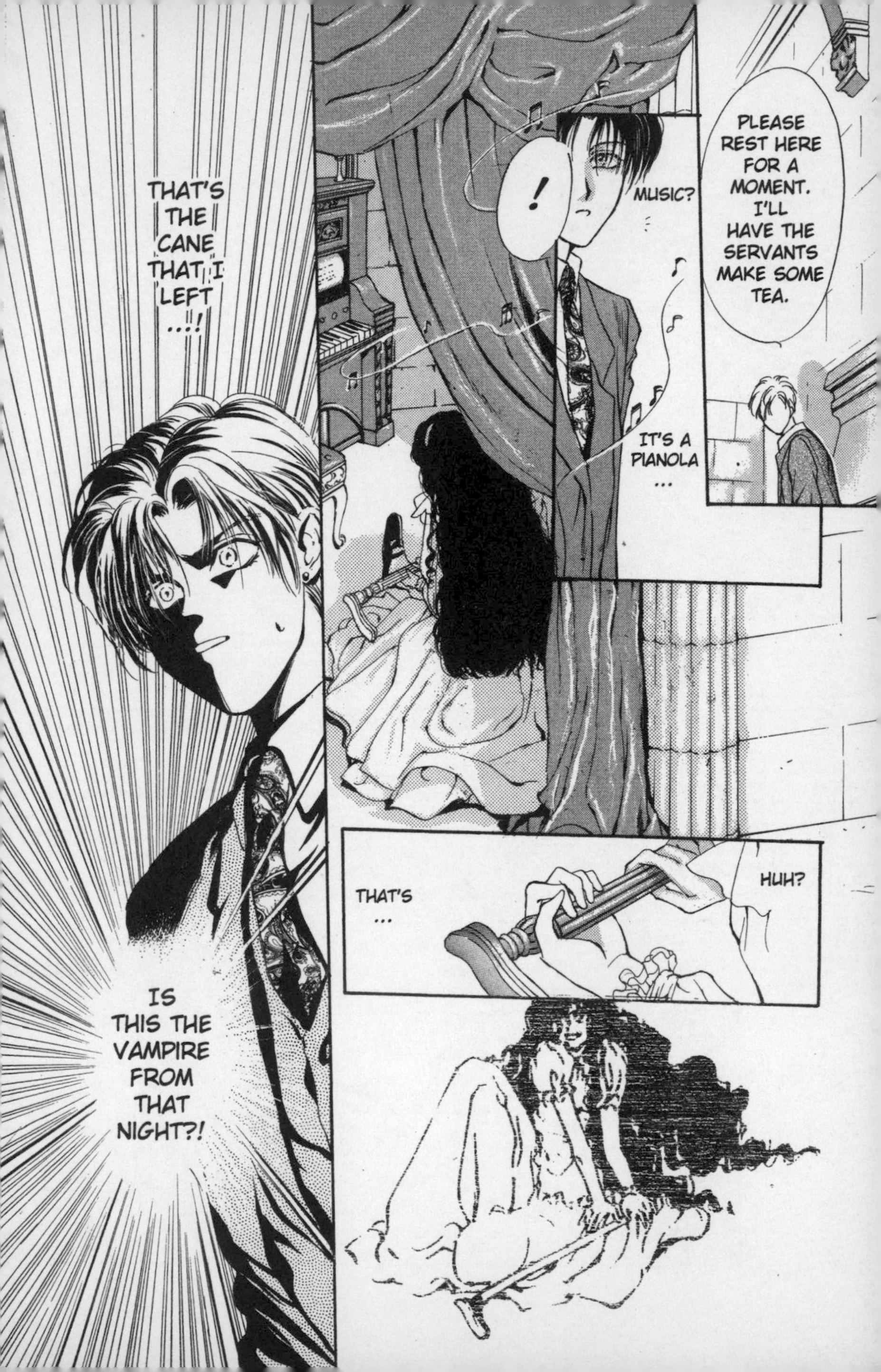
PLEASE REST HERE FOR A MOMENT. I'LL HAVE THE SERVANTS MAKE SOME TEA.
MUSIC?
!
IT'S A PIANOLA ...
HUH?
THAT'S ...
THAT'S THE CANE THAT I LEFT ...!
IS THIS THE VAMPIRE FROM THAT NIGHT?!

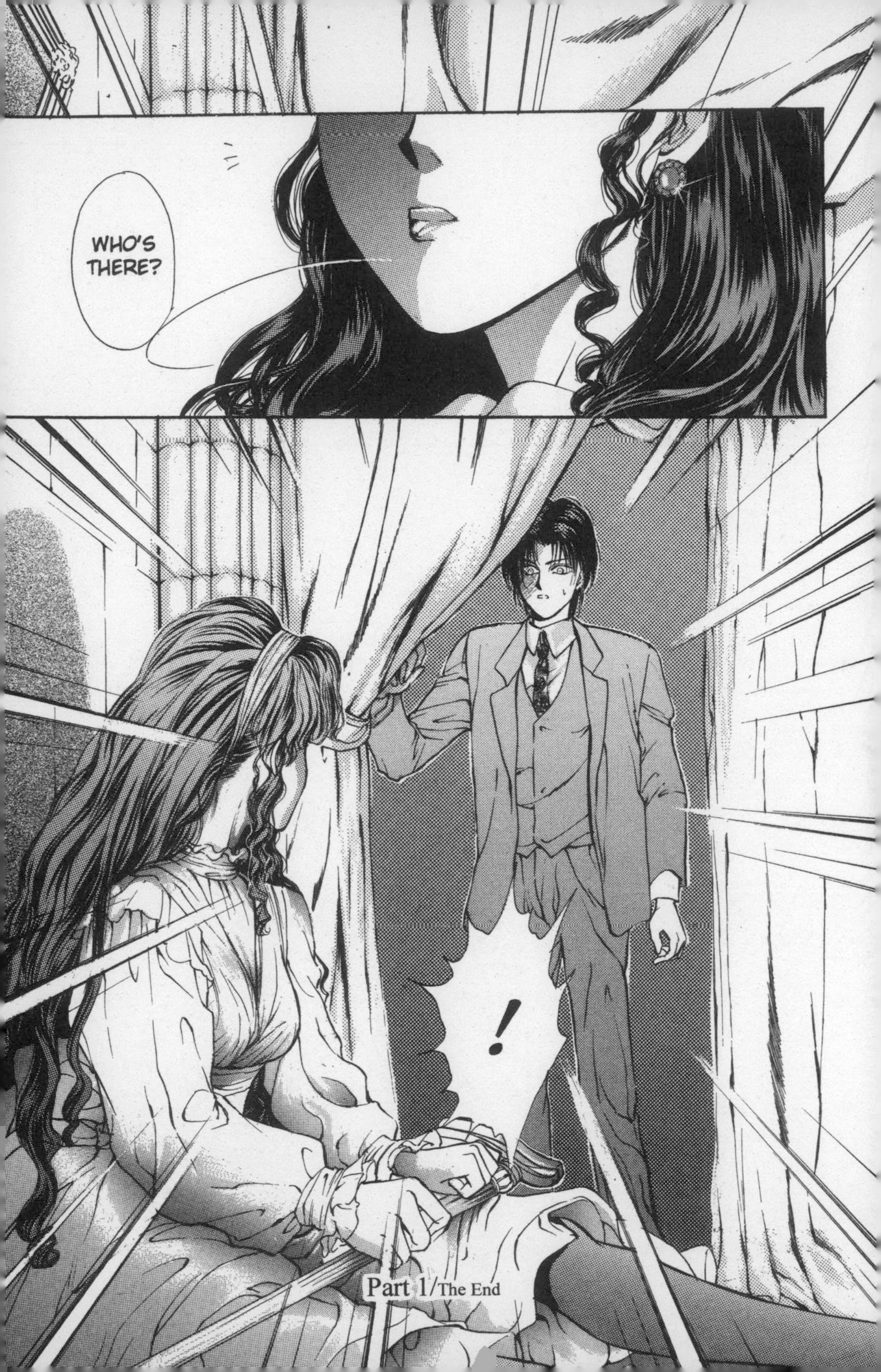
WHO'S THERE?
!
Part 1/The End

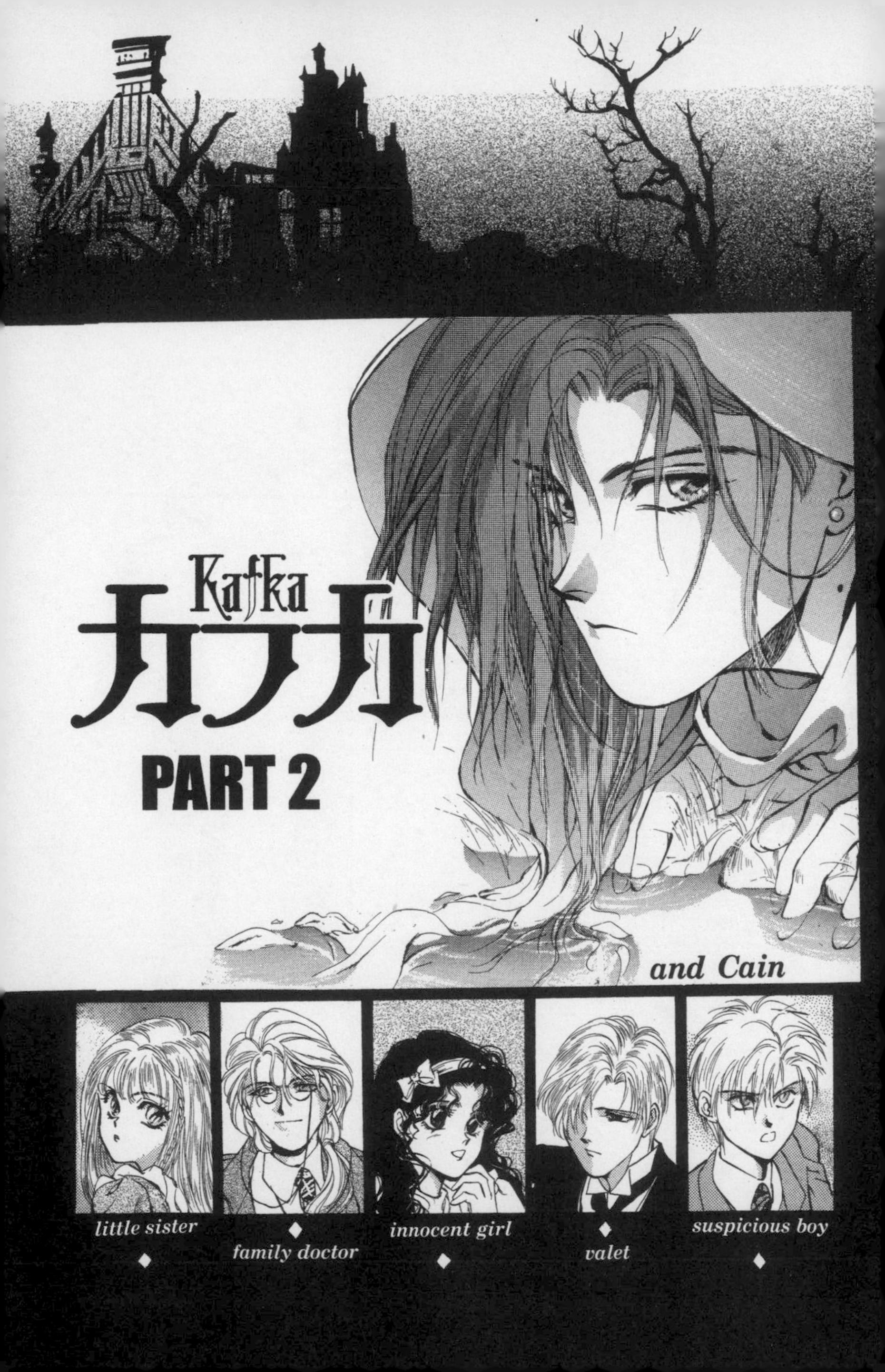

Kafka
カフカ
PART 2
and Cain
little sister
family doctor
innocent girl
valet
suspicious boy

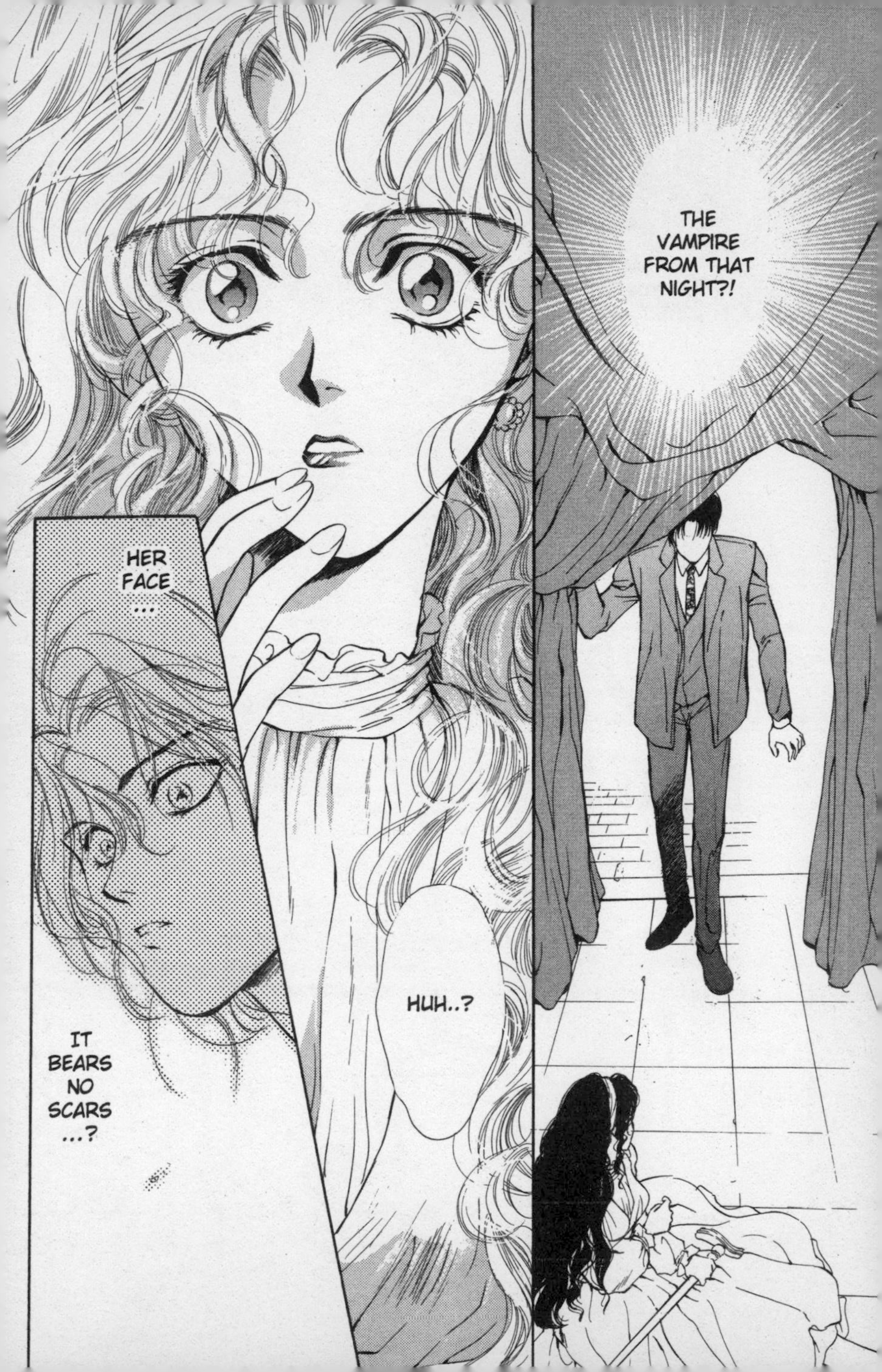
THE VAMPIRE FROM THAT NIGHT?!
HUH..?
HER FACE ...
IT BEARS NO SCARS ...?

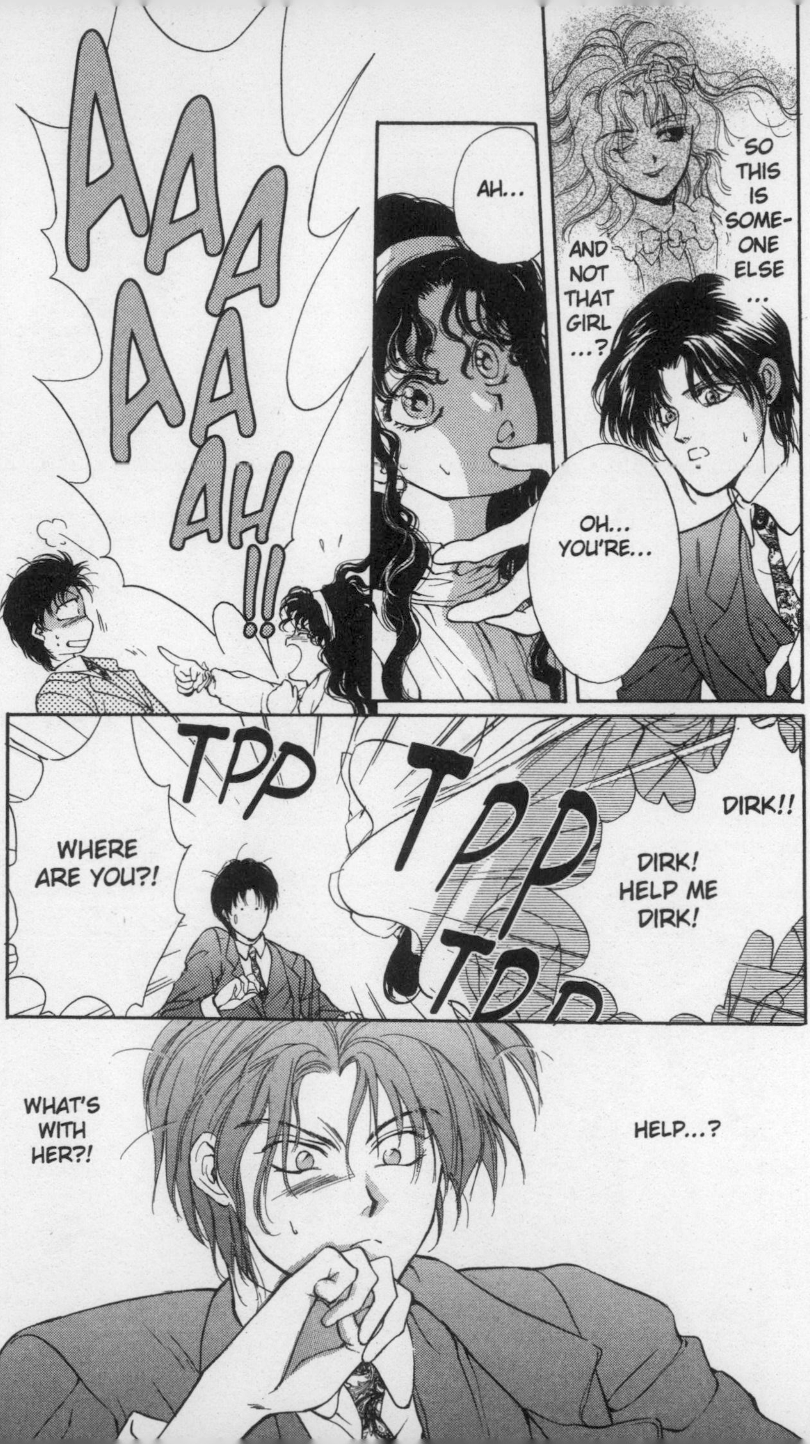
SO THIS IS SOMEONE ELSE ...
AND NOT THAT GIRL ...?
OH... YOU'RE...
AH...
AAAAAAH!!
DIRK!!
TPP
DIRK! HELP ME DIRK!
TPP
WHERE ARE YOU?!
HELP...?
WHAT'S WITH HER?!

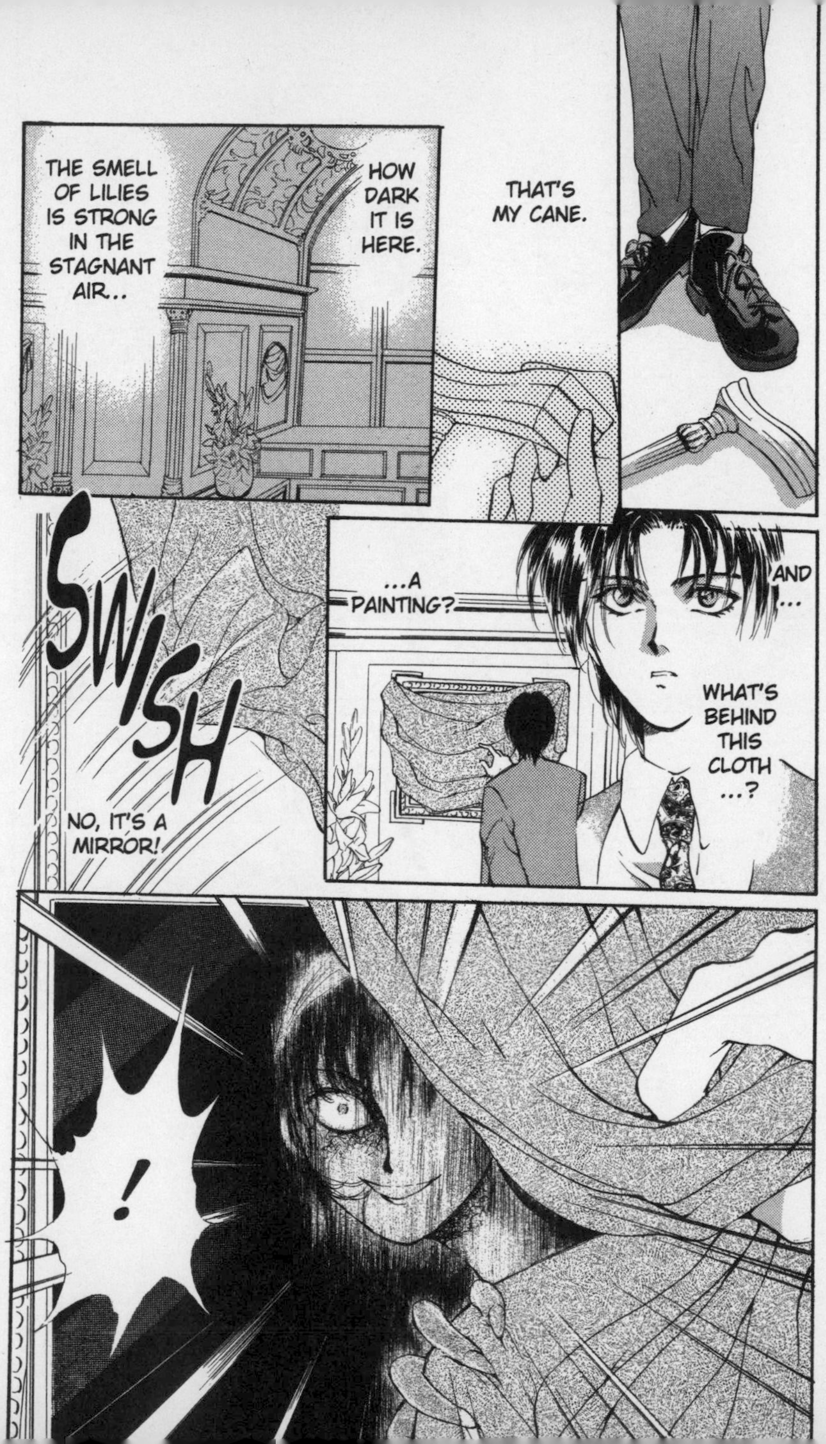
THAT'S MY CANE.
HOW DARK IT IS HERE.
THE SMELL OF LILIES IS STRONG IN THE STAGNANT AIR...
AND ...
WHAT'S BEHIND THIS CLOTH ...?
...A PAINTING?
SWISH
NO, IT'S A MIRROR!
!

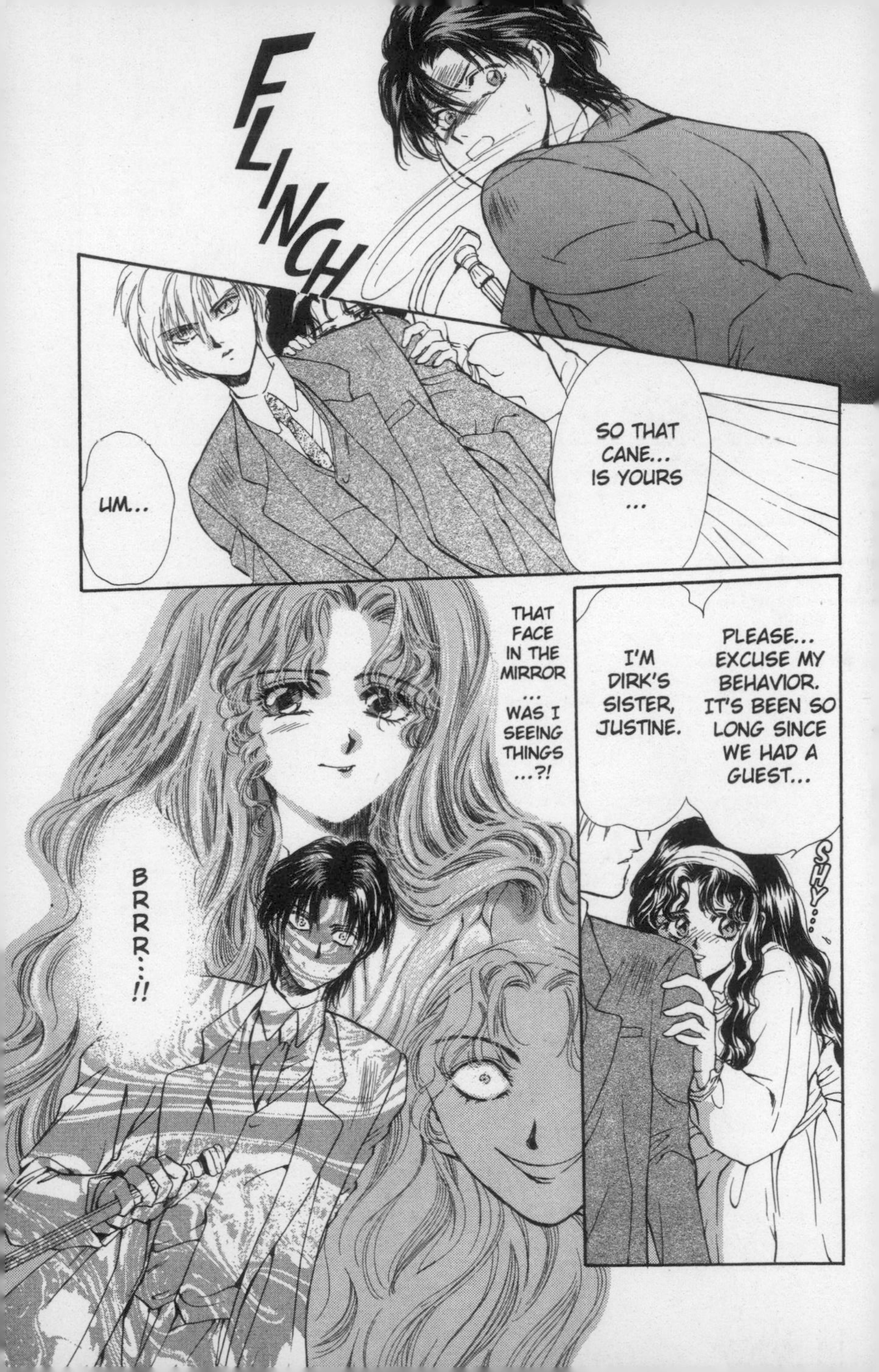
FLINCH
SO THAT CANE... IS YOURS ...
UM...
PLEASE... EXCUSE MY BEHAVIOR. IT'S BEEN SO LONG SINCE WE HAD A GUEST...
I'M DIRK'S SISTER, JUSTINE.
SHY...
THAT FACE IN THE MIRROR ... WAS I SEEING THINGS ...?!
BRRR...!!

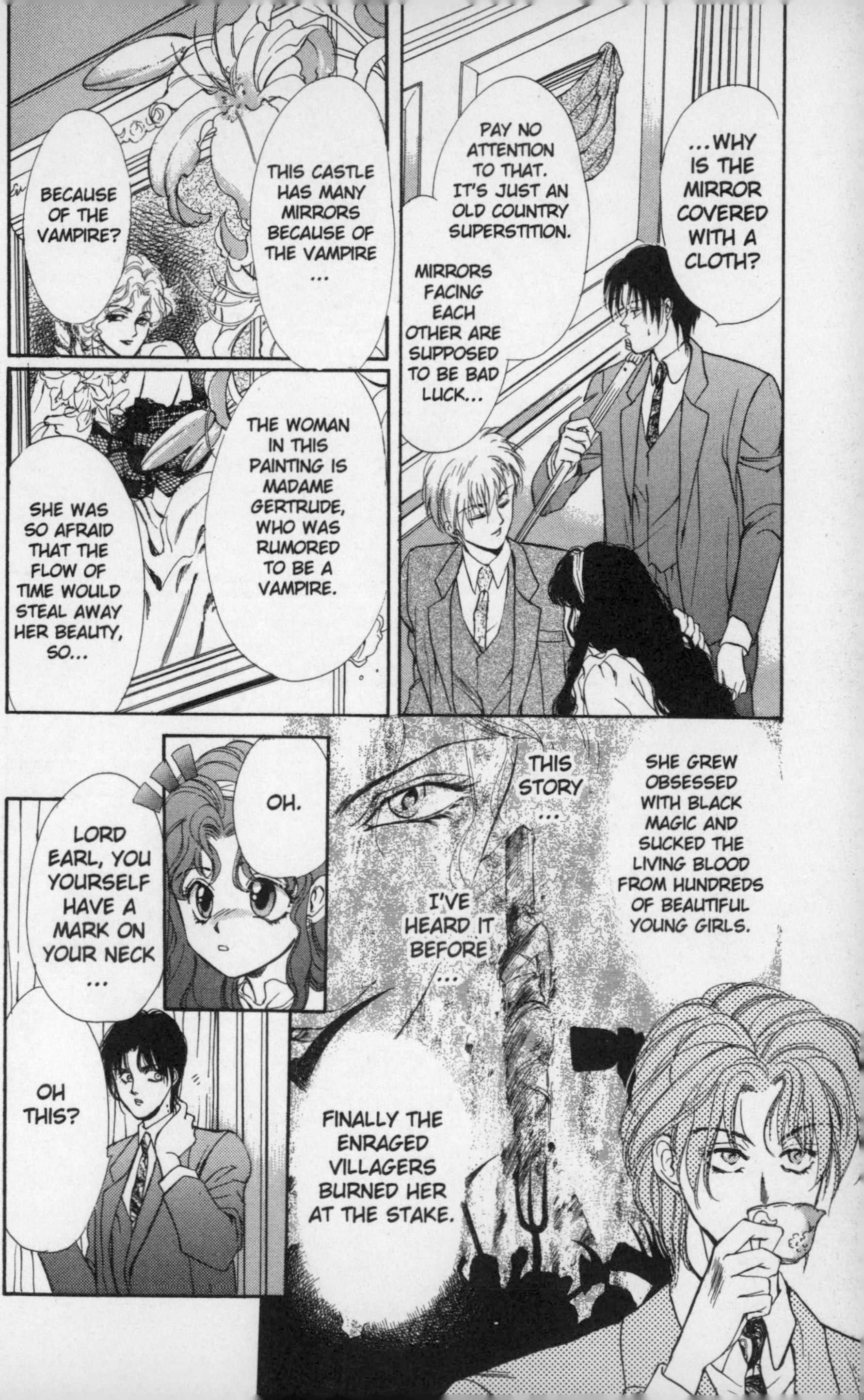
...WHY IS THE MIRROR COVERED WITH A CLOTH?
PAY NO ATTENTION TO THAT. IT'S JUST AN OLD COUNTRY SUPERSTITION.
MIRRORS FACING EACH OTHER ARE SUPPOSED TO BE BAD LUCK...
THIS CASTLE HAS MANY MIRRORS BECAUSE OF THE VAMPIRE ...
BECAUSE OF THE VAMPIRE?
THE WOMAN IN THIS PAINTING IS MADAME GERTRUDE, WHO WAS RUMORED TO BE A VAMPIRE.
SHE WAS SO AFRAID THAT THE FLOW OF TIME WOULD STEAL AWAY HER BEAUTY, SO...
SHE GREW OBSESSED WITH BLACK MAGIC AND SUCKED THE LIVING BLOOD FROM HUNDREDS OF BEAUTIFUL YOUNG GIRLS.
THIS STORY ...
I'VE HEARD IT BEFORE ...
FINALLY THE ENRAGED VILLAGERS BURNED HER AT THE STAKE.
OH.
LORD EARL, YOU YOURSELF HAVE A MARK ON YOUR NECK ...
OH THIS?

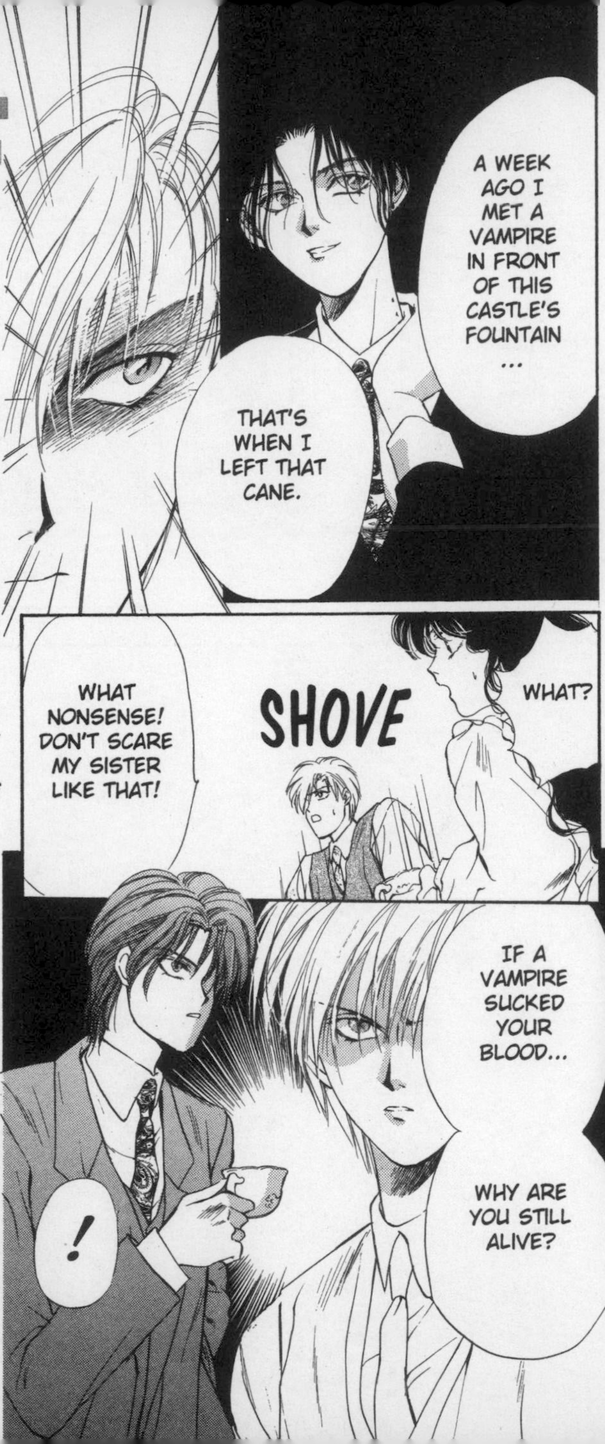
A WEEK AGO I MET A VAMPIRE IN FRONT OF THIS CASTLE'S FOUNTAIN...
THAT'S WHEN I LEFT THAT CANE.
WHAT?
SHOVE
WHAT NONSENSE! DON'T SCARE MY SISTER LIKE THAT!
IF A VAMPIRE SUCKED YOUR BLOOD...
WHY ARE YOU STILL ALIVE?
!

WILD ♦ TALK

This is the episode about which some readers called Cain "nasty." Yes, let me tell you right now. Cain is a player...Vulnerable girls seem to be his type. Of course he's pretty picky about their faces too. Around this time I got a lot of letters from big fans of Riff. He really doesn't appear that much in the story, so it's kind of strange. Hmm...This is a vampire story and I love vampire stories, so I rented my darling Gary Oldman's Dracula but...ended up not using it after all. Still, I'd like to redo that story and make it nastier (what?) and more beautiful. I once wanted to be a vampire. Really!

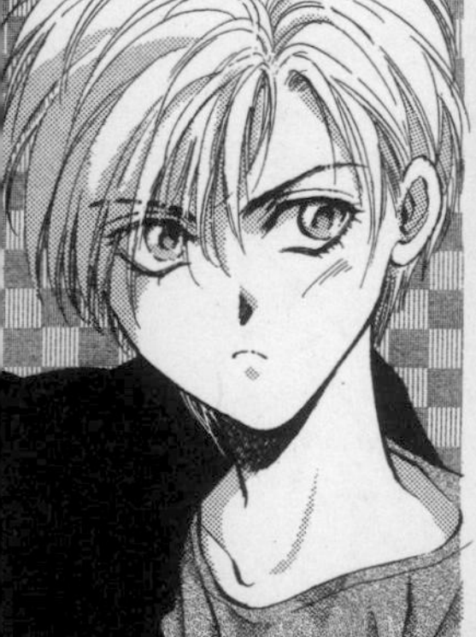

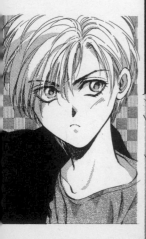

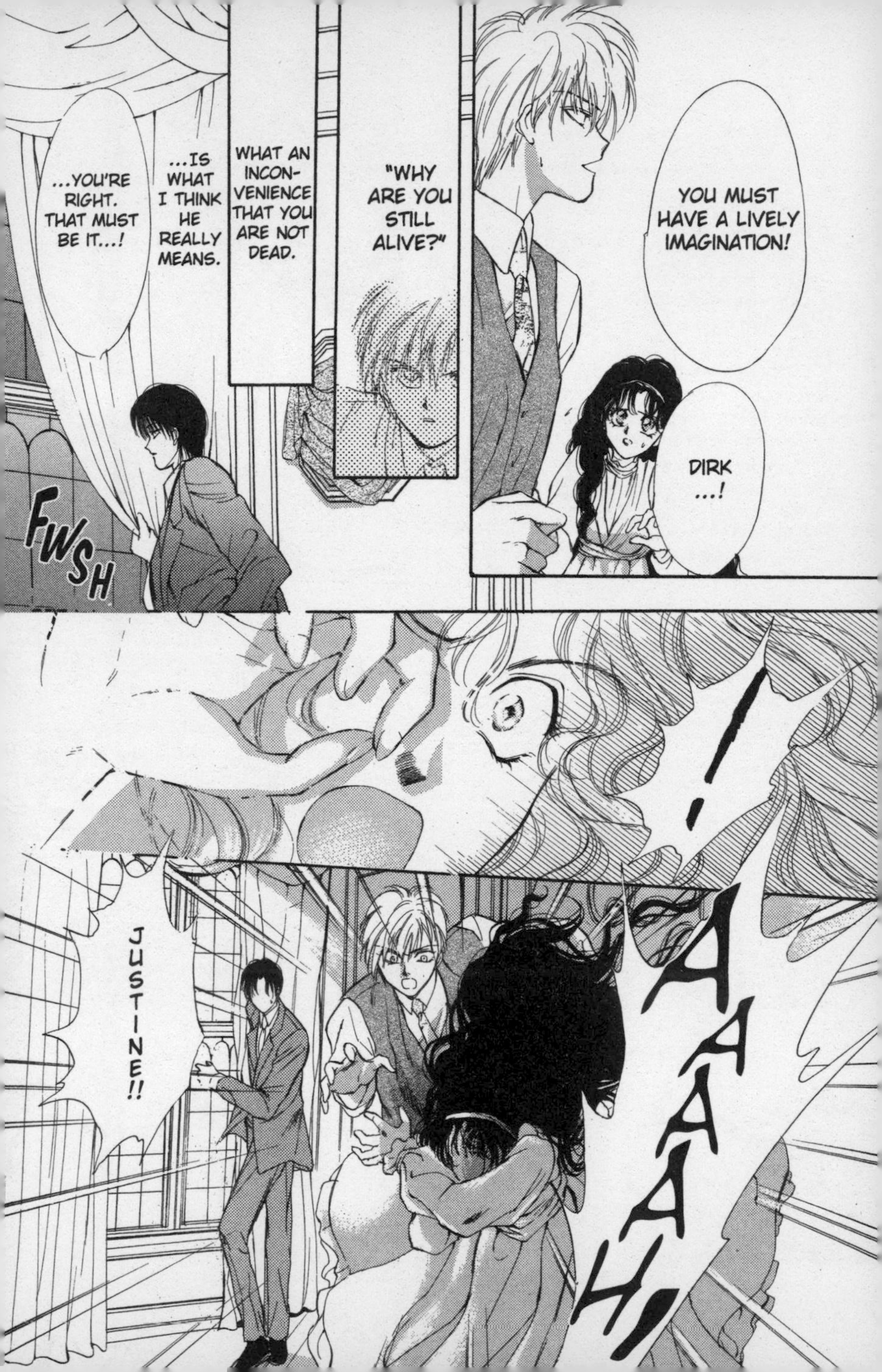
YOU MUST HAVE A LIVELY IMAGINATION!
DIRK ...!
"WHY ARE YOU STILL ALIVE?"
WHAT AN INCON-VENIENCE THAT YOU ARE NOT DEAD.
...IS WHAT I THINK HE REALLY MEANS.
...YOU'RE RIGHT. THAT MUST BE IT...!
FWSH
!
AAAAH!
JUSTINE!!

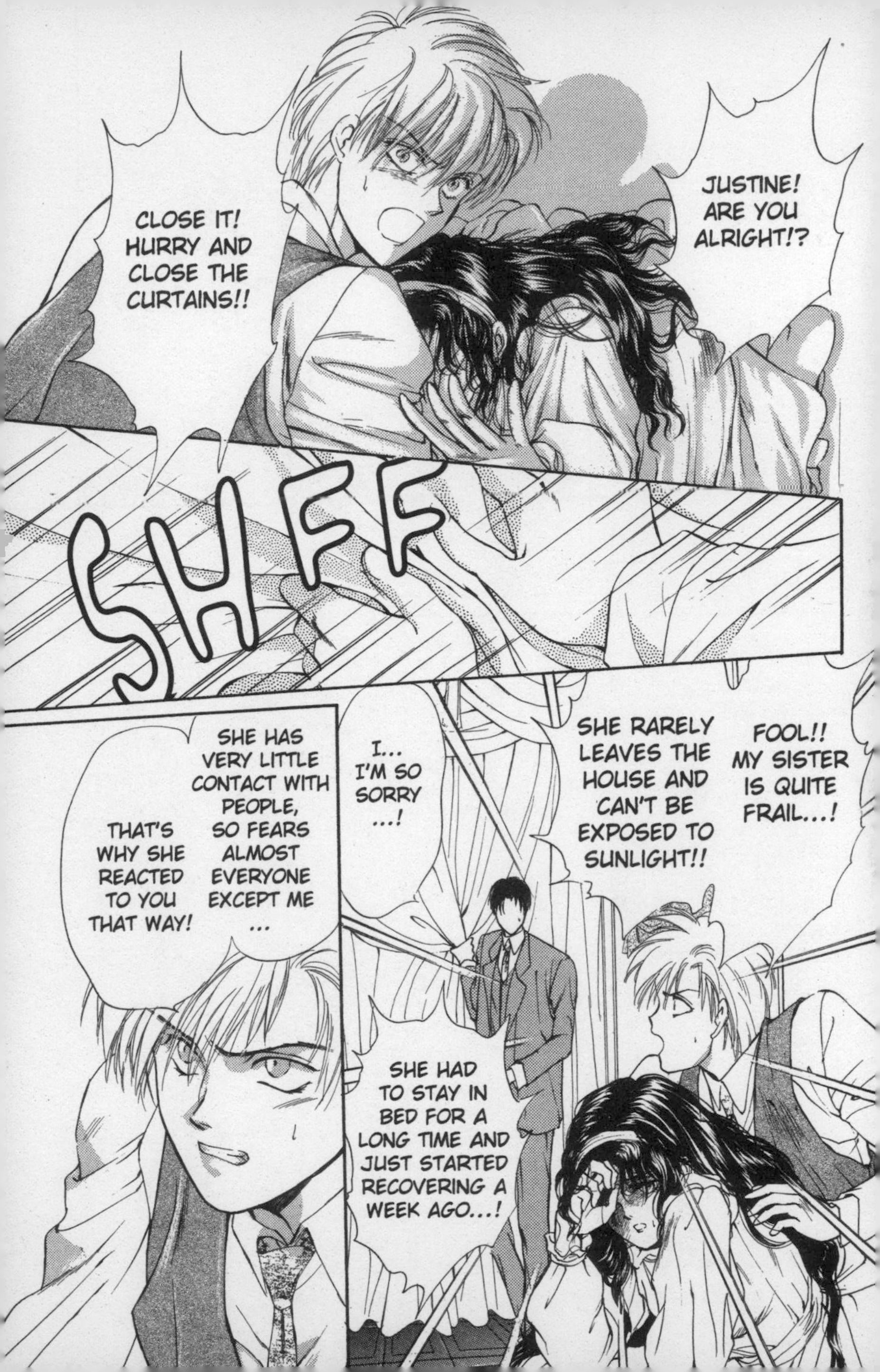
JUSTINE! ARE YOU ALRIGHT!?
CLOSE IT! HURRY AND CLOSE THE CURTAINS!!
SHFF
FOOL!! MY SISTER IS QUITE FRAIL...!
SHE RARELY LEAVES THE HOUSE AND CAN'T BE EXPOSED TO SUNLIGHT!!
SHE HAD TO STAY IN BED FOR A LONG TIME AND JUST STARTED RECOVERING A WEEK AGO...!
I... I'M SO SORRY ...!
SHE HAS VERY LITTLE CONTACT WITH PEOPLE, SO FEARS ALMOST EVERYONE EXCEPT ME ...
THAT'S WHY SHE REACTED TO YOU THAT WAY!

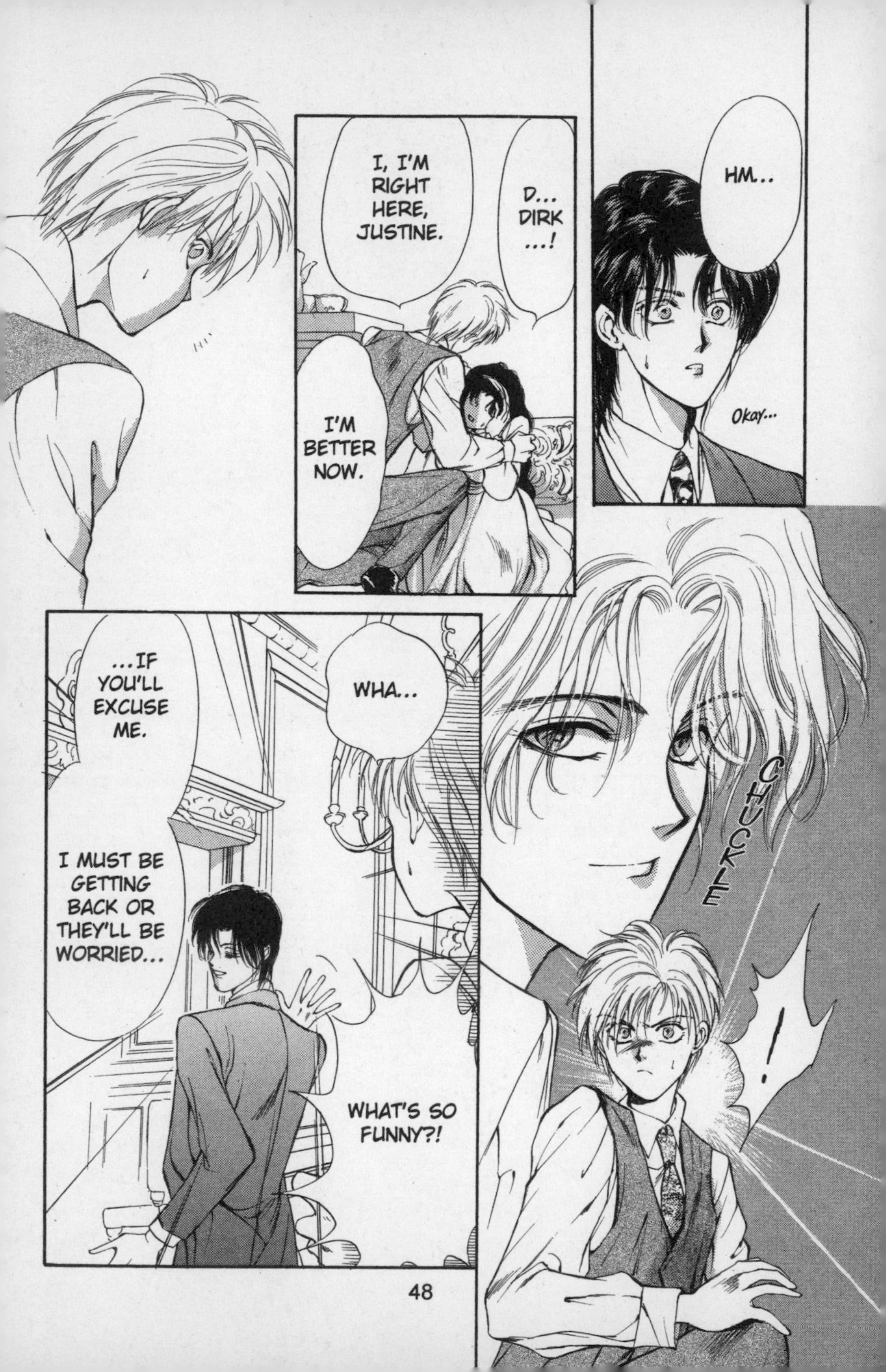
HM...
Okay...
D... DIRK ...!
I, I'M RIGHT HERE, JUSTINE.
I'M BETTER NOW.
CHUCKLE
!
WHA...
...IF YOU'LL EXCUSE ME.
I MUST BE GETTING BACK OR THEY'LL BE WORRIED...
WHAT'S SO FUNNY?!

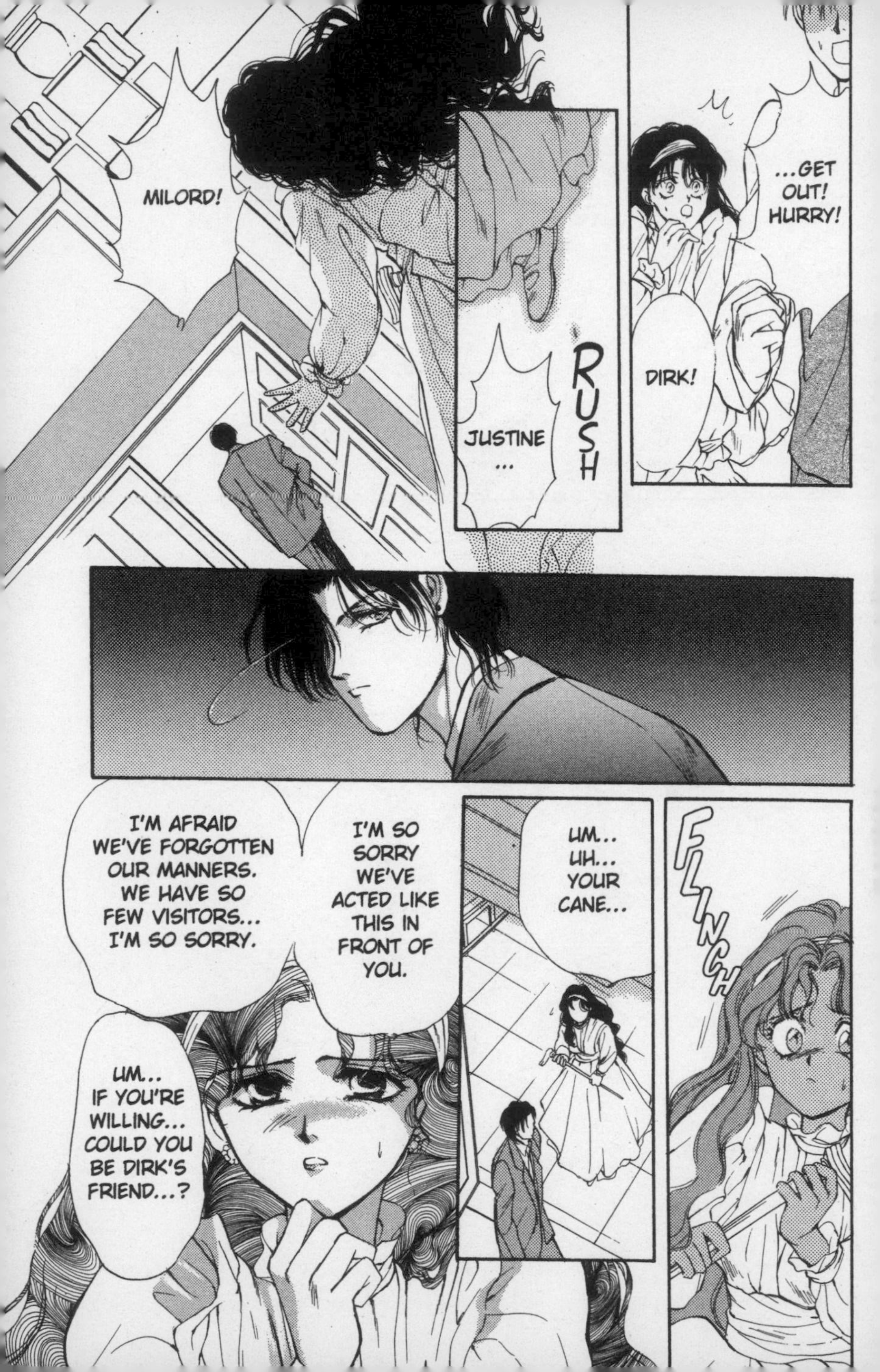
...GET OUT! HURRY!
DIRK!
RUSH
JUSTINE ...
MILORD!
FLINCH
UM.. UH... YOUR CANE...
I'M SO SORRY WE'VE ACTED LIKE THIS IN FRONT OF YOU.
I'M AFRAID WE'VE FORGOTTEN OUR MANNERS. WE HAVE SO FEW VISITORS... I'M SO SORRY.
UM... IF YOU'RE WILLING... COULD YOU BE DIRK'S FRIEND...?

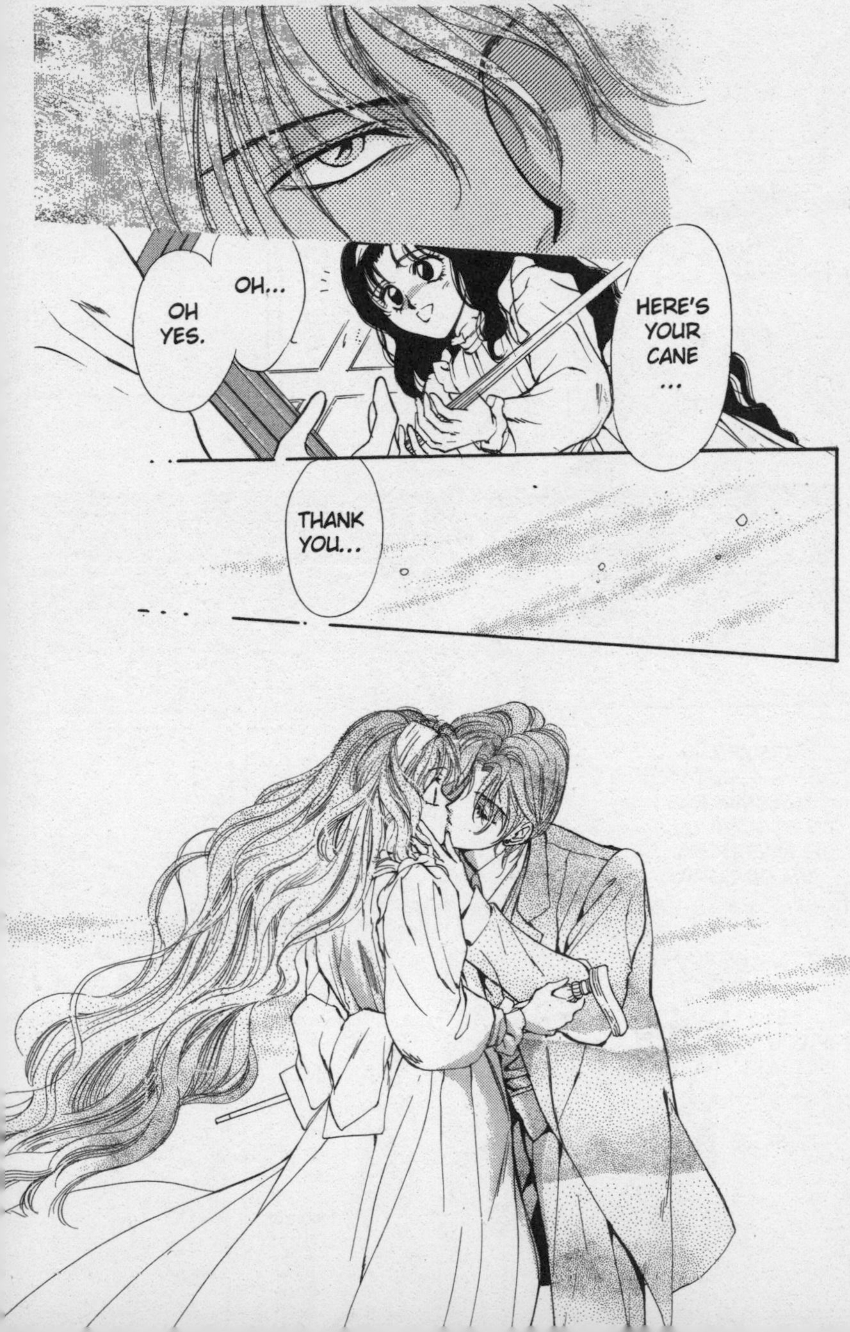
HERE'S YOUR CANE ...
OH... OH YES.
THANK YOU...

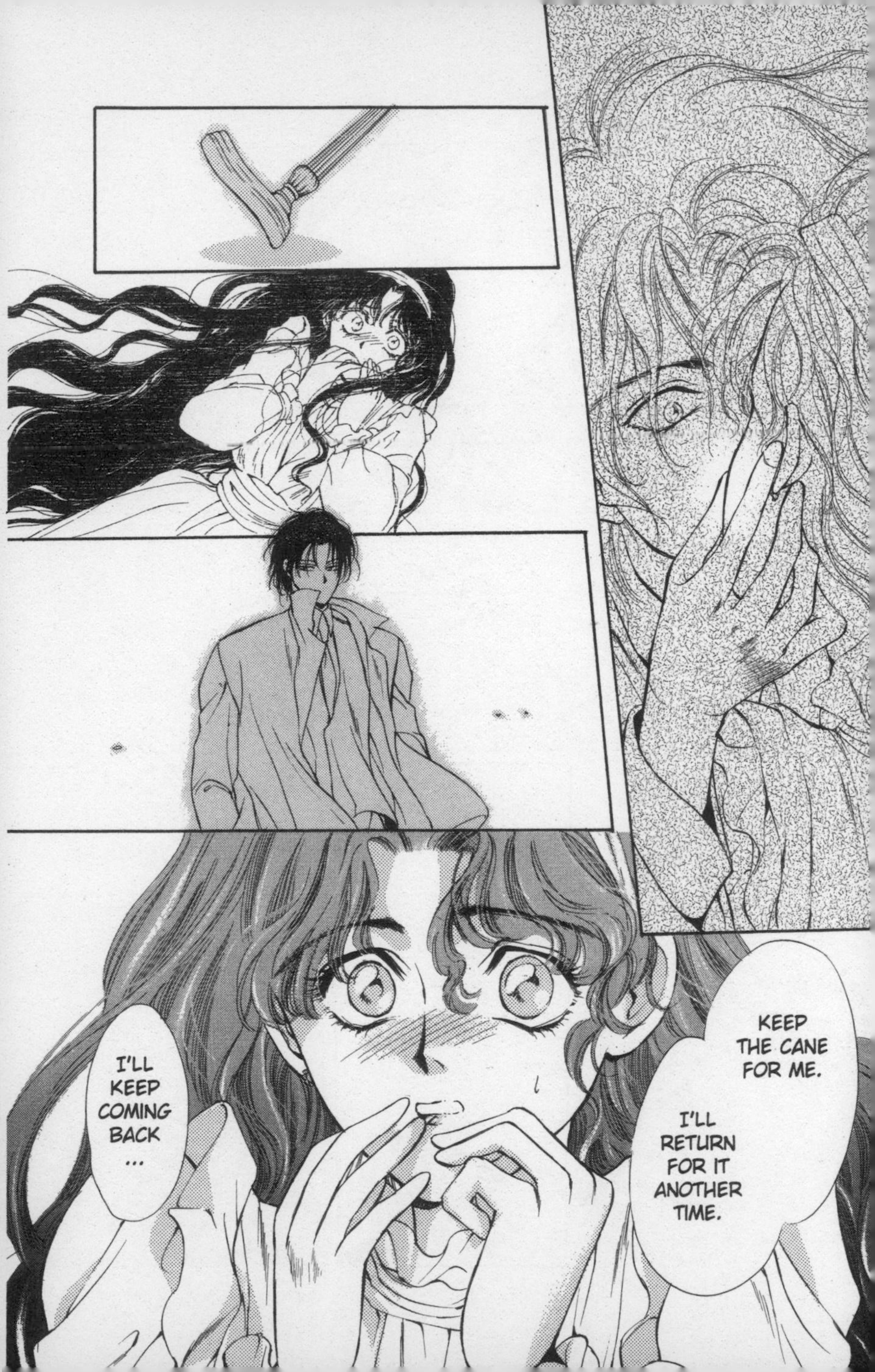
KEEP THE CANE FOR ME.
I'LL RETURN FOR IT ANOTHER TIME.
I'LL KEEP COMING BACK ...

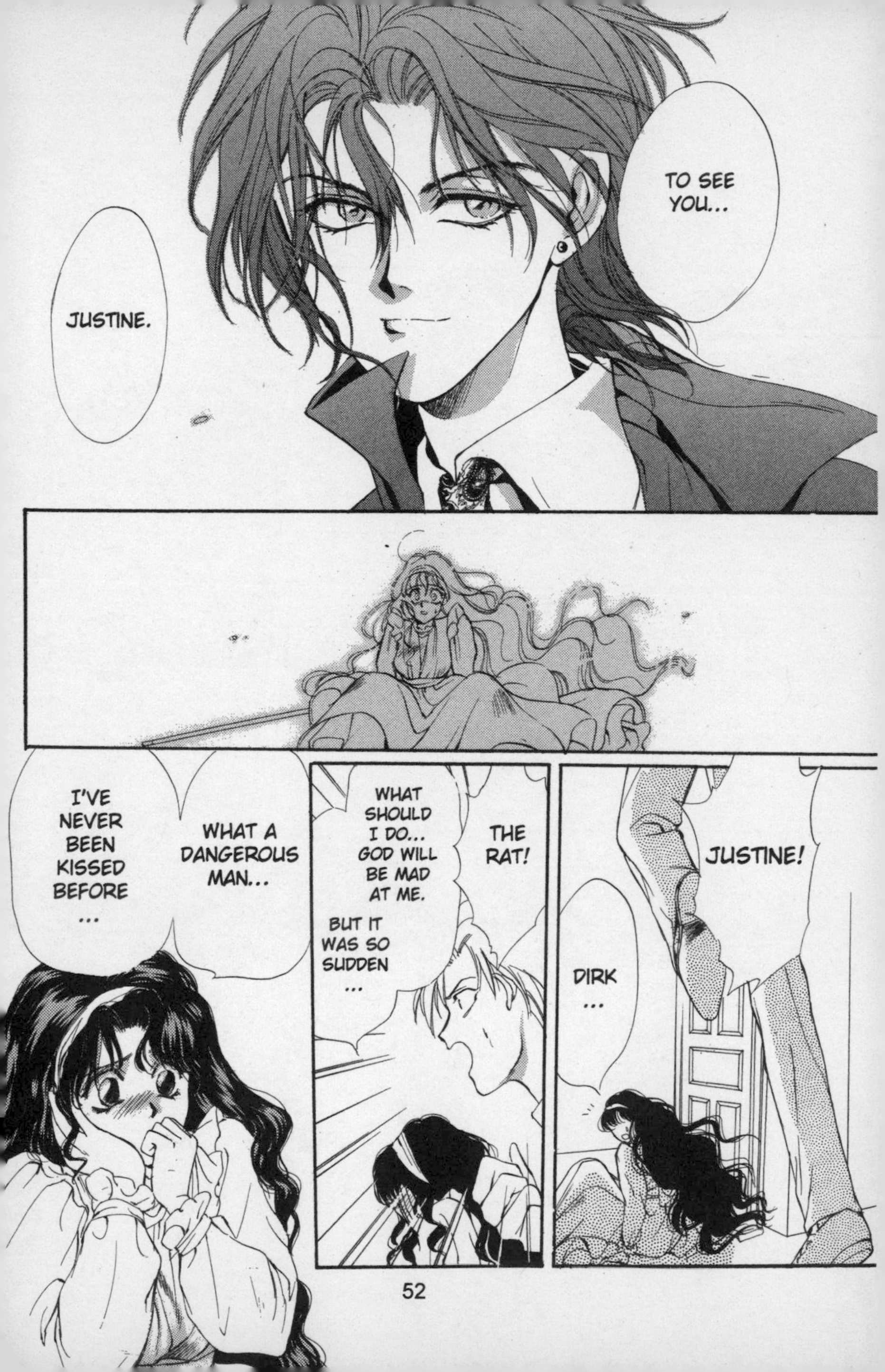
TO SEE YOU...
JUSTINE.
JUSTINE!
DIRK ...
THE RAT!
WHAT SHOULD I DO... GOD WILL BE MAD AT ME.
BUT IT WAS SO SUDDEN ...
WHAT A DANGEROUS MAN...
I'VE NEVER BEEN KISSED BEFORE ...

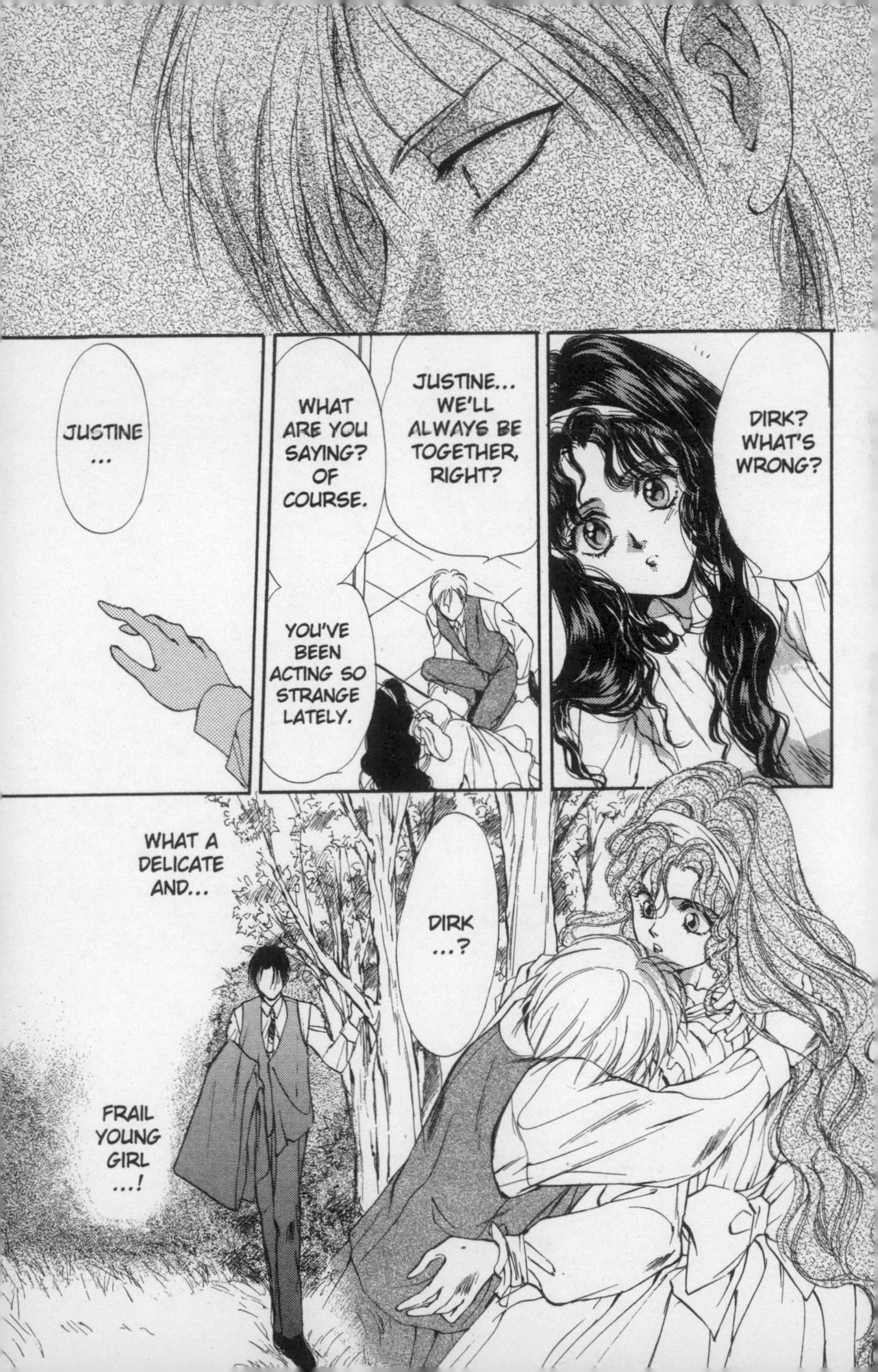
DIRK? WHAT'S WRONG?
JUSTINE... WE'LL ALWAYS BE TOGETHER, RIGHT?
WHAT ARE YOU SAYING? OF COURSE.
YOU'VE BEEN ACTING SO STRANGE LATELY.
JUSTINE ...
DIRK ...?
WHAT A DELICATE AND...
FRAIL YOUNG GIRL ...!

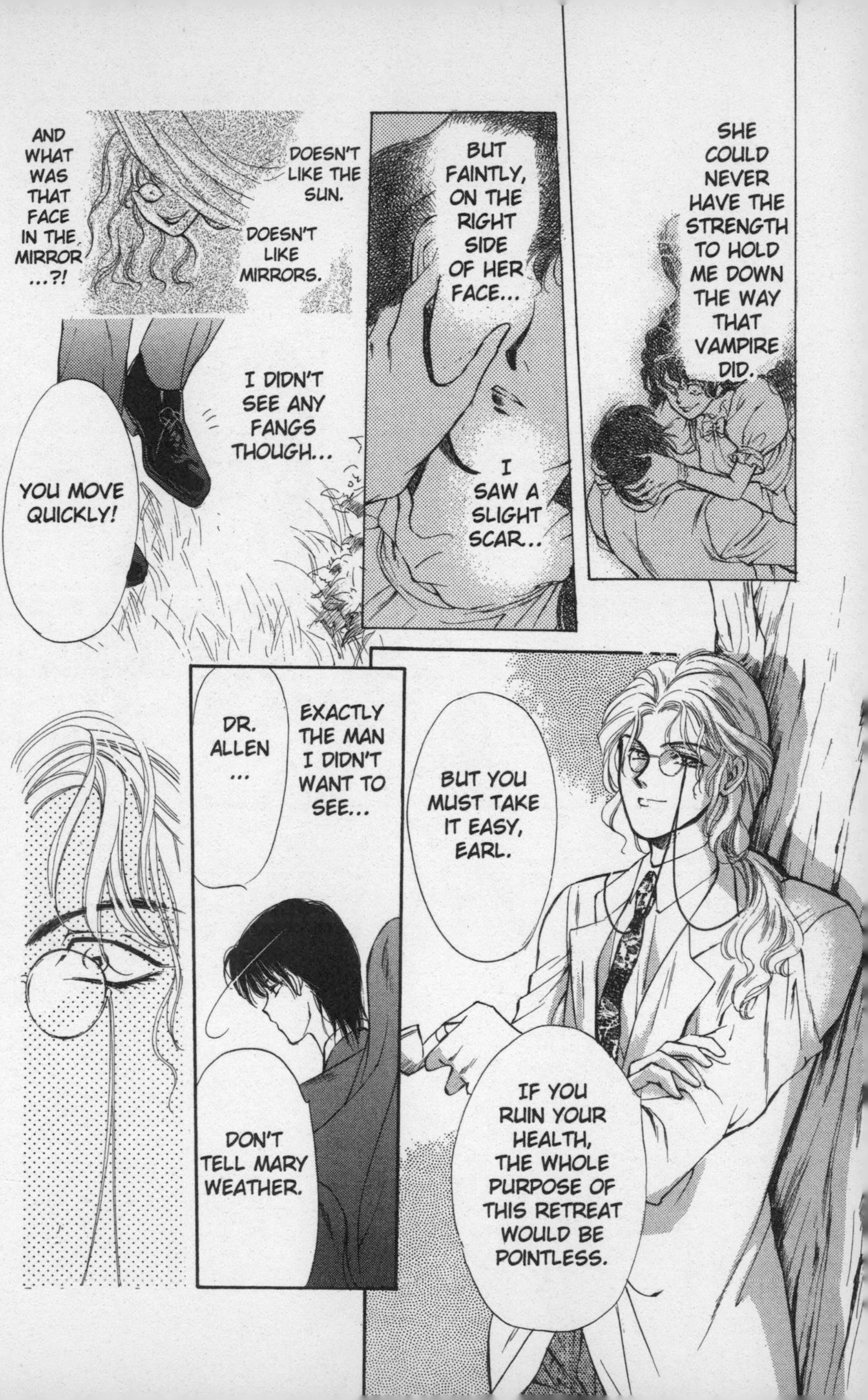
SHE COULD NEVER HAVE THE STRENGTH TO HOLD ME DOWN THE WAY THAT VAMPIRE DID.
BUT FAINTLY, ON THE RIGHT SIDE OF HER FACE...
I SAW A SLIGHT SCAR...
DOESN'T LIKE THE SUN.
DOESN'T LIKE MIRRORS.
AND WHAT WAS THAT FACE IN THE MIRROR...?!
I DIDN'T SEE ANY FANGS THOUGH...
YOU MOVE QUICKLY!
BUT YOU MUST TAKE IT EASY, EARL.
IF YOU RUIN YOUR HEALTH, THE WHOLE PURPOSE OF THIS RETREAT WOULD BE POINTLESS.
DR. ALLEN ...
EXACTLY THE MAN I DIDN'T WANT TO SEE...
DON'T TELL MARY WEATHER.

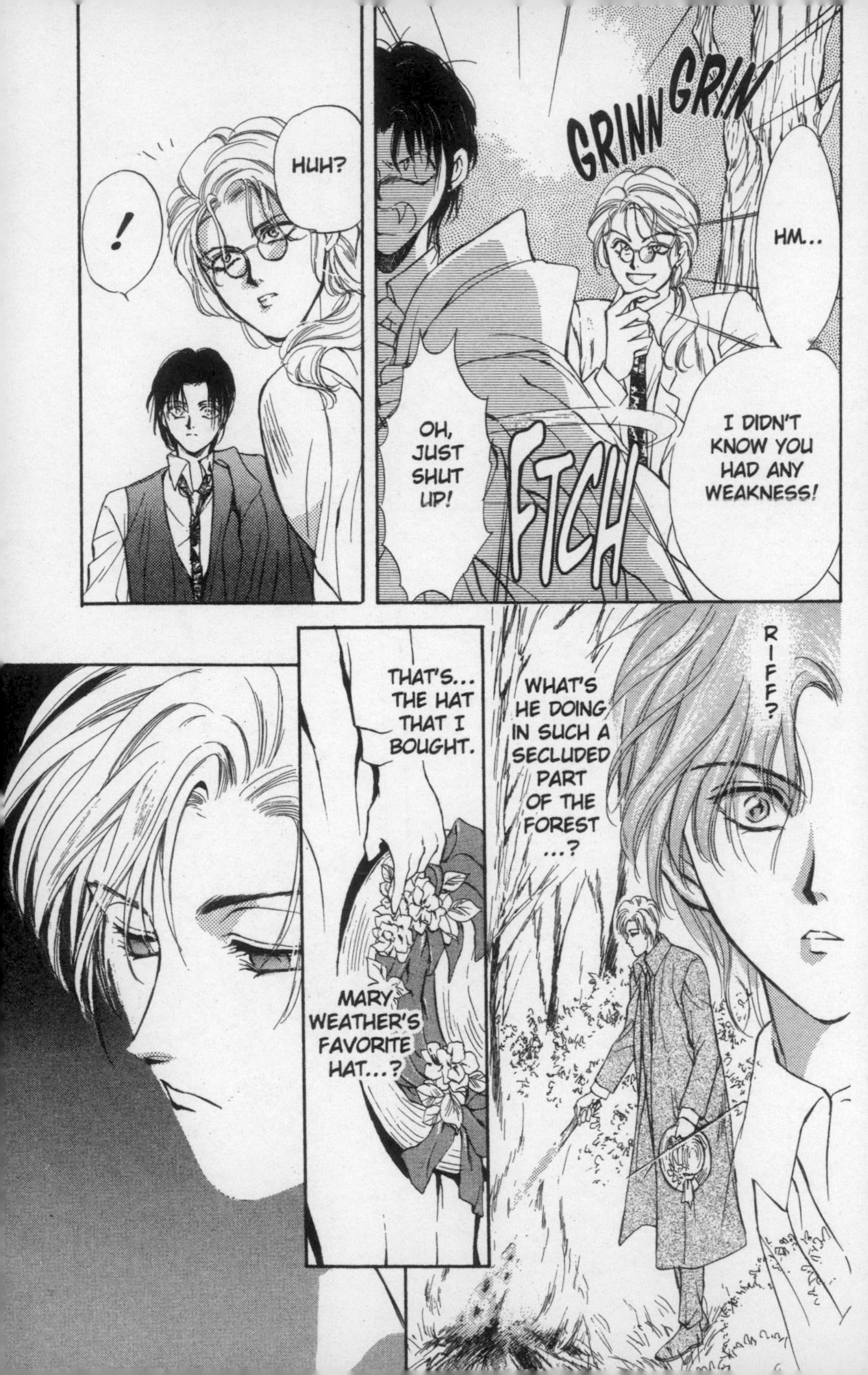
GRINN GRIN
HM...
I DIDN'T KNOW YOU HAD ANY WEAKNESS!
OH, JUST SHUT UP!
FTCH
HUH?
!
RIFF?
WHAT'S HE DOING IN SUCH A SECLUDED PART OF THE FOREST ...?
THAT'S... THE HAT THAT I BOUGHT.
MARY WEATHER'S FAVORITE HAT...?

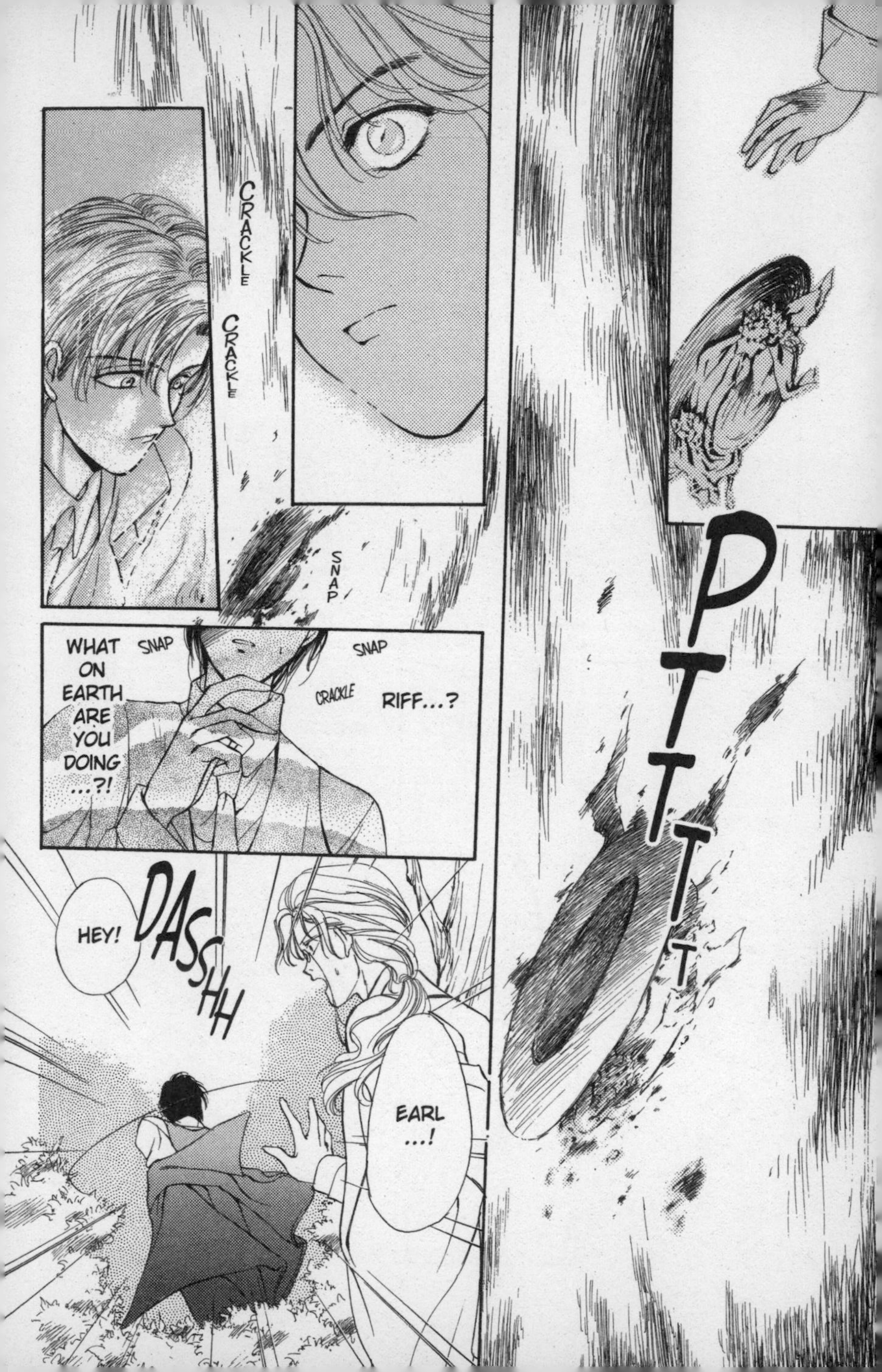
PTTTT
CRACKLE
CRACKLE
SNAP
SNAP
RIFF...?
CRACKLE
SNAP
WHAT ON EARTH ARE YOU DOING ...?!
EARL ...!
DASSHH
HEY!

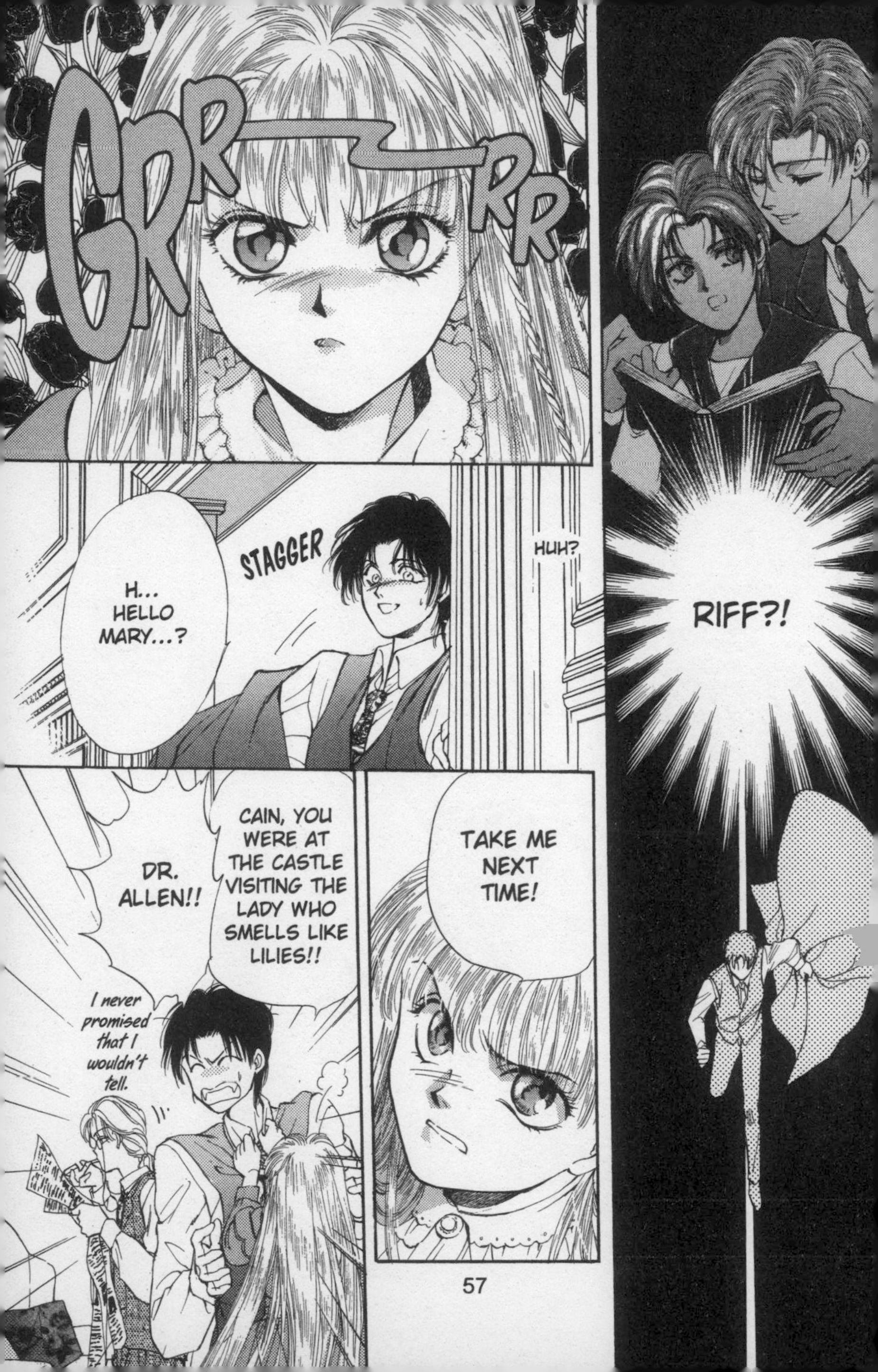
RIFF?!
GRRR
HUH?
STAGGER
H... HELLO MARY...?
TAKE ME NEXT TIME!
CAIN, YOU WERE AT THE CASTLE VISITING THE LADY WHO SMELLS LIKE LILIES!!
DR. ALLEN!!
I never promised that I wouldn't tell.

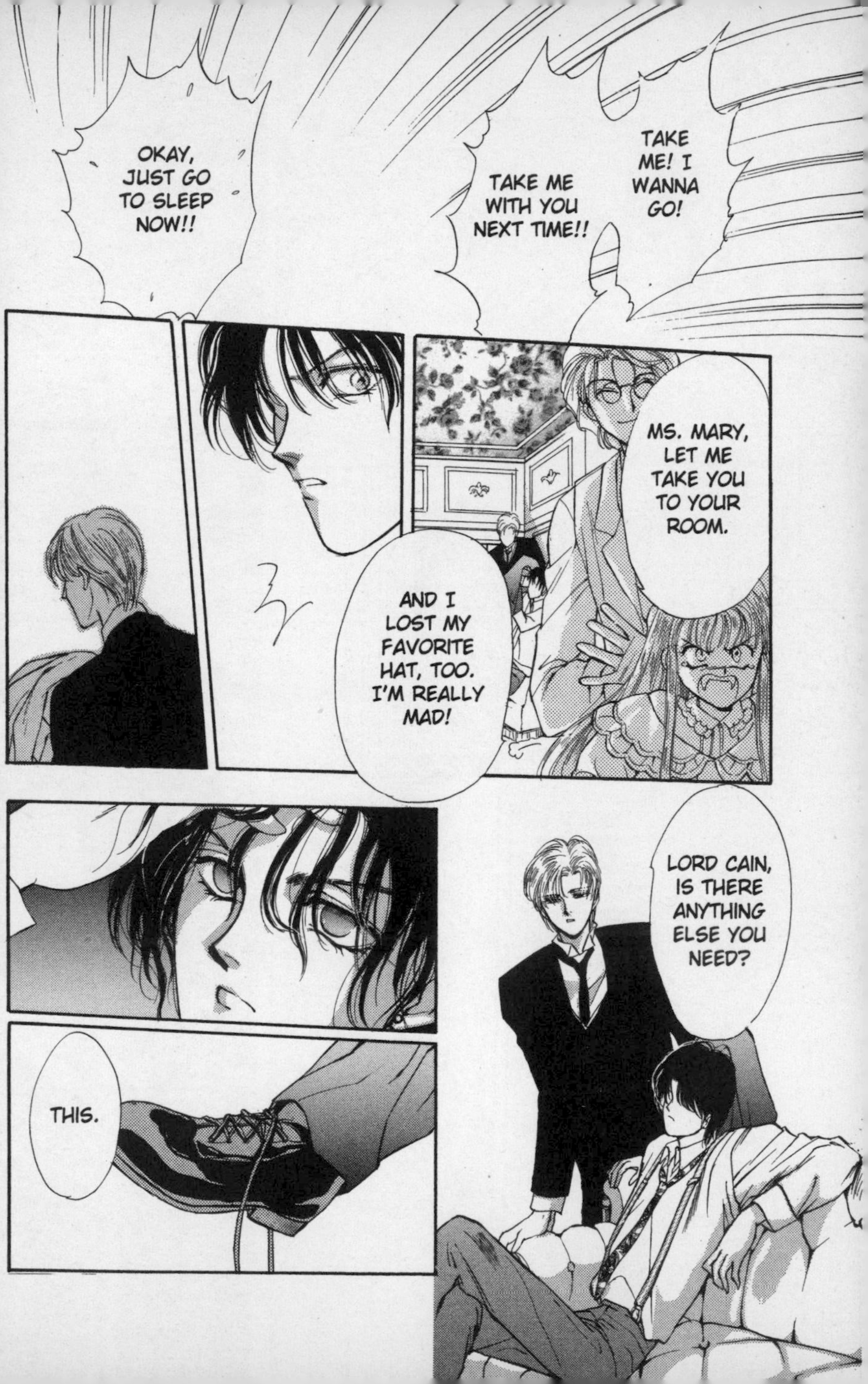
TAKE ME! I WANNA GO!
TAKE ME WITH YOU NEXT TIME!!
OKAY, JUST GO TO SLEEP NOW!!
MS. MARY, LET ME TAKE YOU TO YOUR ROOM.
AND I LOST MY FAVORITE HAT, TOO. I'M REALLY MAD!
LORD CAIN, IS THERE ANYTHING ELSE YOU NEED?
THIS.

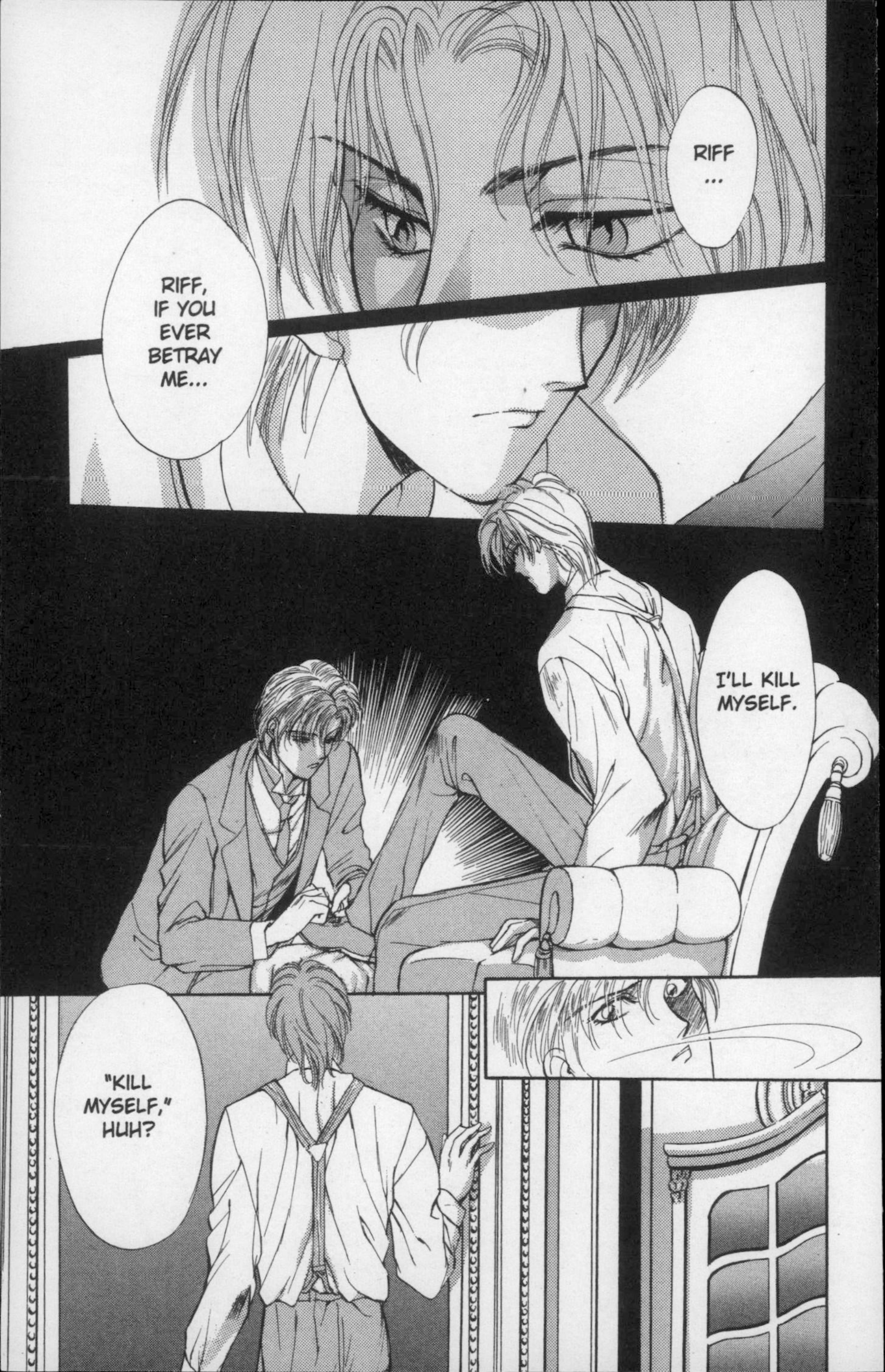
RIFF ...
RIFF, IF YOU EVER BETRAY ME...
I'LL KILL MYSELF.
"KILL MYSELF," HUH?

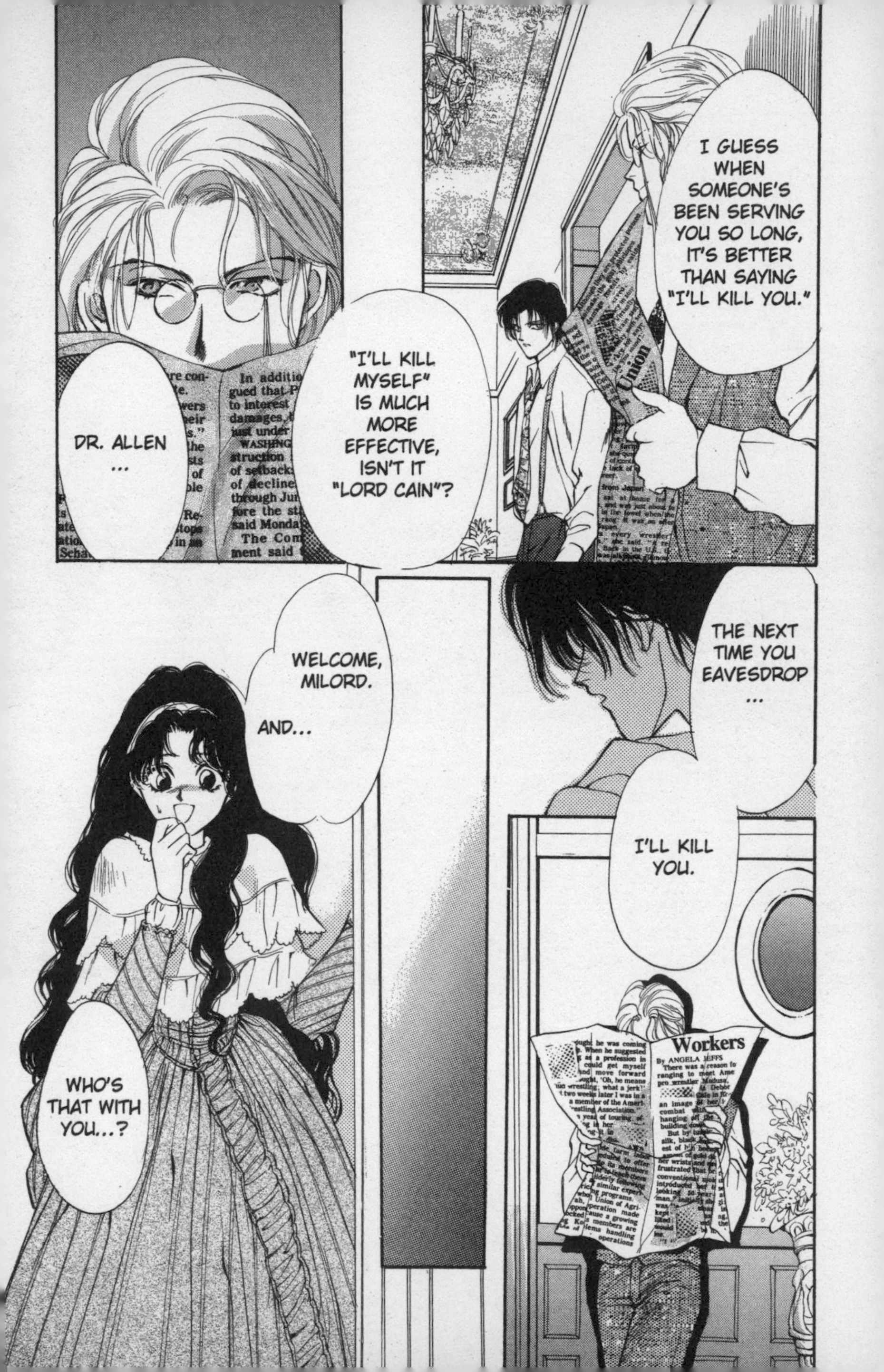
I GUESS WHEN SOMEONE'S BEEN SERVING YOU SO LONG, IT'S BETTER THAN SAYING "I'LL KILL YOU."
"I'LL KILL MYSELF" IS MUCH MORE EFFECTIVE, ISN'T IT "LORD CAIN"?
DR. ALLEN ...
THE NEXT TIME YOU EAVESDROP ...
I'LL KILL YOU.
Workers
By ANGELA JEFFS
WELCOME, MILORD.
AND...
WHO'S THAT WITH YOU...?

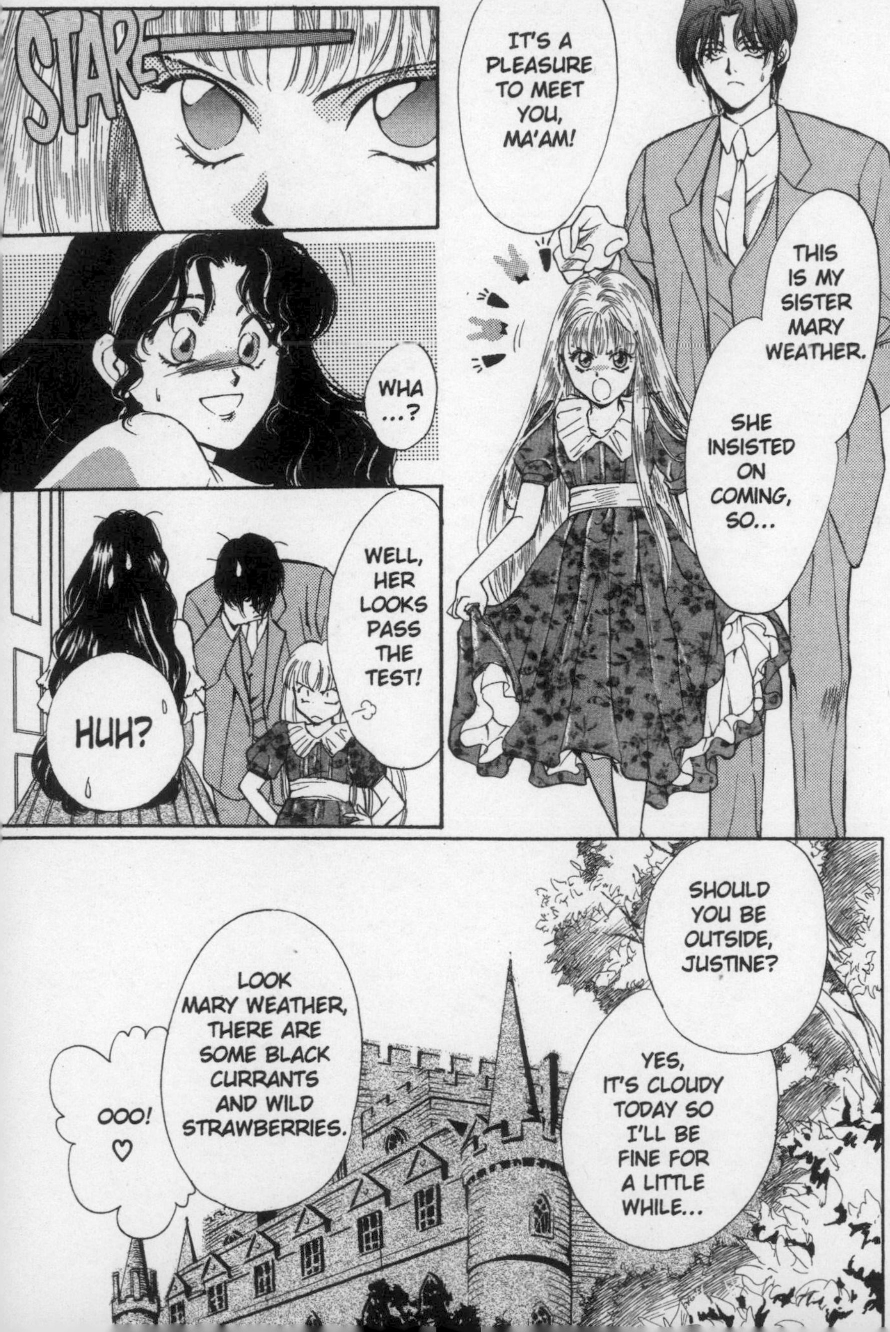
THIS IS MY SISTER MARY WEATHER.
SHE INSISTED ON COMING, SO...
IT'S A PLEASURE TO MEET YOU, MA'AM!
STARE
WHA ...?
WELL, HER LOOKS PASS THE TEST!
HUH?
SHOULD YOU BE OUTSIDE, JUSTINE?
YES, IT'S CLOUDY TODAY SO I'LL BE FINE FOR A LITTLE WHILE...
LOOK MARY WEATHER, THERE ARE SOME BLACK CURRANTS AND WILD STRAWBERRIES.
OOO! ♡

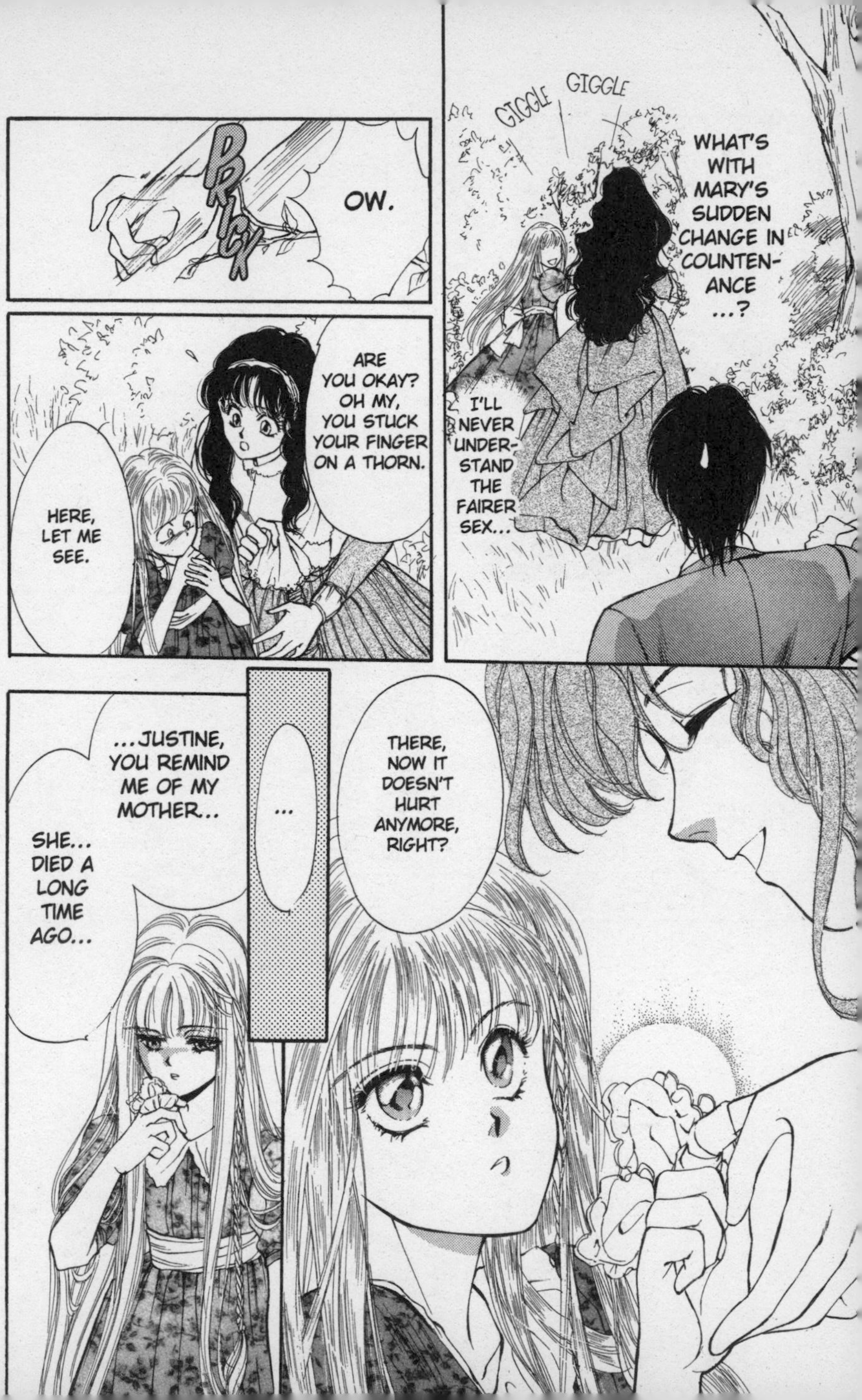
GIGGLE GIGGLE
WHAT'S WITH MARY'S SUDDEN CHANGE IN COUNTENANCE...?
I'LL NEVER UNDERSTAND THE FAIRER SEX...
PRICK
OW.
ARE YOU OKAY? OH MY, YOU STUCK YOUR FINGER ON A THORN.
HERE, LET ME SEE.
THERE, NOW IT DOESN'T HURT ANYMORE, RIGHT?
...
...JUSTINE, YOU REMIND ME OF MY MOTHER...
SHE... DIED A LONG TIME AGO...

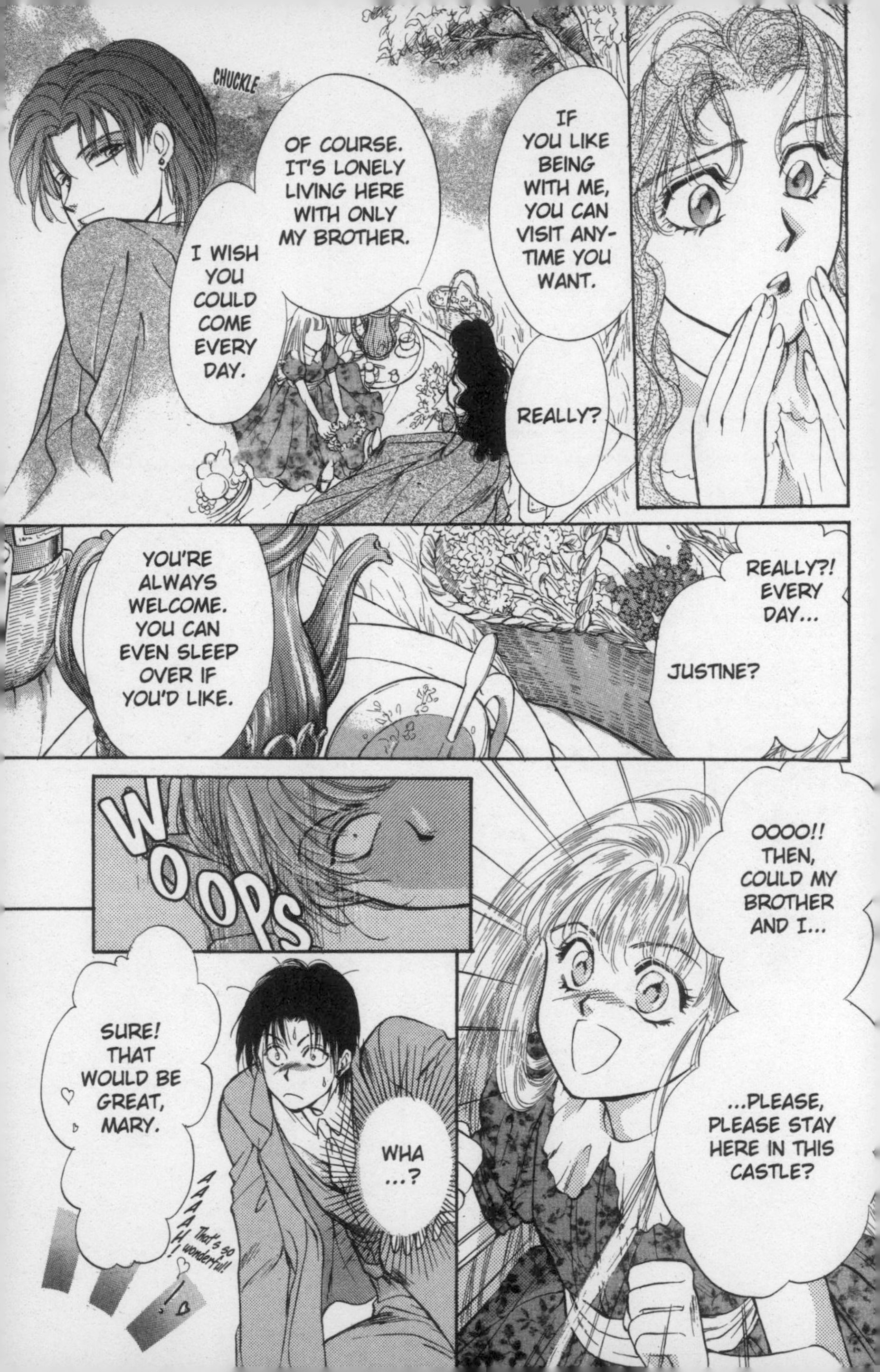
IF YOU LIKE BEING WITH ME, YOU CAN VISIT ANY-TIME YOU WANT.
REALLY?
CHUCKLE
OF COURSE. IT'S LONELY LIVING HERE WITH ONLY MY BROTHER.
I WISH YOU COULD COME EVERY DAY.
REALLY?! EVERY DAY...
JUSTINE?
YOU'RE ALWAYS WELCOME. YOU CAN EVEN SLEEP OVER IF YOU'D LIKE.
OOOO!! THEN, COULD MY BROTHER AND I...
...PLEASE, PLEASE STAY HERE IN THIS CASTLE?
WOOPS
WHA ...?
SURE! THAT WOULD BE GREAT, MARY.
AAAAAH! That's so wonderful!

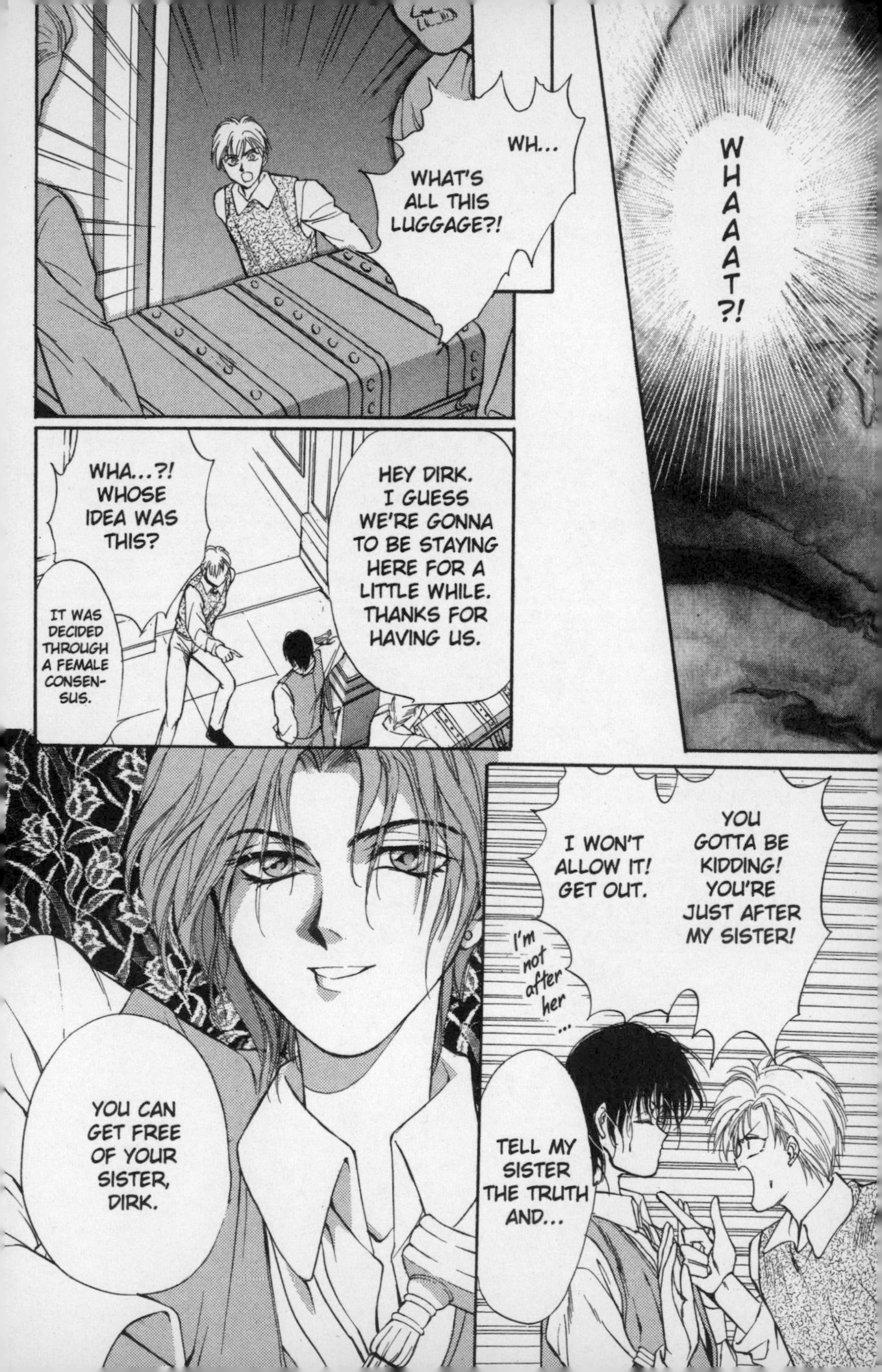
WHAAAT?!
WH...
WHAT'S ALL THIS LUGGAGE?!
HEY DIRK. I GUESS WE'RE GONNA TO BE STAYING HERE FOR A LITTLE WHILE. THANKS FOR HAVING US.
WHA...?! WHOSE IDEA WAS THIS?
IT WAS DECIDED THROUGH A FEMALE CONSEN-SUS.
YOU GOTTA BE KIDDING! YOU'RE JUST AFTER MY SISTER!
I WON'T ALLOW IT! GET OUT.
I'm not after her...
TELL MY SISTER THE TRUTH AND...
YOU CAN GET FREE OF YOUR SISTER, DIRK.

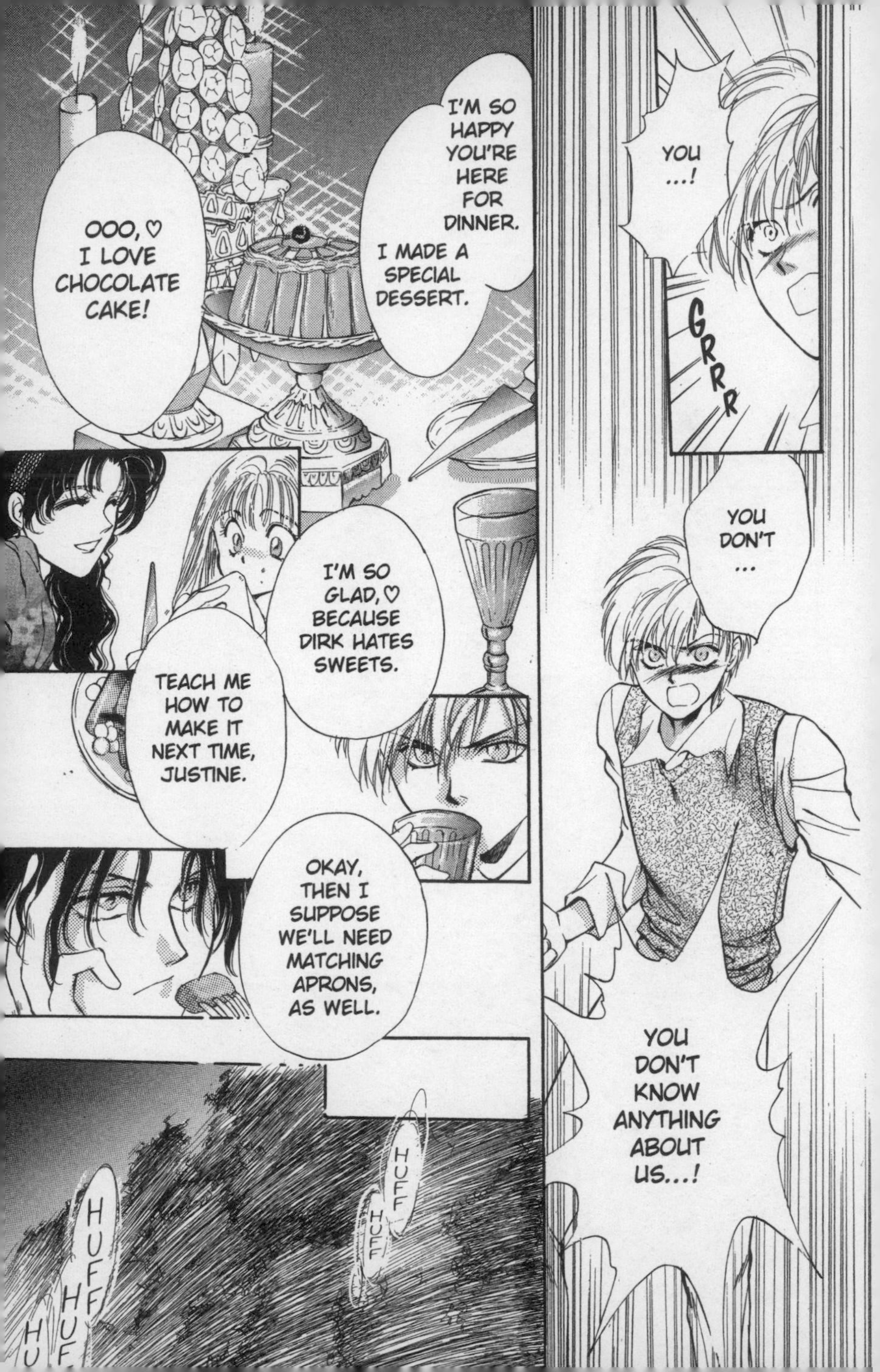
YOU ...!
GRRR
YOU DON'T ...
YOU DON'T KNOW ANYTHING ABOUT US...!
I'M SO HAPPY YOU'RE HERE FOR DINNER.
I MADE A SPECIAL DESSERT.
OOO, ♡ I LOVE CHOCOLATE CAKE!
I'M SO GLAD, ♡ BECAUSE DIRK HATES SWEETS.
TEACH ME HOW TO MAKE IT NEXT TIME, JUSTINE.
OKAY, THEN I SUPPOSE WE'LL NEED MATCHING APRONS, AS WELL.
HUFF HUFF
HUFF HUFF

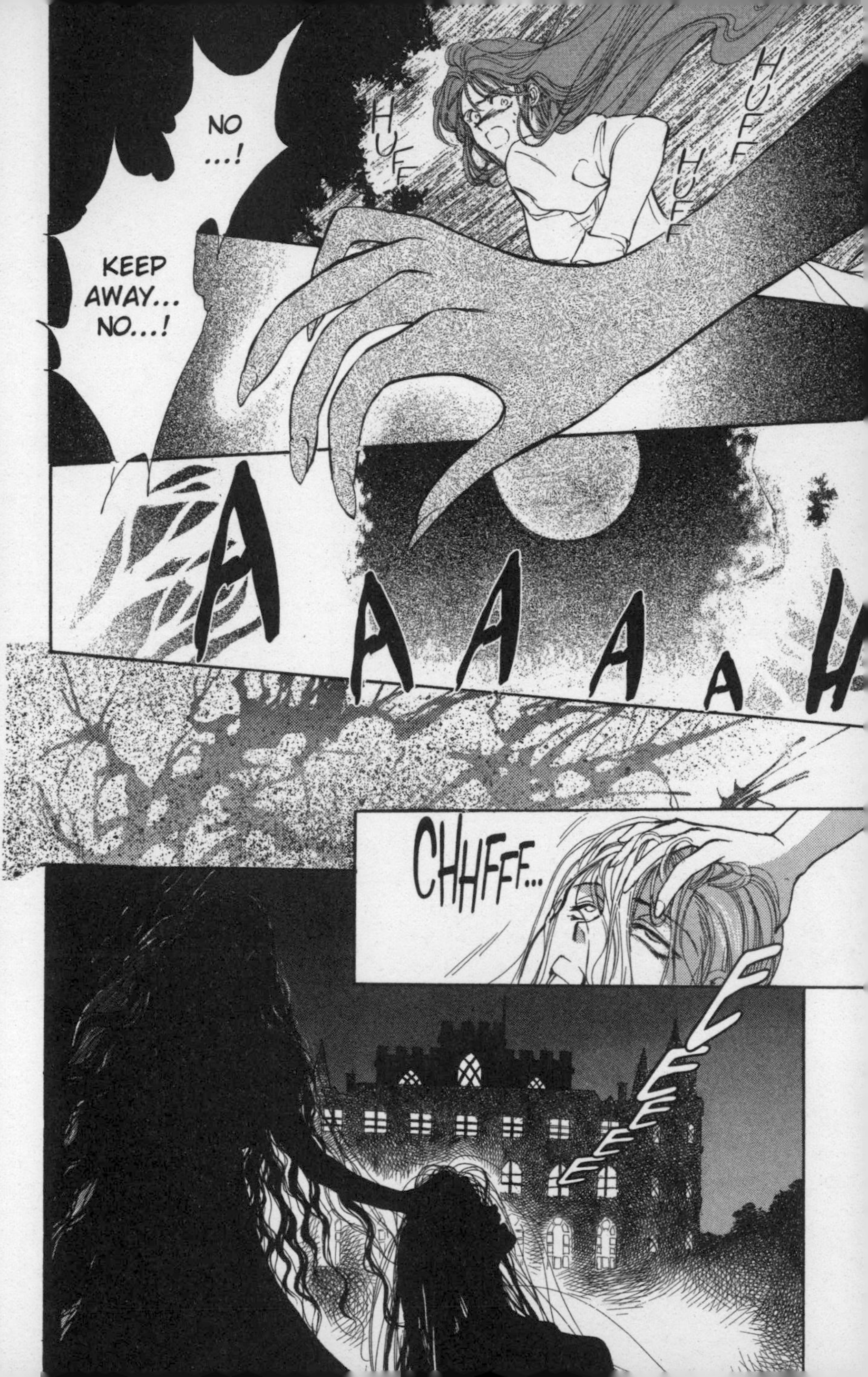
HUFF
HUFF
HUFF
NO ...!
KEEP AWAY... NO...!
AAAAAH
CHHFFF...
EEEEEEE

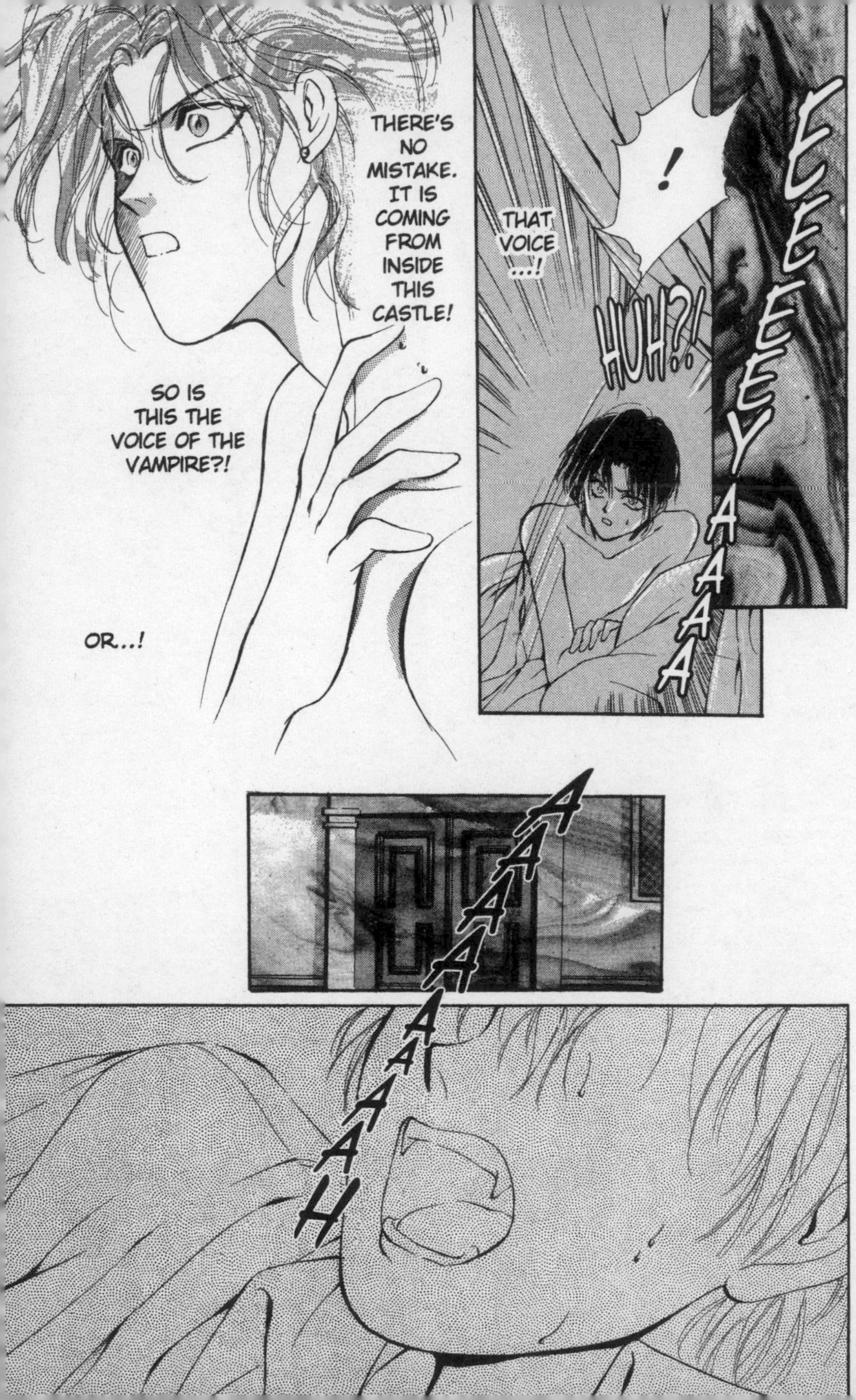
!
THAT VOICE ...!
HUH?!
EEEEEEEYAAAA
THERE'S NO MISTAKE. IT IS COMING FROM INSIDE THIS CASTLE!
SO IS THIS THE VOICE OF THE VAMPIRE?!
OR...!
AAAAAAAAH

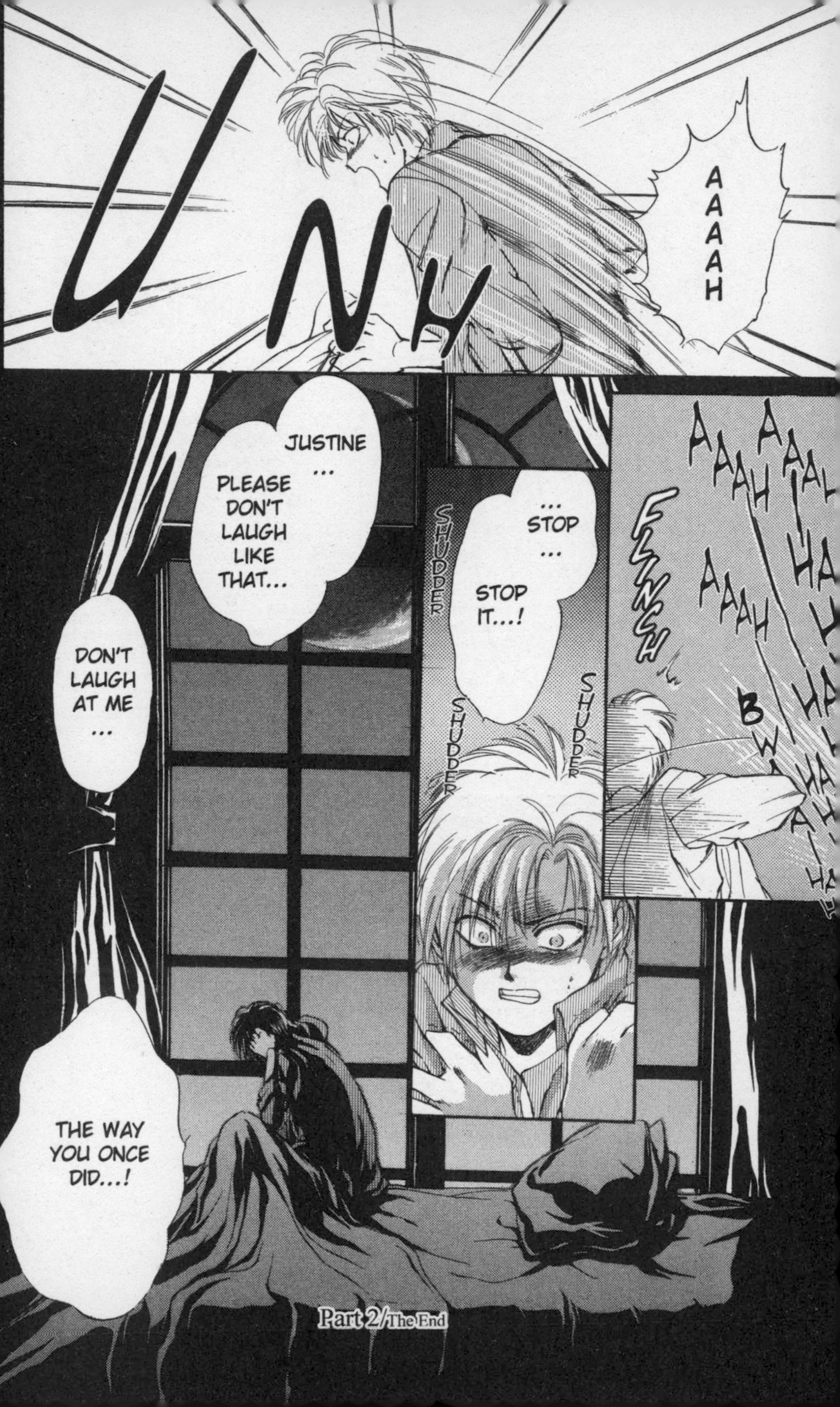
AAAAH
UNH
AAAH
AAAH
FLINCH
...STOP... STOP IT...!
SHUDDER
SHUDDER
SHUDDER
JUSTINE... PLEASE DON'T LAUGH LIKE THAT...
DON'T LAUGH AT ME...
THE WAY YOU ONCE DID...!
Part 2/The End

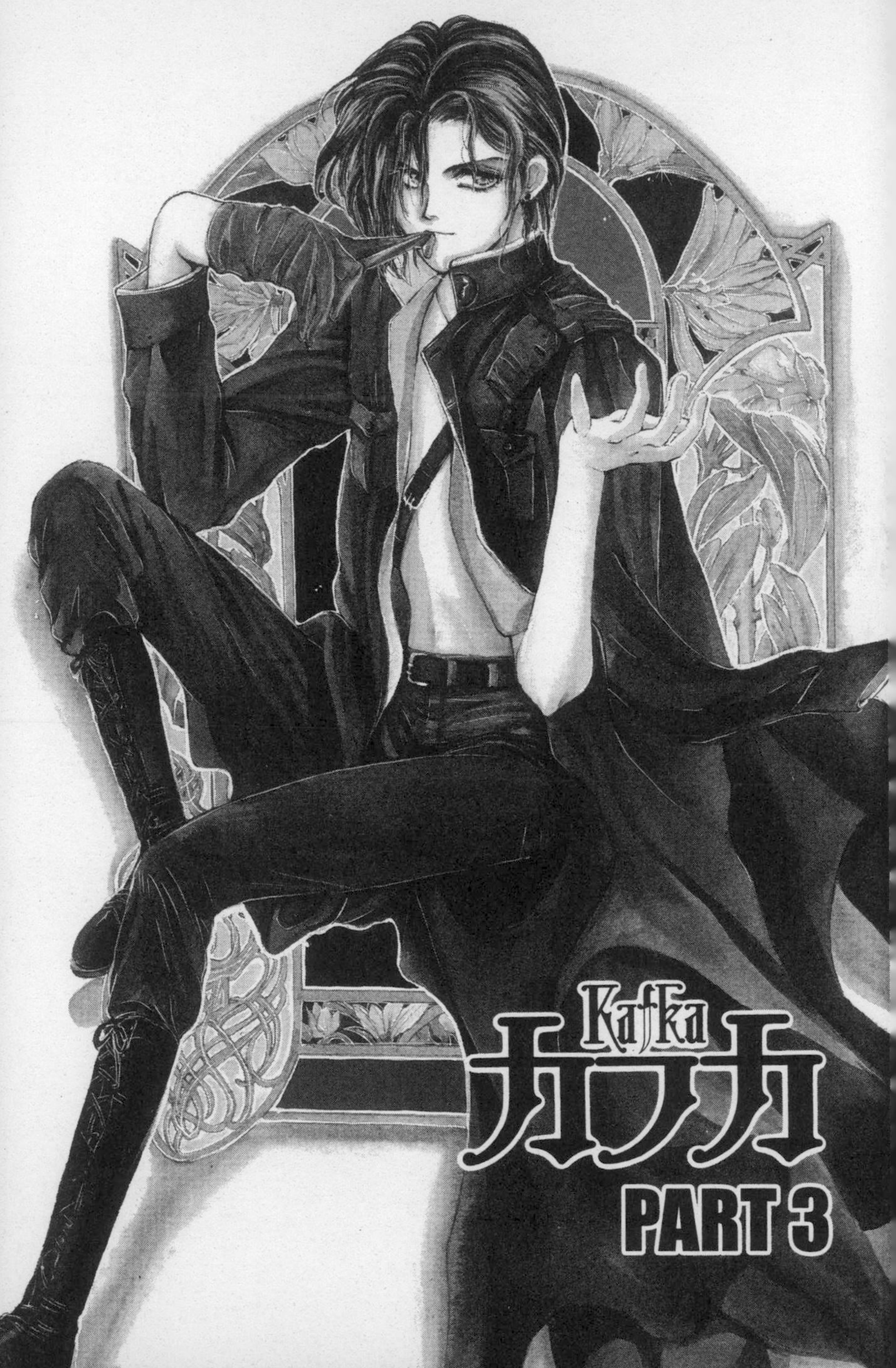
Kafka
カフカ
PART 3

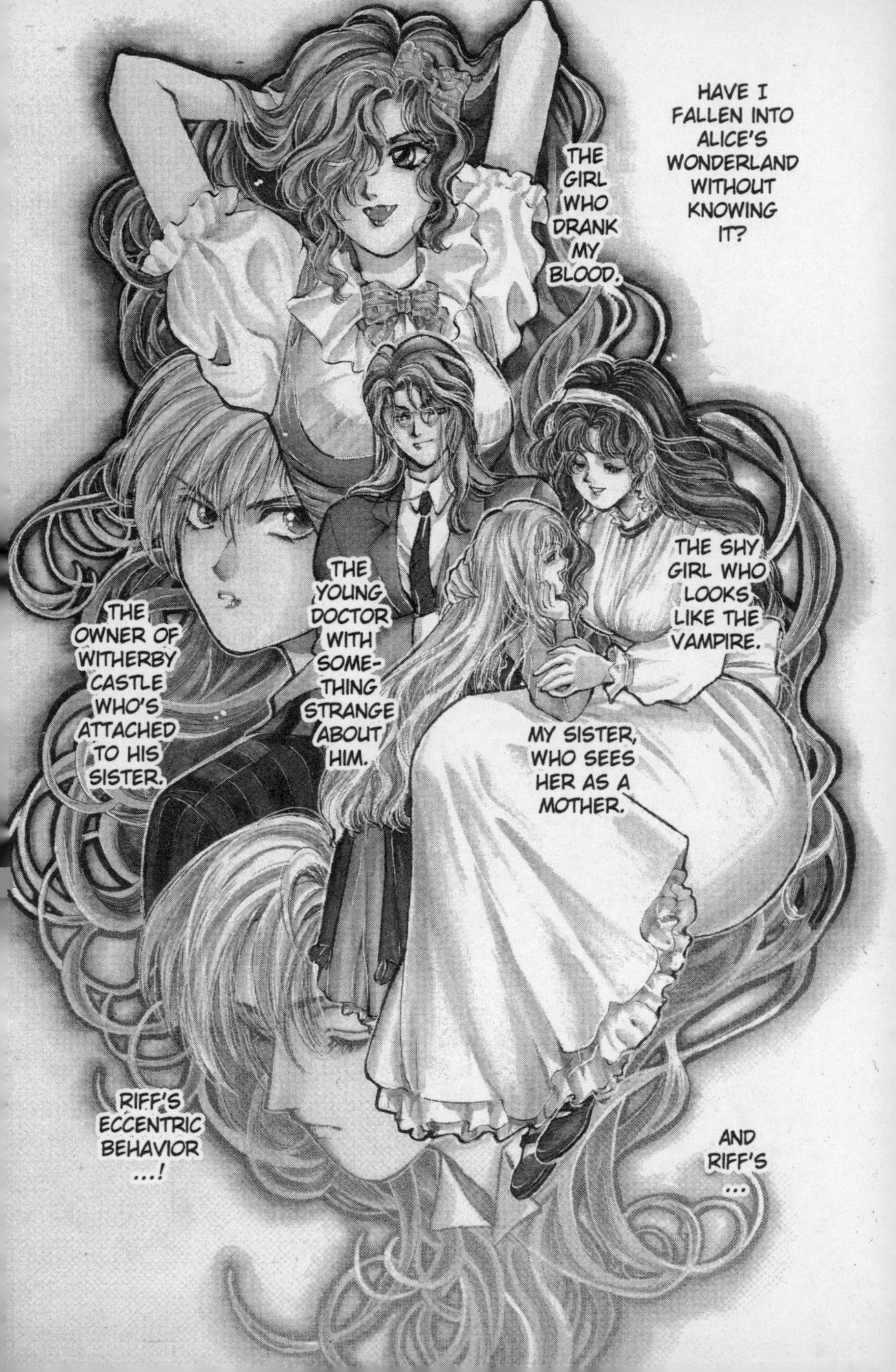
HAVE I FALLEN INTO ALICE'S WONDERLAND WITHOUT KNOWING IT?
THE GIRL WHO DRANK MY BLOOD.
THE SHY GIRL WHO LOOKS LIKE THE VAMPIRE.
MY SISTER, WHO SEES HER AS A MOTHER.
THE YOUNG DOCTOR WITH SOME-THING STRANGE ABOUT HIM.
THE OWNER OF WITHERBY CASTLE WHO'S ATTACHED TO HIS SISTER.
RIFF'S ECCENTRIC BEHAVIOR ...!
AND RIFF'S ...

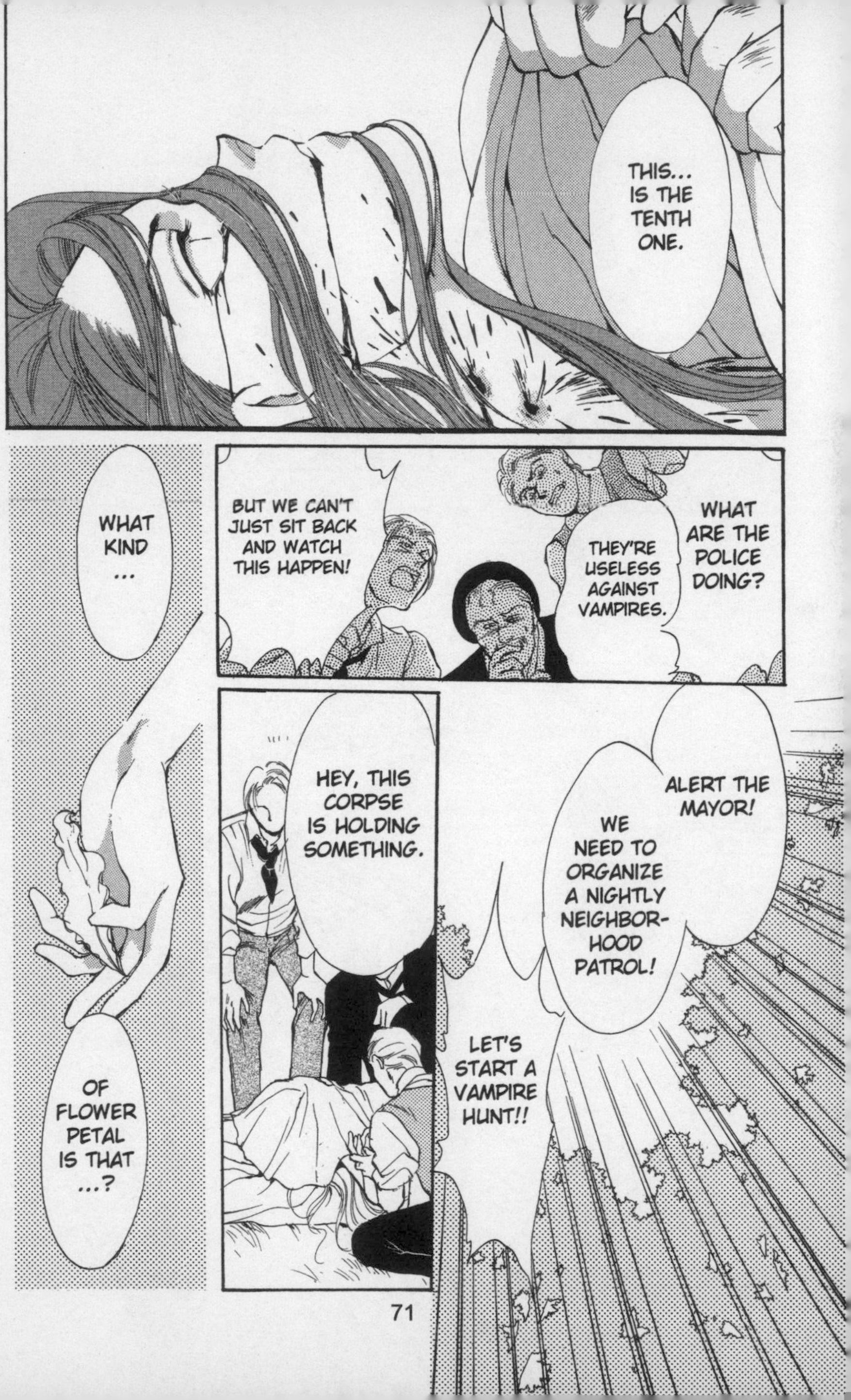
THIS... IS THE TENTH ONE.
WHAT ARE THE POLICE DOING?
THEY'RE USELESS AGAINST VAMPIRES.
BUT WE CAN'T JUST SIT BACK AND WATCH THIS HAPPEN!
ALERT THE MAYOR!
WE NEED TO ORGANIZE A NIGHTLY NEIGHBOR-HOOD PATROL!
LET'S START A VAMPIRE HUNT!!
HEY, THIS CORPSE IS HOLDING SOMETHING.
WHAT KIND ...
OF FLOWER PETAL IS THAT ...?

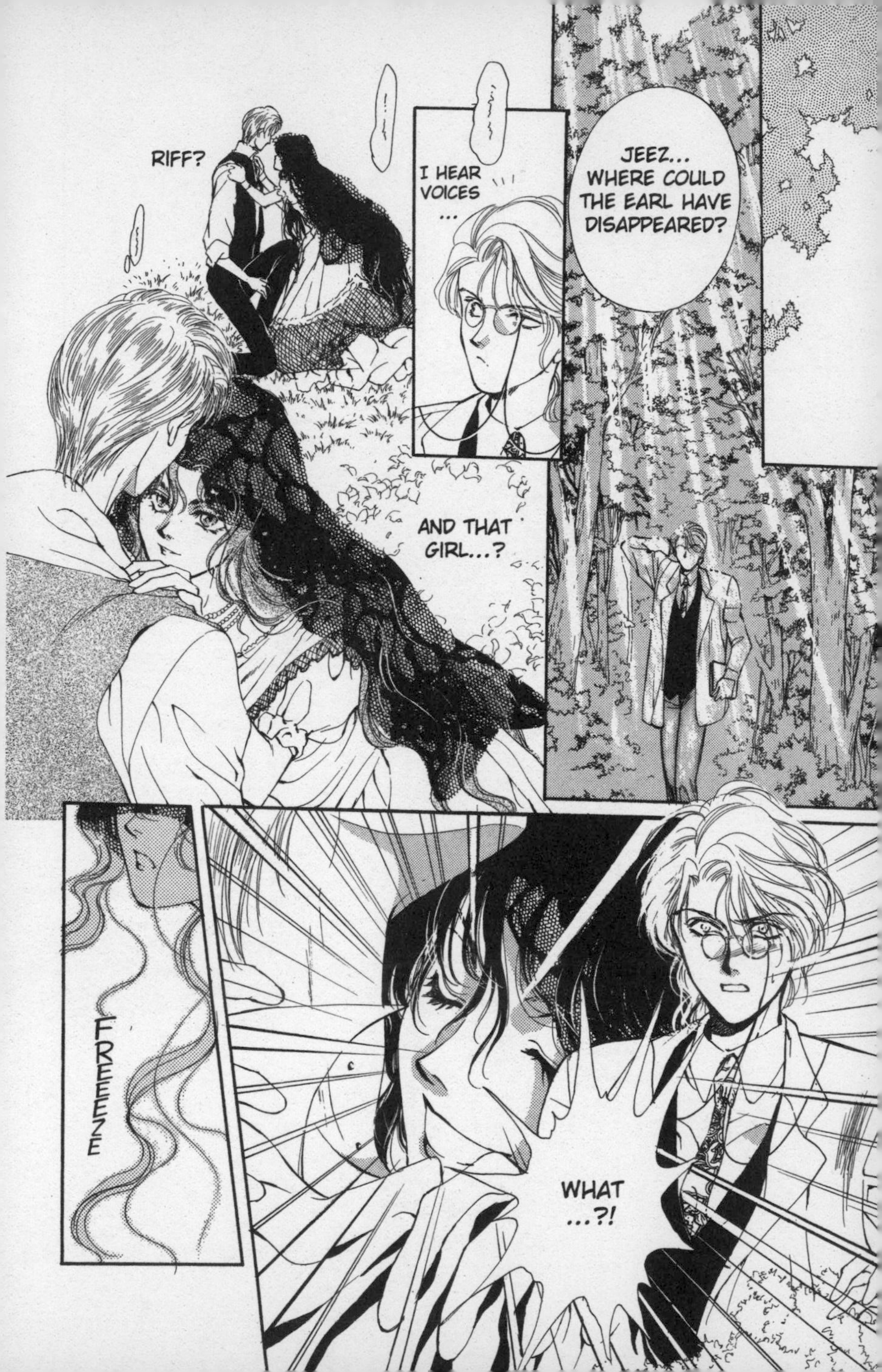
JEEZ... WHERE COULD THE EARL HAVE DISAPPEARED?
I HEAR VOICES ...
RIFF?
AND THAT GIRL...?
WHAT ...?!
FREEEZE

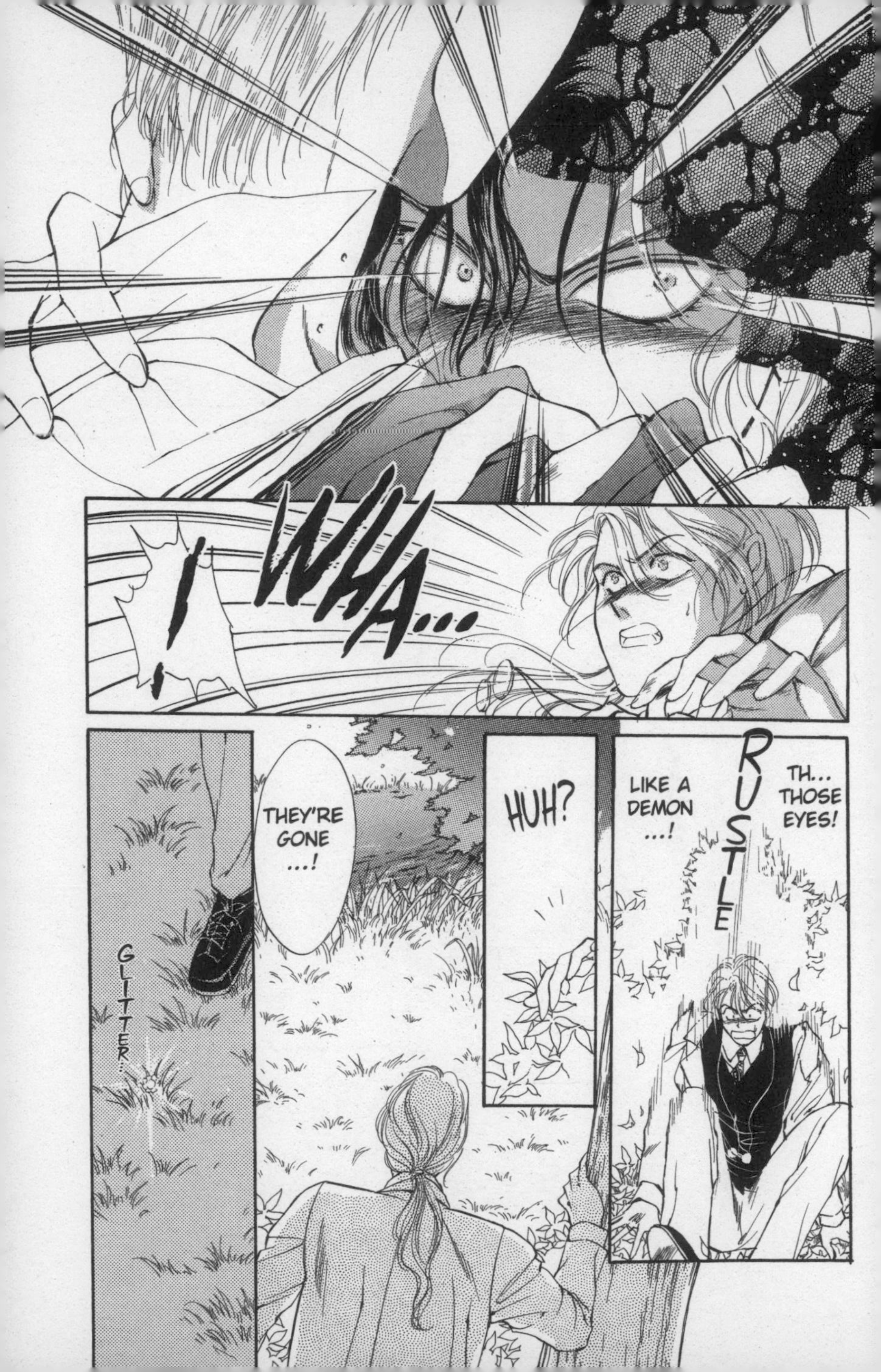
WHA...!
TH... THOSE EYES!
RUSTLE
LIKE A DEMON ...!
HUH?
THEY'RE GONE ...!
GLITTER...

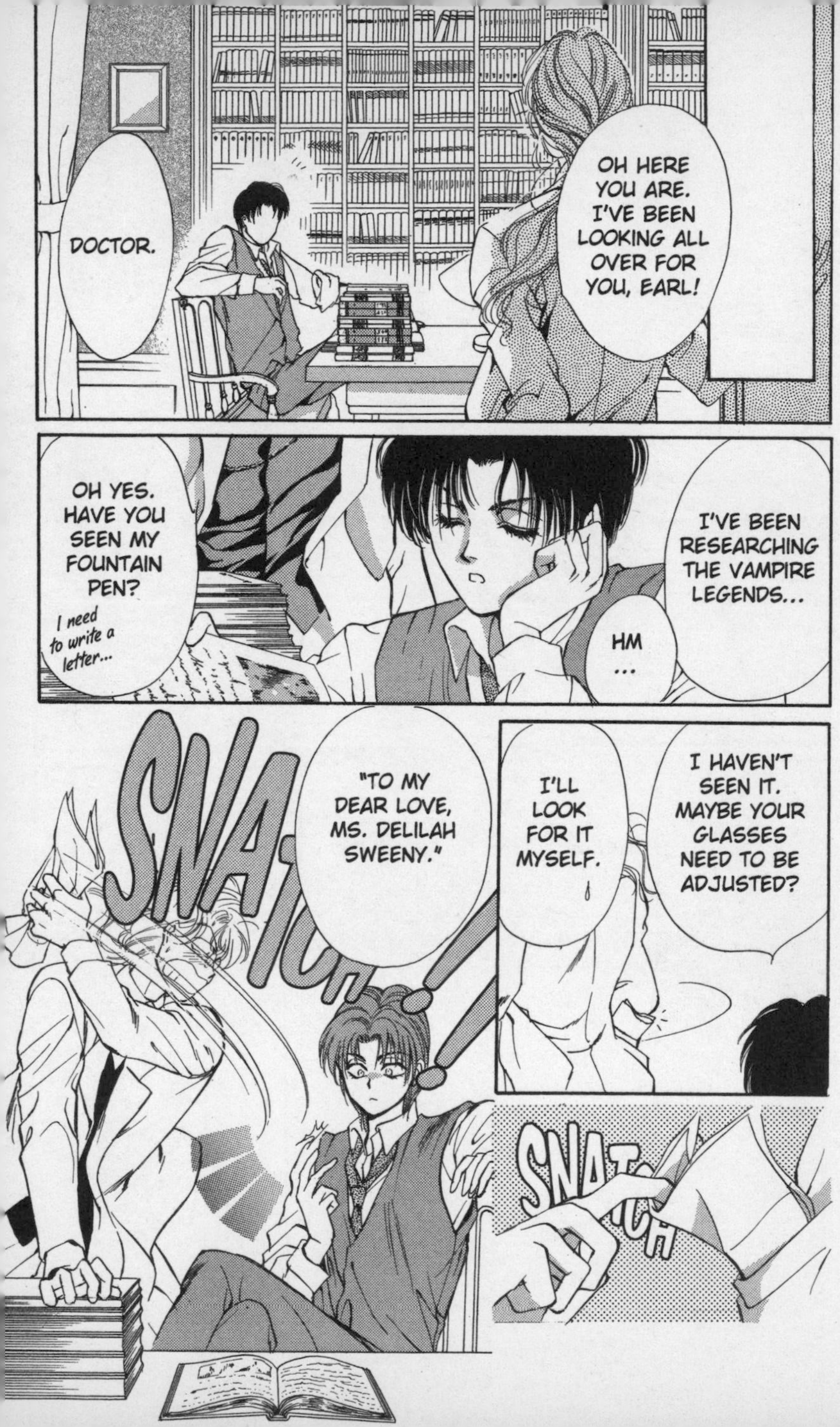
OH HERE YOU ARE. I'VE BEEN LOOKING ALL OVER FOR YOU, EARL!
DOCTOR.
I'VE BEEN RESEARCHING THE VAMPIRE LEGENDS...
HM ...
OH YES. HAVE YOU SEEN MY FOUNTAIN PEN?
I need to write a letter...
I HAVEN'T SEEN IT. MAYBE YOUR GLASSES NEED TO BE ADJUSTED?
I'LL LOOK FOR IT MYSELF.
SNATCH
SNATCH
"TO MY DEAR LOVE, MS. DELILAH SWEENY."

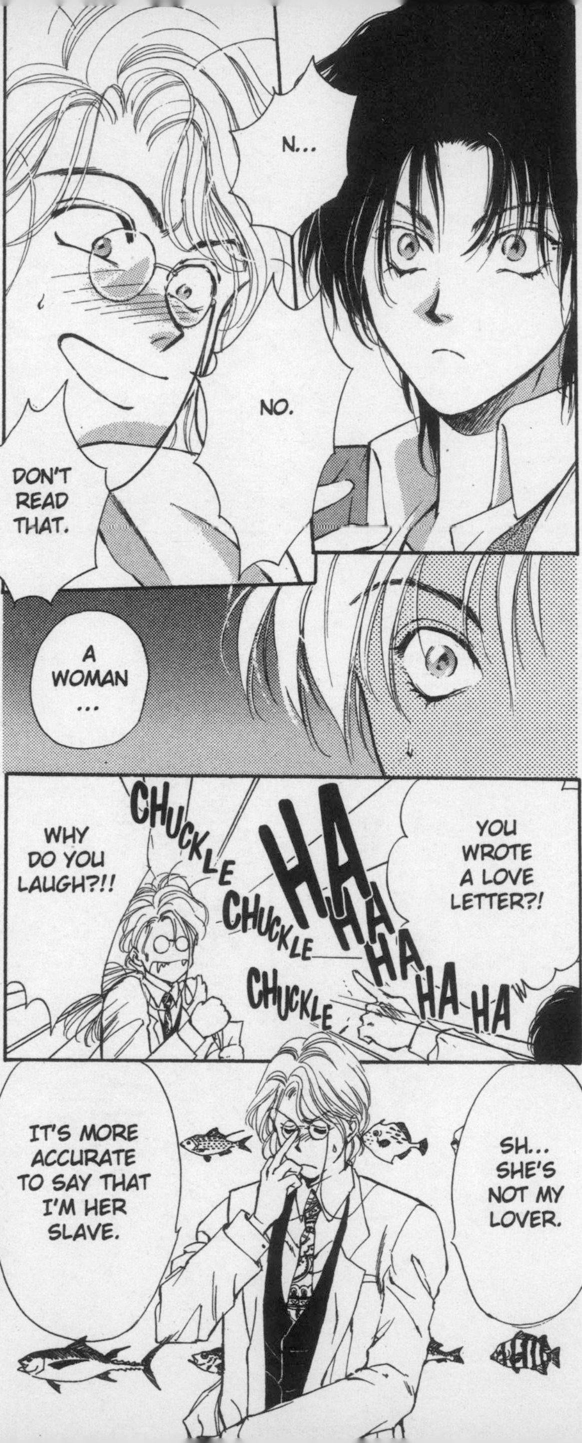
N...
NO.
DON'T READ THAT.
A WOMAN ...
YOU WROTE A LOVE LETTER?!
HA HA HA HA HA HA
CHUCKLE CHUCKLE CHUCKLE
WHY DO YOU LAUGH?!!
SH... SHE'S NOT MY LOVER.
IT'S MORE ACCURATE TO SAY THAT I'M HER SLAVE.

WILD ♦ TALK

The Riff fans are angry (?!) Volume 3. Hey you guys, he's not the main focus of the story. Thanks to this, Dr. Allen has become very unpopular with the fans for no reason at all. Personally, I really liked him. But they say he can't take the place of Riff. By the way, the drink called Pearl is flat beer with sugar, gin, herbs, etc. added to it. Gross! Riff has some really embarrassing lines in the last scene, which is in part spurred on by Mary. Mary realizes that Cain's love for her is like the love you might have for a dog or cat, and it upsets her. But she can't bear to leave his side. Hey, it's getting a bit serious isn't it?

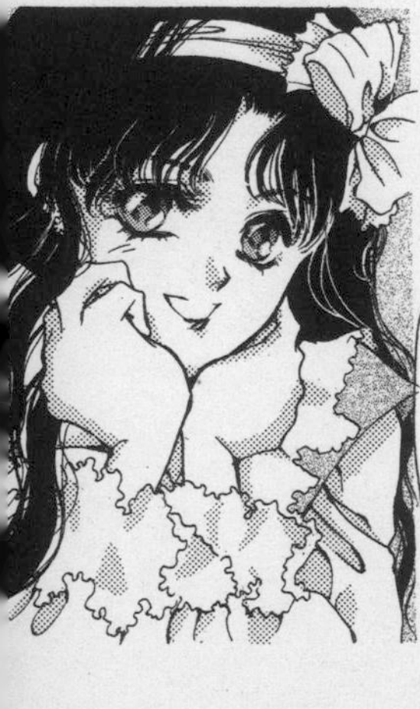

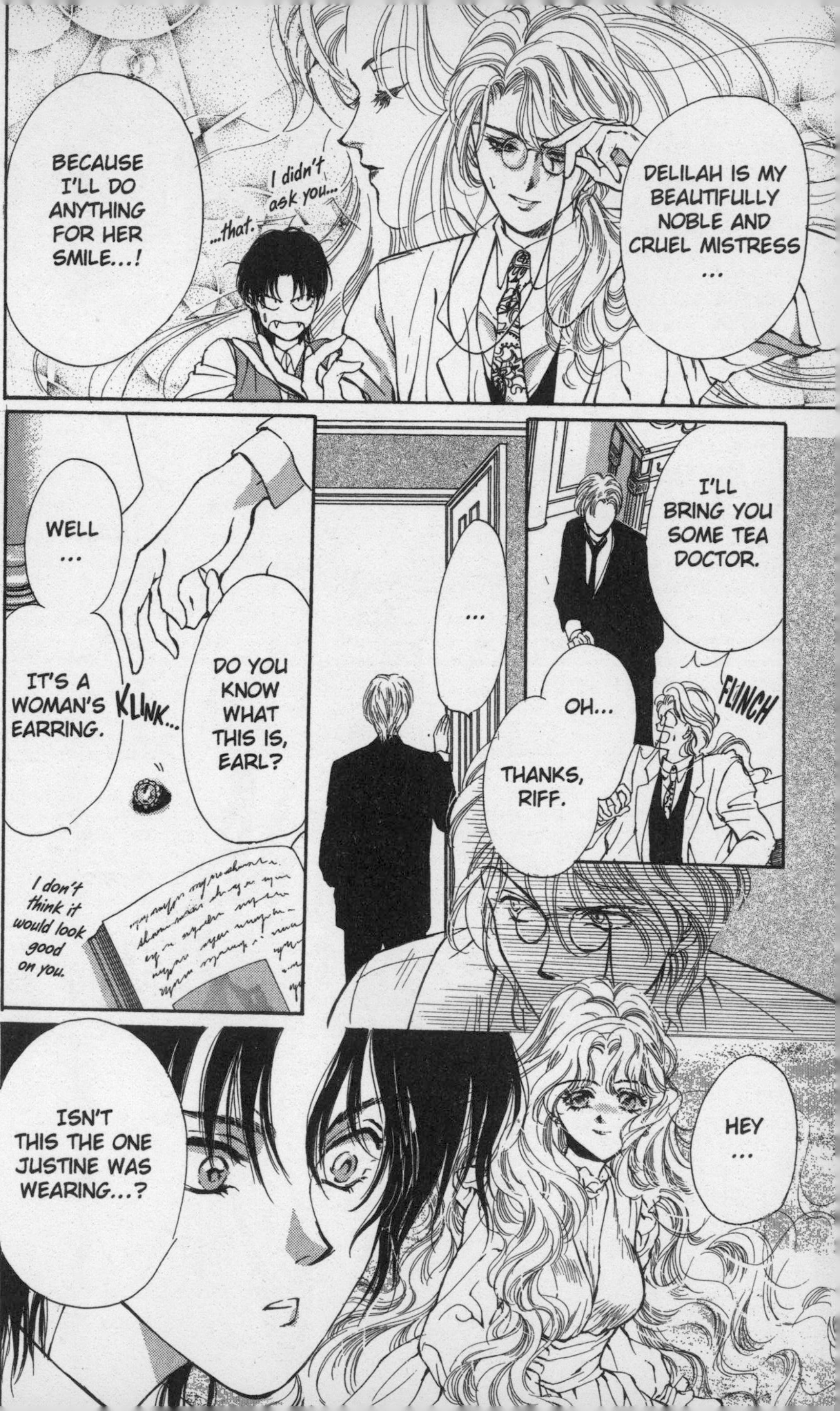
DELILAH IS MY BEAUTIFULLY NOBLE AND CRUEL MISTRESS ...
I didn't ask you...
...that.
BECAUSE I'LL DO ANYTHING FOR HER SMILE...!
I'LL BRING YOU SOME TEA DOCTOR.
FLINCH
OH...
THANKS, RIFF.
...
DO YOU KNOW WHAT THIS IS, EARL?
WELL ...
IT'S A WOMAN'S EARRING.
KLINK...
I don't think it would look good on you.
HEY ...
ISN'T THIS THE ONE JUSTINE WAS WEARING...?

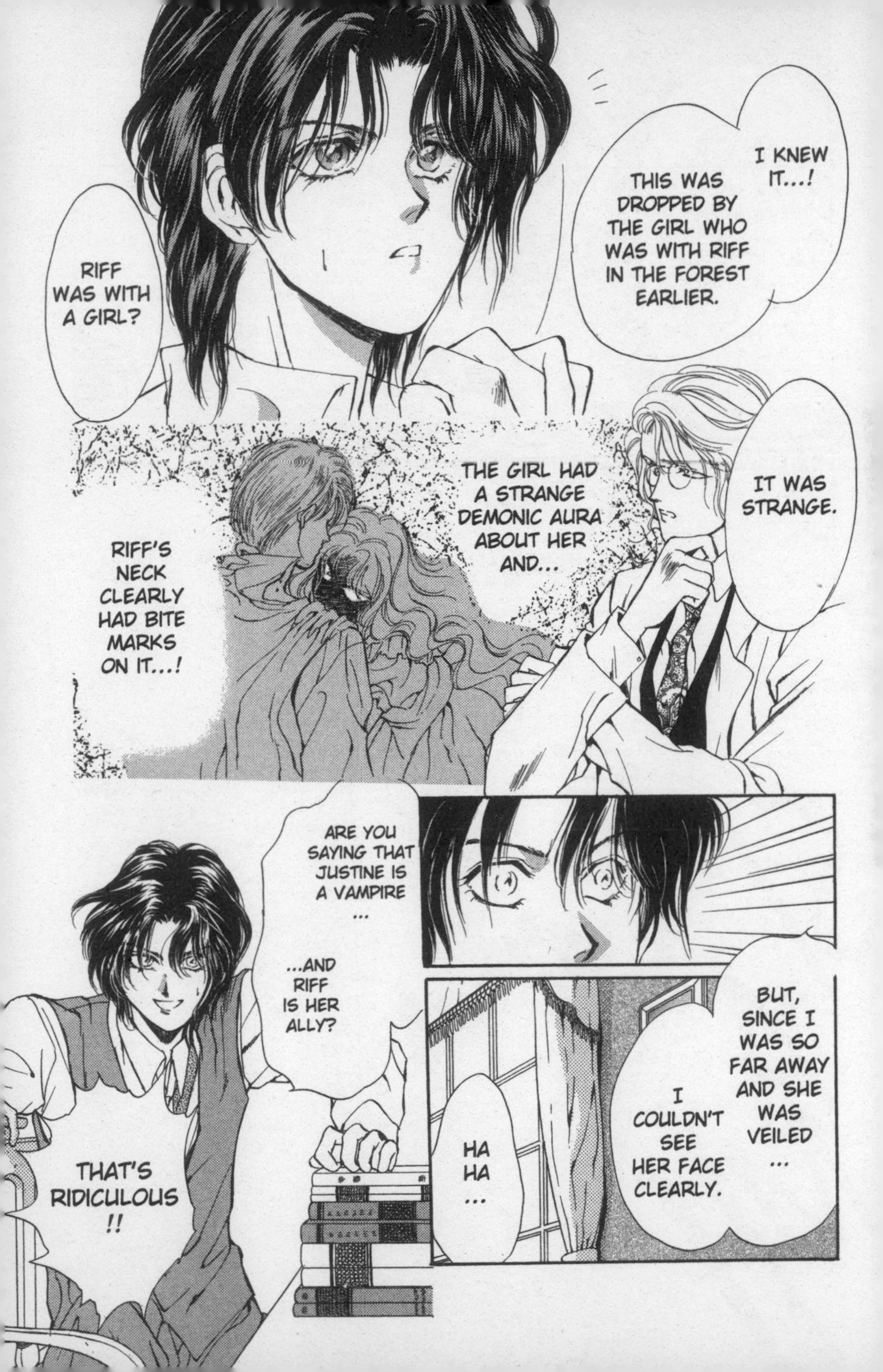

I KNEW IT...!
THIS WAS DROPPED BY THE GIRL WHO WAS WITH RIFF IN THE FOREST EARLIER.
RIFF WAS WITH A GIRL?
IT WAS STRANGE.
THE GIRL HAD A STRANGE DEMONIC AURA ABOUT HER AND...
RIFF'S NECK CLEARLY HAD BITE MARKS ON IT...!
BUT, SINCE I WAS SO FAR AWAY AND SHE WAS VEILED...
I COULDN'T SEE HER FACE CLEARLY.
HA HA...
ARE YOU SAYING THAT JUSTINE IS A VAMPIRE...
...AND RIFF IS HER ALLY?
THAT'S RIDICULOUS!!

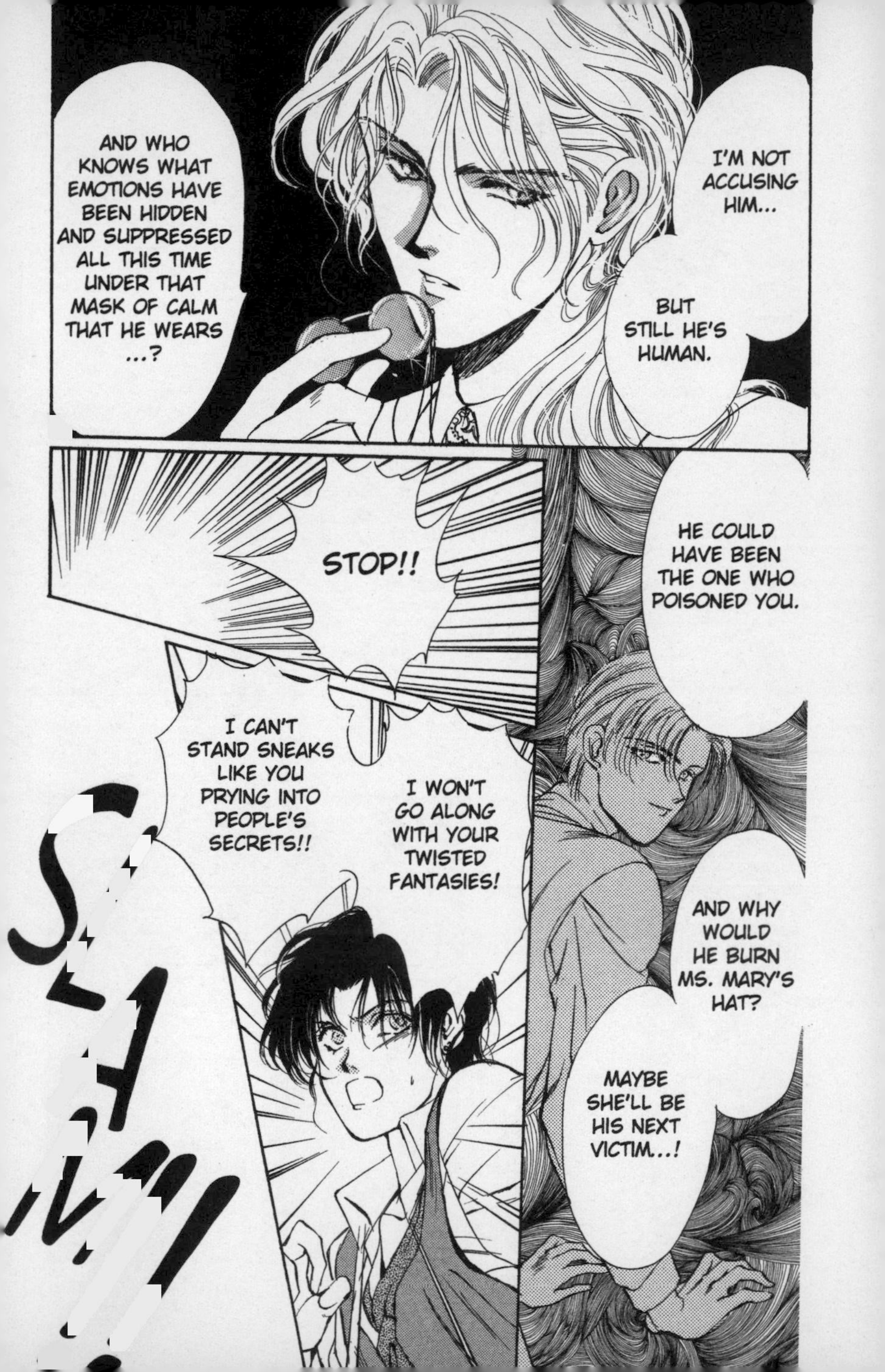
I'M NOT ACCUSING HIM...
BUT STILL HE'S HUMAN.
AND WHO KNOWS WHAT EMOTIONS HAVE BEEN HIDDEN AND SUPPRESSED ALL THIS TIME UNDER THAT MASK OF CALM THAT HE WEARS ...?
HE COULD HAVE BEEN THE ONE WHO POISONED YOU.
AND WHY WOULD HE BURN MS. MARY'S HAT?
MAYBE SHE'LL BE HIS NEXT VICTIM...!
STOP!!
I WON'T GO ALONG WITH YOUR TWISTED FANTASIES!
I CAN'T STAND SNEAKS LIKE YOU PRYING INTO PEOPLE'S SECRETS!!

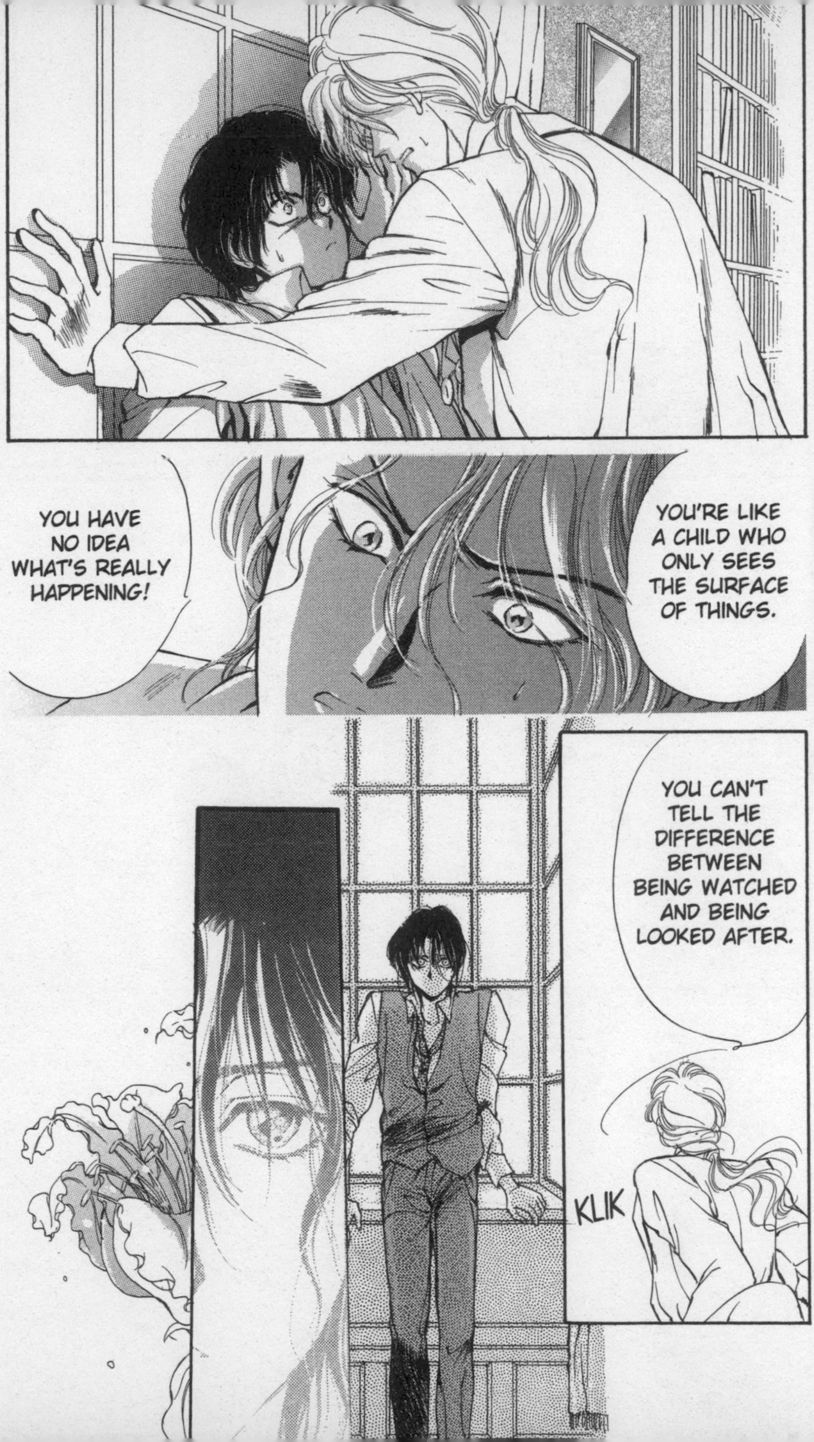
YOU'RE LIKE A CHILD WHO ONLY SEES THE SURFACE OF THINGS.
YOU HAVE NO IDEA WHAT'S REALLY HAPPENING!
YOU CAN'T TELL THE DIFFERENCE BETWEEN BEING WATCHED AND BEING LOOKED AFTER.
KLIK

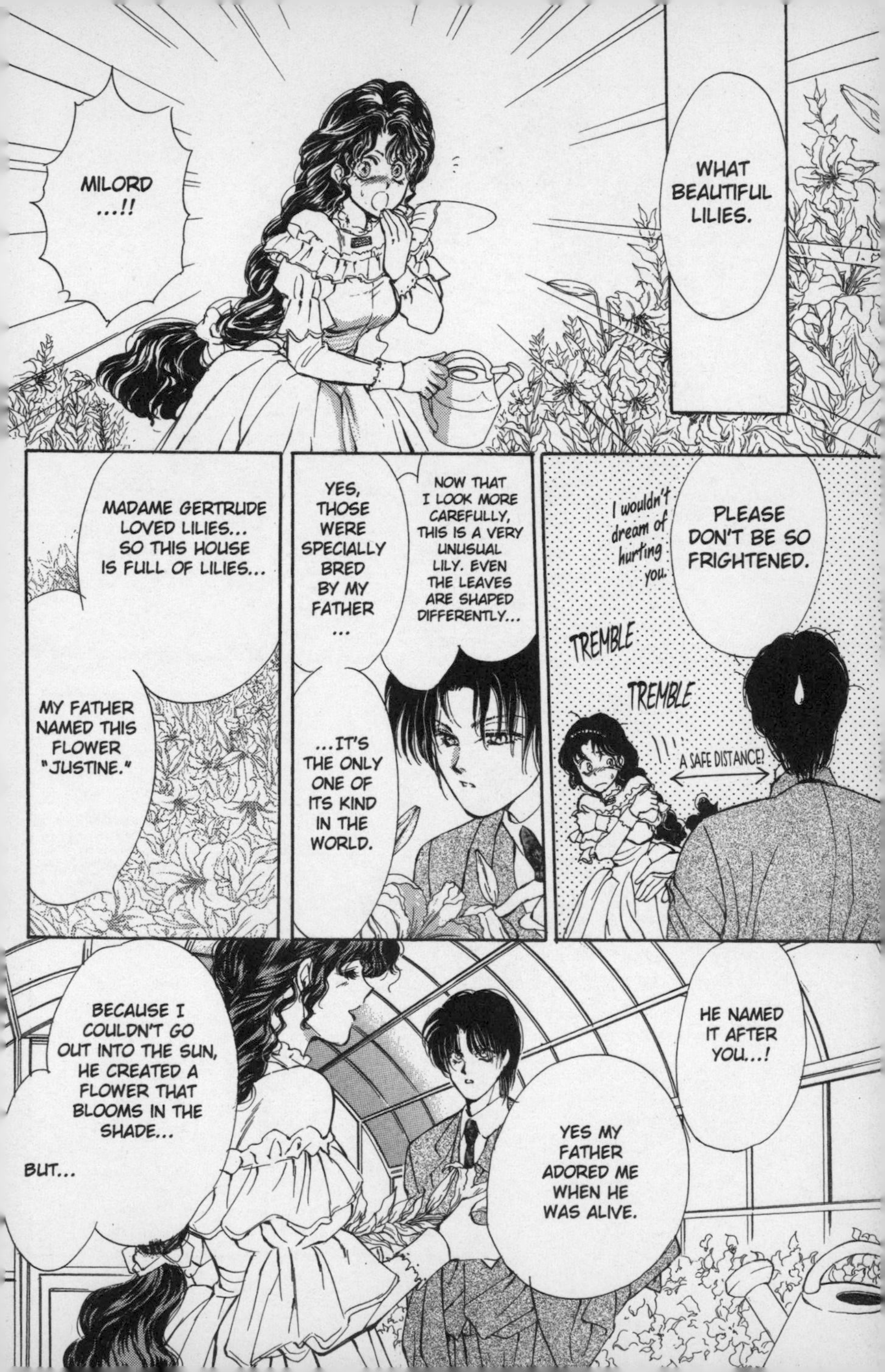
WHAT BEAUTIFUL LILIES.
MILORD ...!!
PLEASE DON'T BE SO FRIGHTENED.
I wouldn't dream of hurting you.
TREMBLE
TREMBLE
A SAFE DISTANCE?
NOW THAT I LOOK MORE CAREFULLY, THIS IS A VERY UNUSUAL LILY. EVEN THE LEAVES ARE SHAPED DIFFERENTLY...
YES, THOSE WERE SPECIALLY BRED BY MY FATHER ...
...IT'S THE ONLY ONE OF ITS KIND IN THE WORLD.
MADAME GERTRUDE LOVED LILIES... SO THIS HOUSE IS FULL OF LILIES...
MY FATHER NAMED THIS FLOWER "JUSTINE."
HE NAMED IT AFTER YOU...!
YES MY FATHER ADORED ME WHEN HE WAS ALIVE.
BECAUSE I COULDN'T GO OUT INTO THE SUN, HE CREATED A FLOWER THAT BLOOMS IN THE SHADE...
BUT...

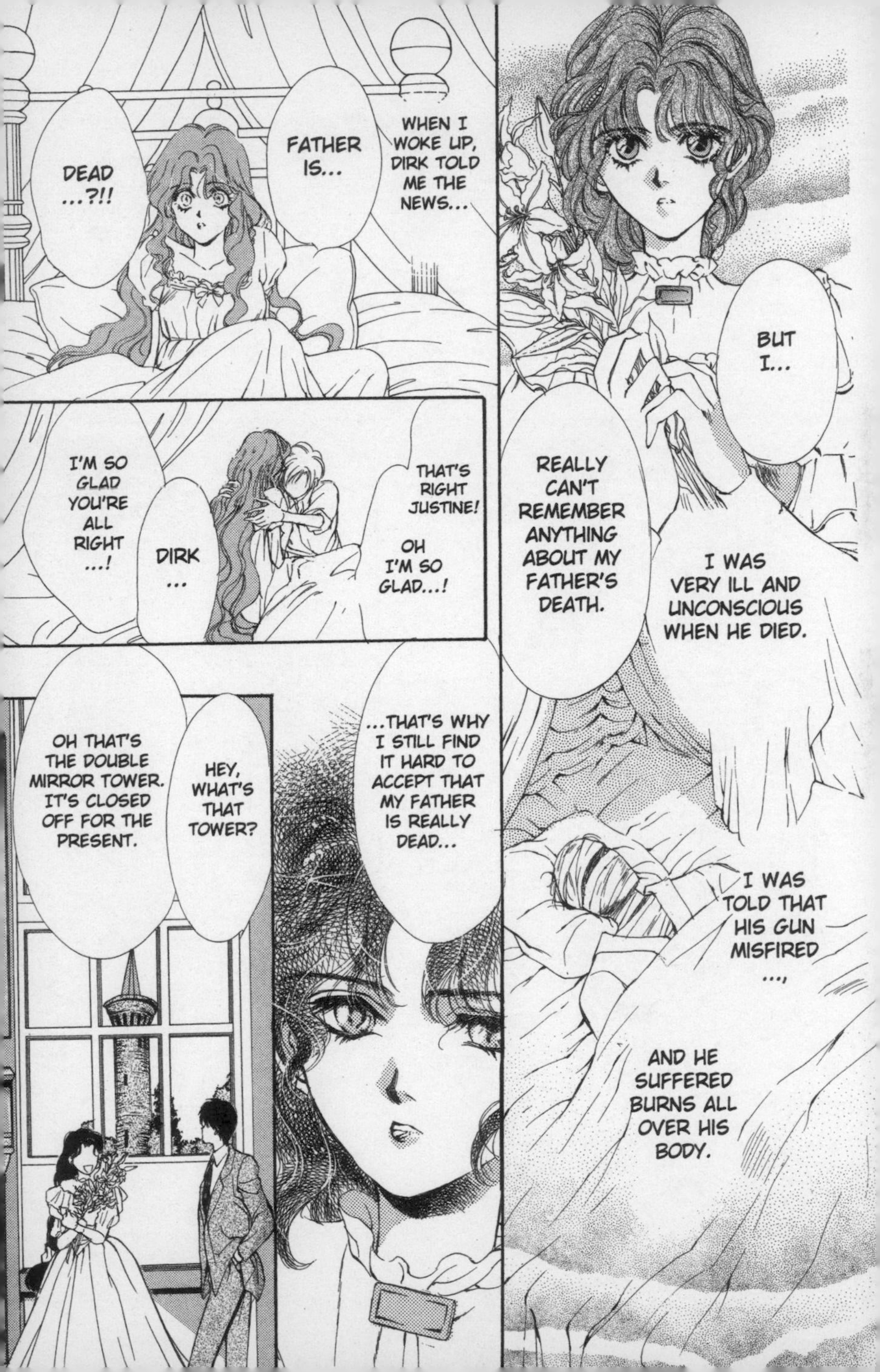
BUT I...
REALLY CAN'T REMEMBER ANYTHING ABOUT MY FATHER'S DEATH.
I WAS VERY ILL AND UNCONSCIOUS WHEN HE DIED.
I WAS TOLD THAT HIS GUN MISFIRED ...,
AND HE SUFFERED BURNS ALL OVER HIS BODY.
WHEN I WOKE UP, DIRK TOLD ME THE NEWS...
FATHER IS...
DEAD ...?!!
THAT'S RIGHT JUSTINE!
OH I'M SO GLAD...!
DIRK ...
I'M SO GLAD YOU'RE ALL RIGHT ...!
...THAT'S WHY I STILL FIND IT HARD TO ACCEPT THAT MY FATHER IS REALLY DEAD...
HEY, WHAT'S THAT TOWER?
OH THAT'S THE DOUBLE MIRROR TOWER. IT'S CLOSED OFF FOR THE PRESENT.

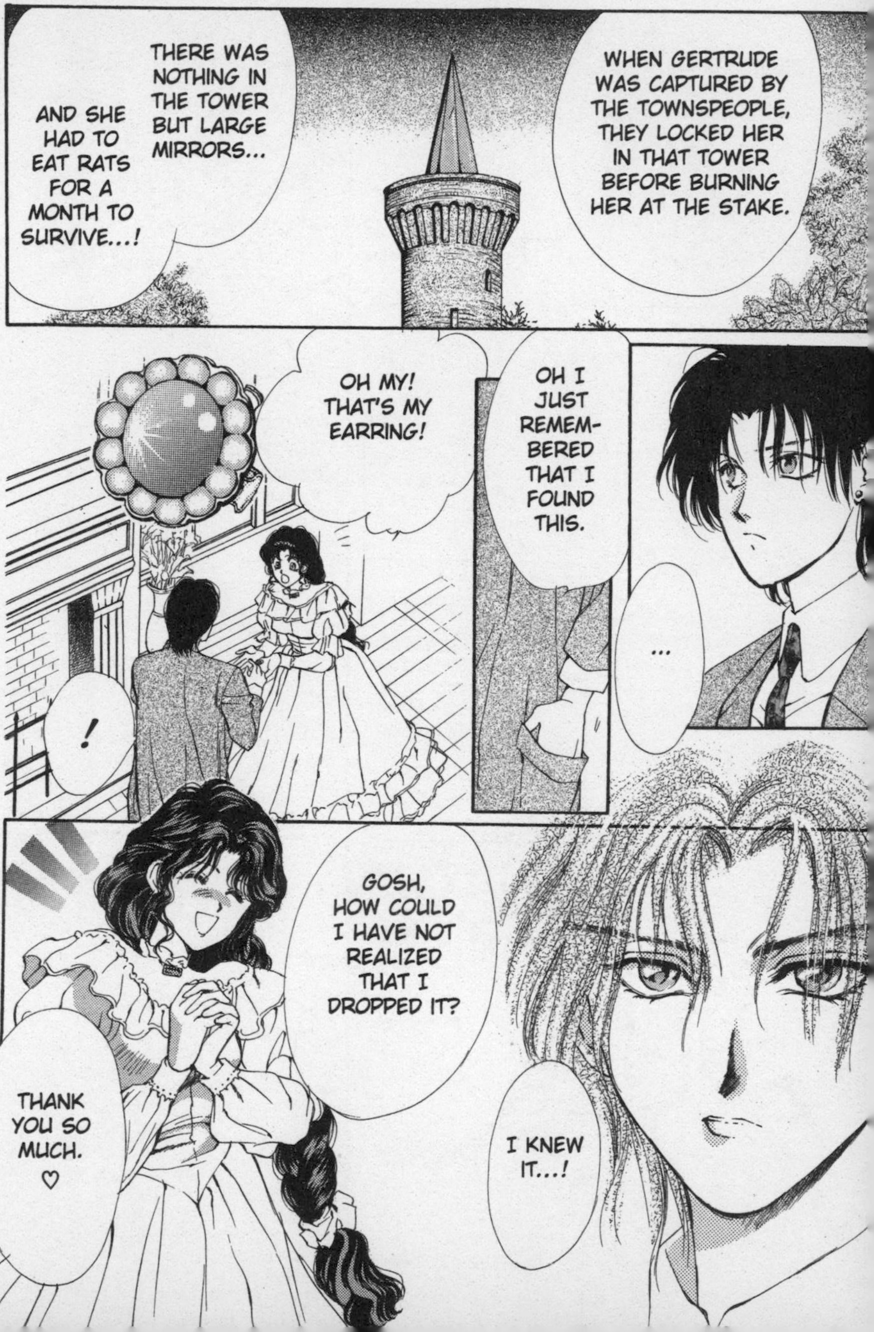
WHEN GERTRUDE WAS CAPTURED BY THE TOWNSPEOPLE, THEY LOCKED HER IN THAT TOWER BEFORE BURNING HER AT THE STAKE.
THERE WAS NOTHING IN THE TOWER BUT LARGE MIRRORS...
AND SHE HAD TO EAT RATS FOR A MONTH TO SURVIVE...!
...
OH I JUST REMEMBERED THAT I FOUND THIS.
OH MY! THAT'S MY EARRING!
!
I KNEW IT...!
GOSH, HOW COULD I HAVE NOT REALIZED THAT I DROPPED IT?
THANK YOU SO MUCH. ♡

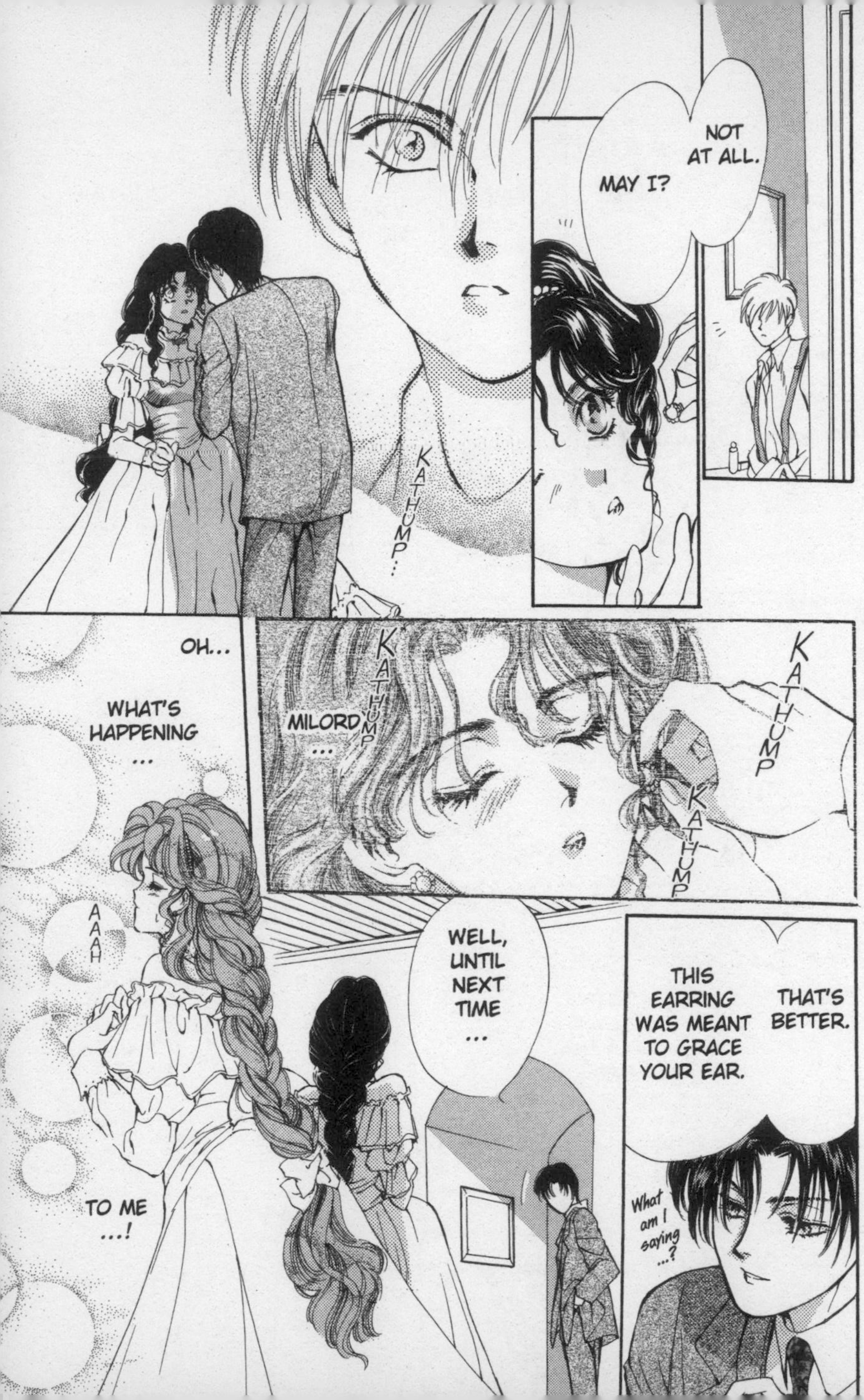
NOT AT ALL.
MAY I?
KATHUMP...
KATHUMP
MILORD ...
KATHUMP
KATHUMP
OH...
WHAT'S HAPPENING ...
THAT'S BETTER.
THIS EARRING WAS MEANT TO GRACE YOUR EAR.
What am I saying ...?
WELL, UNTIL NEXT TIME ...
AAAH
TO ME ...!

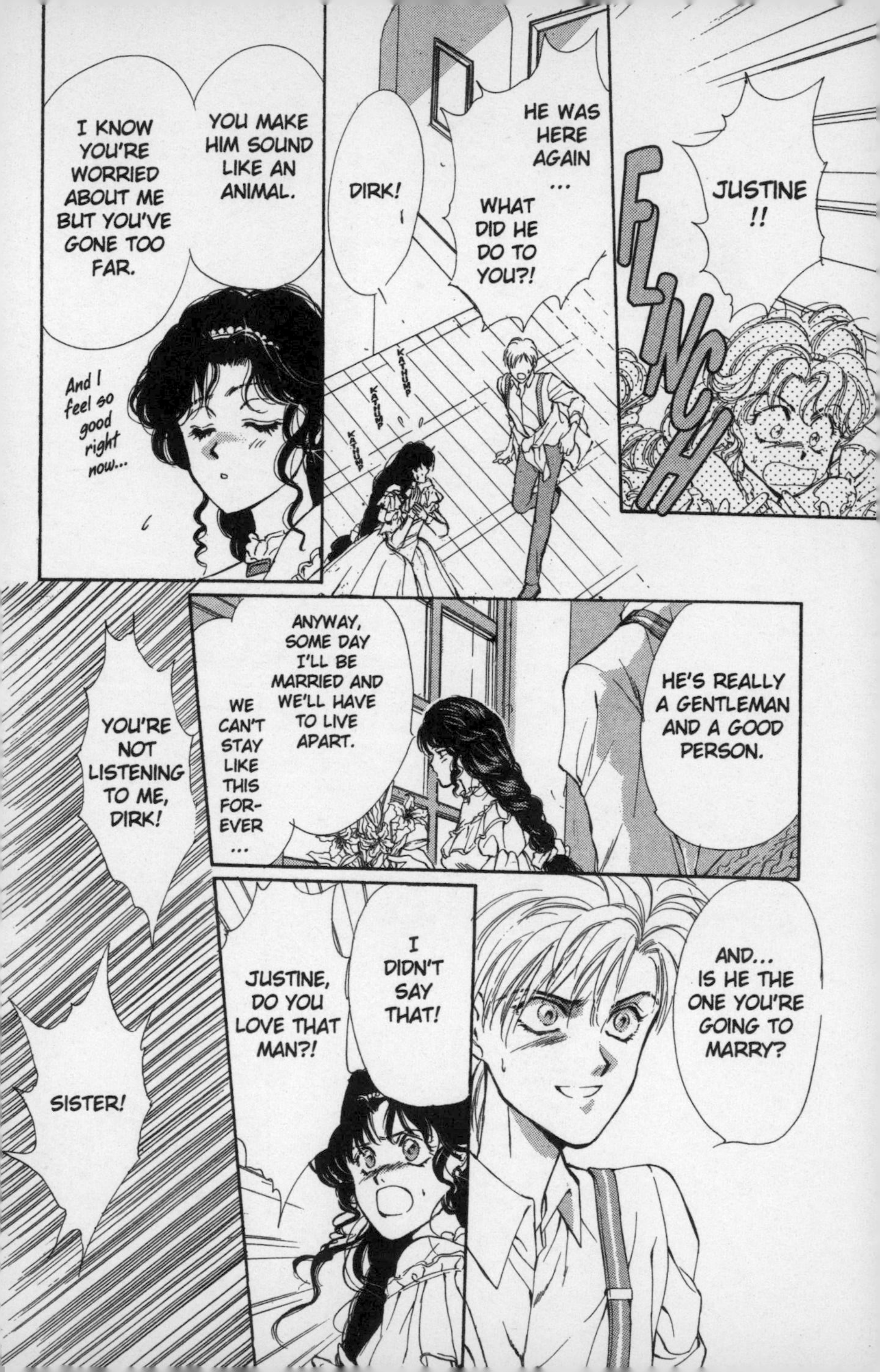
JUSTINE !!
FLINCH
HE WAS HERE AGAIN ...
WHAT DID HE DO TO YOU?!
DIRK!
KATHUMP
KATHUMP
KATHUMP
YOU MAKE HIM SOUND LIKE AN ANIMAL.
I KNOW YOU'RE WORRIED ABOUT ME BUT YOU'VE GONE TOO FAR.
And I feel so good right now...
HE'S REALLY A GENTLEMAN AND A GOOD PERSON.
ANYWAY, SOME DAY I'LL BE MARRIED AND WE'LL HAVE TO LIVE APART.
WE CAN'T STAY LIKE THIS FOR-EVER ...
AND... IS HE THE ONE YOU'RE GOING TO MARRY?
I DIDN'T SAY THAT!
JUSTINE, DO YOU LOVE THAT MAN?!
YOU'RE NOT LISTENING TO ME, DIRK!
SISTER!

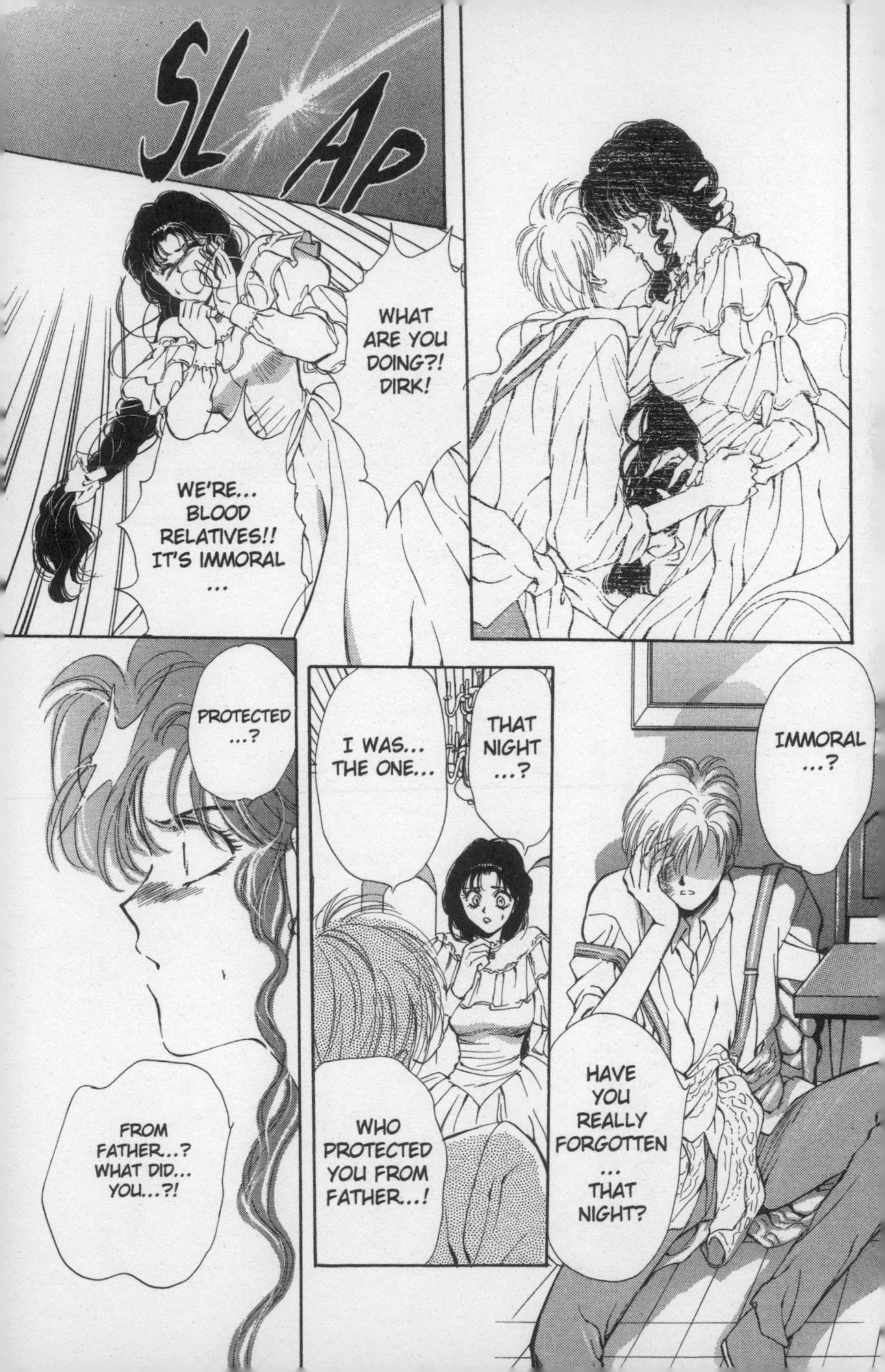
SLAP
WHAT ARE YOU DOING?! DIRK!
WE'RE... BLOOD RELATIVES!! IT'S IMMORAL ...
IMMORAL ...?
HAVE YOU REALLY FORGOTTEN ... THAT NIGHT?
THAT NIGHT ...?
I WAS... THE ONE...
WHO PROTECTED YOU FROM FATHER...!
PROTECTED ...?
FROM FATHER...? WHAT DID... YOU...?!

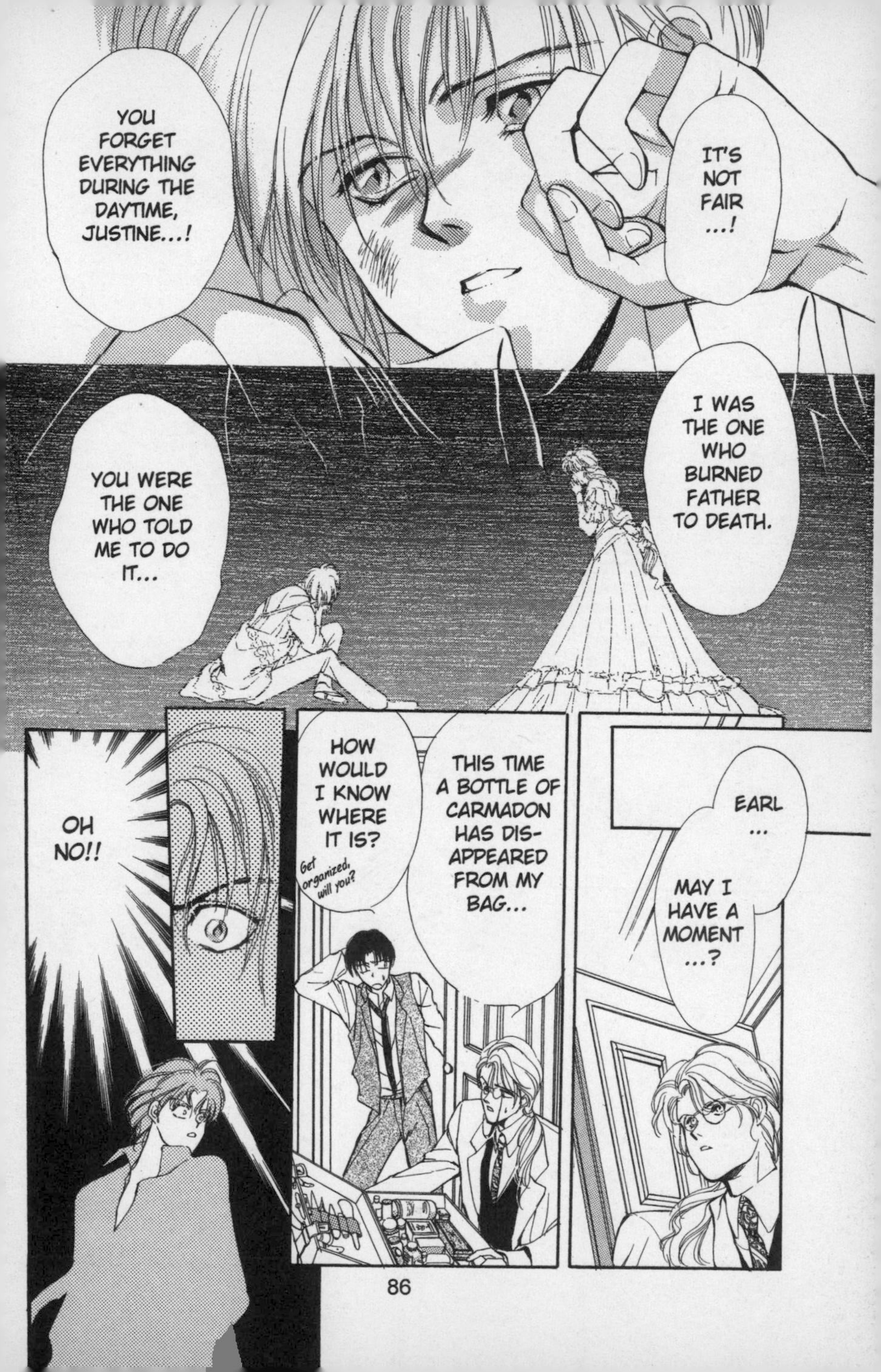
IT'S NOT FAIR ...!
YOU FORGET EVERYTHING DURING THE DAYTIME, JUSTINE...!
I WAS THE ONE WHO BURNED FATHER TO DEATH.
YOU WERE THE ONE WHO TOLD ME TO DO IT...
EARL ...
MAY I HAVE A MOMENT ...?
THIS TIME A BOTTLE OF CARMADON HAS DIS-APPEARED FROM MY BAG...
HOW WOULD I KNOW WHERE IT IS?
Get organized, will you?
OH NO!!

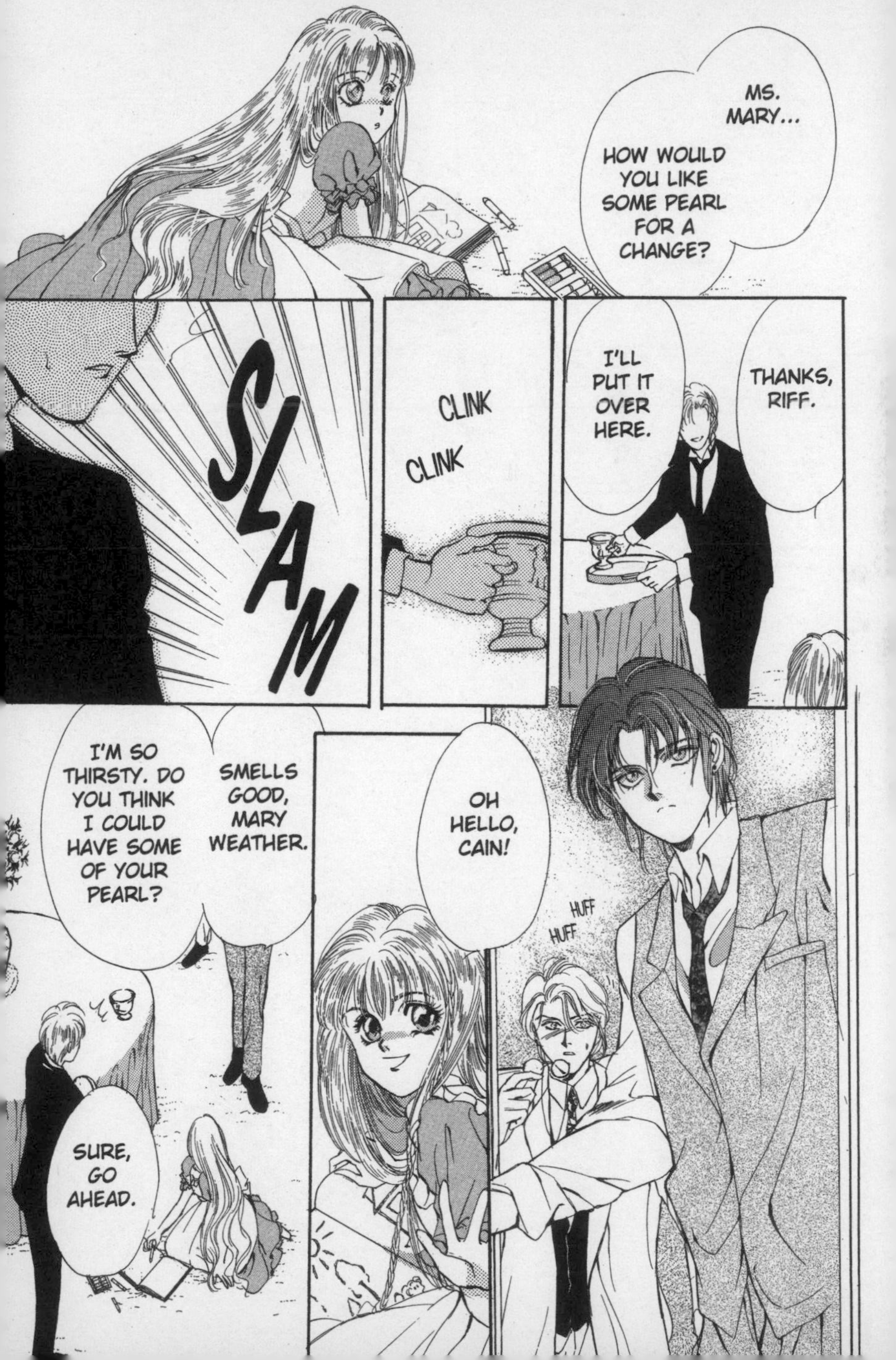

MS. MARY...
HOW WOULD YOU LIKE SOME PEARL FOR A CHANGE?
THANKS, RIFF.
I'LL PUT IT OVER HERE.
CLINK
CLINK
SLAM
HUFF
HUFF
OH HELLO, CAIN!
SMELLS GOOD, MARY WEATHER.
I'M SO THIRSTY. DO YOU THINK I COULD HAVE SOME OF YOUR PEARL?
SURE, GO AHEAD.

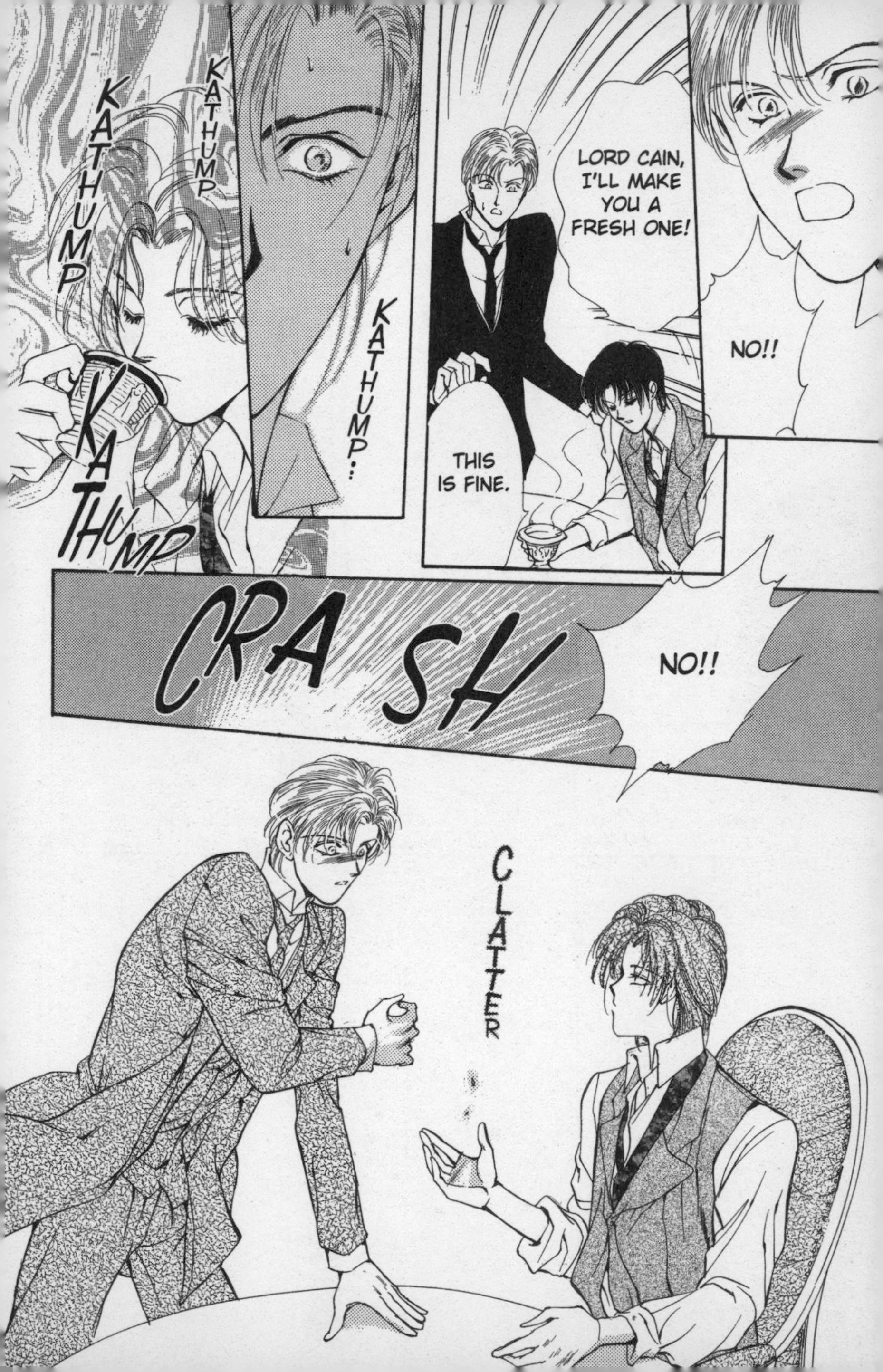
NO!!
LORD CAIN, I'LL MAKE YOU A FRESH ONE!
THIS IS FINE.
KATHUMP
KATHUMP...
KATHUMP
KATHUMP
KATHUMP
CRASH
NO!!
CLATTER

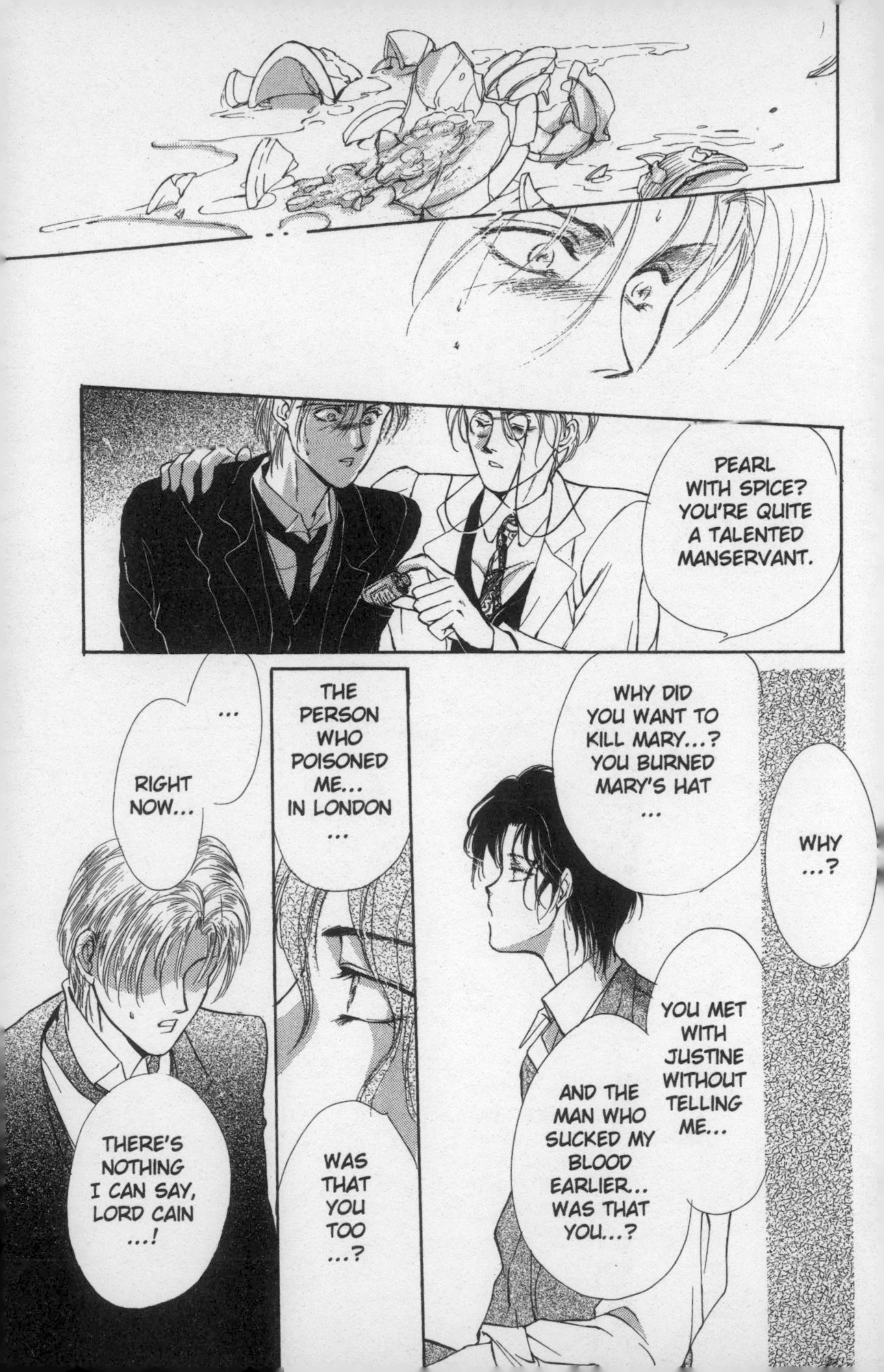
PEARL WITH SPICE? YOU'RE QUITE A TALENTED MANSERVANT.
WHY ...?
WHY DID YOU WANT TO KILL MARY...? YOU BURNED MARY'S HAT ...
YOU MET WITH JUSTINE WITHOUT TELLING ME...
AND THE MAN WHO SUCKED MY BLOOD EARLIER... WAS THAT YOU...?
THE PERSON WHO POISONED ME... IN LONDON ...
WAS THAT YOU TOO ...?
...
RIGHT NOW...
THERE'S NOTHING I CAN SAY, LORD CAIN ...!

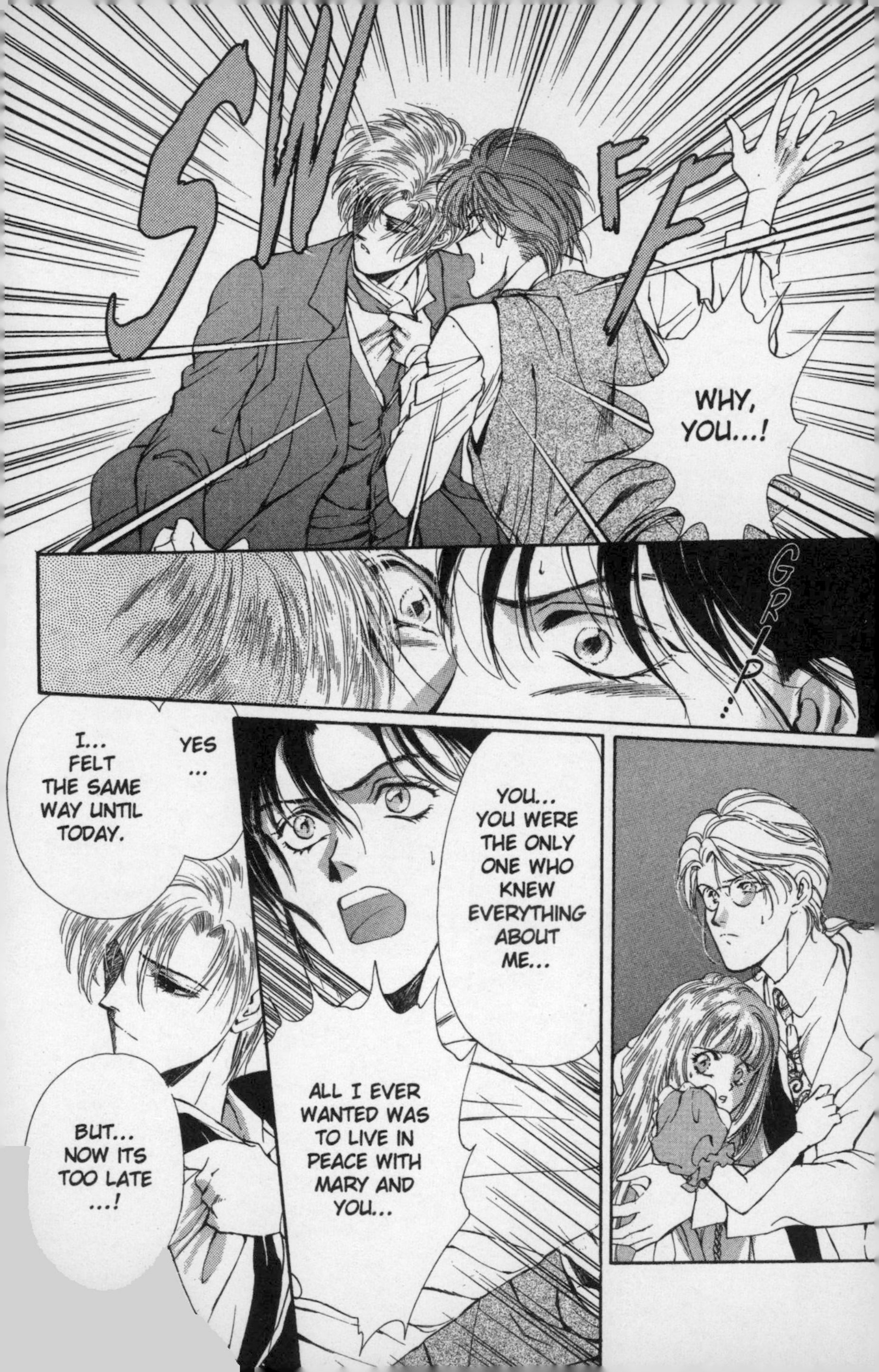
SWFF
WHY, YOU...!
GRIP...
YOU... YOU WERE THE ONLY ONE WHO KNEW EVERYTHING ABOUT ME...
ALL I EVER WANTED WAS TO LIVE IN PEACE WITH MARY AND YOU...
YES...
I... FELT THE SAME WAY UNTIL TODAY.
BUT... NOW ITS TOO LATE ...!

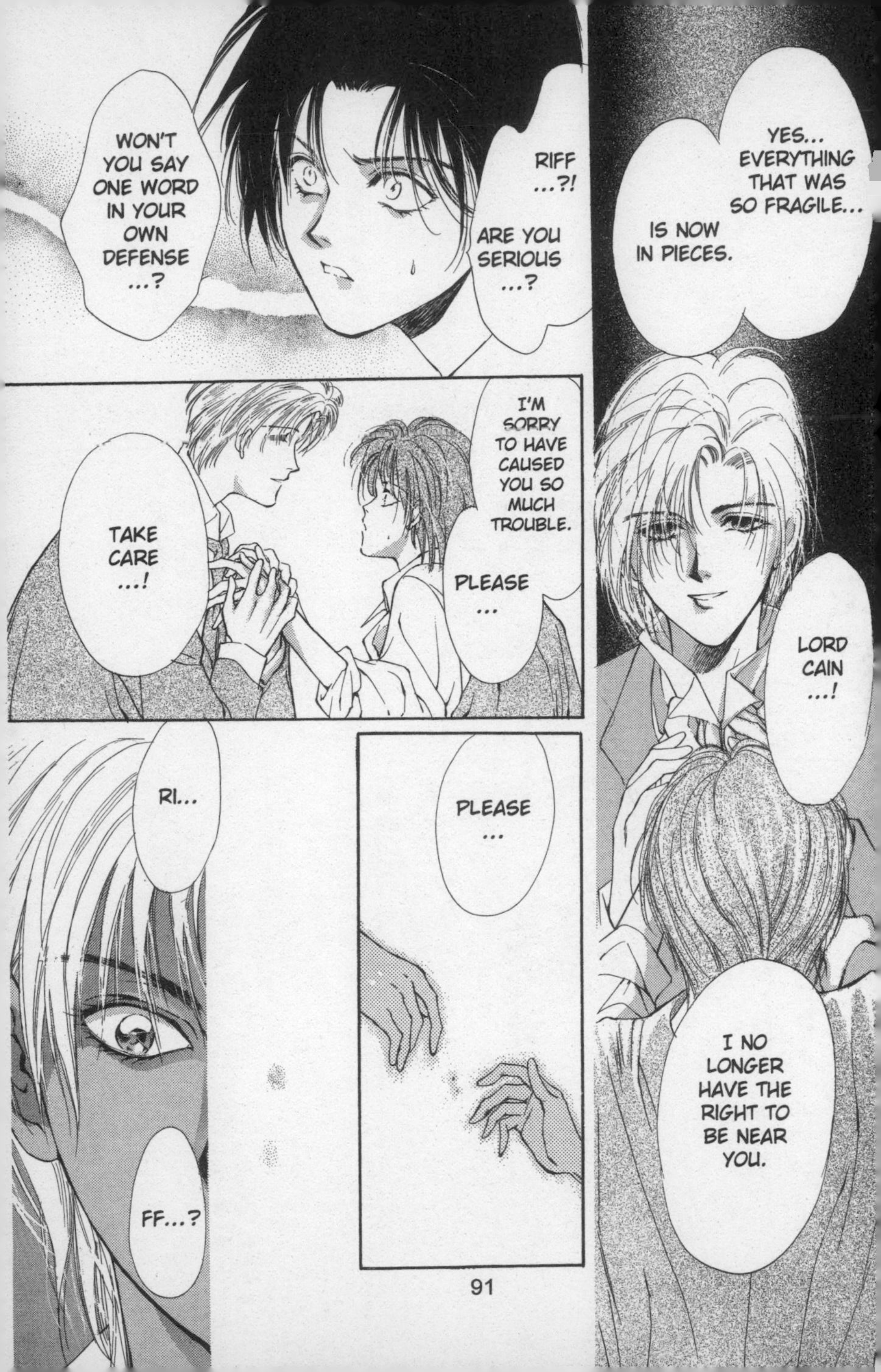
YES... EVERYTHING THAT WAS SO FRAGILE...
IS NOW IN PIECES.
LORD CAIN ...!
I NO LONGER HAVE THE RIGHT TO BE NEAR YOU.
RIFF ...?!
ARE YOU SERIOUS ...?
WON'T YOU SAY ONE WORD IN YOUR OWN DEFENSE ...?
I'M SORRY TO HAVE CAUSED YOU SO MUCH TROUBLE.
PLEASE ...
TAKE CARE ...!
PLEASE ...
RI...
FF...?

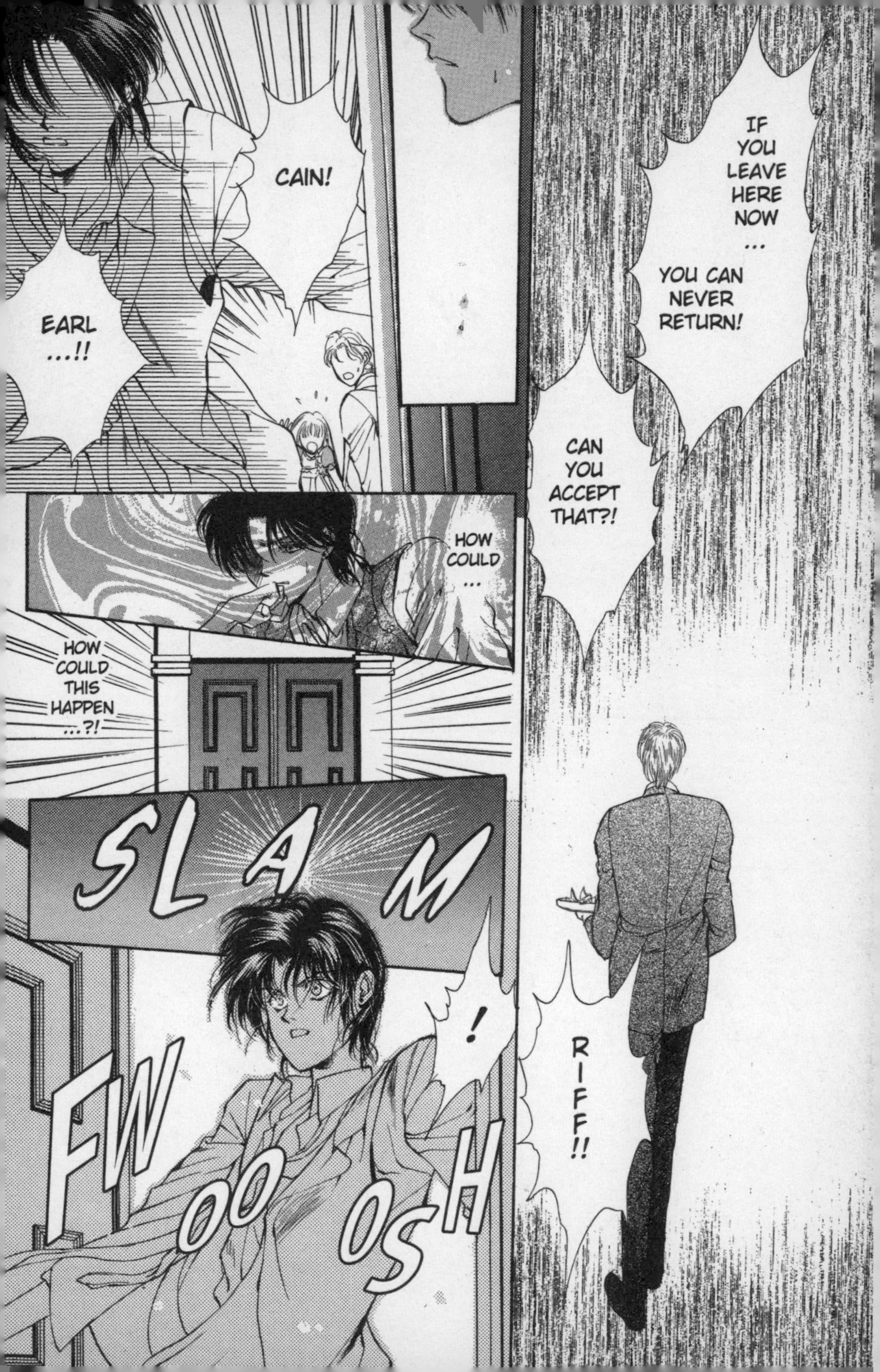
IF YOU LEAVE HERE NOW ...
YOU CAN NEVER RETURN!
CAN YOU ACCEPT THAT?!
RIFF!!
CAIN!
EARL ...!!
HOW COULD ...
HOW COULD THIS HAPPEN ...?!
SLAM
!
FWOOOSH

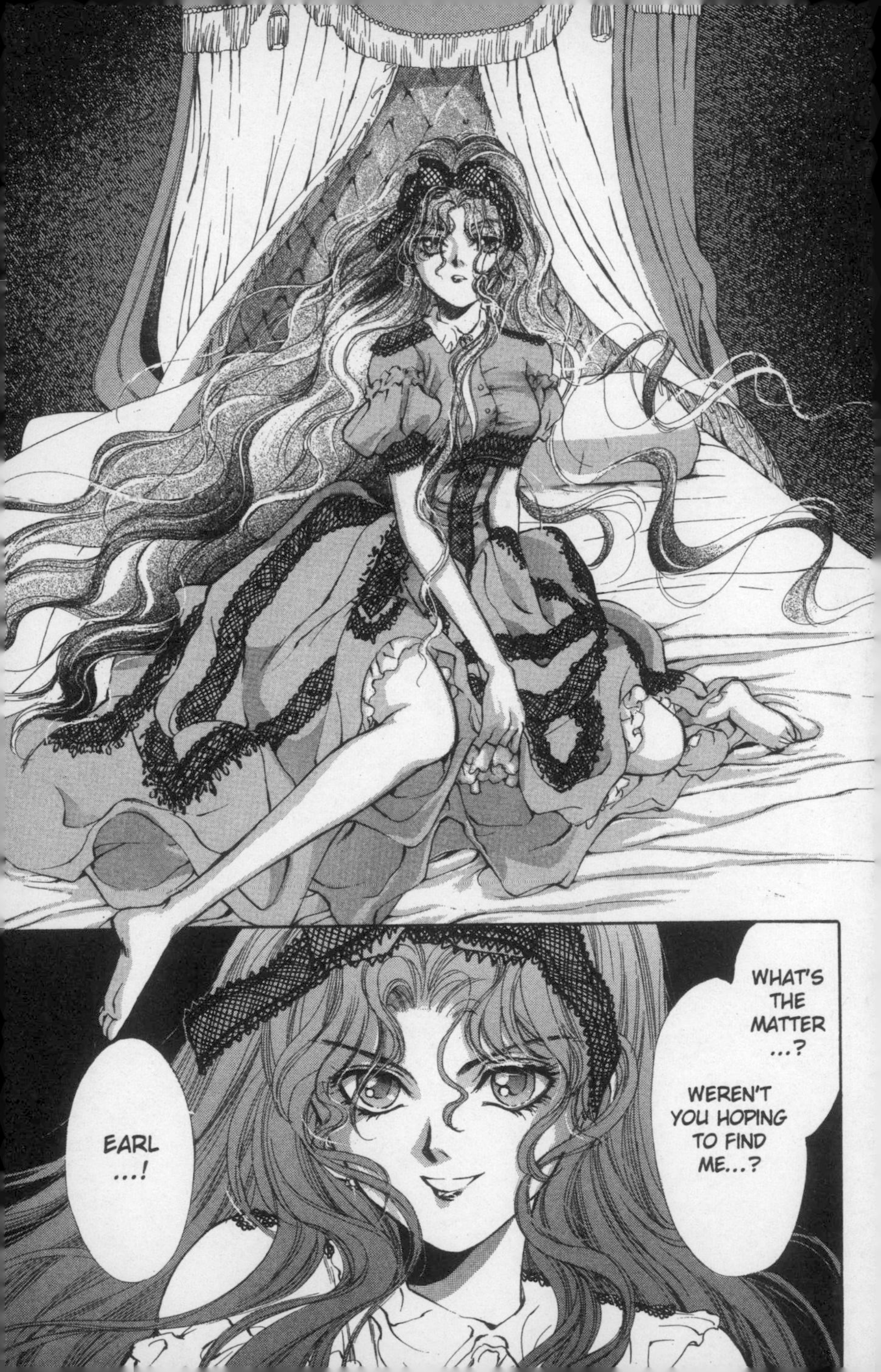
WHAT'S THE MATTER ...?
WEREN'T YOU HOPING TO FIND ME...?
EARL ...!

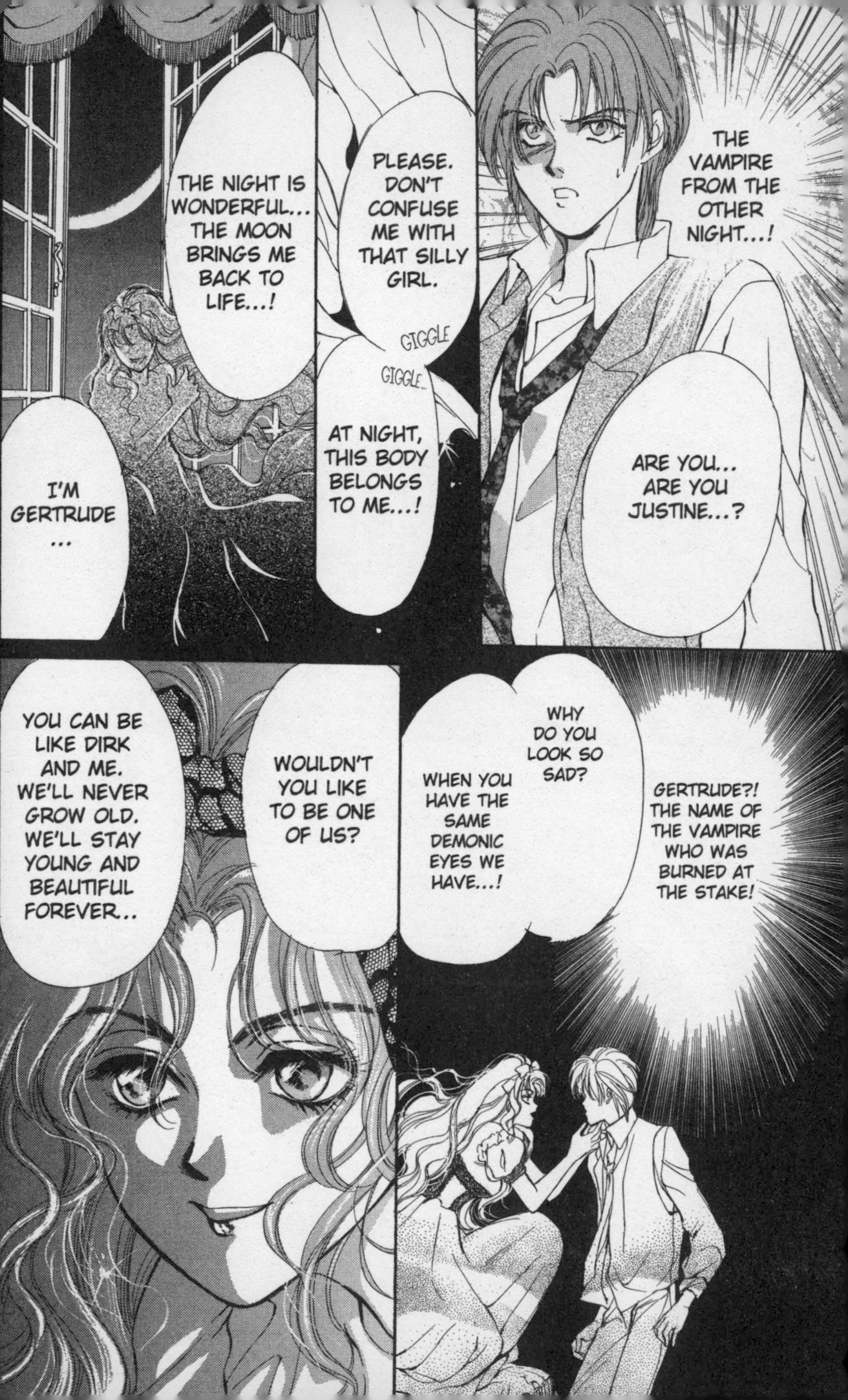
THE VAMPIRE FROM THE OTHER NIGHT...!
ARE YOU... ARE YOU JUSTINE...?
PLEASE. DON'T CONFUSE ME WITH THAT SILLY GIRL.
GIGGLE
GIGGLE...
AT NIGHT, THIS BODY BELONGS TO ME...!
THE NIGHT IS WONDERFUL... THE MOON BRINGS ME BACK TO LIFE...!
I'M GERTRUDE ...
GERTRUDE?! THE NAME OF THE VAMPIRE WHO WAS BURNED AT THE STAKE!
WHY DO YOU LOOK SO SAD?
WHEN YOU HAVE THE SAME DEMONIC EYES WE HAVE...!
WOULDN'T YOU LIKE TO BE ONE OF US?
YOU CAN BE LIKE DIRK AND ME. WE'LL NEVER GROW OLD. WE'LL STAY YOUNG AND BEAUTIFUL FOREVER...

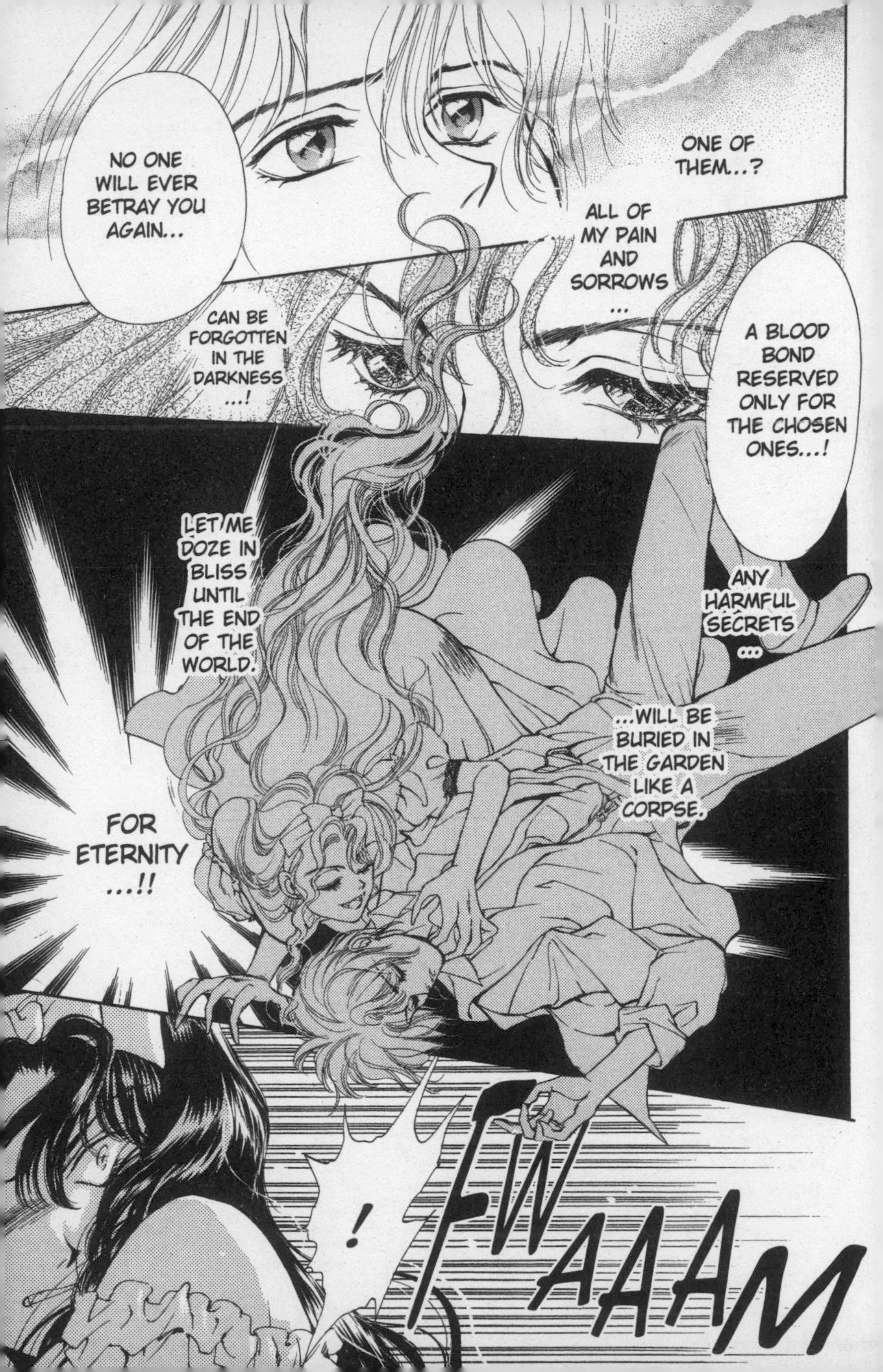
ONE OF THEM...?
NO ONE WILL EVER BETRAY YOU AGAIN...
ALL OF MY PAIN AND SORROWS ...
CAN BE FORGOTTEN IN THE DARKNESS ...!
A BLOOD BOND RESERVED ONLY FOR THE CHOSEN ONES...!
ANY HARMFUL SECRETS ...
...WILL BE BURIED IN THE GARDEN LIKE A CORPSE.
LET ME DOZE IN BLISS UNTIL THE END OF THE WORLD.
FOR ETERNITY ...!!
!
FWAAAM

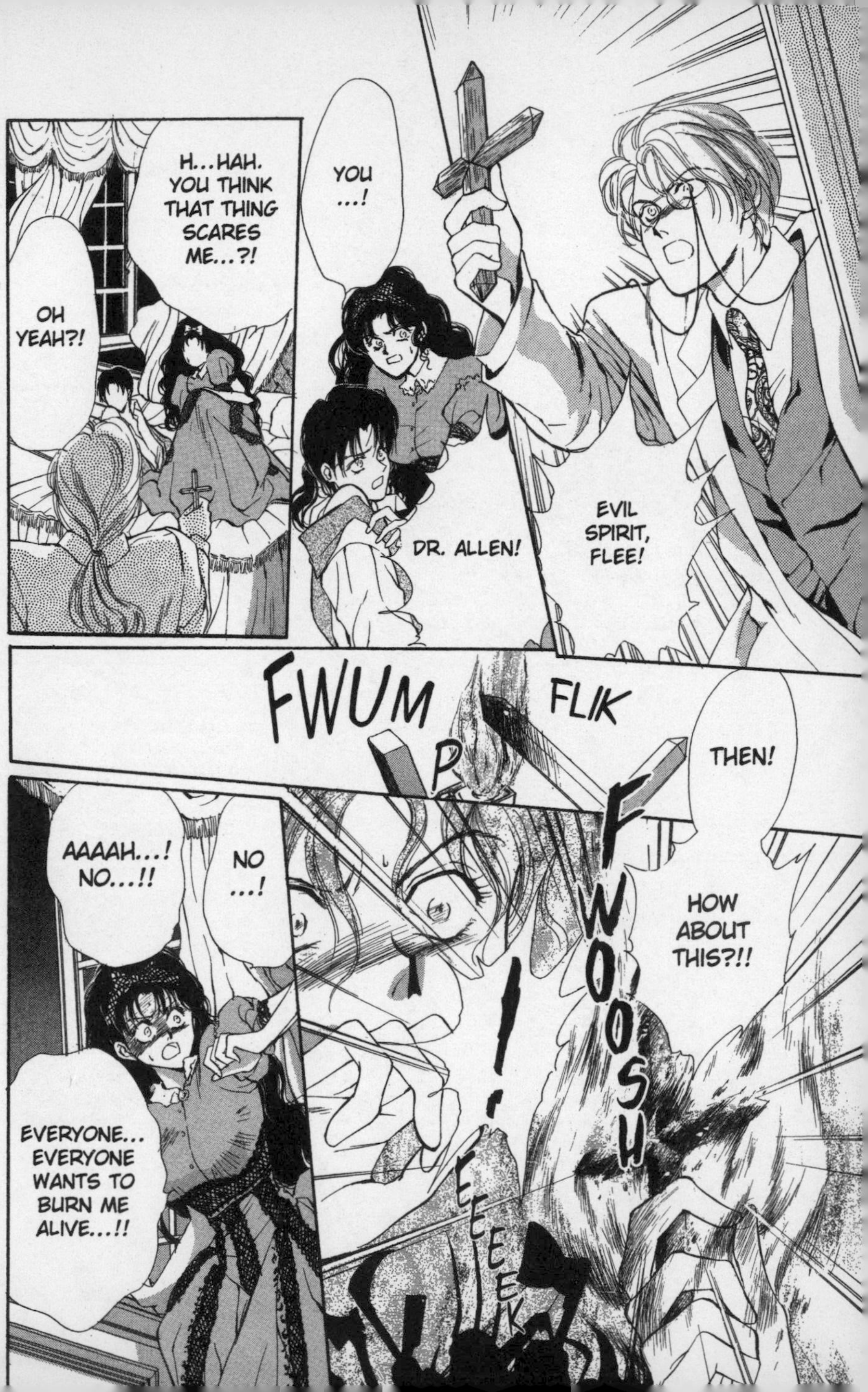
EVIL SPIRIT, FLEE!
DR. ALLEN!
YOU ...!
H...HAH. YOU THINK THAT THING SCARES ME...?!
OH YEAH?!
FLIK
P
FWUM
THEN!
HOW ABOUT THIS?!!
FWOOSH
!!
EEEEK
NO ...!
AAAAH...! NO...!!
EVERYONE... EVERYONE WANTS TO BURN ME ALIVE...!!

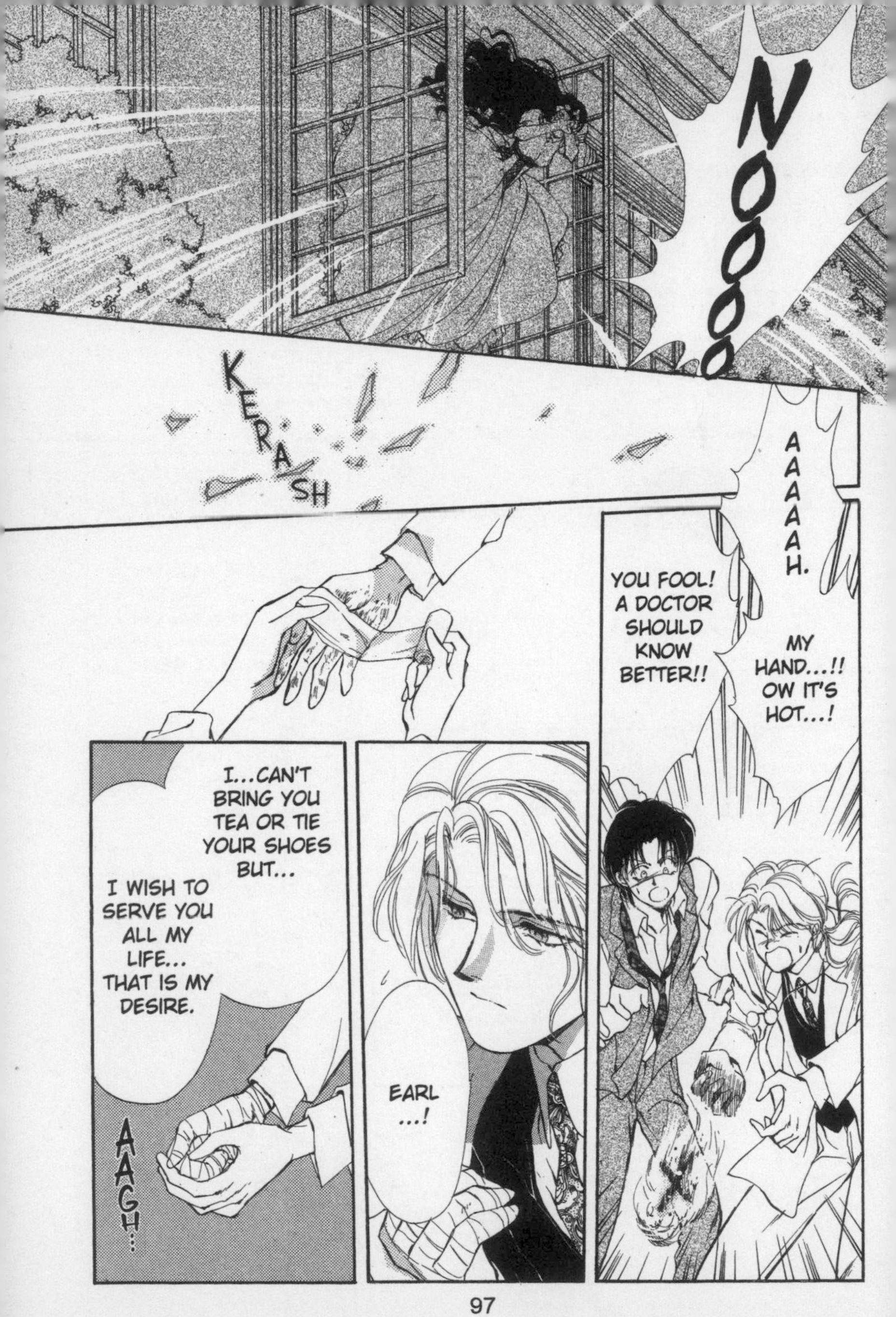
NOOOOO
KERASH
AAAAAAH.
MY HAND...!! OW IT'S HOT...!
YOU FOOL! A DOCTOR SHOULD KNOW BETTER!!
EARL ...!
I...CAN'T BRING YOU TEA OR TIE YOUR SHOES BUT...
I WISH TO SERVE YOU ALL MY LIFE... THAT IS MY DESIRE.
AAGH...

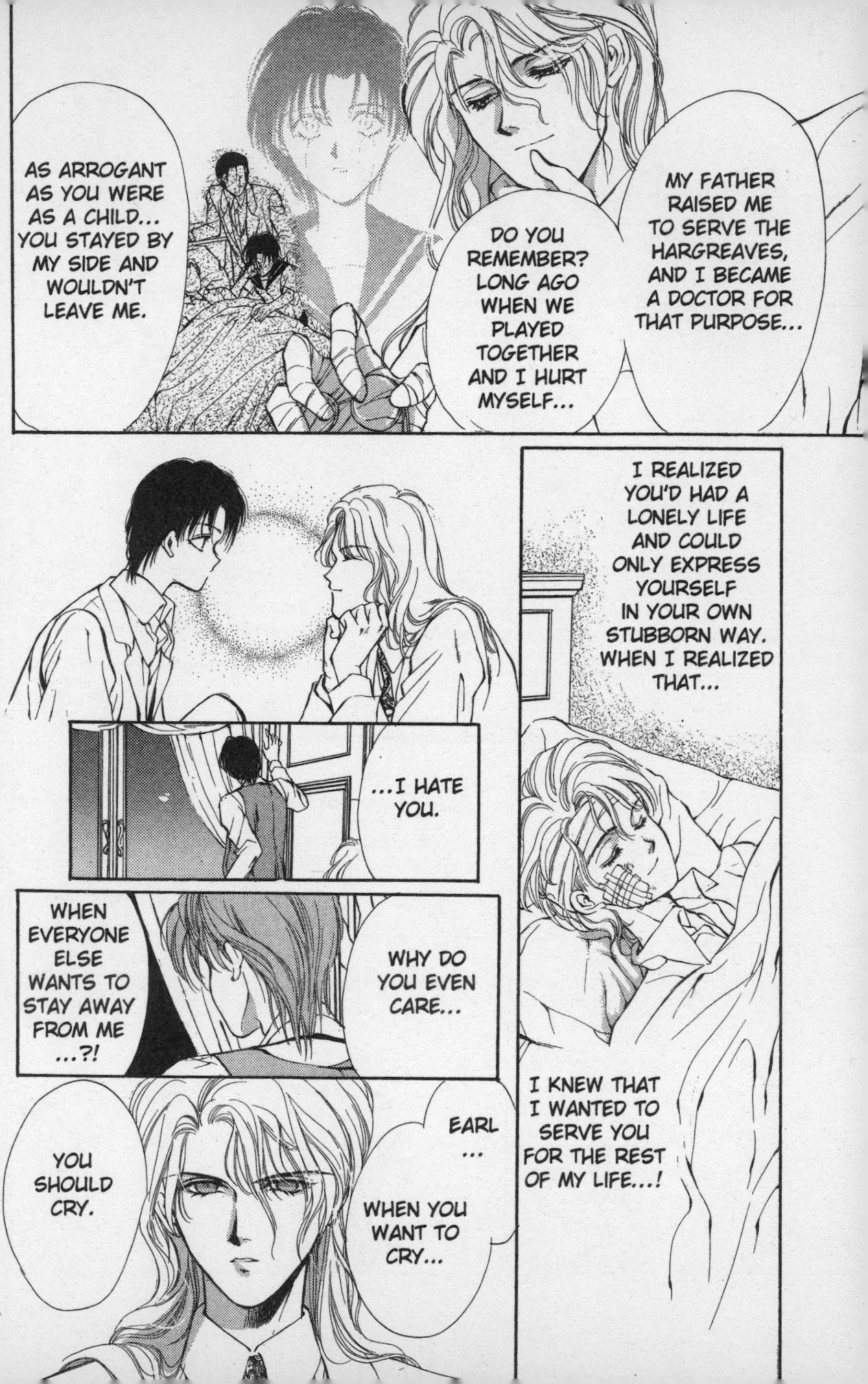
MY FATHER RAISED ME TO SERVE THE HARGREAVES, AND I BECAME A DOCTOR FOR THAT PURPOSE...
DO YOU REMEMBER? LONG AGO WHEN WE PLAYED TOGETHER AND I HURT MYSELF...
AS ARROGANT AS YOU WERE AS A CHILD... YOU STAYED BY MY SIDE AND WOULDN'T LEAVE ME.
I REALIZED YOU'D HAD A LONELY LIFE AND COULD ONLY EXPRESS YOURSELF IN YOUR OWN STUBBORN WAY. WHEN I REALIZED THAT...
I KNEW THAT I WANTED TO SERVE YOU FOR THE REST OF MY LIFE...!
...I HATE YOU.
WHY DO YOU EVEN CARE...
WHEN EVERYONE ELSE WANTS TO STAY AWAY FROM ME ...?!
EARL ...
WHEN YOU WANT TO CRY...
YOU SHOULD CRY.

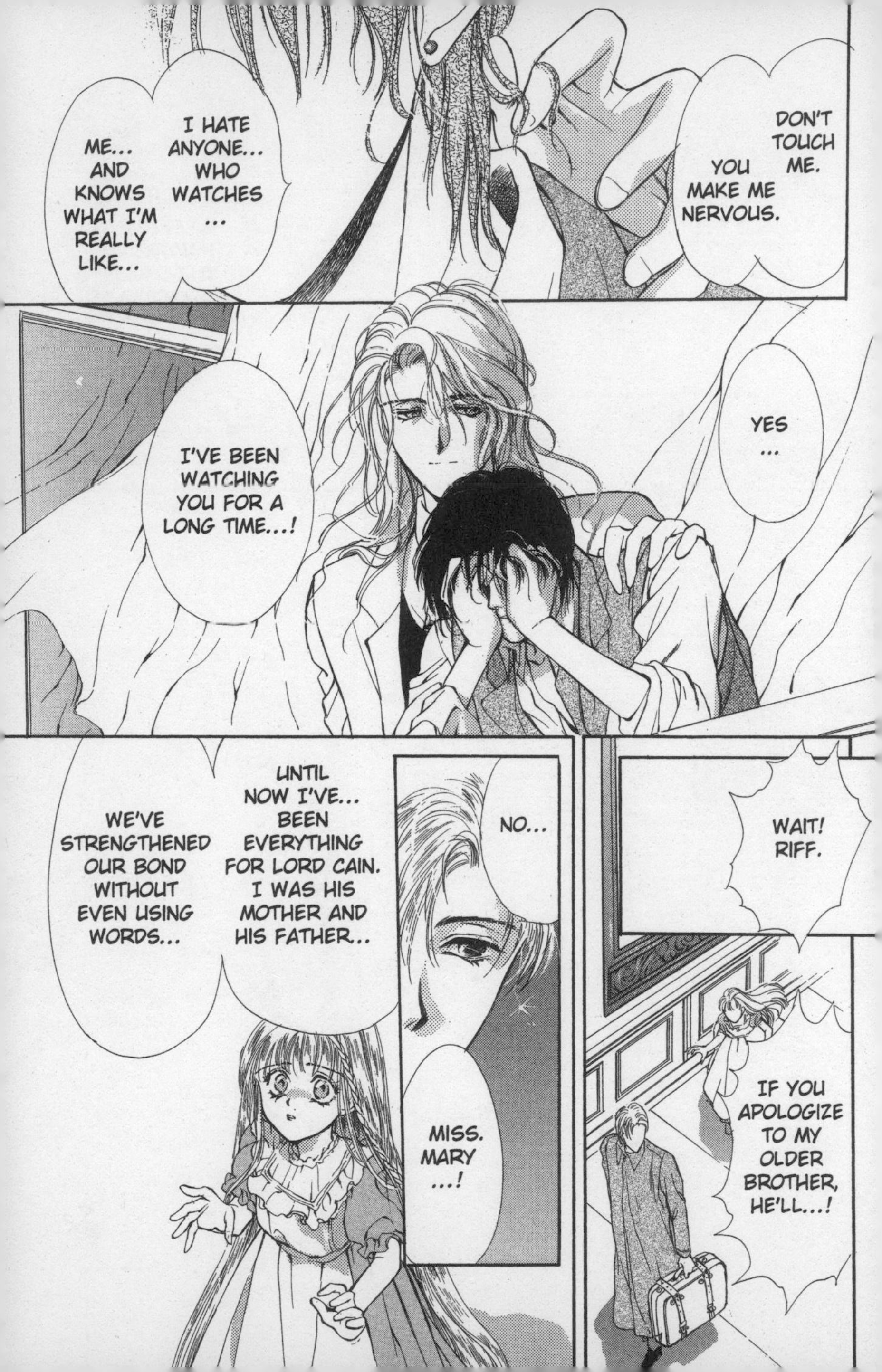
DON'T TOUCH ME. YOU MAKE ME NERVOUS.
I HATE ANYONE... WHO WATCHES ... ME... AND KNOWS WHAT I'M REALLY LIKE...
YES ...
I'VE BEEN WATCHING YOU FOR A LONG TIME...!
WAIT! RIFF.
IF YOU APOLOGIZE TO MY OLDER BROTHER, HE'LL...!
NO...
MISS. MARY ...!
UNTIL NOW I'VE... BEEN EVERYTHING FOR LORD CAIN. I WAS HIS MOTHER AND HIS FATHER...
WE'VE STRENGTHENED OUR BOND WITHOUT EVEN USING WORDS...

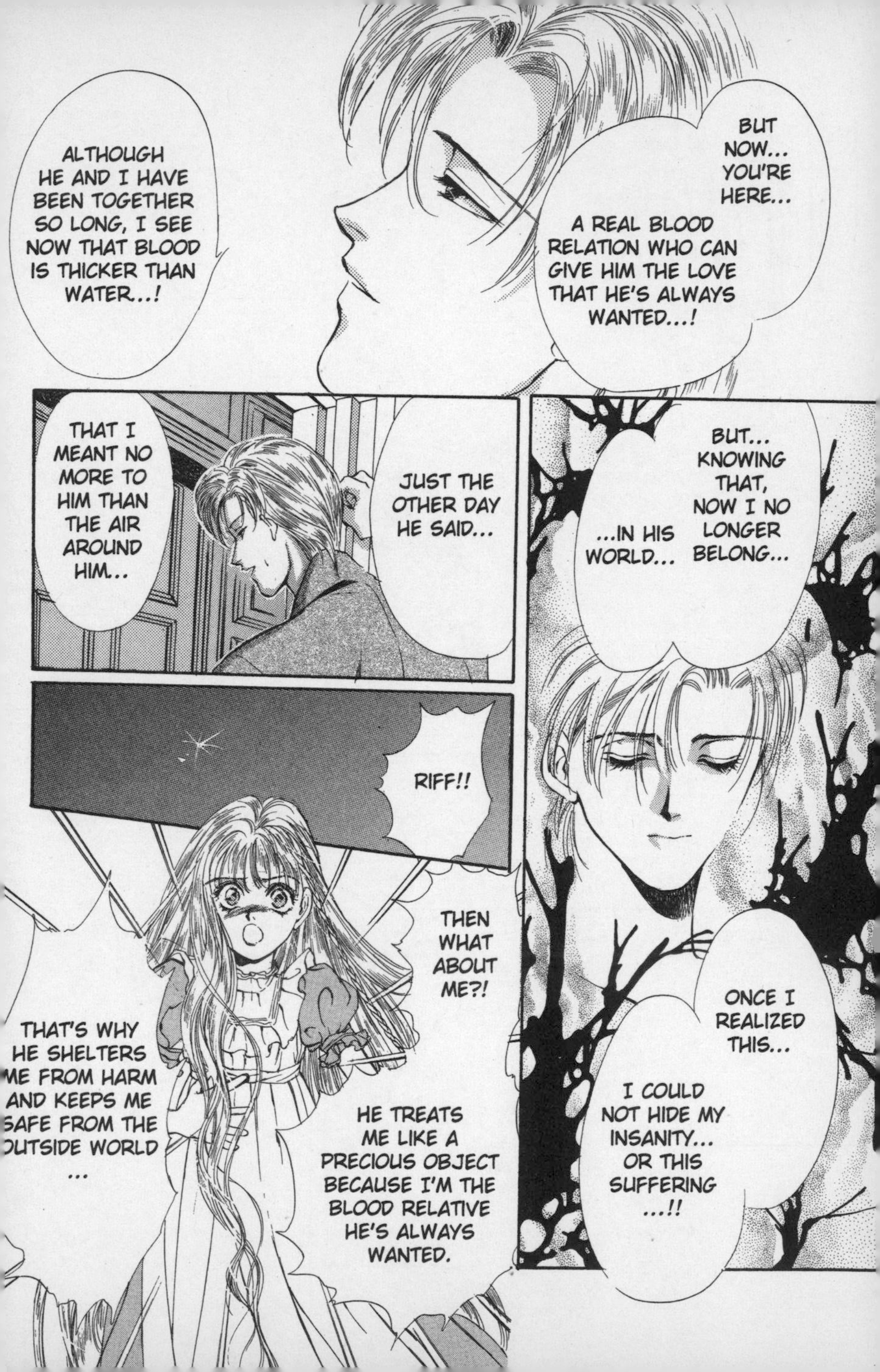
BUT NOW... YOU'RE HERE...
A REAL BLOOD RELATION WHO CAN GIVE HIM THE LOVE THAT HE'S ALWAYS WANTED...!
ALTHOUGH HE AND I HAVE BEEN TOGETHER SO LONG, I SEE NOW THAT BLOOD IS THICKER THAN WATER...!
BUT... KNOWING THAT, NOW I NO LONGER BELONG...
...IN HIS WORLD...
ONCE I REALIZED THIS...
I COULD NOT HIDE MY INSANITY... OR THIS SUFFERING ...!!
JUST THE OTHER DAY HE SAID...
THAT I MEANT NO MORE TO HIM THAN THE AIR AROUND HIM...
RIFF!!
THEN WHAT ABOUT ME?!
HE TREATS ME LIKE A PRECIOUS OBJECT BECAUSE I'M THE BLOOD RELATIVE HE'S ALWAYS WANTED.
THAT'S WHY HE SHELTERS ME FROM HARM AND KEEPS ME SAFE FROM THE OUTSIDE WORLD ...

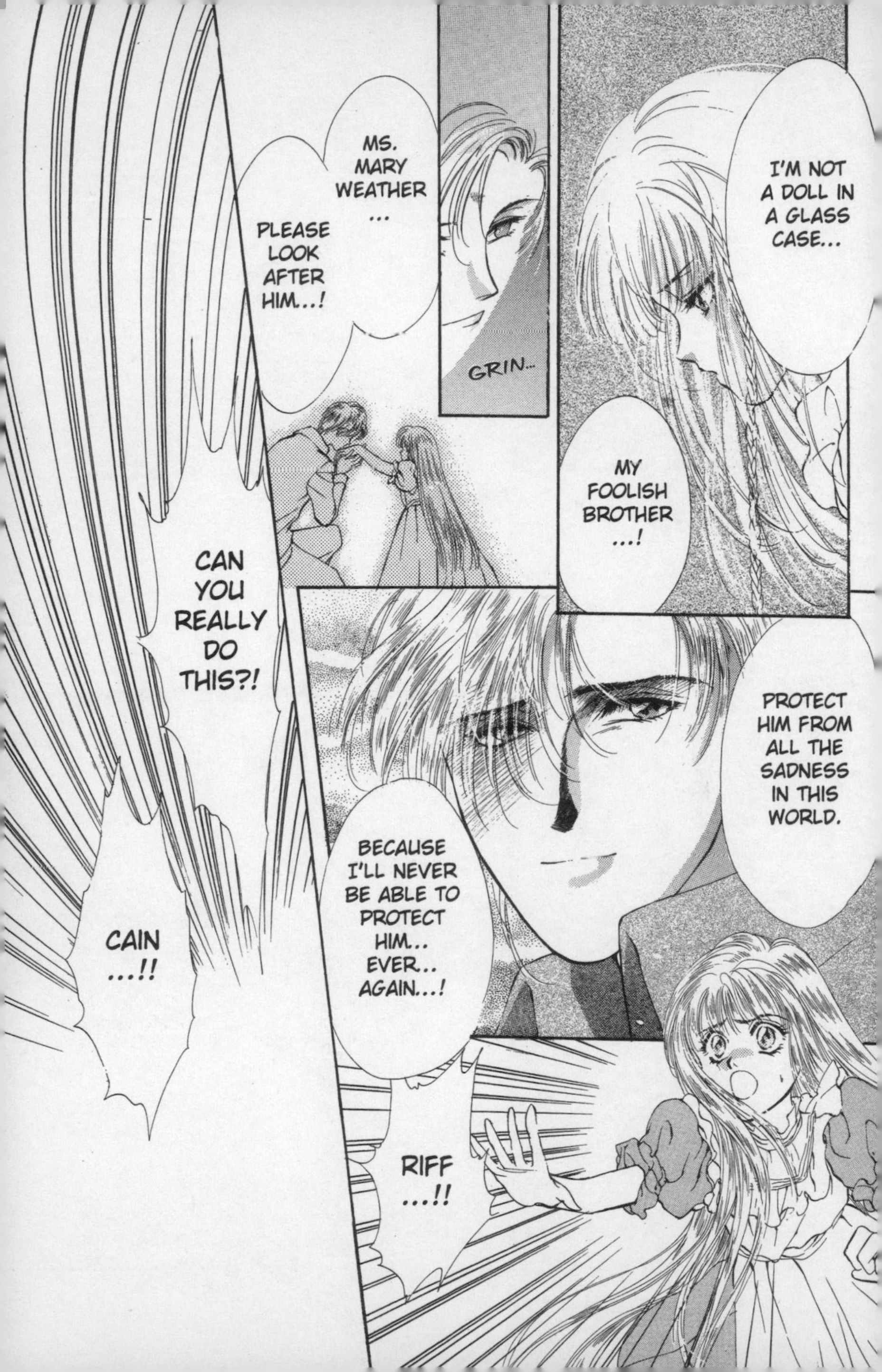
I'M NOT A DOLL IN A GLASS CASE...
MY FOOLISH BROTHER ...!
MS. MARY WEATHER ...
PLEASE LOOK AFTER HIM...!
GRIN...
PROTECT HIM FROM ALL THE SADNESS IN THIS WORLD.
BECAUSE I'LL NEVER BE ABLE TO PROTECT HIM... EVER... AGAIN...!
RIFF ...!!
CAN YOU REALLY DO THIS?!
CAIN ...!!

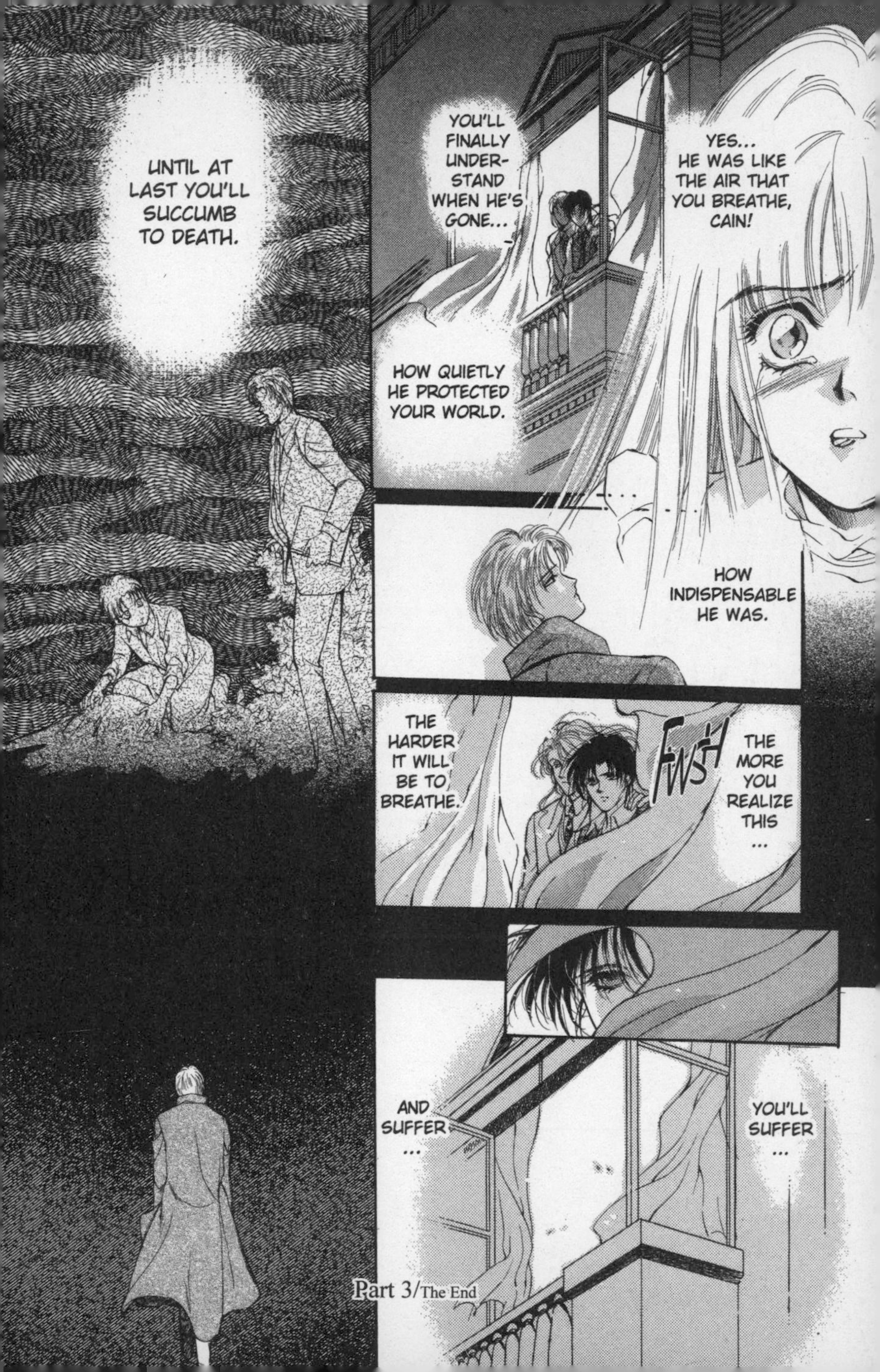
YES... HE WAS LIKE THE AIR THAT YOU BREATHE, CAIN!
YOU'LL FINALLY UNDERSTAND WHEN HE'S GONE...
HOW QUIETLY HE PROTECTED YOUR WORLD.
HOW INDISPENSABLE HE WAS.
FWSH
THE MORE YOU REALIZE THIS ...
THE HARDER IT WILL BE TO BREATHE.
YOU'LL SUFFER ...
AND SUFFER ...
UNTIL AT LAST YOU'LL SUCCUMB TO DEATH.
Part 3/The End

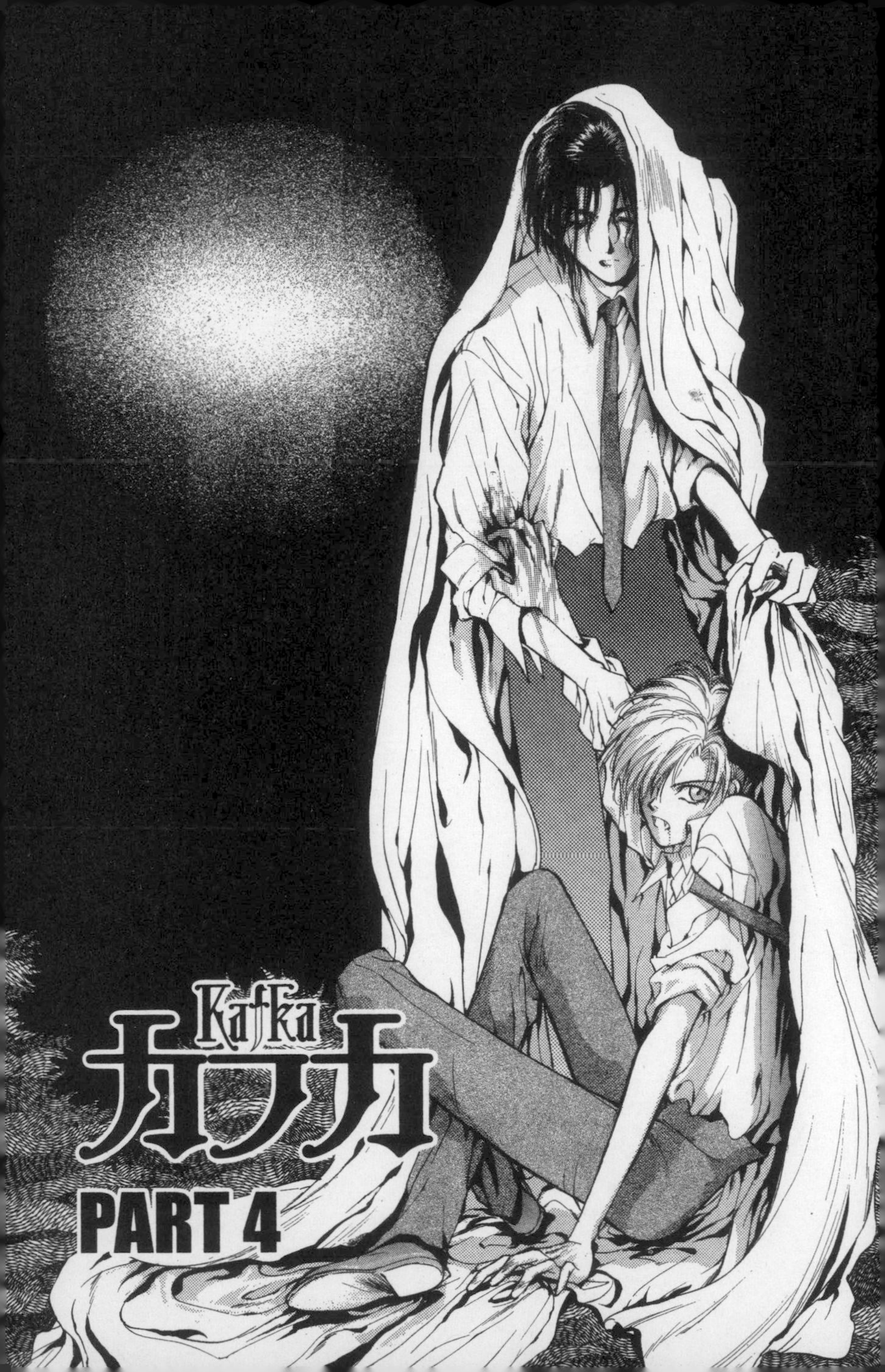
Kafka
カフカ
PART 4

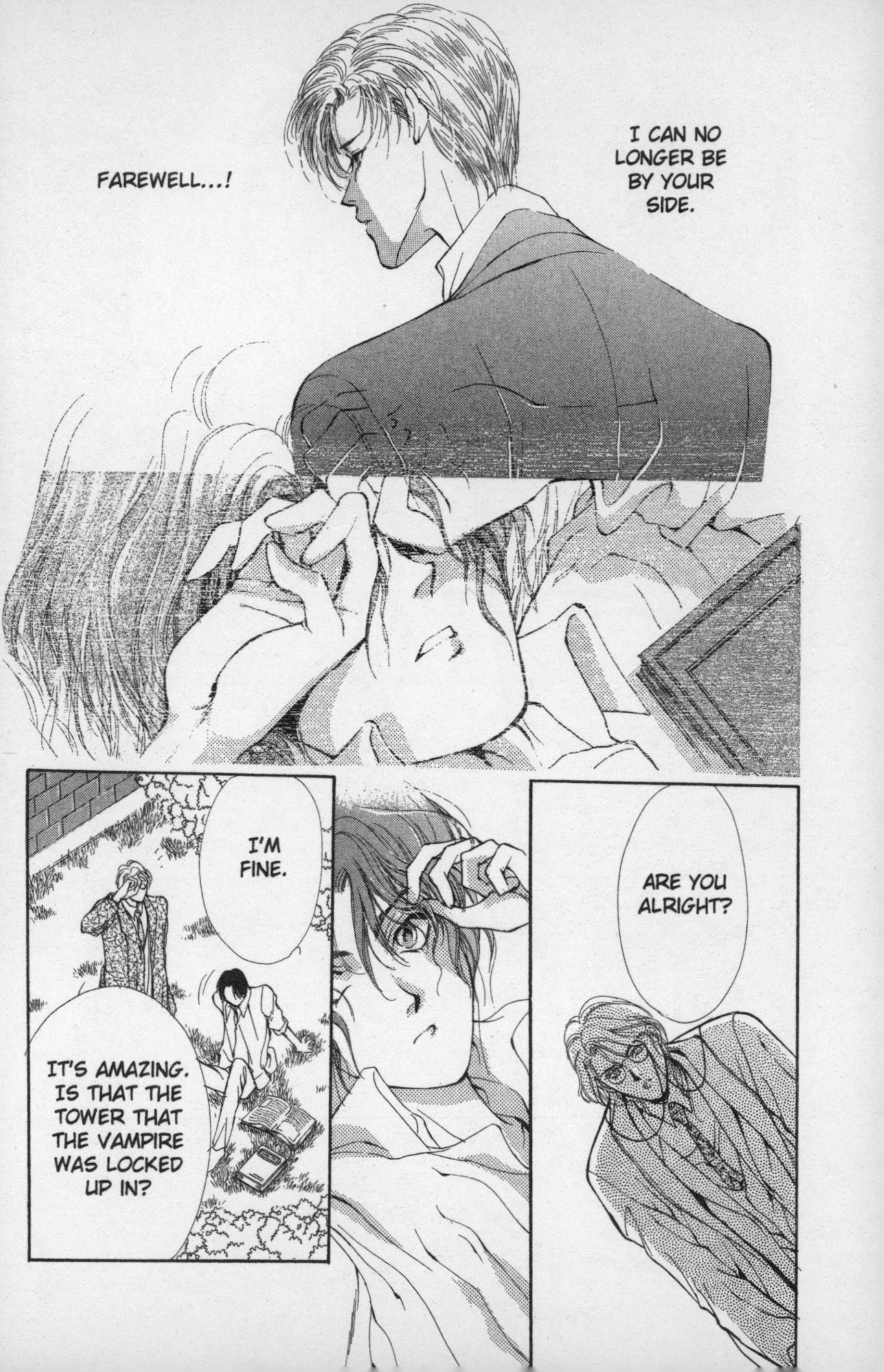
I CAN NO LONGER BE BY YOUR SIDE.
FAREWELL...!
ARE YOU ALRIGHT?
I'M FINE.
IT'S AMAZING. IS THAT THE TOWER THAT THE VAMPIRE WAS LOCKED UP IN?

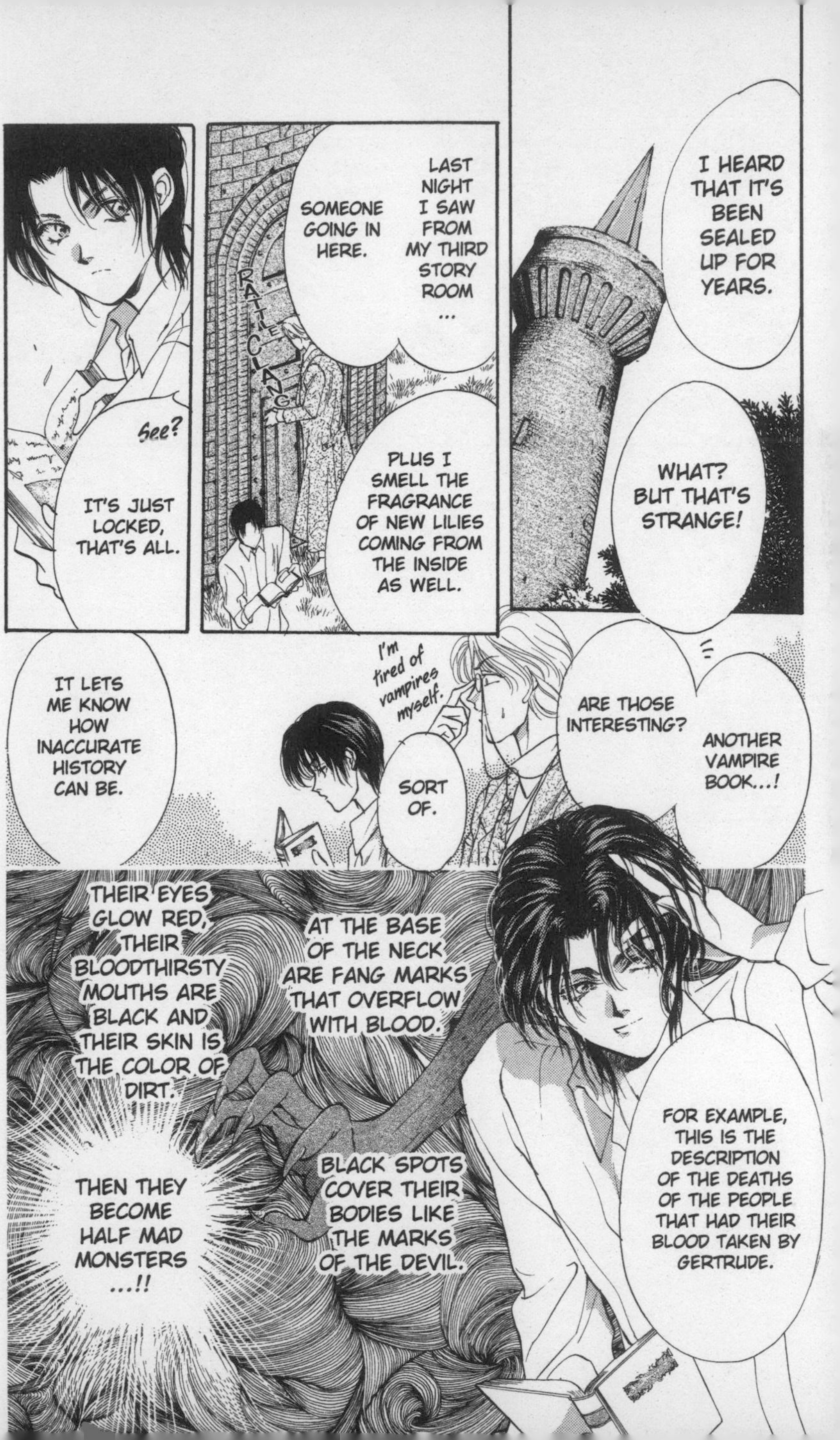
I HEARD THAT IT'S BEEN SEALED UP FOR YEARS.
WHAT? BUT THAT'S STRANGE!
LAST NIGHT I SAW FROM MY THIRD STORY ROOM ...
SOMEONE GOING IN HERE.
RATTLE CLANG
PLUS I SMELL THE FRAGRANCE OF NEW LILIES COMING FROM THE INSIDE AS WELL.
See?
IT'S JUST LOCKED, THAT'S ALL.
ANOTHER VAMPIRE BOOK...!
ARE THOSE INTERESTING?
I'm tired of vampires myself.
SORT OF.
IT LETS ME KNOW HOW INACCURATE HISTORY CAN BE.
FOR EXAMPLE, THIS IS THE DESCRIPTION OF THE DEATHS OF THE PEOPLE THAT HAD THEIR BLOOD TAKEN BY GERTRUDE.
AT THE BASE OF THE NECK ARE FANG MARKS THAT OVERFLOW WITH BLOOD.
THEIR EYES GLOW RED, THEIR BLOODTHIRSTY MOUTHS ARE BLACK AND THEIR SKIN IS THE COLOR OF DIRT.
BLACK SPOTS COVER THEIR BODIES LIKE THE MARKS OF THE DEVIL.
THEN THEY BECOME HALF MAD MONSTERS ...!!

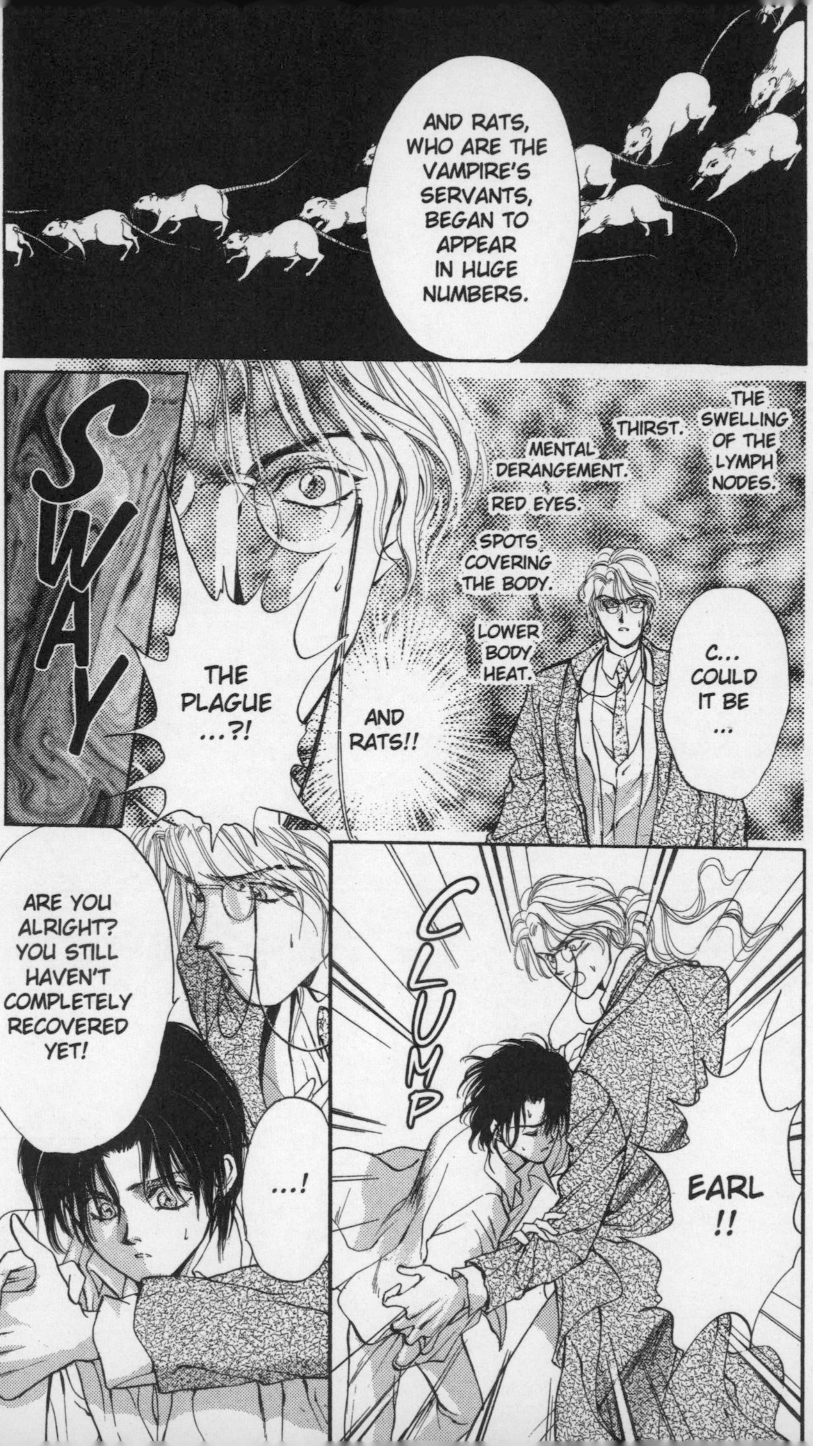
AND RATS, WHO ARE THE VAMPIRE'S SERVANTS, BEGAN TO APPEAR IN HUGE NUMBERS.
THE SWELLING OF THE LYMPH NODES.
THIRST.
MENTAL DERANGEMENT.
RED EYES.
SPOTS COVERING THE BODY.
LOWER BODY HEAT.
C... COULD IT BE ...
SWAY
AND RATS!!
THE PLAGUE ...?!
CLUMP
EARL !!
ARE YOU ALRIGHT? YOU STILL HAVEN'T COMPLETELY RECOVERED YET!
...!

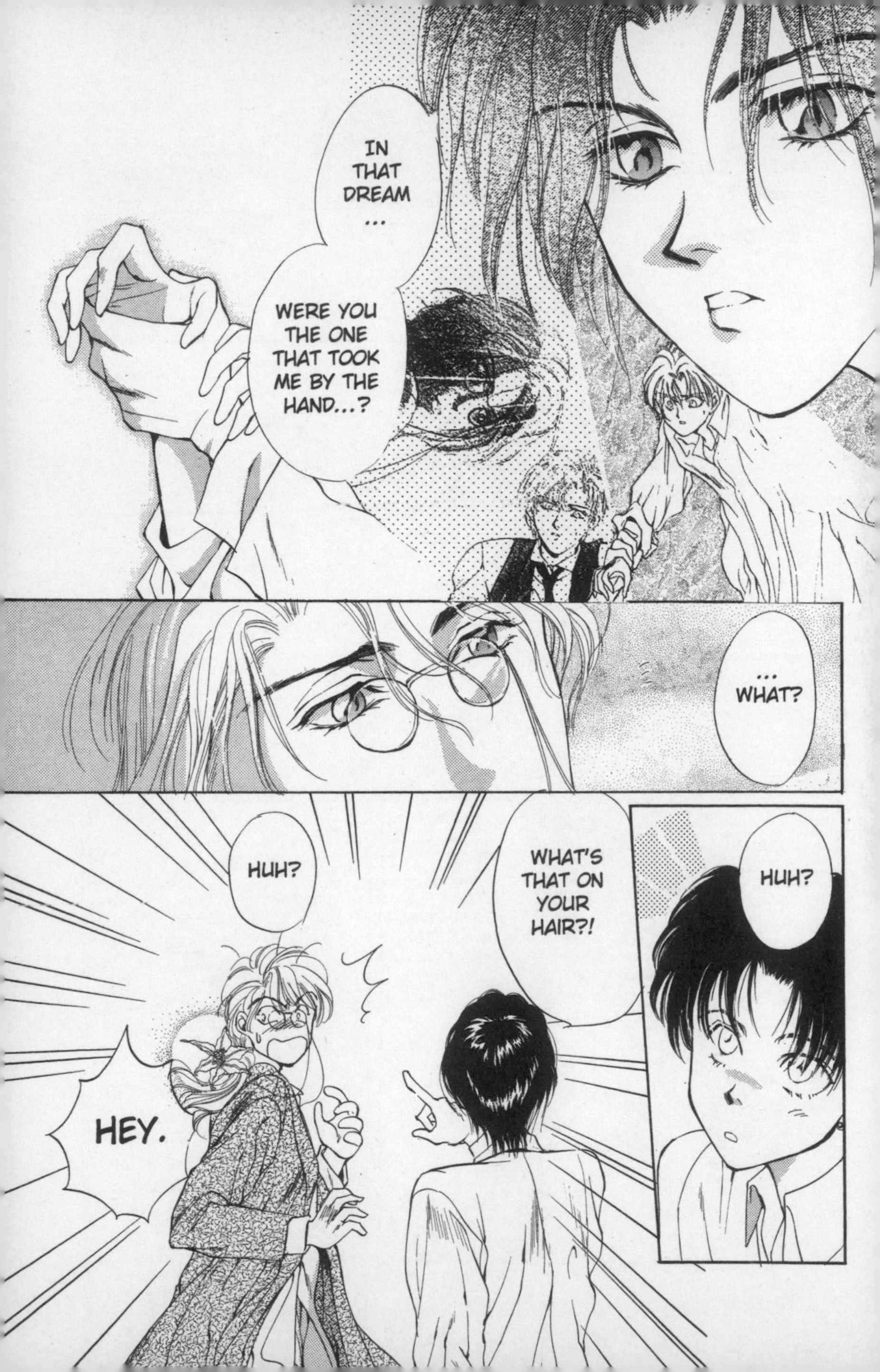
IN THAT DREAM ...
WERE YOU THE ONE THAT TOOK ME BY THE HAND...?
... WHAT?
HUH?
WHAT'S THAT ON YOUR HAIR?!
HUH?
HEY.

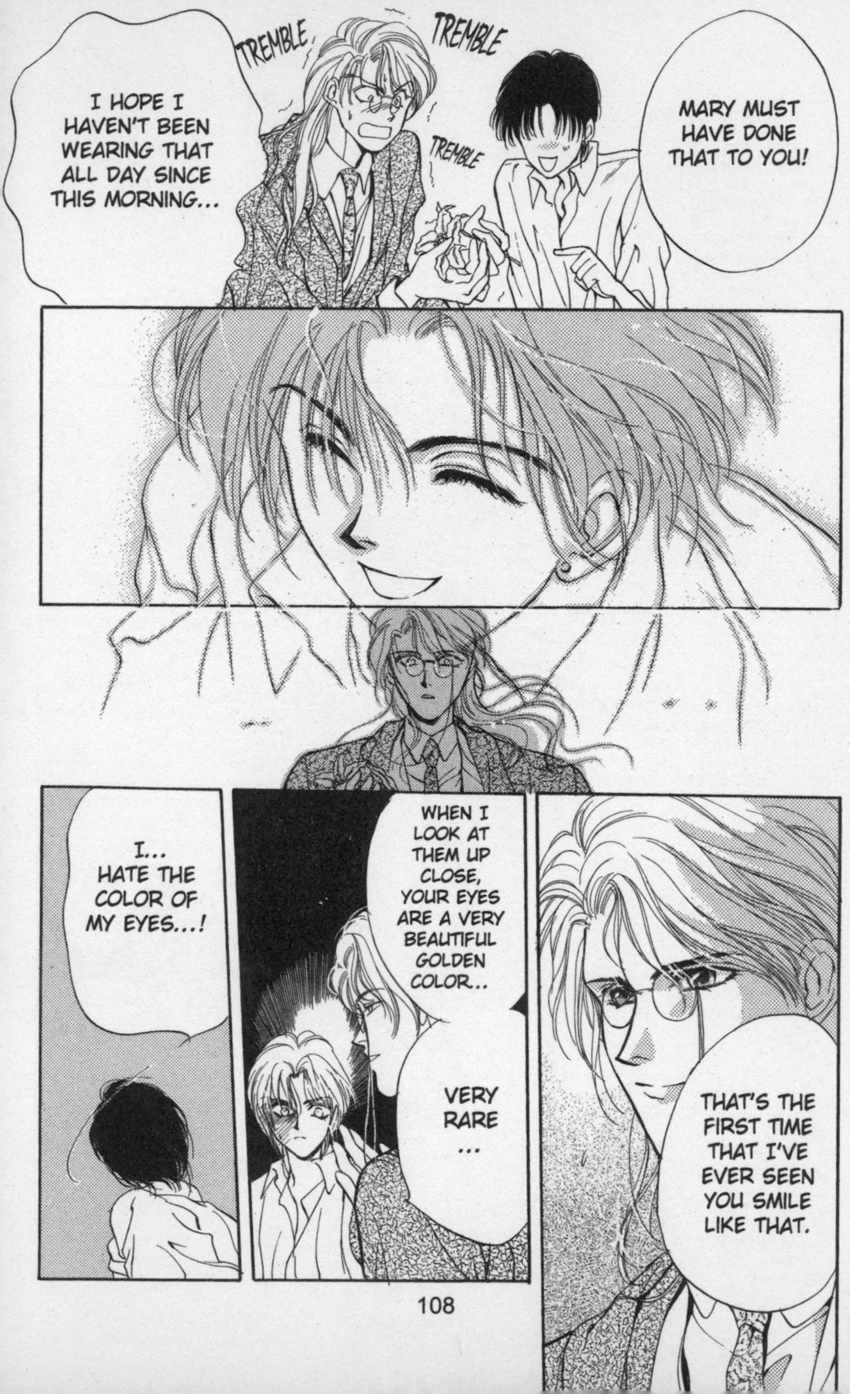
MARY MUST HAVE DONE THAT TO YOU!
TREMBLE
TREMBLE
TREMBLE
I HOPE I HAVEN'T BEEN WEARING THAT ALL DAY SINCE THIS MORNING...
THAT'S THE FIRST TIME THAT I'VE EVER SEEN YOU SMILE LIKE THAT.
WHEN I LOOK AT THEM UP CLOSE, YOUR EYES ARE A VERY BEAUTIFUL GOLDEN COLOR..
VERY RARE ...
I... HATE THE COLOR OF MY EYES...!

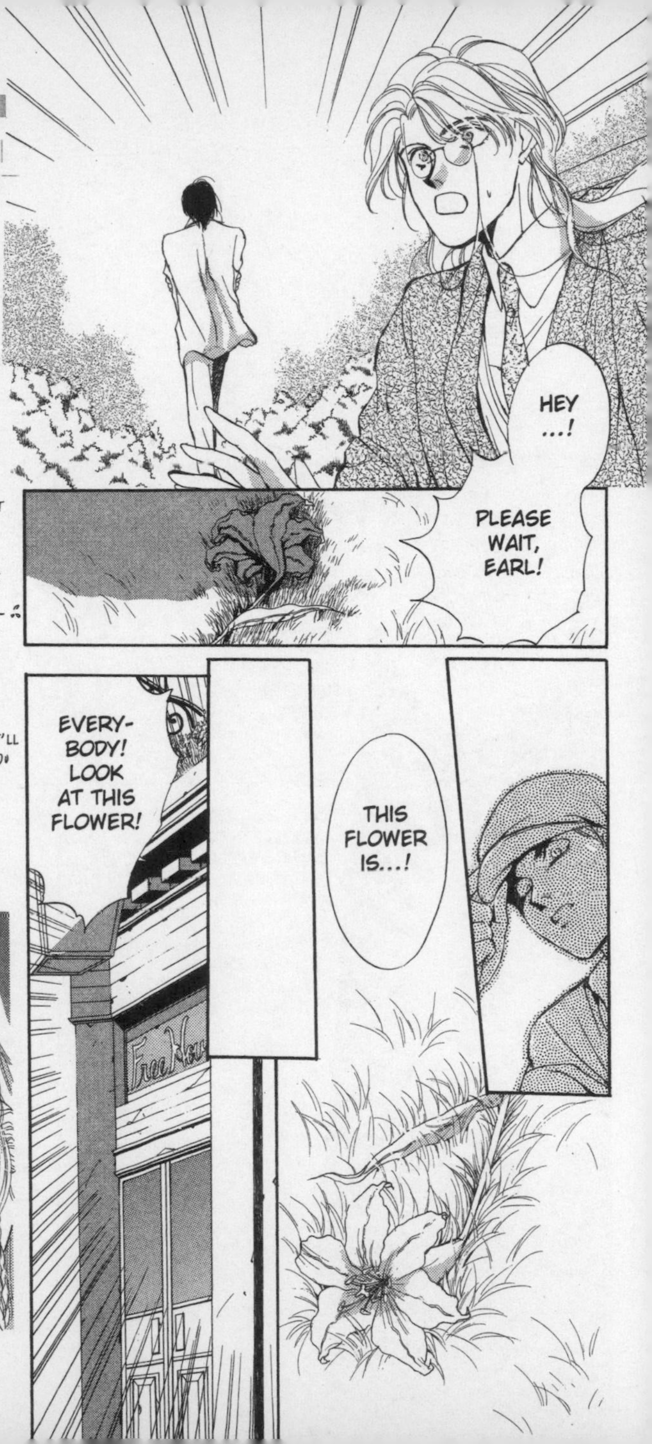
HEY ...!
PLEASE WAIT, EARL!
THIS FLOWER IS...!
EVERY-BODY! LOOK AT THIS FLOWER!

WILD ♦ TALK

NOW THAT I THINK ABOUT IT, ONE READER ASKED ME "WHAT COLOR ARE CAIN'S EYES?" AS IT'S STATED IN THE SOUND OF A BOY HATCHING, HIS EYES ARE GOLD WITH A TOUCH OF GREEN. IF YOU'D LIKE TO SEE WHAT THAT LOOKS LIKE, THEN TAKE A LOOK AT THE EYES OF A CAT. BY THE WAY MY DARLING CAT, MIRUCHAN HAS EYES LIKE THAT. MEOW. ALSO SOMETIMES JENNIFER CONNELLY'S EYES SORT OF LOOK LIKE THAT IN SOME OF HER PICTURES...I WILL ADMIT THAT THIS CURRENT STORY HAD A PRETTY RISQUÉ THEME. IT REALLY EMBARRASSED ME AT THE TIME! IT'S NOT SOMETHING THAT I WOULD SHOW MY PARENTS.~ DRAWING THE "NUDE" MADE ME SO EMBARRASSED THAT I ALMOST DIED. (ALTHOUGH SOME PEOPLE ASK ME "WHY?") PANT PANT AAAAAH NOOOOH. EVEN MY MANAGER SAID "IT'LL BE FINE." BUT AS FOR ME... ANYWAY CAIN'S COUSIN, SUZETTE AND HIS REAL MOTHER AUGUSTA SHARE SOME SIMILARITIES. READ ON AND YOU'LL FIND OUT WHY.

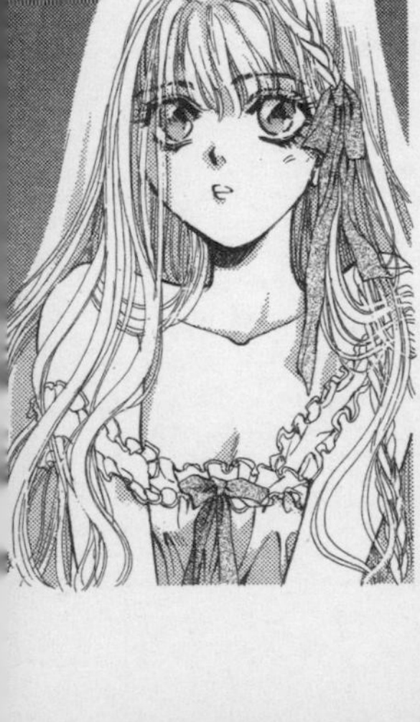

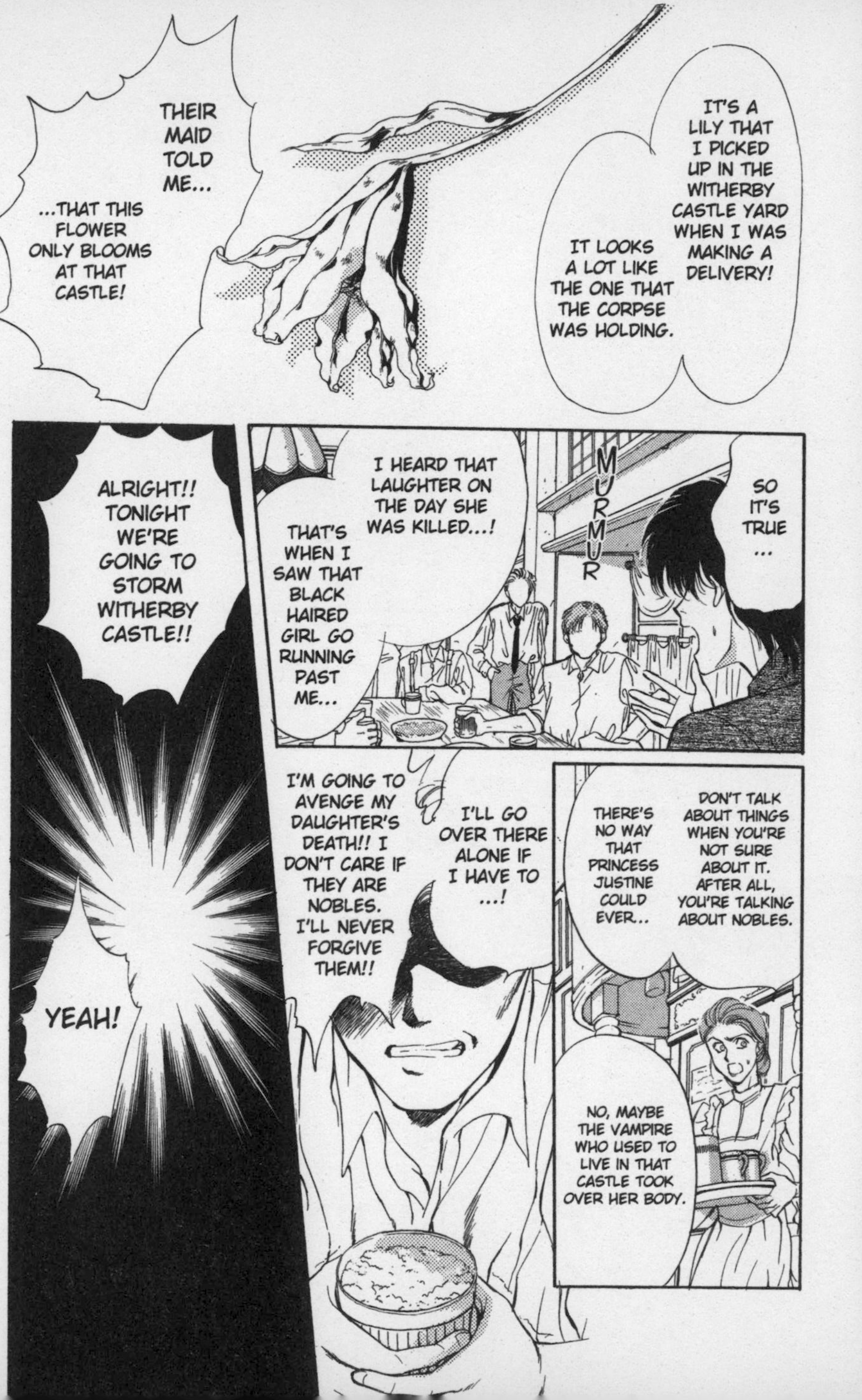
IT'S A LILY THAT I PICKED UP IN THE WITHERBY CASTLE YARD WHEN I WAS MAKING A DELIVERY!
IT LOOKS A LOT LIKE THE ONE THAT THE CORPSE WAS HOLDING.
THEIR MAID TOLD ME...
...THAT THIS FLOWER ONLY BLOOMS AT THAT CASTLE!
SO IT'S TRUE ...
MURMUR
I HEARD THAT LAUGHTER ON THE DAY SHE WAS KILLED...!
THAT'S WHEN I SAW THAT BLACK HAIRED GIRL GO RUNNING PAST ME...
DON'T TALK ABOUT THINGS WHEN YOU'RE NOT SURE ABOUT IT. AFTER ALL, YOU'RE TALKING ABOUT NOBLES.
THERE'S NO WAY THAT PRINCESS JUSTINE COULD EVER...
NO, MAYBE THE VAMPIRE WHO USED TO LIVE IN THAT CASTLE TOOK OVER HER BODY.
I'M GOING TO AVENGE MY DAUGHTER'S DEATH!! I DON'T CARE IF THEY ARE NOBLES. I'LL NEVER FORGIVE THEM!!
I'LL GO OVER THERE ALONE IF I HAVE TO ...!
ALRIGHT!! TONIGHT WE'RE GOING TO STORM WITHERBY CASTLE!!
YEAH!

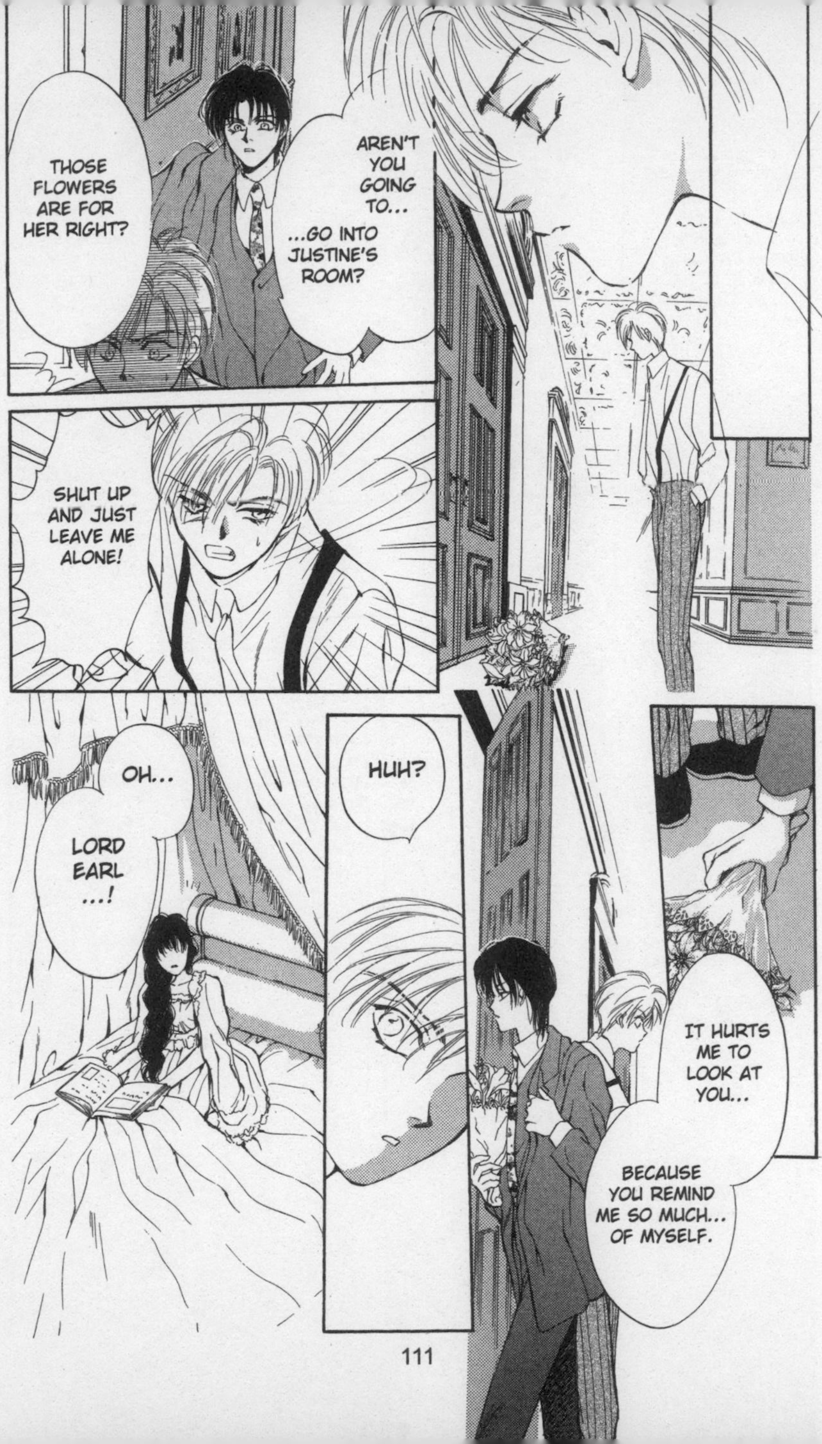
AREN'T YOU GOING TO...
...GO INTO JUSTINE'S ROOM?
THOSE FLOWERS ARE FOR HER RIGHT?
SHUT UP AND JUST LEAVE ME ALONE!
IT HURTS ME TO LOOK AT YOU...
BECAUSE YOU REMIND ME SO MUCH... OF MYSELF.
HUH?
OH...
LORD EARL ...!

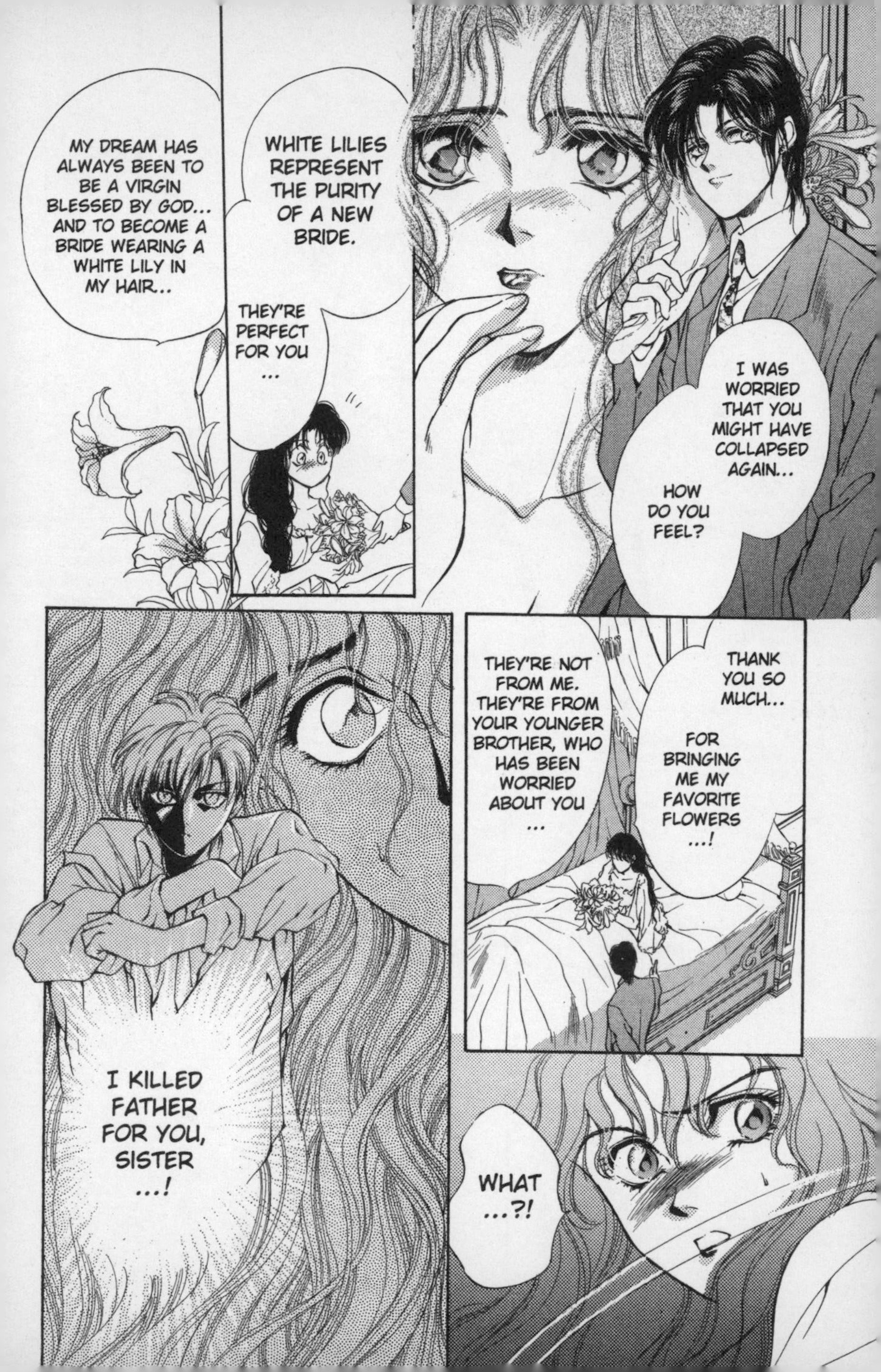
I WAS WORRIED THAT YOU MIGHT HAVE COLLAPSED AGAIN...
HOW DO YOU FEEL?
WHITE LILIES REPRESENT THE PURITY OF A NEW BRIDE.
THEY'RE PERFECT FOR YOU ...
MY DREAM HAS ALWAYS BEEN TO BE A VIRGIN BLESSED BY GOD... AND TO BECOME A BRIDE WEARING A WHITE LILY IN MY HAIR...
THANK YOU SO MUCH...
FOR BRINGING ME MY FAVORITE FLOWERS ...!
THEY'RE NOT FROM ME. THEY'RE FROM YOUR YOUNGER BROTHER, WHO HAS BEEN WORRIED ABOUT YOU ...
WHAT ...?!
I KILLED FATHER FOR YOU, SISTER ...!

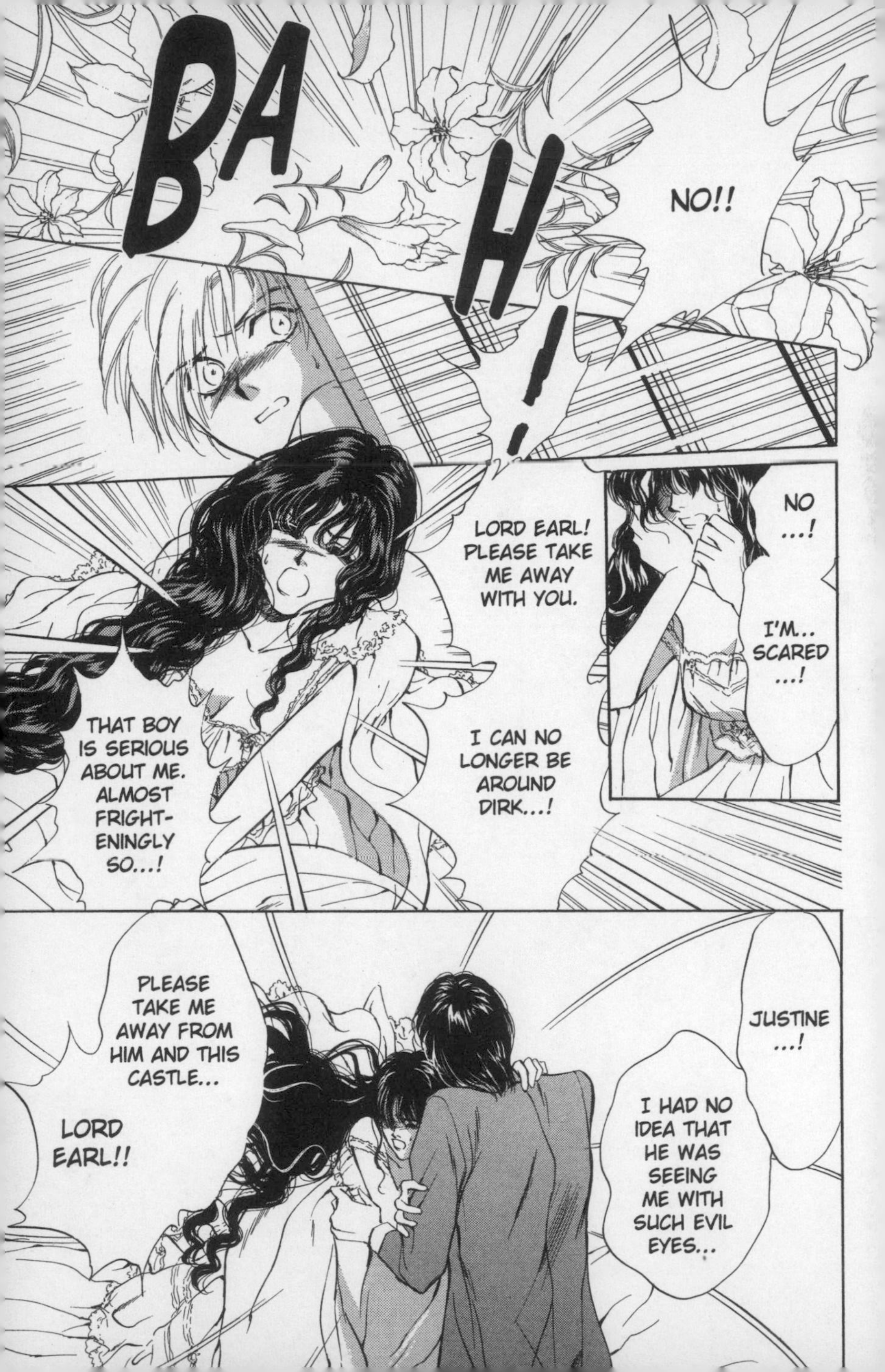
BAHI!
NO!!
NO ...!
I'M... SCARED ...!
LORD EARL! PLEASE TAKE ME AWAY WITH YOU.
I CAN NO LONGER BE AROUND DIRK...!
THAT BOY IS SERIOUS ABOUT ME. ALMOST FRIGHT-ENINGLY SO...!
JUSTINE ...!
I HAD NO IDEA THAT HE WAS SEEING ME WITH SUCH EVIL EYES...
PLEASE TAKE ME AWAY FROM HIM AND THIS CASTLE...
LORD EARL!!

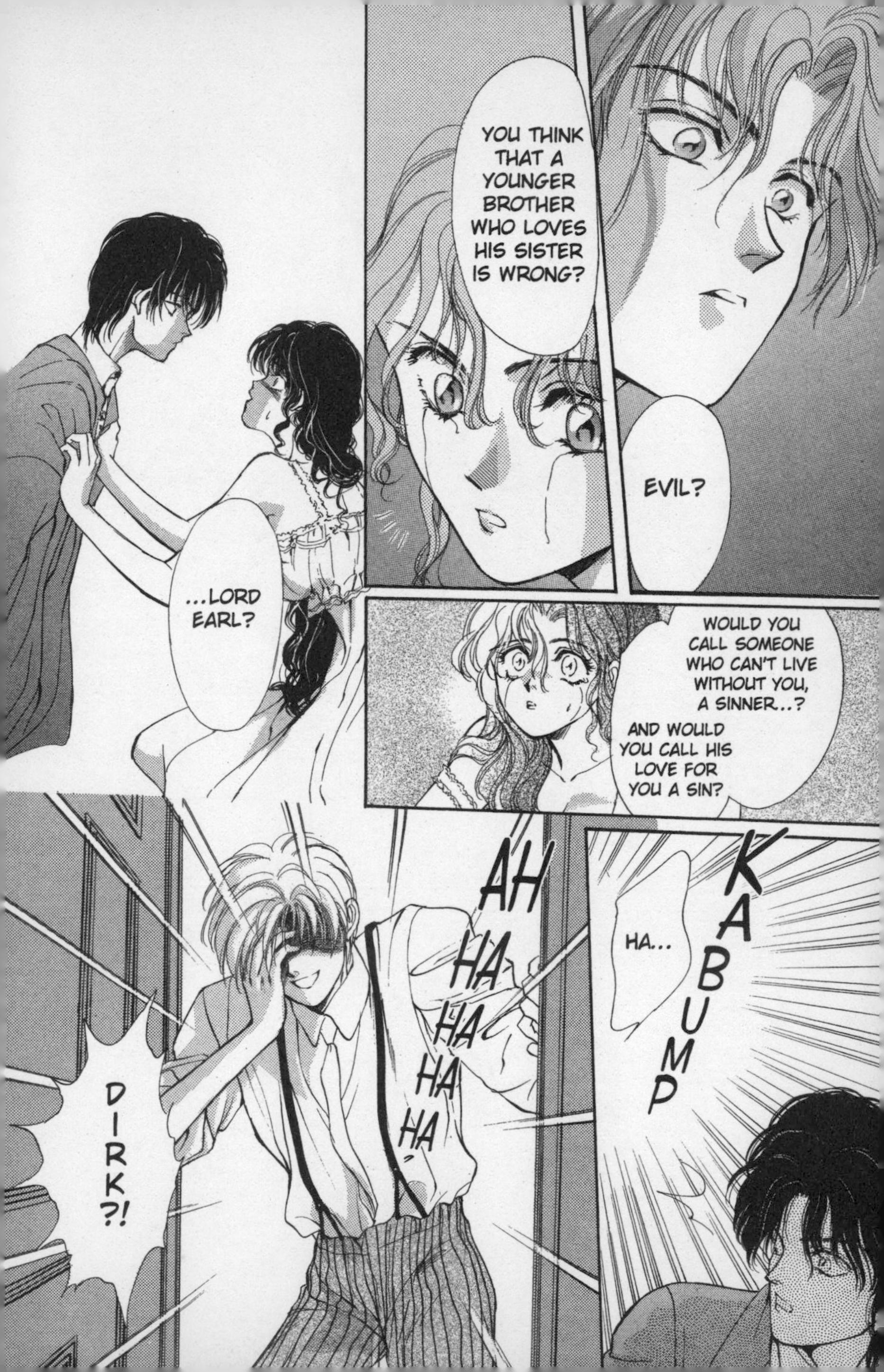
YOU THINK THAT A YOUNGER BROTHER WHO LOVES HIS SISTER IS WRONG?
EVIL?
WOULD YOU CALL SOMEONE WHO CAN'T LIVE WITHOUT YOU, A SINNER...?
AND WOULD YOU CALL HIS LOVE FOR YOU A SIN?
...LORD EARL?
HA...
KABUMP
AH HA HA HA HA HA
DIRK?!

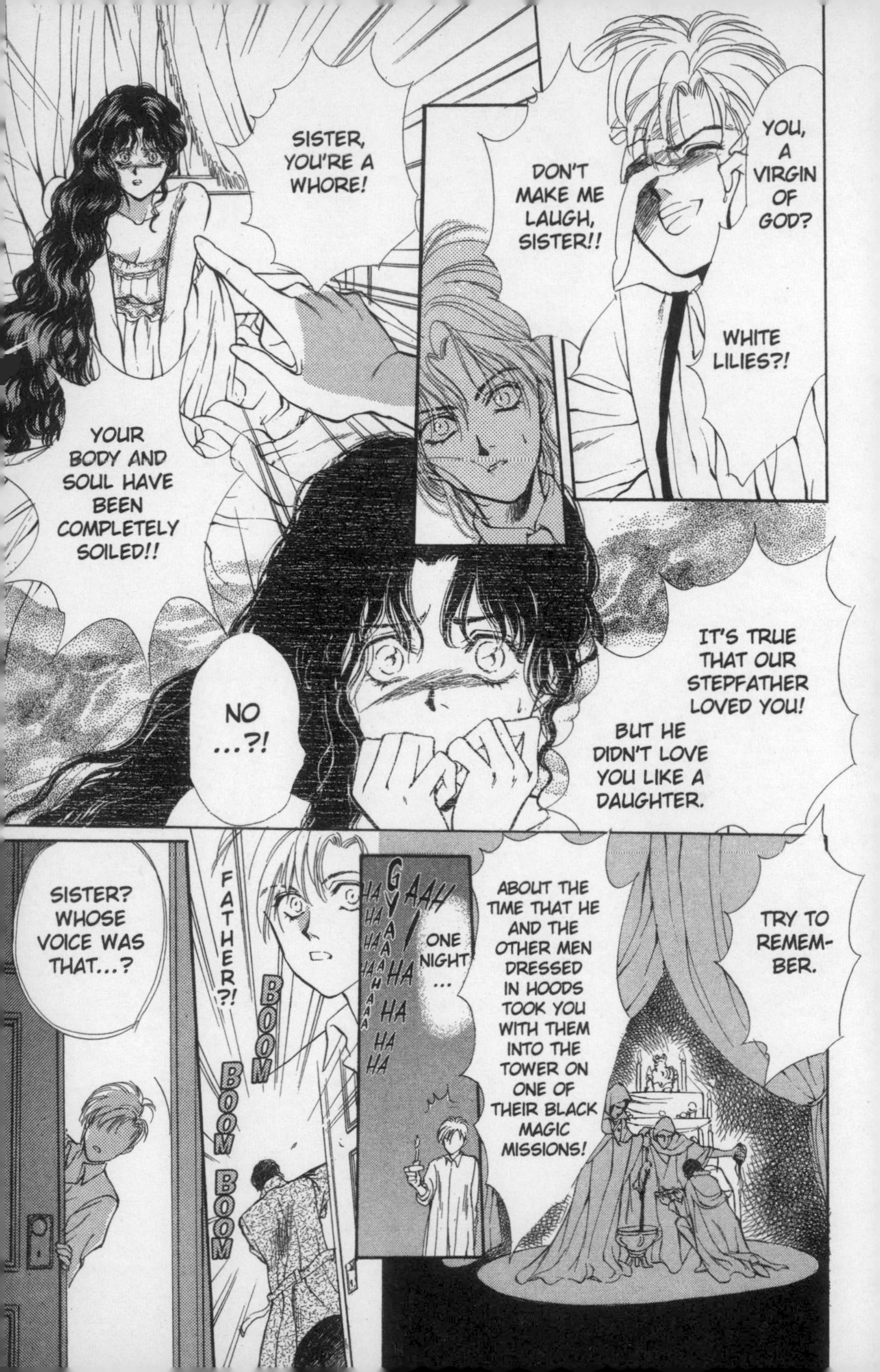
YOU, A VIRGIN OF GOD?
DON'T MAKE ME LAUGH, SISTER!!
WHITE LILIES?!
SISTER, YOU'RE A WHORE!
YOUR BODY AND SOUL HAVE BEEN COMPLETELY SOILED!!
IT'S TRUE THAT OUR STEPFATHER LOVED YOU!
BUT HE DIDN'T LOVE YOU LIKE A DAUGHTER.
NO ...?!
TRY TO REMEM-BER.
ABOUT THE TIME THAT HE AND THE OTHER MEN DRESSED IN HOODS TOOK YOU WITH THEM INTO THE TOWER ON ONE OF THEIR BLACK MAGIC MISSIONS!
ONE NIGHT ...
GYAAAAAH! HA HA HA HA HA
HA HA HA HA HAAAA
FATHER?!
BOOM BOOM
BOOM BOOM
SISTER? WHOSE VOICE WAS THAT...?

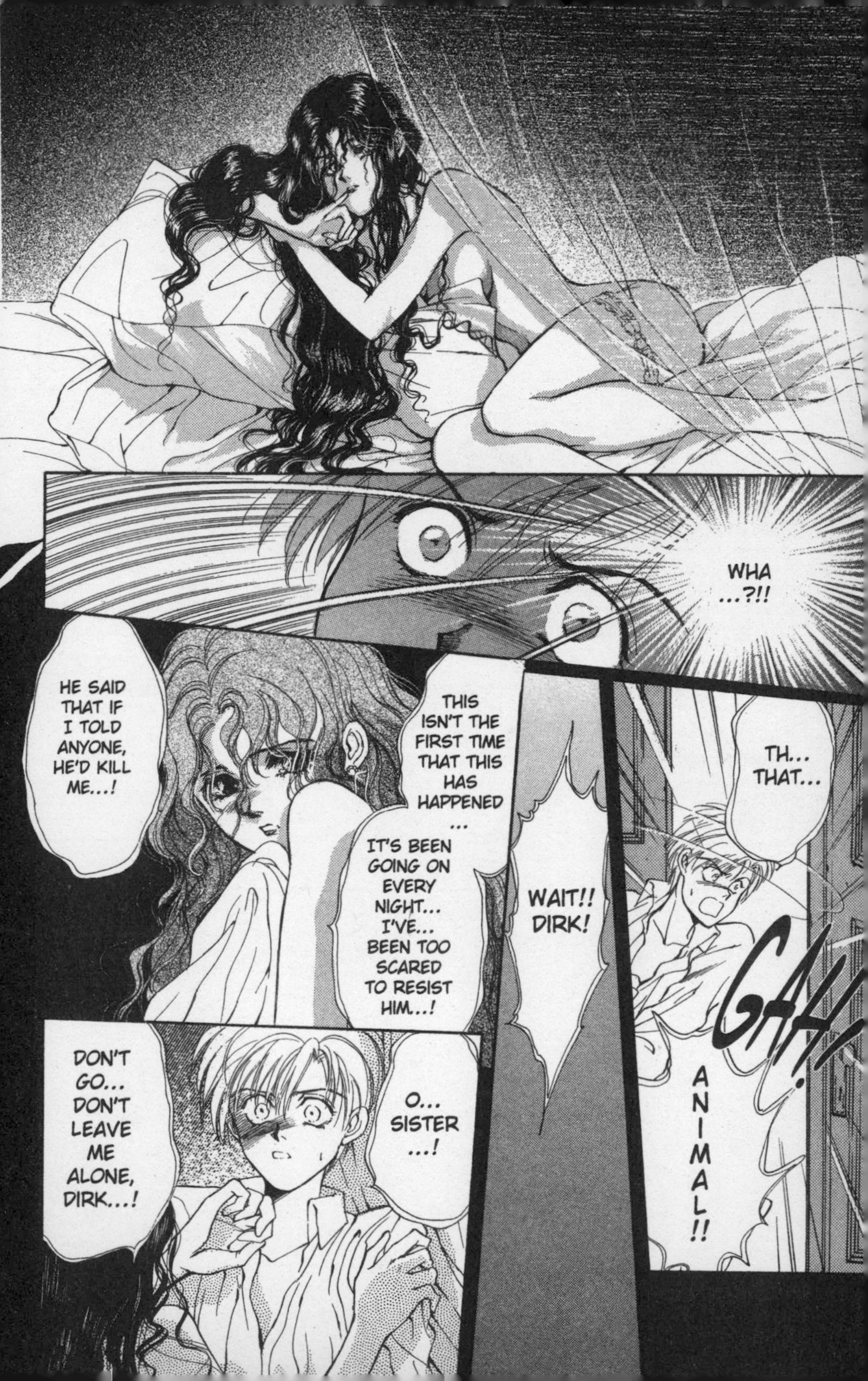
WHA ...?!!
TH... THAT...
GAH!
ANIMAL!!
WAIT!! DIRK!
THIS ISN'T THE FIRST TIME THAT THIS HAS HAPPENED ...
IT'S BEEN GOING ON EVERY NIGHT... I'VE... BEEN TOO SCARED TO RESIST HIM...!
HE SAID THAT IF I TOLD ANYONE, HE'D KILL ME...!
O... SISTER ...!
DON'T GO... DON'T LEAVE ME ALONE, DIRK...!

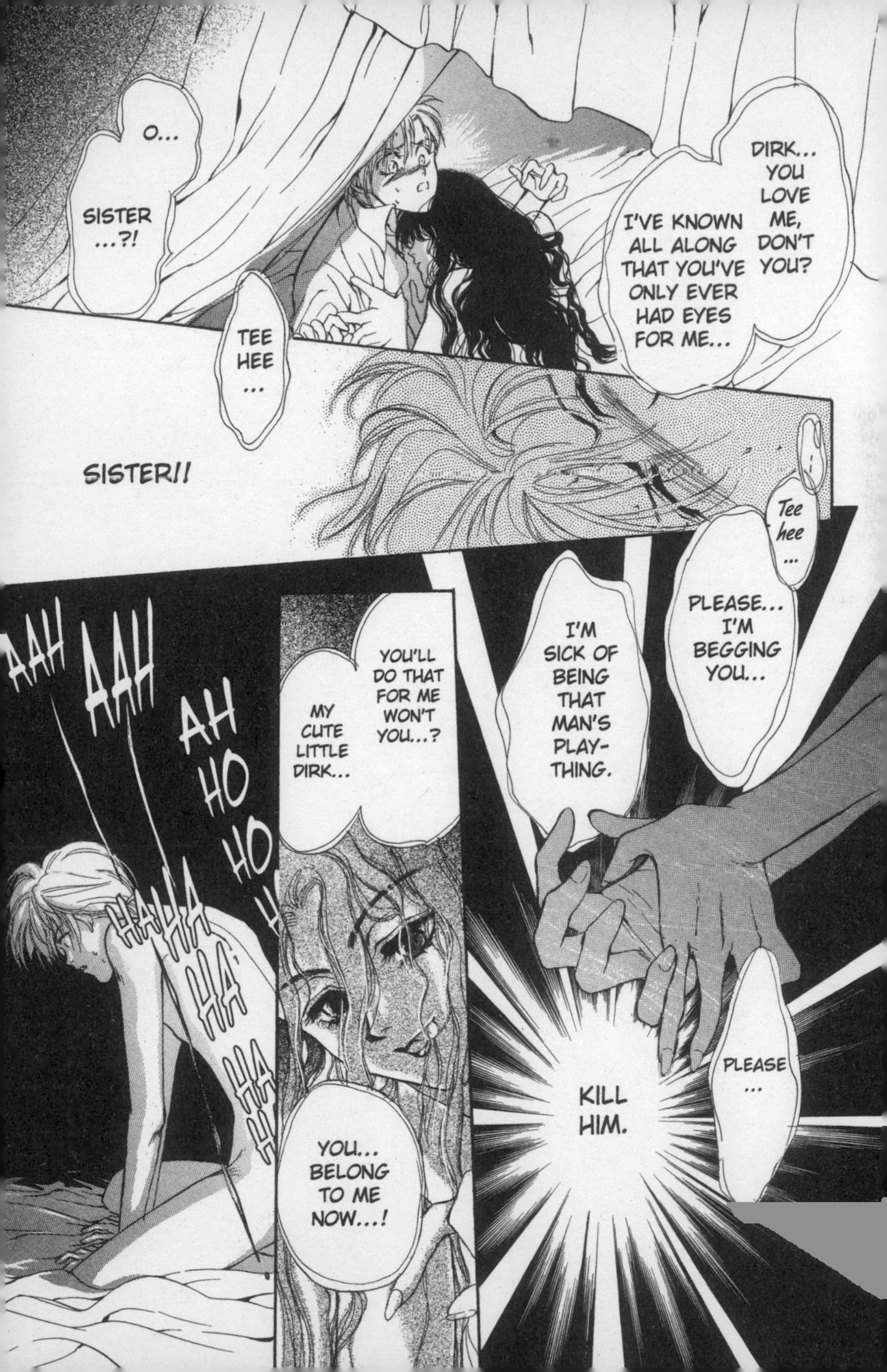

DIRK... YOU LOVE ME, DON'T YOU?
I'VE KNOWN ALL ALONG THAT YOU'VE ONLY EVER HAD EYES FOR ME...
O... SISTER ...?!
TEE HEE ...
Tee hee ...
SISTER!!
PLEASE... I'M BEGGING YOU...
I'M SICK OF BEING THAT MAN'S PLAY-THING.
PLEASE ...
KILL HIM.
YOU'LL DO THAT FOR ME WON'T YOU...?
MY CUTE LITTLE DIRK...
YOU... BELONG TO ME NOW...!
AAH AAH AH HO HO
HAHA HA HA

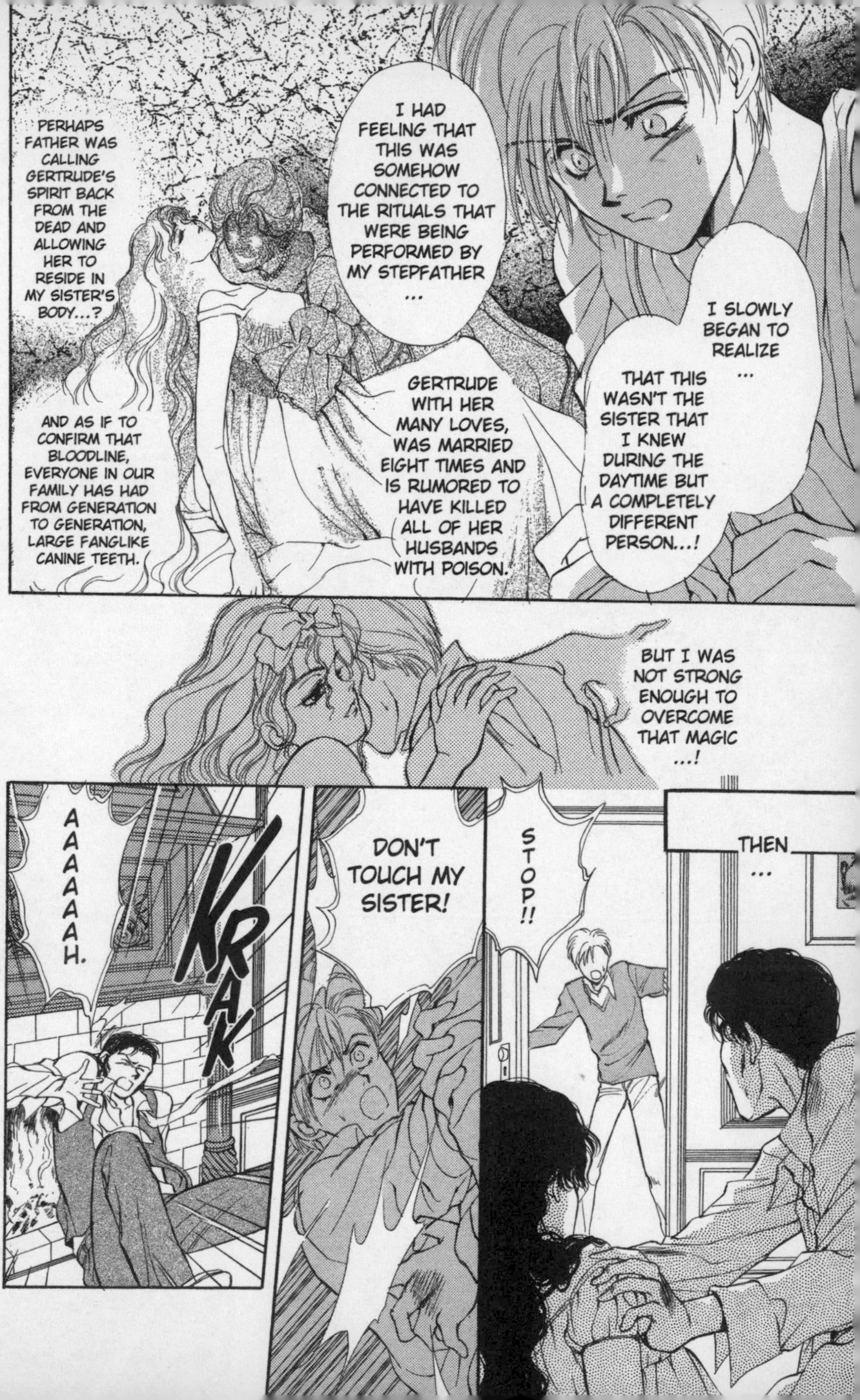
I HAD FEELING THAT THIS WAS SOMEHOW CONNECTED TO THE RITUALS THAT WERE BEING PERFORMED BY MY STEPFATHER ...
I SLOWLY BEGAN TO REALIZE ...
THAT THIS WASN'T THE SISTER THAT I KNEW DURING THE DAYTIME BUT A COMPLETELY DIFFERENT PERSON...!
PERHAPS FATHER WAS CALLING GERTRUDE'S SPIRIT BACK FROM THE DEAD AND ALLOWING HER TO RESIDE IN MY SISTER'S BODY...?
GERTRUDE WITH HER MANY LOVES, WAS MARRIED EIGHT TIMES AND IS RUMORED TO HAVE KILLED ALL OF HER HUSBANDS WITH POISON.
AND AS IF TO CONFIRM THAT BLOODLINE, EVERYONE IN OUR FAMILY HAS HAD FROM GENERATION TO GENERATION, LARGE FANGLIKE CANINE TEETH.
BUT I WAS NOT STRONG ENOUGH TO OVERCOME THAT MAGIC ...!
THEN ...
STOP!!
DON'T TOUCH MY SISTER!
KRAK
AAAAAAAH.

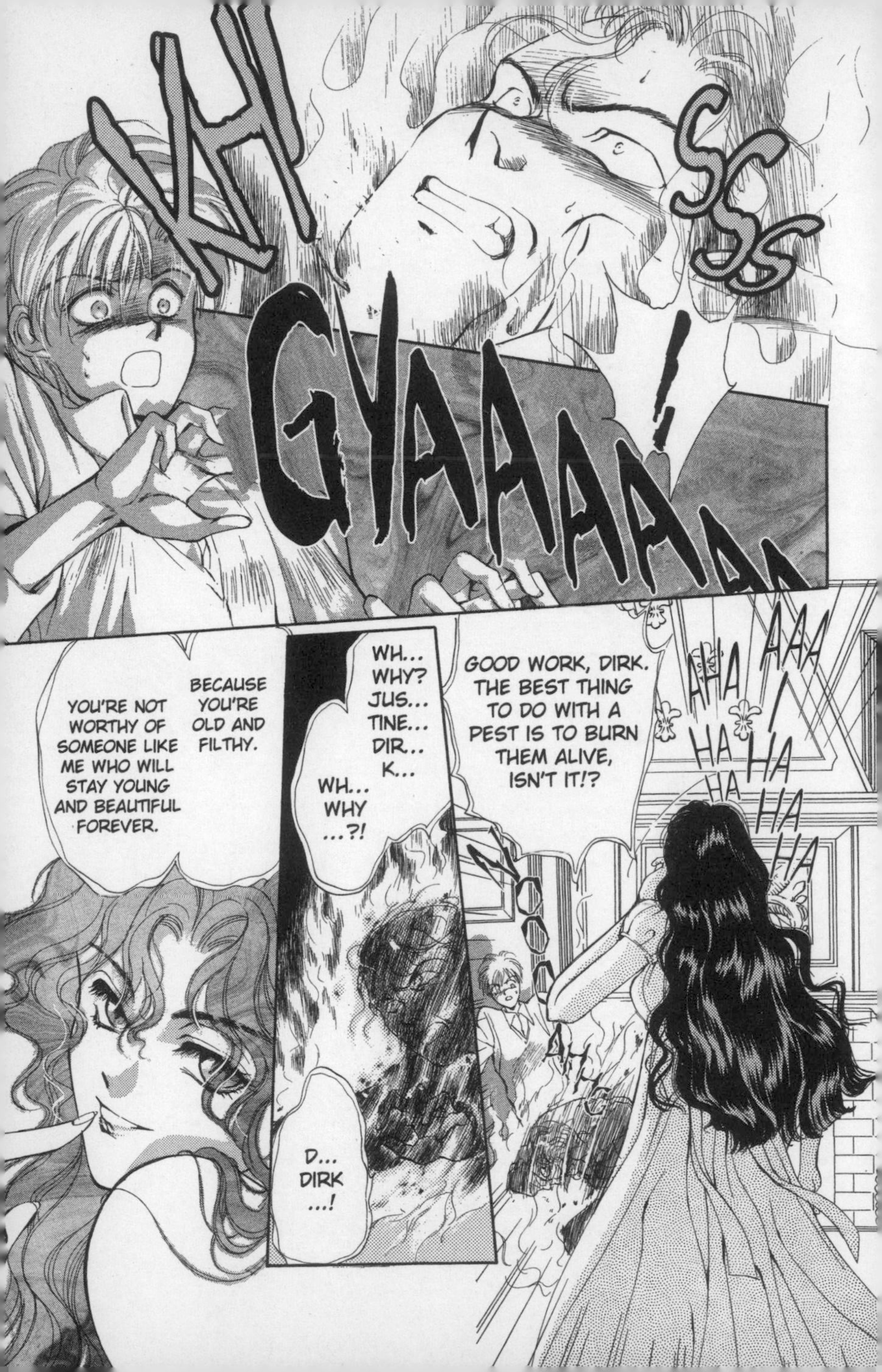
GYAAAA
AHA HA HA HA AAA! HA HA HA HA
GOOD WORK, DIRK. THE BEST THING TO DO WITH A PEST IS TO BURN THEM ALIVE, ISN'T IT!?
WH... WHY? JUS... TINE... DIR... K...
WH... WHY ...?!
D... DIRK ...!
BECAUSE YOU'RE OLD AND FILTHY.
YOU'RE NOT WORTHY OF SOMEONE LIKE ME WHO WILL STAY YOUNG AND BEAUTIFUL FOREVER.

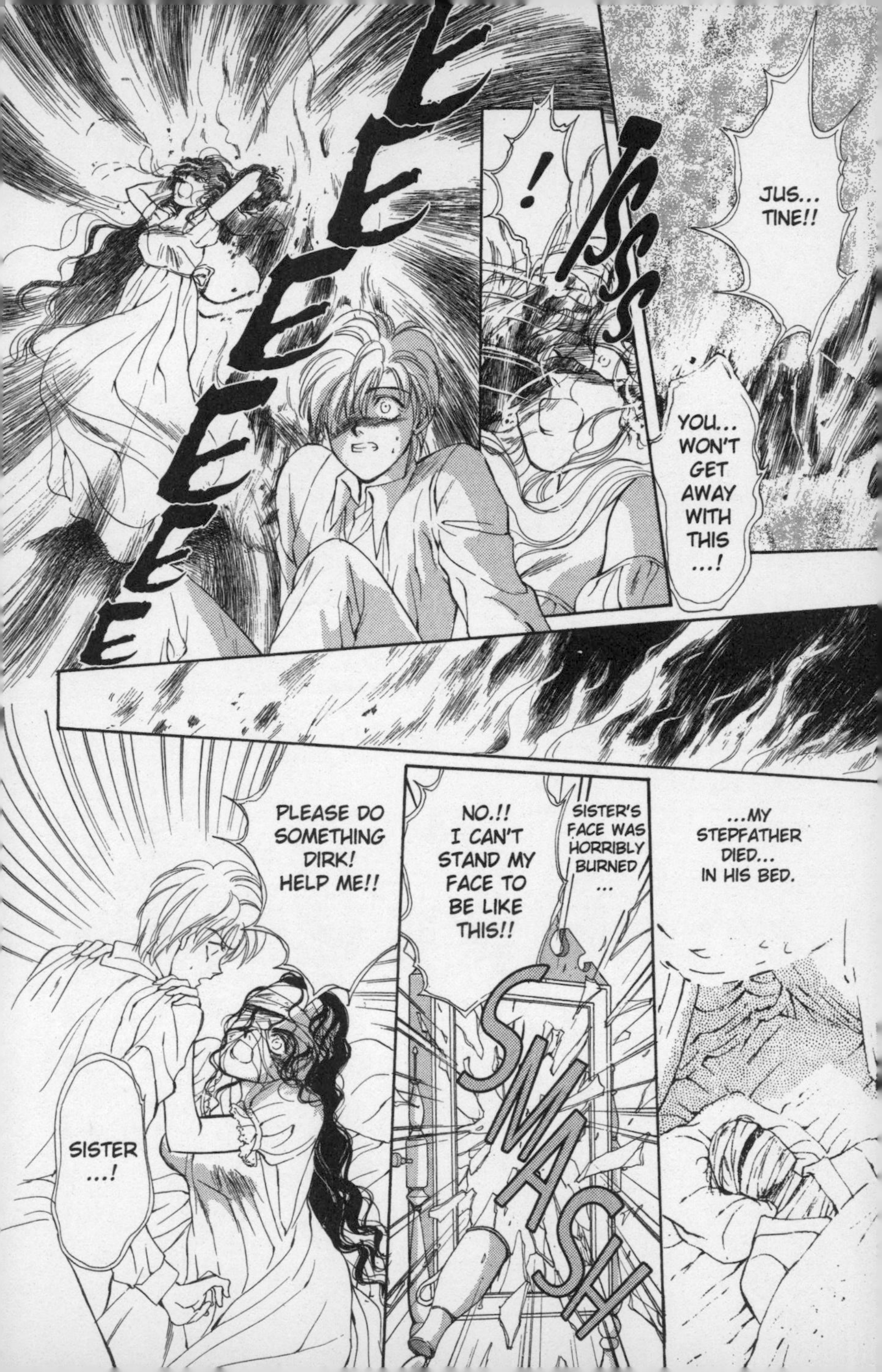
JUS... TINE!!
YOU... WON'T GET AWAY WITH THIS ...!
!
TSSS
EEEEEEEE
...MY STEPFATHER DIED... IN HIS BED.
SISTER'S FACE WAS HORRIBLY BURNED ...
NO.!! I CAN'T STAND MY FACE TO BE LIKE THIS!!
SMASH
PLEASE DO SOMETHING DIRK! HELP ME!!
SISTER ...!

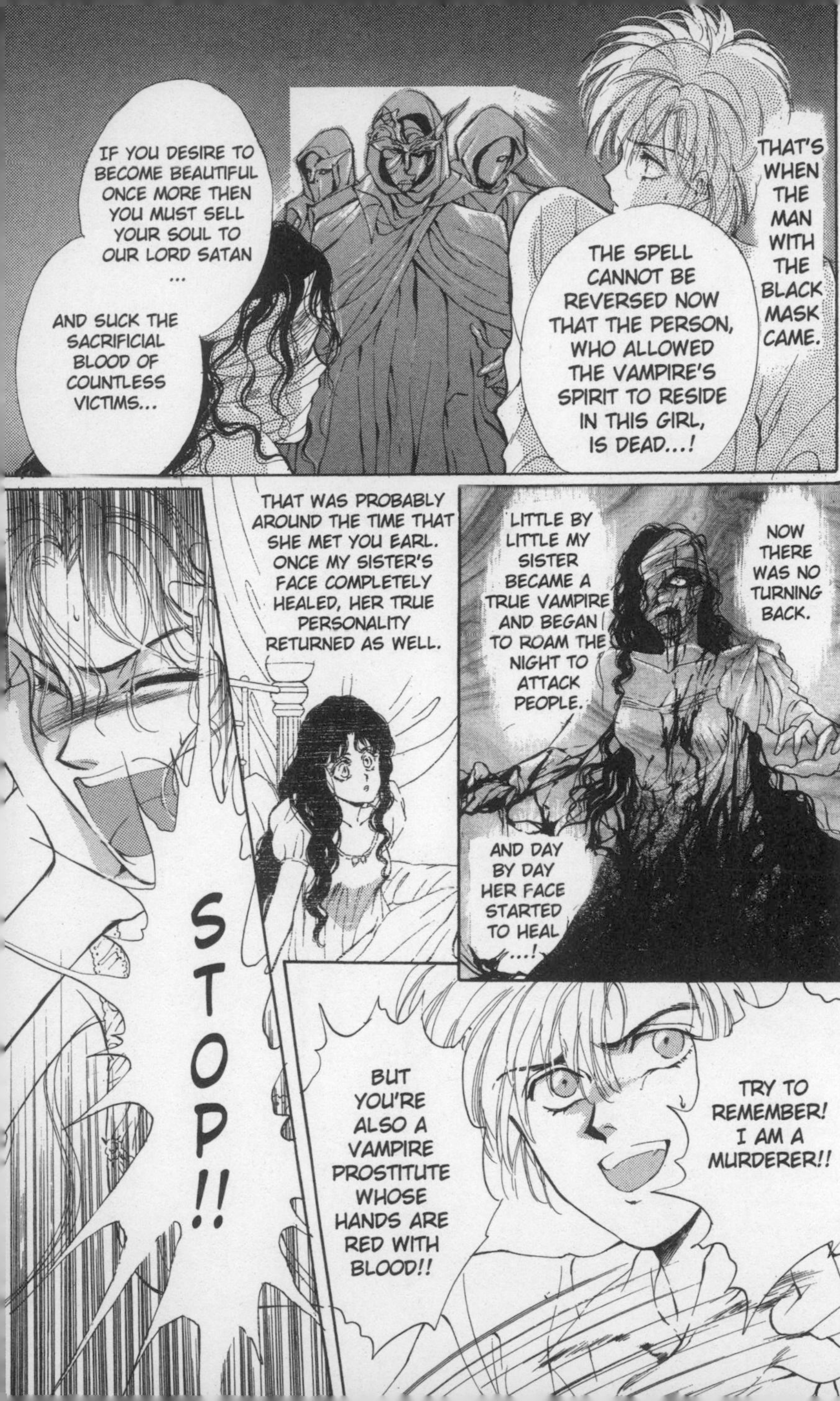
THAT'S WHEN THE MAN WITH THE BLACK MASK CAME.
THE SPELL CANNOT BE REVERSED NOW THAT THE PERSON, WHO ALLOWED THE VAMPIRE'S SPIRIT TO RESIDE IN THIS GIRL, IS DEAD...!
IF YOU DESIRE TO BECOME BEAUTIFUL ONCE MORE THEN YOU MUST SELL YOUR SOUL TO OUR LORD SATAN ...
AND SUCK THE SACRIFICIAL BLOOD OF COUNTLESS VICTIMS...
NOW THERE WAS NO TURNING BACK.
LITTLE BY LITTLE MY SISTER BECAME A TRUE VAMPIRE AND BEGAN TO ROAM THE NIGHT TO ATTACK PEOPLE.
AND DAY BY DAY HER FACE STARTED TO HEAL ...!
THAT WAS PROBABLY AROUND THE TIME THAT SHE MET YOU EARL. ONCE MY SISTER'S FACE COMPLETELY HEALED, HER TRUE PERSONALITY RETURNED AS WELL.
TRY TO REMEMBER! I AM A MURDERER!!
BUT YOU'RE ALSO A VAMPIRE PROSTITUTE WHOSE HANDS ARE RED WITH BLOOD!!
STOP!!

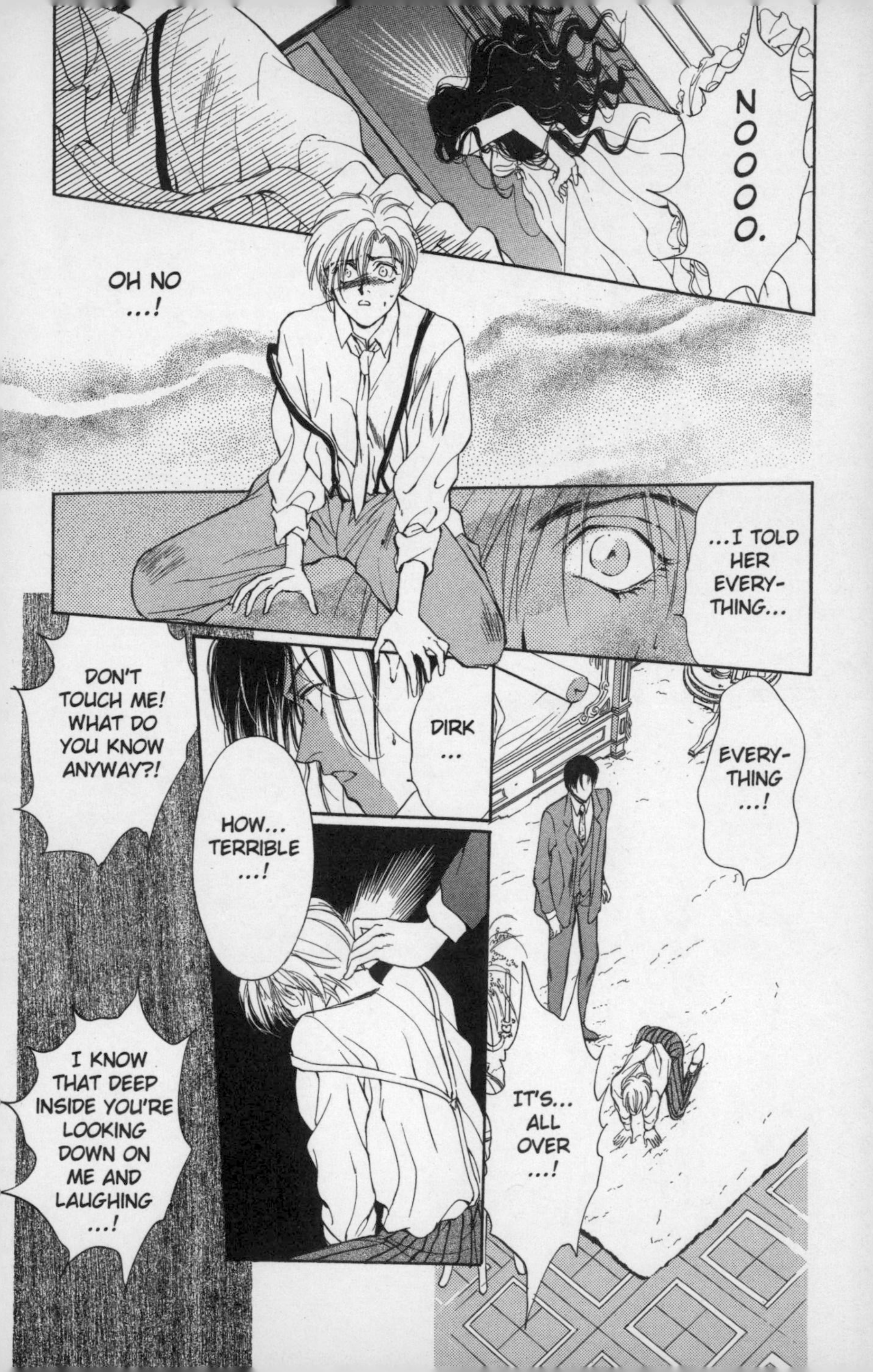
NOOOO.
OH NO ...!
...I TOLD HER EVERY-THING...
EVERY-THING ...!
IT'S... ALL OVER ...!
DIRK ...
HOW... TERRIBLE ...!
DON'T TOUCH ME! WHAT DO YOU KNOW ANYWAY?!
I KNOW THAT DEEP INSIDE YOU'RE LOOKING DOWN ON ME AND LAUGHING ...!

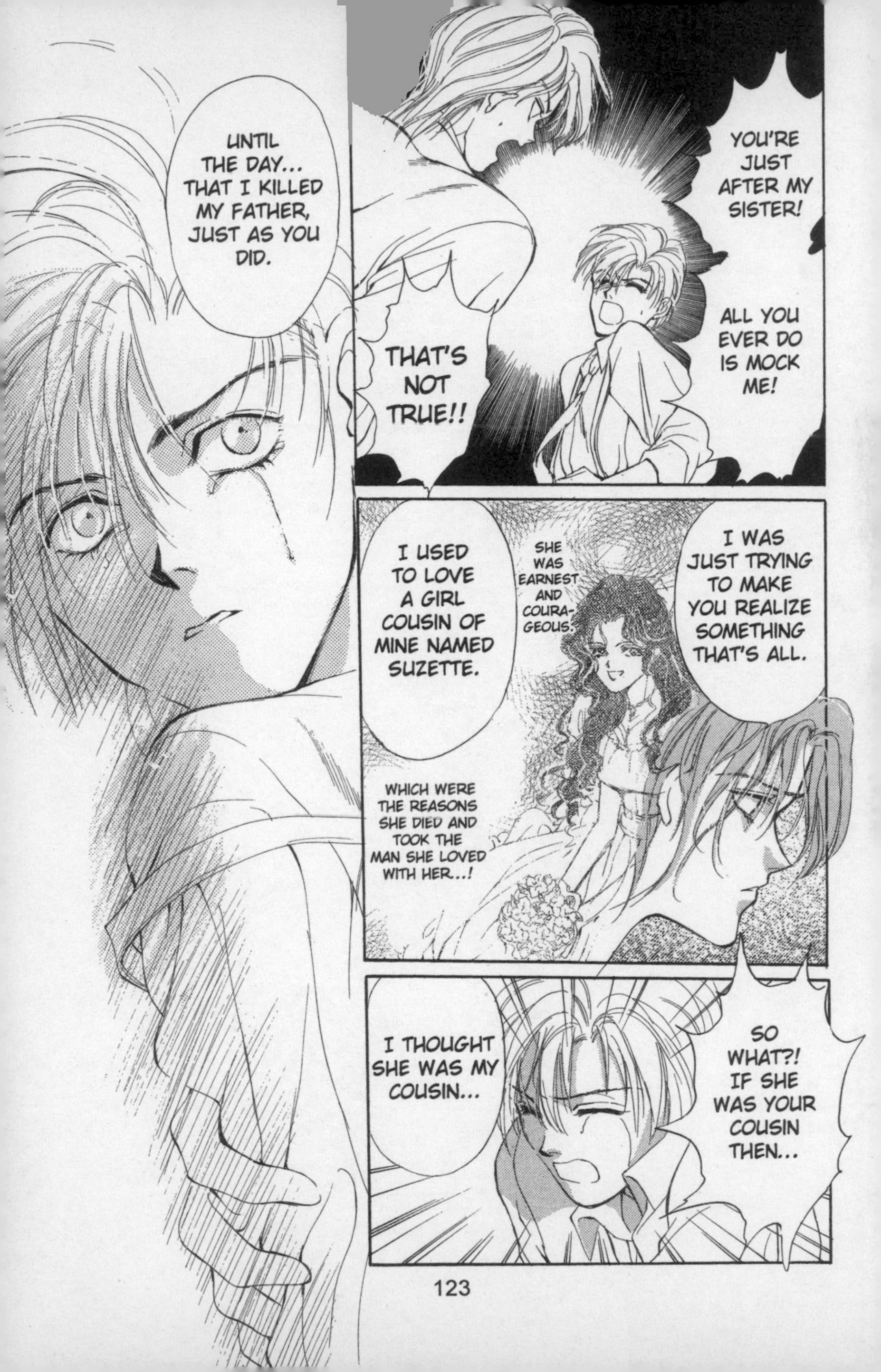
YOU'RE JUST AFTER MY SISTER!
ALL YOU EVER DO IS MOCK ME!
THAT'S NOT TRUE!!
I WAS JUST TRYING TO MAKE YOU REALIZE SOMETHING THAT'S ALL.
SHE WAS EARNEST AND COURAGEOUS.
I USED TO LOVE A GIRL COUSIN OF MINE NAMED SUZETTE.
WHICH WERE THE REASONS SHE DIED AND TOOK THE MAN SHE LOVED WITH HER...!
SO WHAT?! IF SHE WAS YOUR COUSIN THEN...
I THOUGHT SHE WAS MY COUSIN...
UNTIL THE DAY... THAT I KILLED MY FATHER, JUST AS YOU DID.

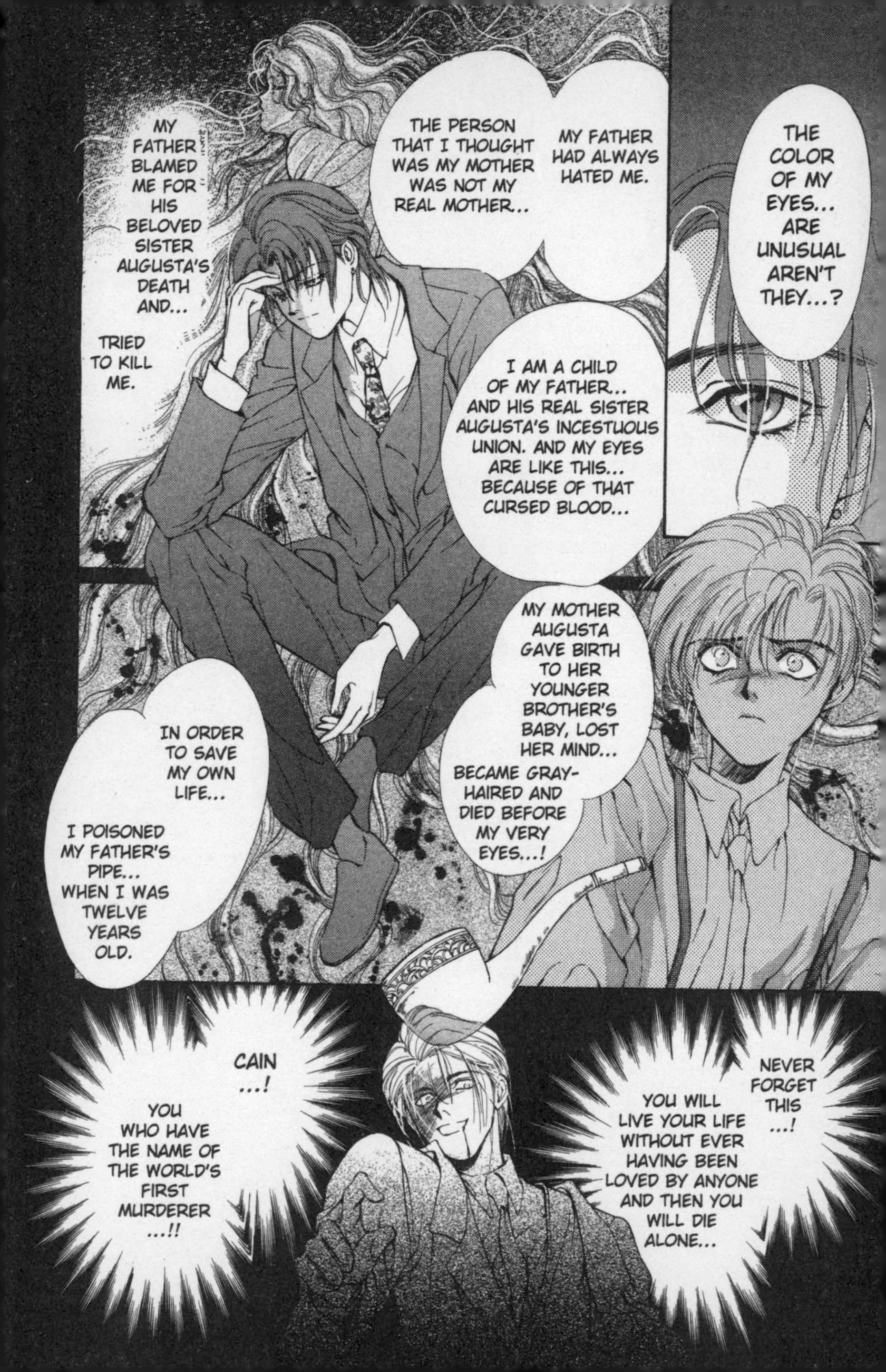
THE COLOR OF MY EYES... ARE UNUSUAL AREN'T THEY...?
MY FATHER HAD ALWAYS HATED ME.
THE PERSON THAT I THOUGHT WAS MY MOTHER WAS NOT MY REAL MOTHER...
MY FATHER BLAMED ME FOR HIS BELOVED SISTER AUGUSTA'S DEATH AND...
TRIED TO KILL ME.
I AM A CHILD OF MY FATHER... AND HIS REAL SISTER AUGUSTA'S INCESTUOUS UNION. AND MY EYES ARE LIKE THIS... BECAUSE OF THAT CURSED BLOOD...
MY MOTHER AUGUSTA GAVE BIRTH TO HER YOUNGER BROTHER'S BABY, LOST HER MIND...
BECAME GRAY-HAIRED AND DIED BEFORE MY VERY EYES...!
IN ORDER TO SAVE MY OWN LIFE...
I POISONED MY FATHER'S PIPE... WHEN I WAS TWELVE YEARS OLD.
NEVER FORGET THIS ...!
YOU WILL LIVE YOUR LIFE WITHOUT EVER HAVING BEEN LOVED BY ANYONE AND THEN YOU WILL DIE ALONE...
CAIN ...!
YOU WHO HAVE THE NAME OF THE WORLD'S FIRST MURDERER ...!!

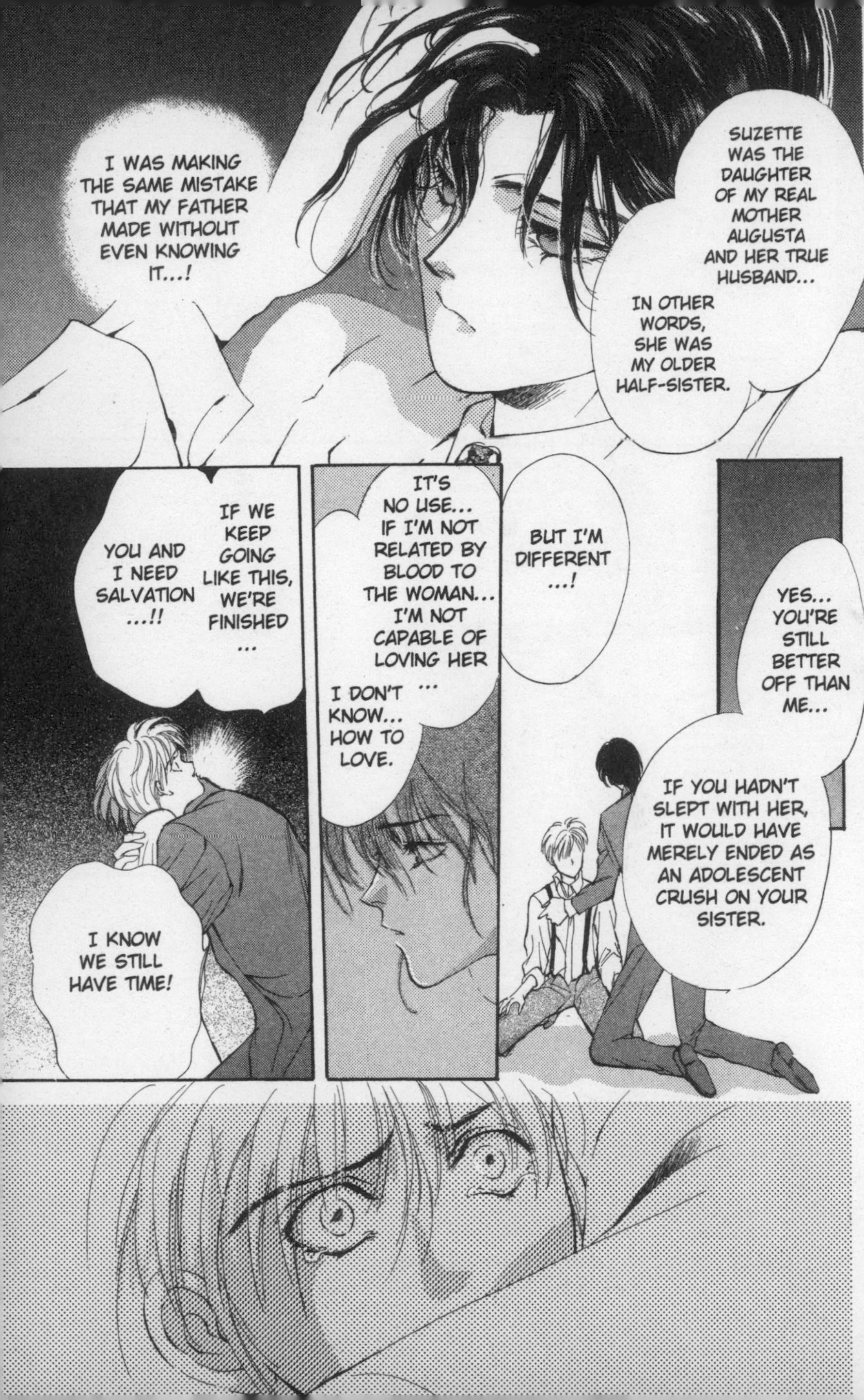
SUZETTE WAS THE DAUGHTER OF MY REAL MOTHER AUGUSTA AND HER TRUE HUSBAND...
IN OTHER WORDS, SHE WAS MY OLDER HALF-SISTER.
I WAS MAKING THE SAME MISTAKE THAT MY FATHER MADE WITHOUT EVEN KNOWING IT...!
YES... YOU'RE STILL BETTER OFF THAN ME...
IF YOU HADN'T SLEPT WITH HER, IT WOULD HAVE MERELY ENDED AS AN ADOLESCENT CRUSH ON YOUR SISTER.
BUT I'M DIFFERENT ...!
IT'S NO USE... IF I'M NOT RELATED BY BLOOD TO THE WOMAN... I'M NOT CAPABLE OF LOVING HER ...
I DON'T KNOW... HOW TO LOVE.
IF WE KEEP GOING LIKE THIS, WE'RE FINISHED ...
YOU AND I NEED SALVATION ...!!
I KNOW WE STILL HAVE TIME!

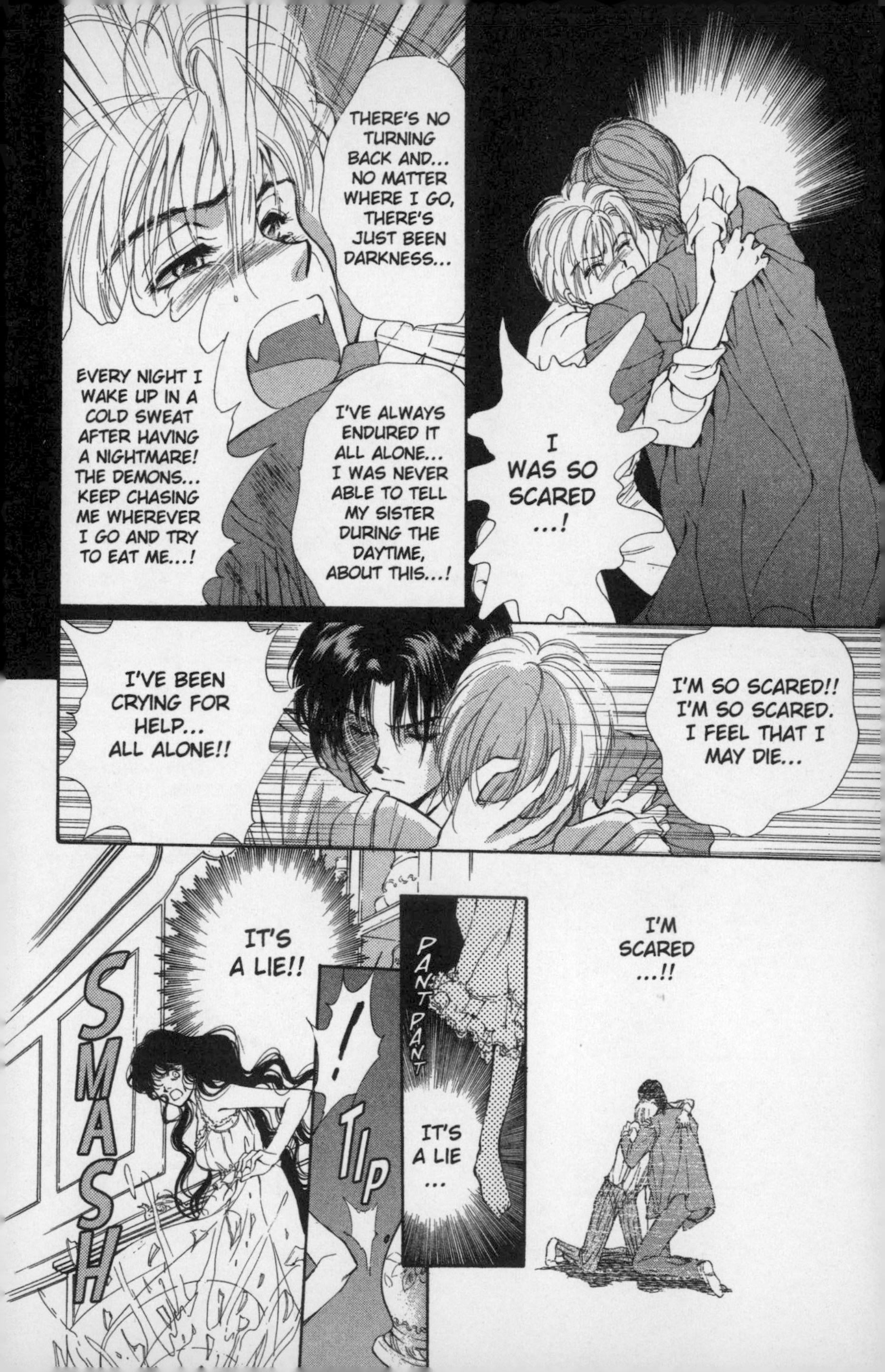
I WAS SO SCARED ...!
THERE'S NO TURNING BACK AND... NO MATTER WHERE I GO, THERE'S JUST BEEN DARKNESS...
I'VE ALWAYS ENDURED IT ALL ALONE... I WAS NEVER ABLE TO TELL MY SISTER DURING THE DAYTIME, ABOUT THIS...!
EVERY NIGHT I WAKE UP IN A COLD SWEAT AFTER HAVING A NIGHTMARE! THE DEMONS... KEEP CHASING ME WHEREVER I GO AND TRY TO EAT ME...!
I'M SO SCARED!! I'M SO SCARED. I FEEL THAT I MAY DIE...
I'VE BEEN CRYING FOR HELP... ALL ALONE!!
I'M SCARED ...!!
PANT PANT
IT'S A LIE ...
!
TIP
IT'S A LIE!!
SMASH

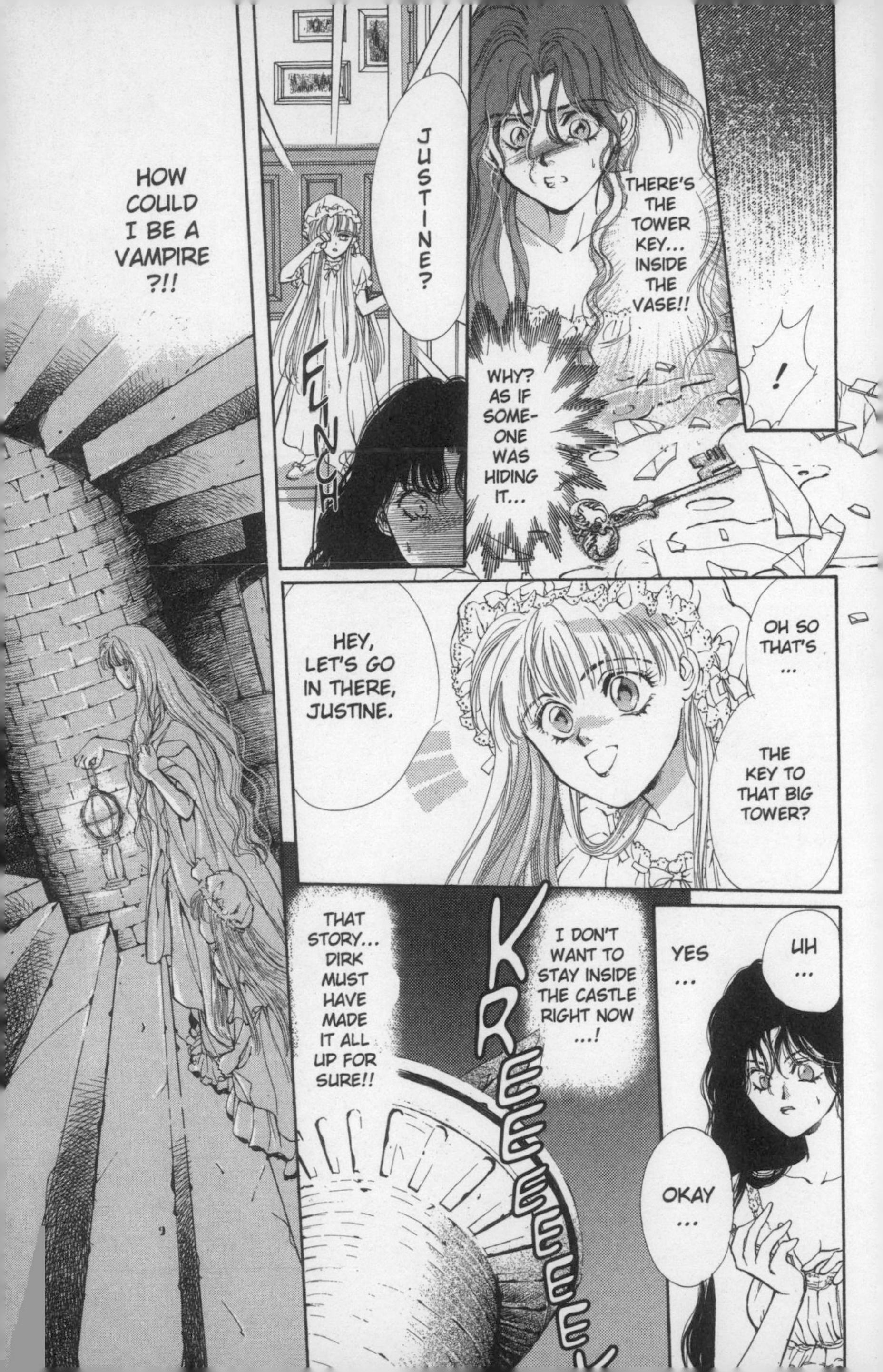

!
THERE'S THE TOWER KEY... INSIDE THE VASE!!
WHY? AS IF SOMEONE WAS HIDING IT...
JUSTINE?
FLINCH
OH SO THAT'S ...
THE KEY TO THAT BIG TOWER?
HEY, LET'S GO IN THERE, JUSTINE.
UH ...
YES ...
OKAY ...
I DON'T WANT TO STAY INSIDE THE CASTLE RIGHT NOW ...!
KREEEEEEK
THAT STORY... DIRK MUST HAVE MADE IT ALL UP FOR SURE!!
HOW COULD I BE A VAMPIRE ?!!

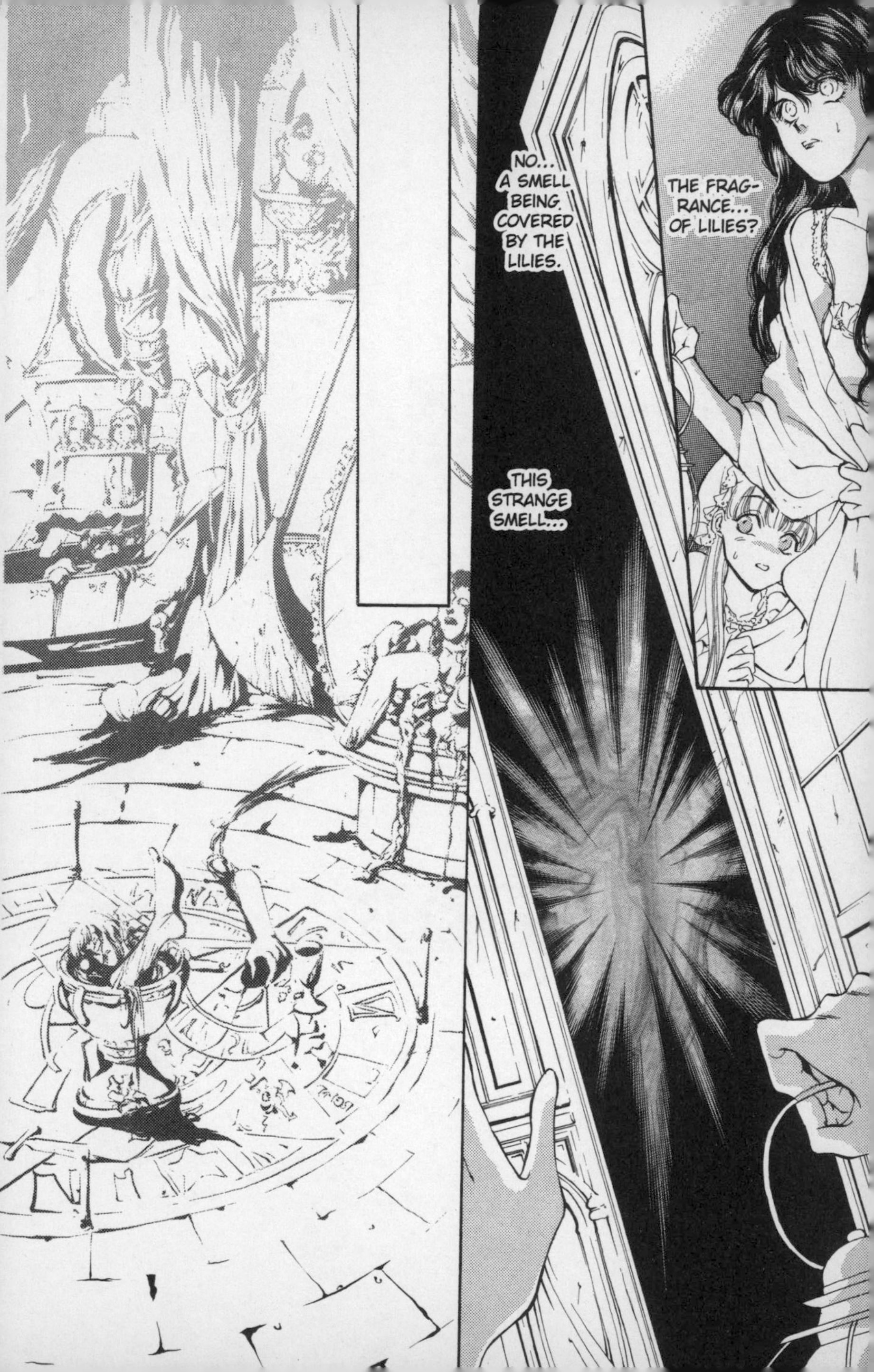
THE FRAGRANCE... OF LILIES?
NO... A SMELL BEING COVERED BY THE LILIES.
THIS STRANGE SMELL...

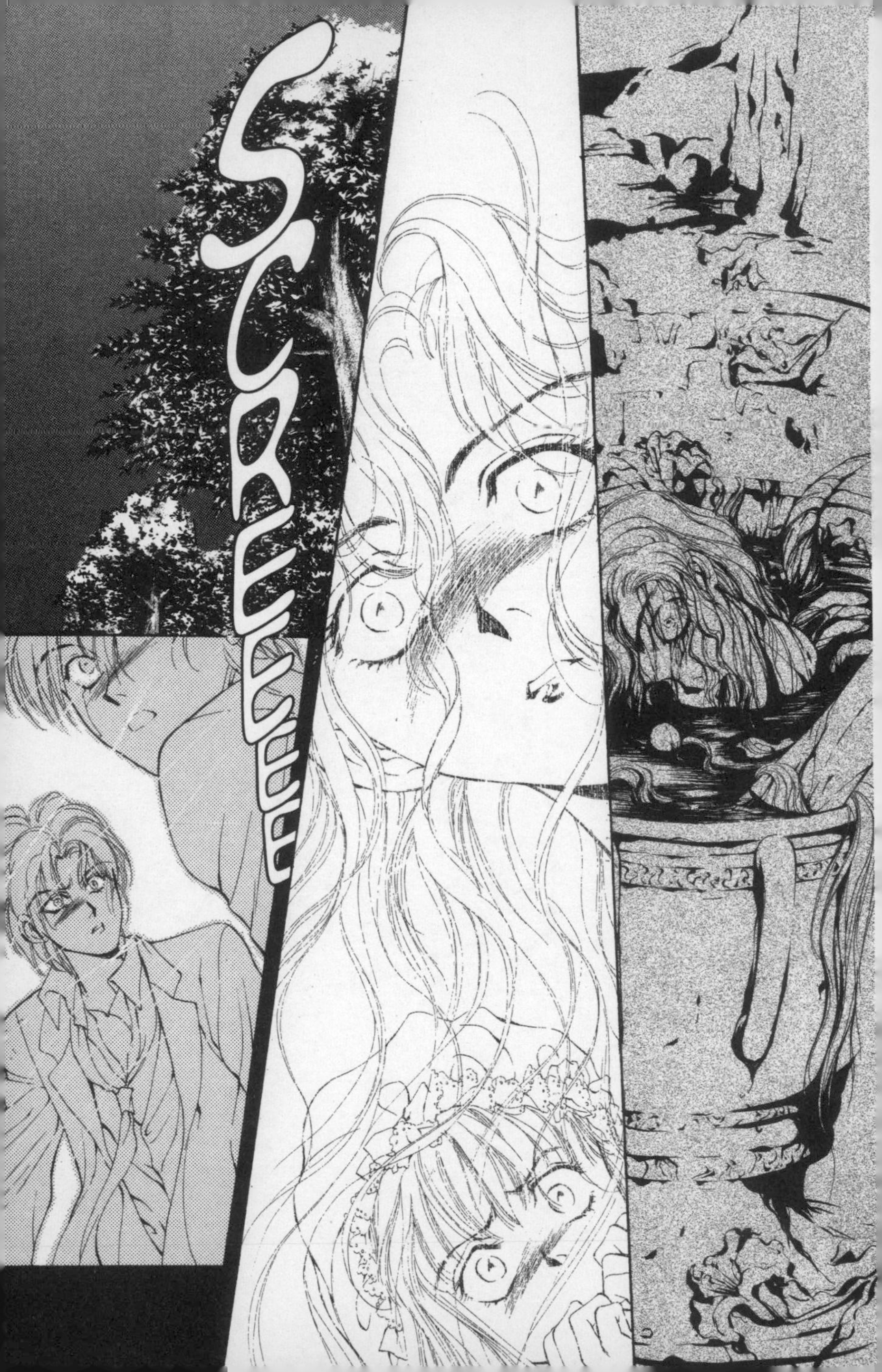
SCREEEEE

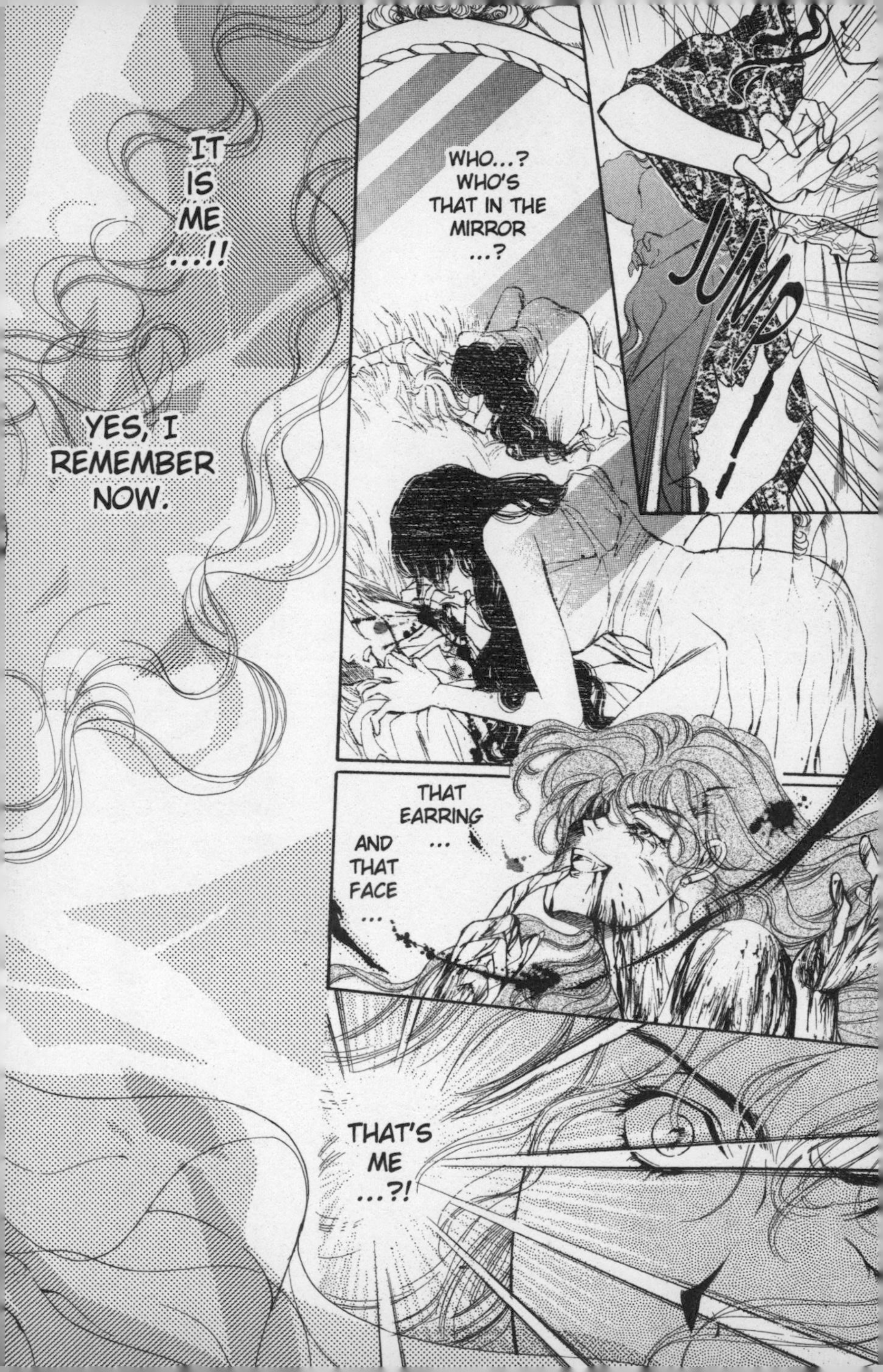
JUMP
WHO...? WHO'S THAT IN THE MIRROR ...?
THAT EARRING ...
AND THAT FACE ...
THAT'S ME ...?!
IT IS ME ...!!
YES, I REMEMBER NOW.

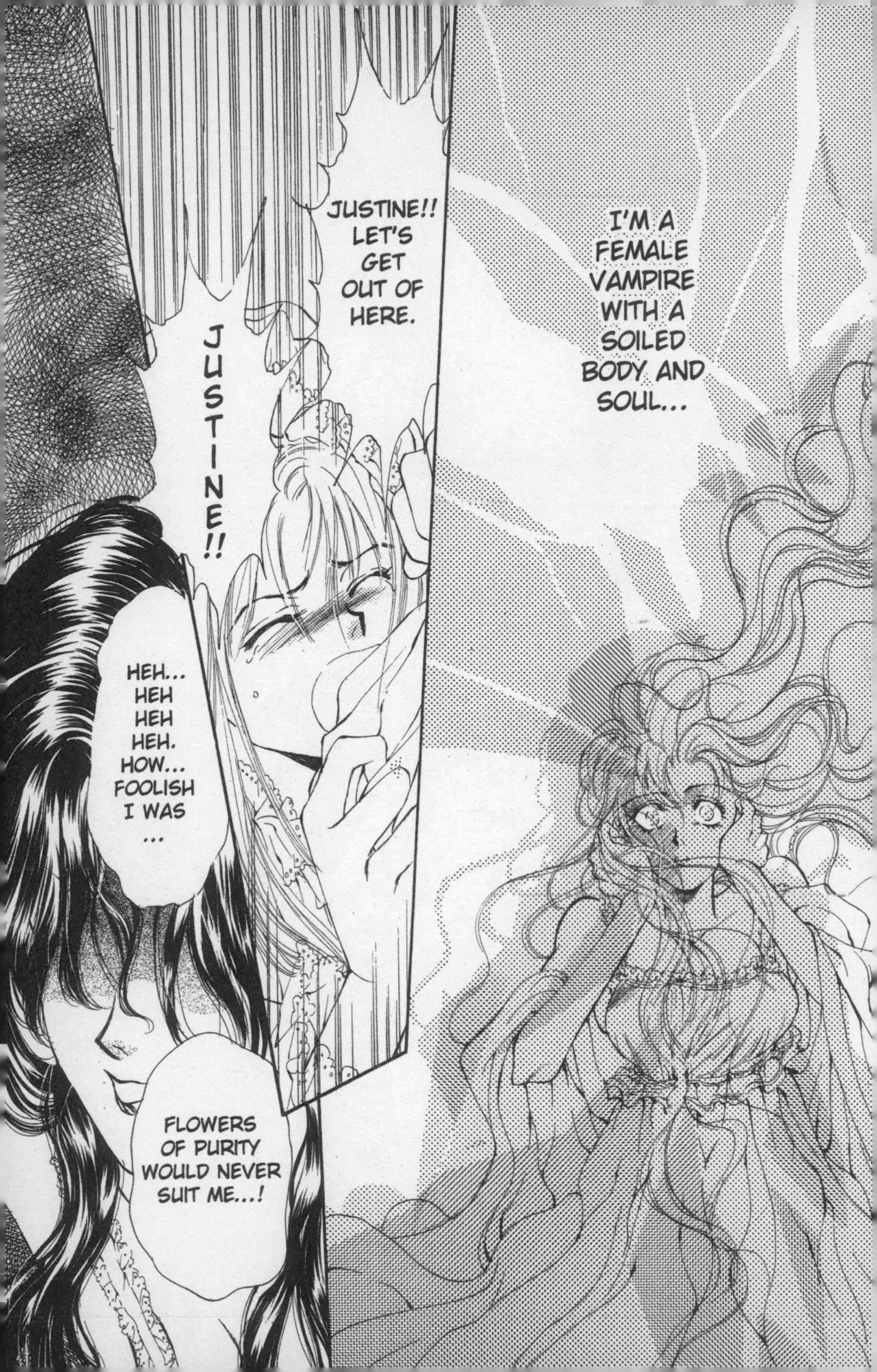
I'M A FEMALE VAMPIRE WITH A SOILED BODY AND SOUL...
JUSTINE!! LET'S GET OUT OF HERE.
JUSTINE!!
HEH... HEH HEH HEH. HOW... FOOLISH I WAS ...
FLOWERS OF PURITY WOULD NEVER SUIT ME...!

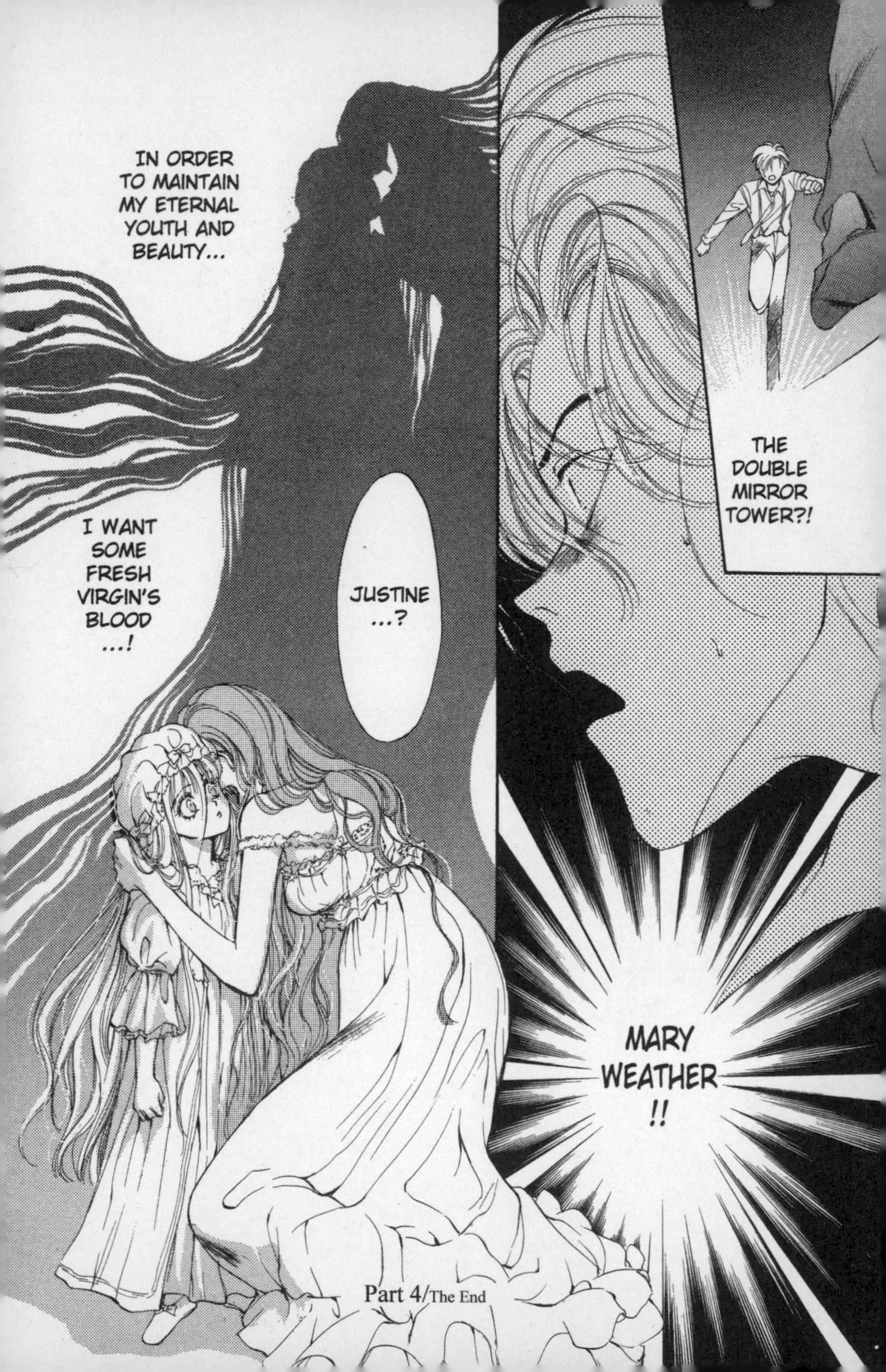
THE DOUBLE MIRROR TOWER?!
MARY WEATHER!!
IN ORDER TO MAINTAIN MY ETERNAL YOUTH AND BEAUTY...
I WANT SOME FRESH VIRGIN'S BLOOD...!
JUSTINE...?
Part 4/The End

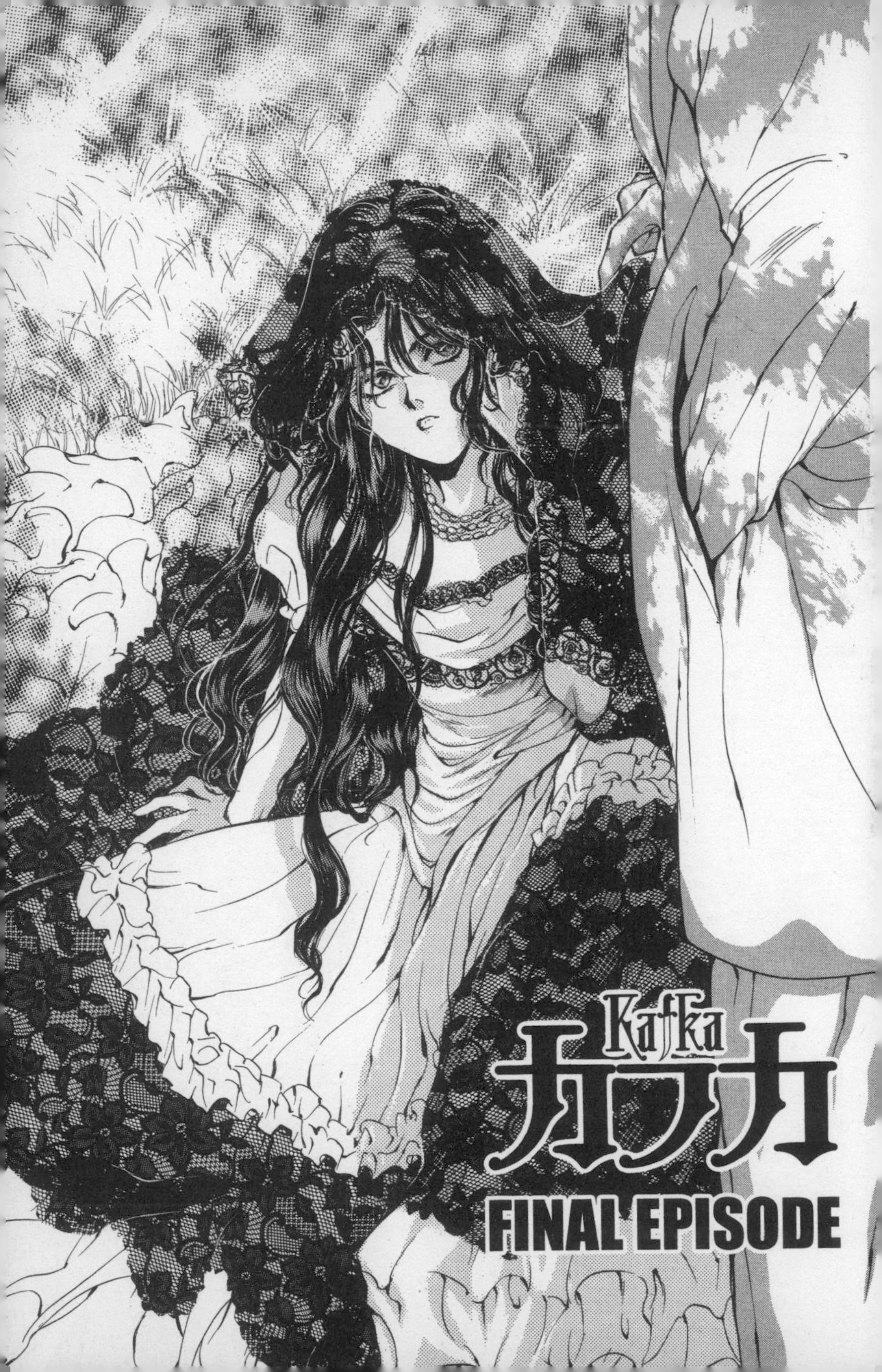
Kafka
カフカ
FINAL EPISODE

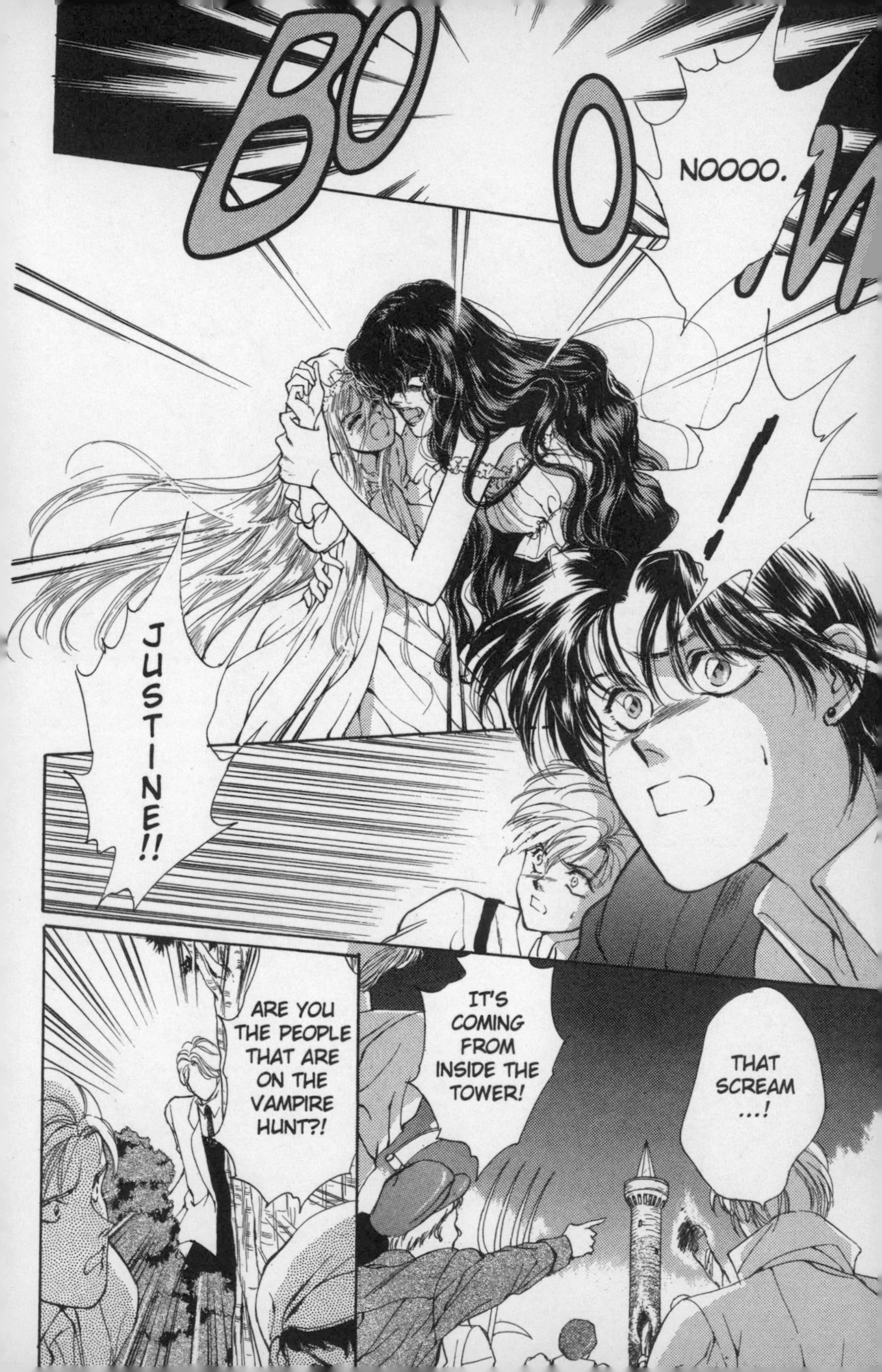
BOO
NOOOO.
!
JUSTINE!!
THAT SCREAM ...!
IT'S COMING FROM INSIDE THE TOWER!
ARE YOU THE PEOPLE THAT ARE ON THE VAMPIRE HUNT?!

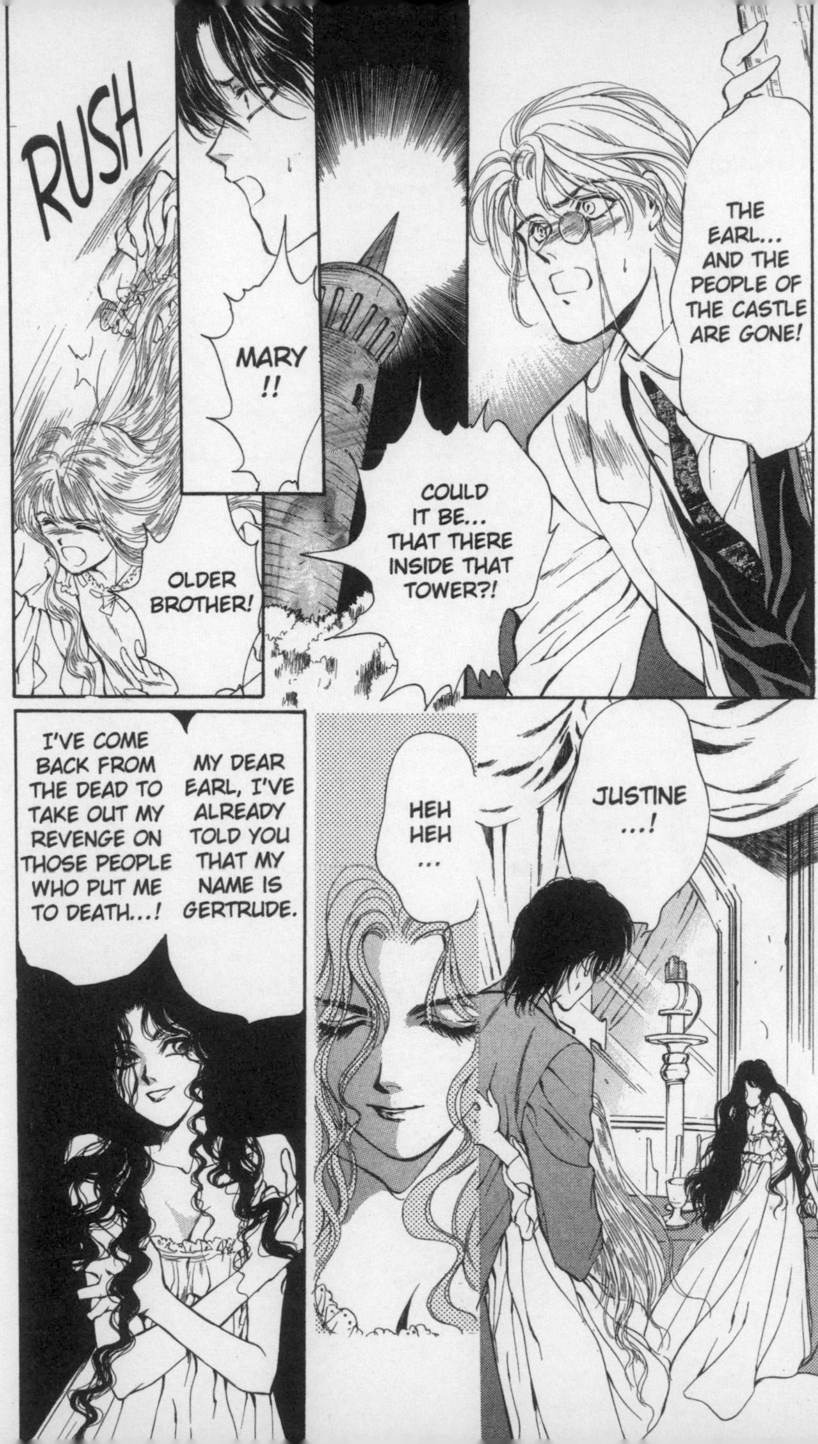
THE EARL... AND THE PEOPLE OF THE CASTLE ARE GONE!
COULD IT BE... THAT THERE INSIDE THAT TOWER?!
MARY !!
RUSH
OLDER BROTHER!
JUSTINE ...!
HEH HEH ...
MY DEAR EARL, I'VE ALREADY TOLD YOU THAT MY NAME IS GERTRUDE.
I'VE COME BACK FROM THE DEAD TO TAKE OUT MY REVENGE ON THOSE PEOPLE WHO PUT ME TO DEATH...!

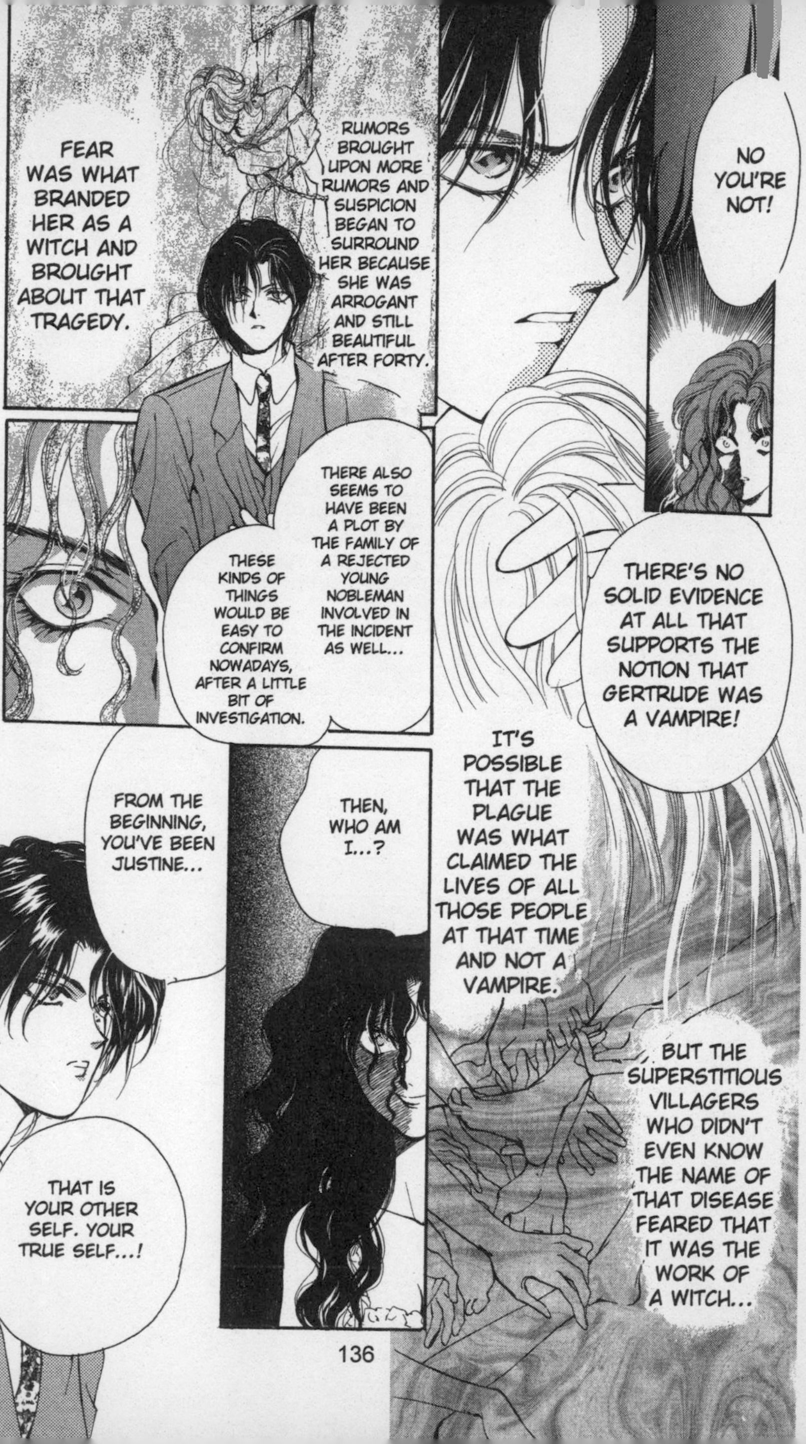
NO YOU'RE NOT!
THERE'S NO SOLID EVIDENCE AT ALL THAT SUPPORTS THE NOTION THAT GERTRUDE WAS A VAMPIRE!
IT'S POSSIBLE THAT THE PLAGUE WAS WHAT CLAIMED THE LIVES OF ALL THOSE PEOPLE AT THAT TIME AND NOT A VAMPIRE.
BUT THE SUPERSTITIOUS VILLAGERS WHO DIDN'T EVEN KNOW THE NAME OF THAT DISEASE FEARED THAT IT WAS THE WORK OF A WITCH...
RUMORS BROUGHT UPON MORE RUMORS AND SUSPICION BEGAN TO SURROUND HER BECAUSE SHE WAS ARROGANT AND STILL BEAUTIFUL AFTER FORTY.
FEAR WAS WHAT BRANDED HER AS A WITCH AND BROUGHT ABOUT THAT TRAGEDY.
THERE ALSO SEEMS TO HAVE BEEN A PLOT BY THE FAMILY OF A REJECTED YOUNG NOBLEMAN INVOLVED IN THE INCIDENT AS WELL...
THESE KINDS OF THINGS WOULD BE EASY TO CONFIRM NOWADAYS, AFTER A LITTLE BIT OF INVESTIGATION.
THEN, WHO AM I...?
FROM THE BEGINNING, YOU'VE BEEN JUSTINE...
THAT IS YOUR OTHER SELF. YOUR TRUE SELF...!

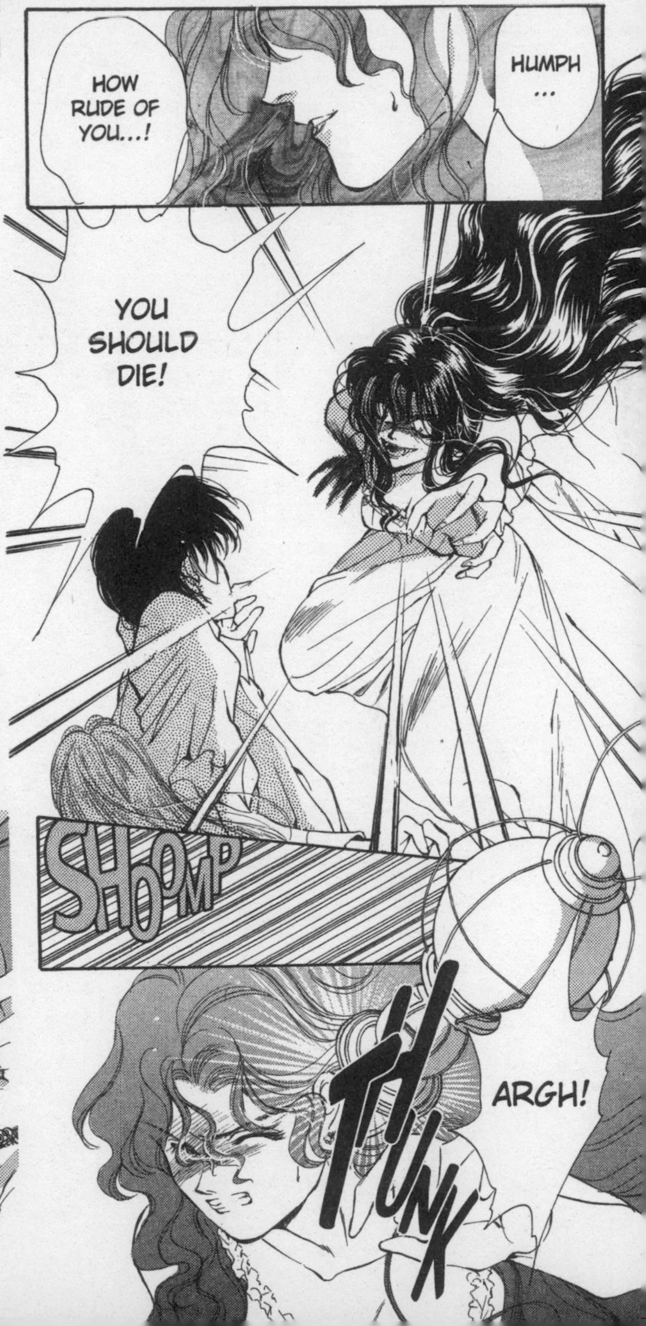
HUMPH ...
HOW RUDE OF YOU...!
YOU SHOULD DIE!
SHOOMP
ARGH!
THUNK

WILD ♦ TALK

HEY THERE AREN'T ENOUGH PAGES THAT CONTINUE AFTER "THE GRAVEL KINGDOM." THIS IS THE FINAL EPISODE. IDIOT. WELL, YOU GUYS SURE WERE MAD! YOU FELT THE "SAME WAY AS MARY!!" I NEVER THOUGHT THAT PEOPLE WOULD GIVE ME SO MUCH FLACK... HMM. I ALSO GOT A LOT OF PEOPLE THAT SAID, "I WAS SERIOUSLY WORRIED." I WONDER IF THEY CRIED. HOW CUTE. OR "GIVE ME BACK THE TEARS THAT I SHED." (OH, IF YOU HAVEN'T READ THE WHOLE STORY YET, READ THIS AFTER YOU FINISH KAFKA OKAY?) SOME PEOPLE SAID THAT THE DOCTOR WAS SUSPICIOUS FROM THE BEGINNING TOO. (I PREDICTED THAT SO THAT'S WHY I WROTE IT THE WAY I DID.) I USUALLY DON'T LIKE LONG HAIRED GUYS BUT I DREW HIM ANYWAY. I GUESS SOME READERS THOUGHT THAT THE FRONT COVER ILLUSTRATION WAS JUSTINE. (YOU GUYS STILL GOT A LONG WAY TO GO.) CHECK OUT HOW I DREW CAIN'S FACE THE SAME WAY AS I USUALLY DO.

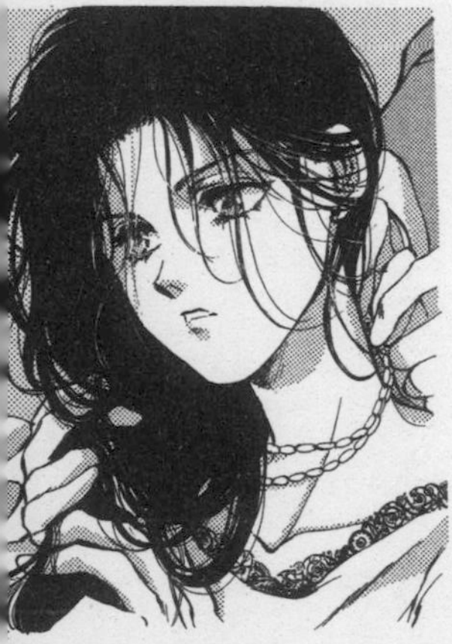

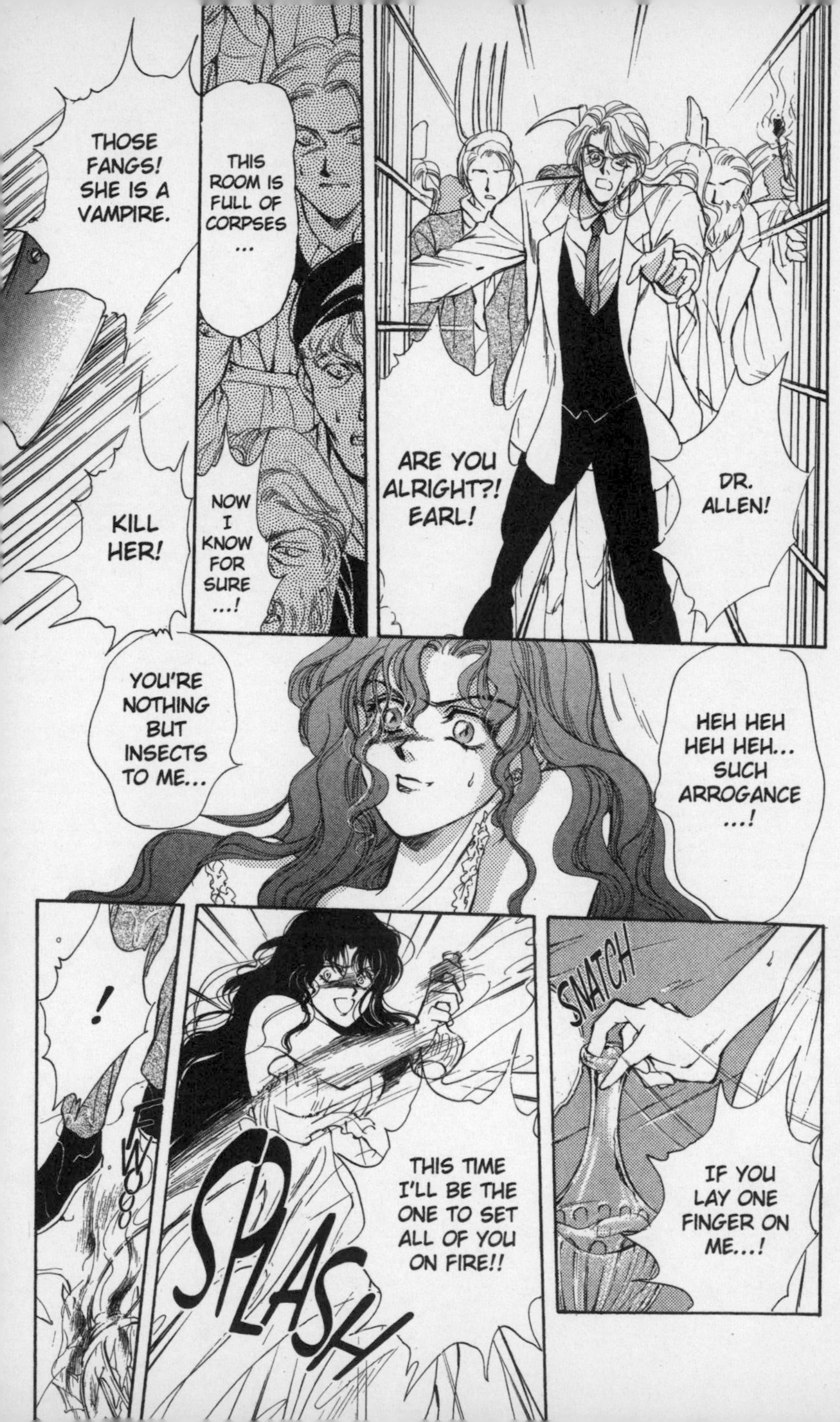
DR. ALLEN!
ARE YOU ALRIGHT?! EARL!
THIS ROOM IS FULL OF CORPSES ...
NOW I KNOW FOR SURE ...!
THOSE FANGS! SHE IS A VAMPIRE.
KILL HER!
HEH HEH HEH HEH... SUCH ARROGANCE ...!
YOU'RE NOTHING BUT INSECTS TO ME...
SNATCH
IF YOU LAY ONE FINGER ON ME...!
THIS TIME I'LL BE THE ONE TO SET ALL OF YOU ON FIRE!!
SPLASH
!
FWOOO

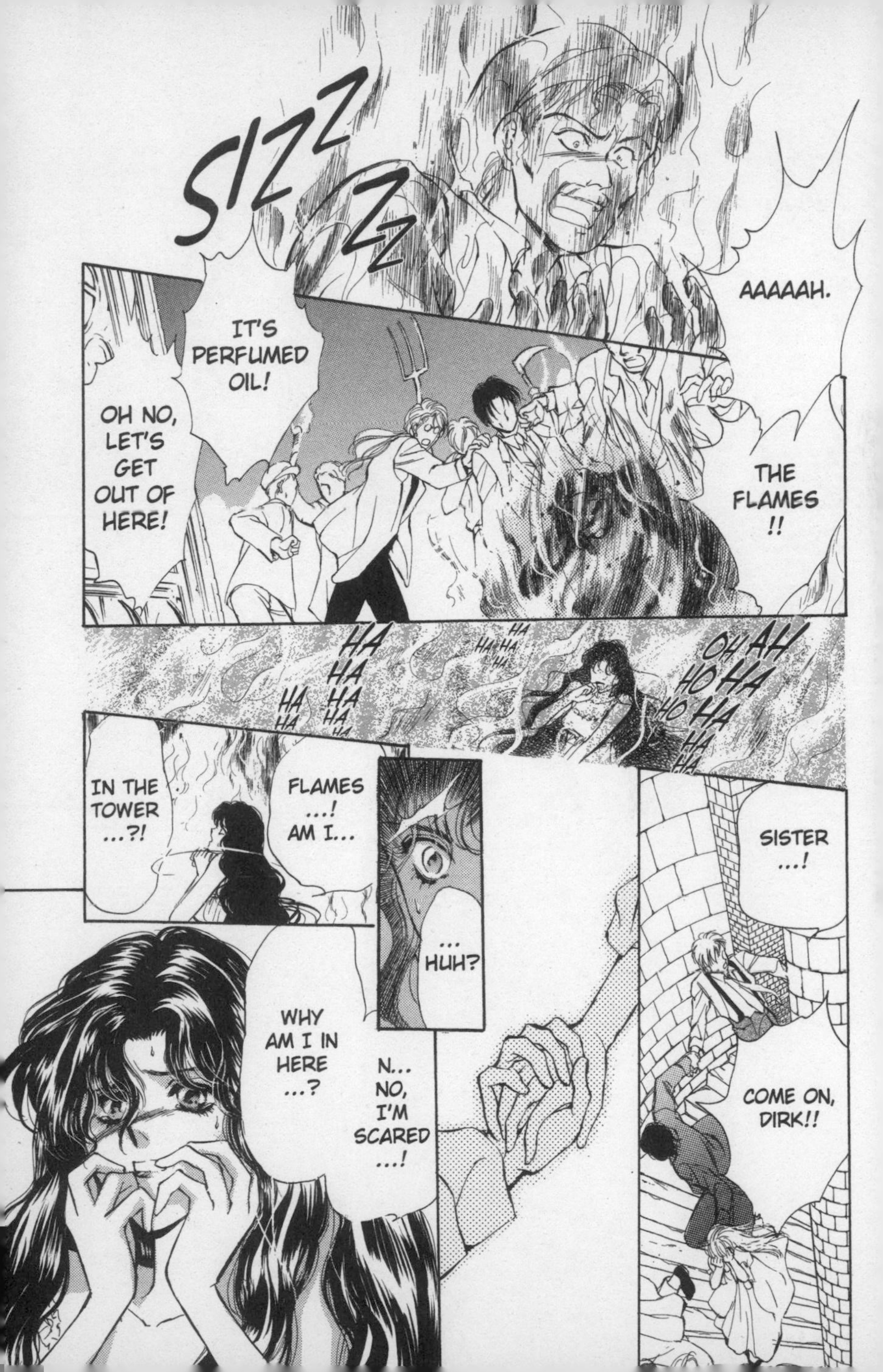
SIZZZ
AAAAAH.
THE FLAMES !!
IT'S PERFUMED OIL!
OH NO, LET'S GET OUT OF HERE!
OH HO HO
AH HA HA HA HA HA
HA HA HA HA
HA HA HA HA HA
HA HA
SISTER ...!
COME ON, DIRK!!
... HUH?
FLAMES ...! AM I...
IN THE TOWER ...?!
WHY AM I IN HERE ...?
N... NO, I'M SCARED ...!

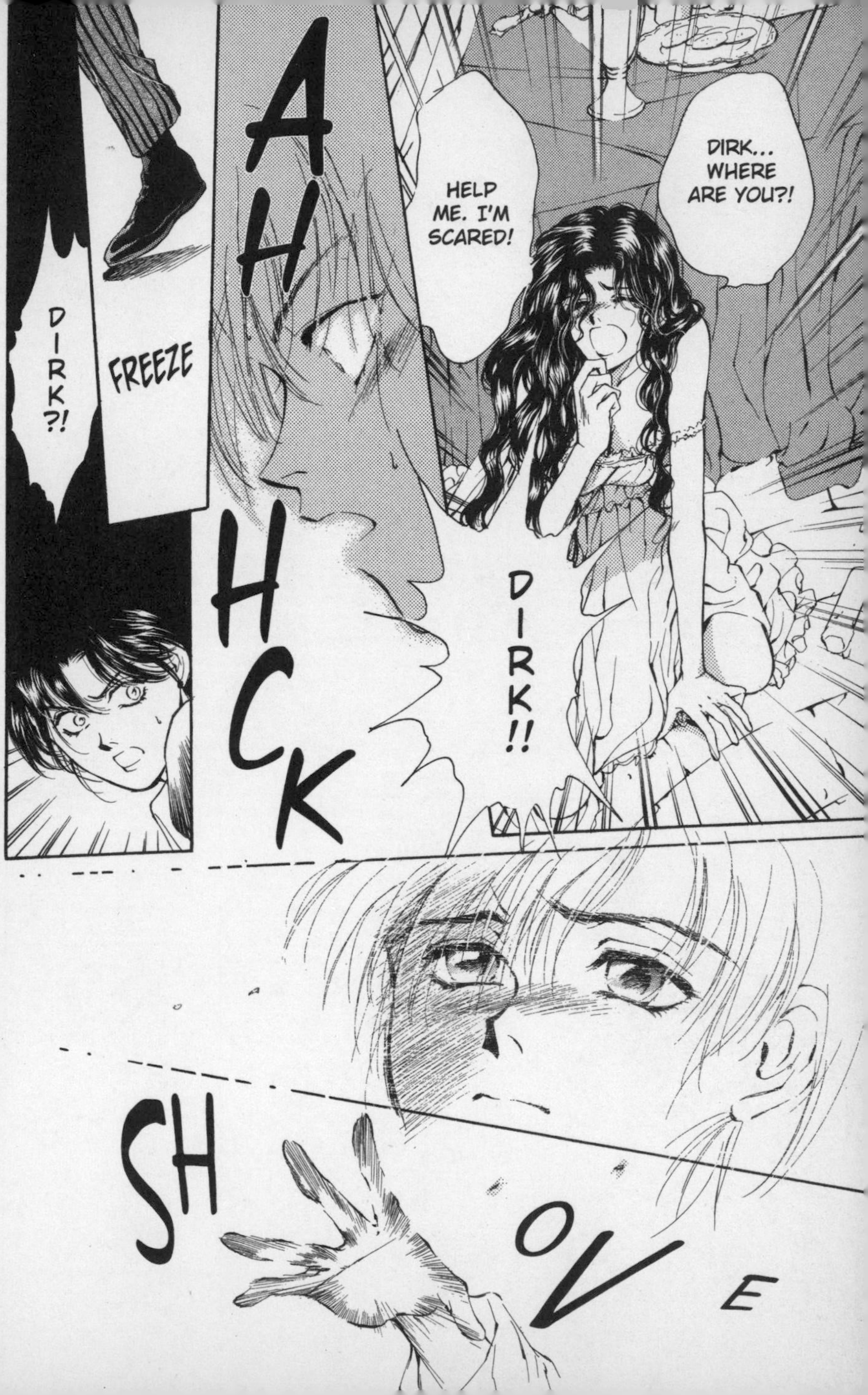
DIRK... WHERE ARE YOU?!
HELP ME. I'M SCARED!
DIRK!!
AHHCK
FREEZE
DIRK?!
SHOVE

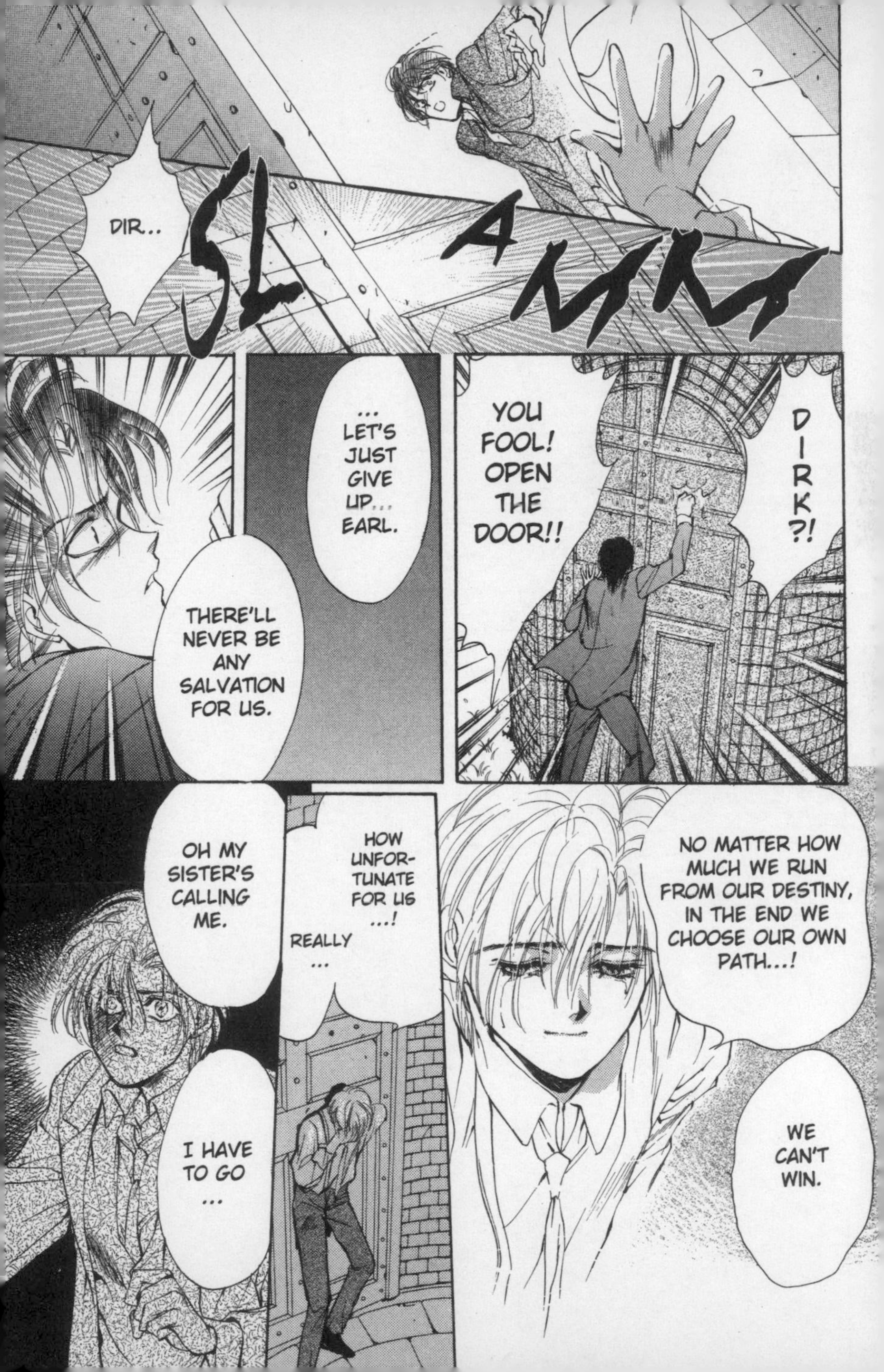
SLAMM
DIR...
DIRK?!
YOU FOOL! OPEN THE DOOR!!
... LET'S JUST GIVE UP... EARL.
THERE'LL NEVER BE ANY SALVATION FOR US.
NO MATTER HOW MUCH WE RUN FROM OUR DESTINY, IN THE END WE CHOOSE OUR OWN PATH...!
WE CAN'T WIN.
HOW UNFORTUNATE FOR US ...!
REALLY ...
OH MY SISTER'S CALLING ME.
I HAVE TO GO ...

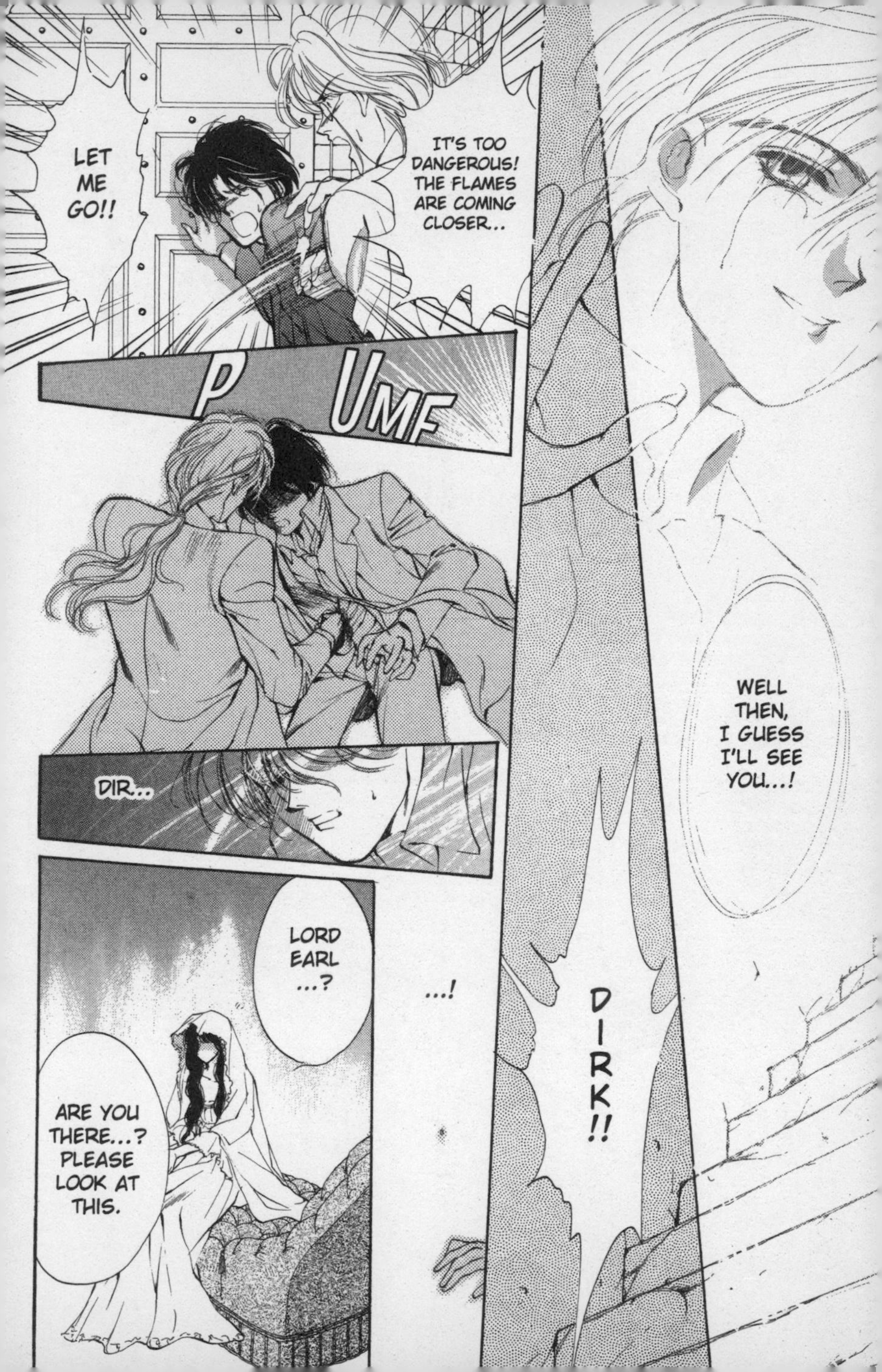
WELL THEN, I GUESS I'LL SEE YOU...!
DIRK!!
IT'S TOO DANGEROUS! THE FLAMES ARE COMING CLOSER...
LET ME GO!!
PUMF
DIR...
LORD EARL ...?
...!
ARE YOU THERE...? PLEASE LOOK AT THIS.

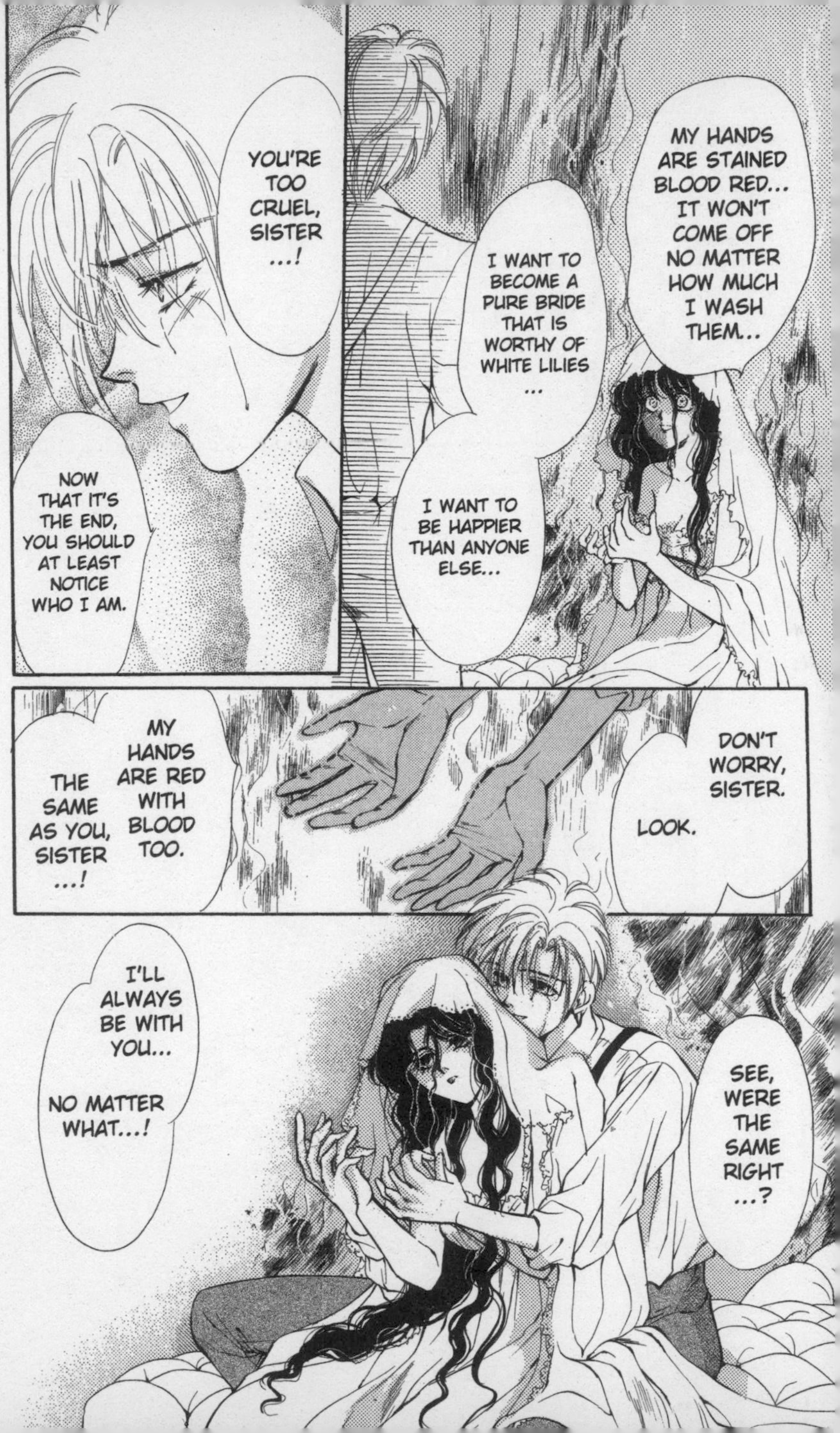
MY HANDS ARE STAINED BLOOD RED... IT WON'T COME OFF NO MATTER HOW MUCH I WASH THEM...
I WANT TO BECOME A PURE BRIDE THAT IS WORTHY OF WHITE LILIES ...
I WANT TO BE HAPPIER THAN ANYONE ELSE...
YOU'RE TOO CRUEL, SISTER ...!
NOW THAT IT'S THE END, YOU SHOULD AT LEAST NOTICE WHO I AM.
DON'T WORRY, SISTER.
LOOK.
MY HANDS ARE RED WITH BLOOD TOO.
THE SAME AS YOU, SISTER ...!
SEE, WERE THE SAME RIGHT ...?
I'LL ALWAYS BE WITH YOU...
NO MATTER WHAT...!

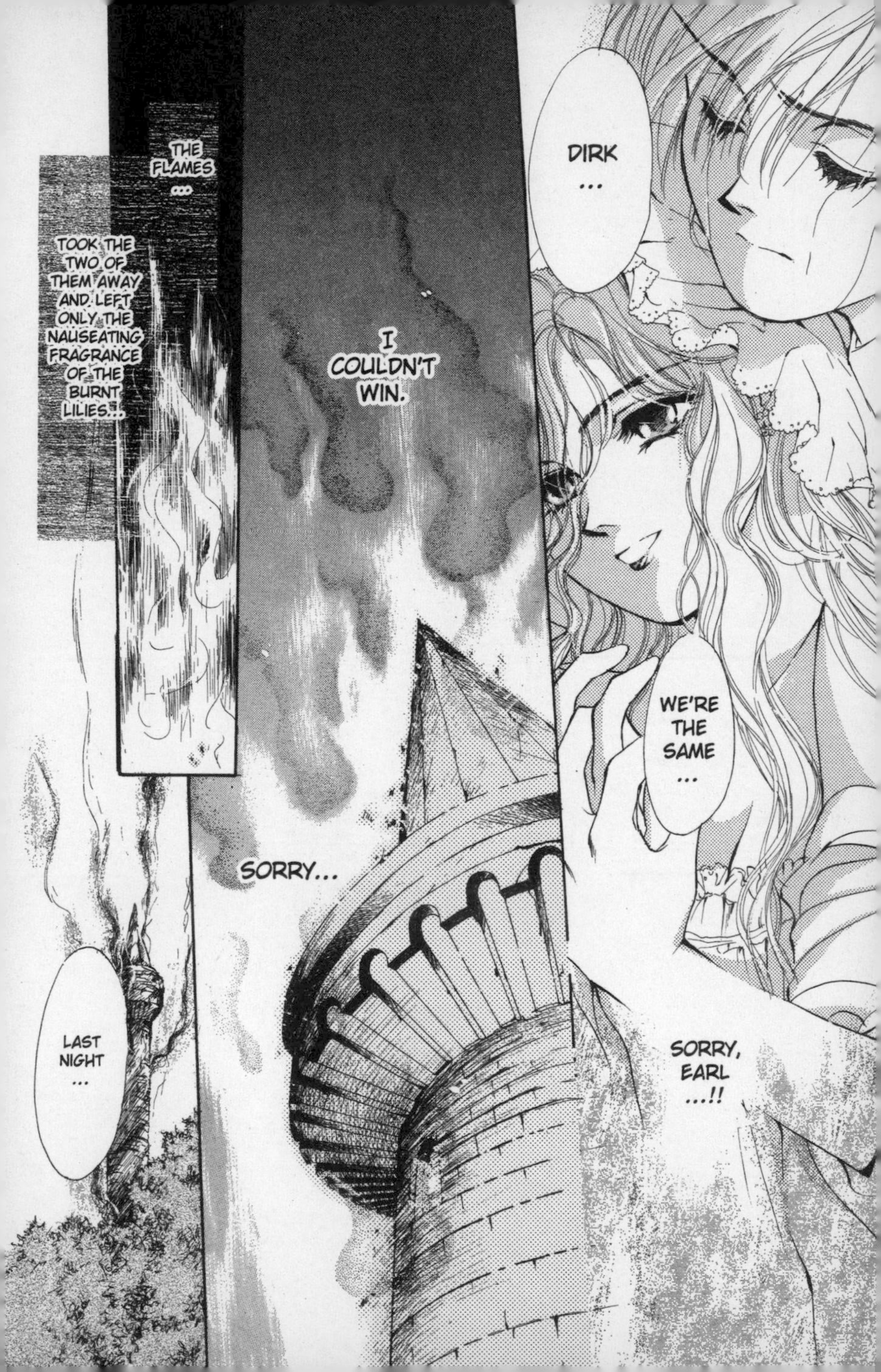
DIRK ...
WE'RE THE SAME ...
SORRY, EARL ...!!
I COULDN'T WIN.
SORRY...
THE FLAMES ...
TOOK THE TWO OF THEM AWAY AND LEFT ONLY THE NAUSEATING FRAGRANCE OF THE BURNT LILIES...
LAST NIGHT ...

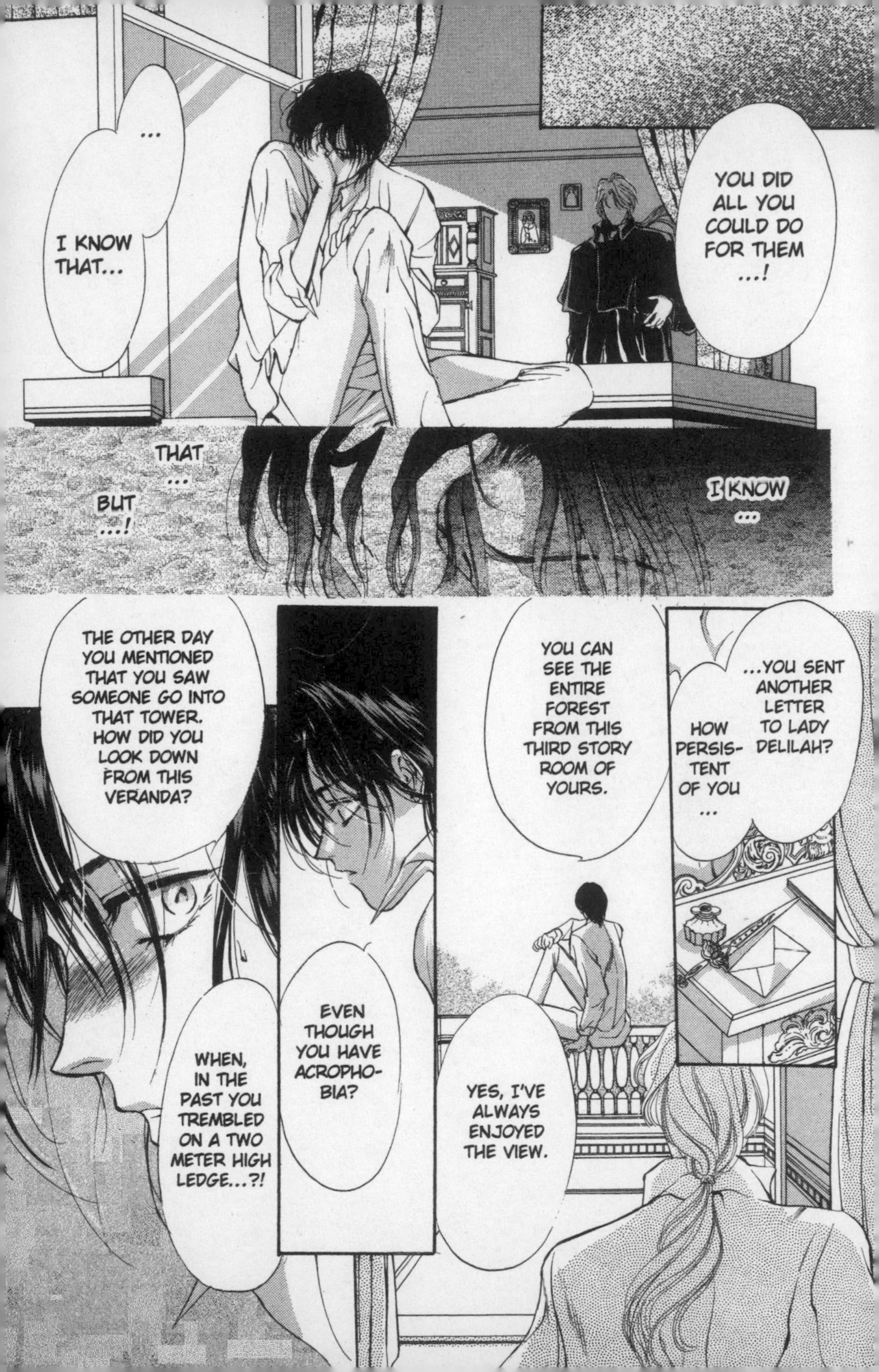
YOU DID ALL YOU COULD DO FOR THEM ...!
... I KNOW THAT...
I KNOW ...
THAT ...
BUT ...!
...YOU SENT ANOTHER LETTER TO LADY DELILAH?
HOW PERSIS-TENT OF YOU ...
YOU CAN SEE THE ENTIRE FOREST FROM THIS THIRD STORY ROOM OF YOURS.
YES, I'VE ALWAYS ENJOYED THE VIEW.
EVEN THOUGH YOU HAVE ACROPHO-BIA?
THE OTHER DAY YOU MENTIONED THAT YOU SAW SOMEONE GO INTO THAT TOWER. HOW DID YOU LOOK DOWN FROM THIS VERANDA?
WHEN, IN THE PAST YOU TREMBLED ON A TWO METER HIGH LEDGE...?!

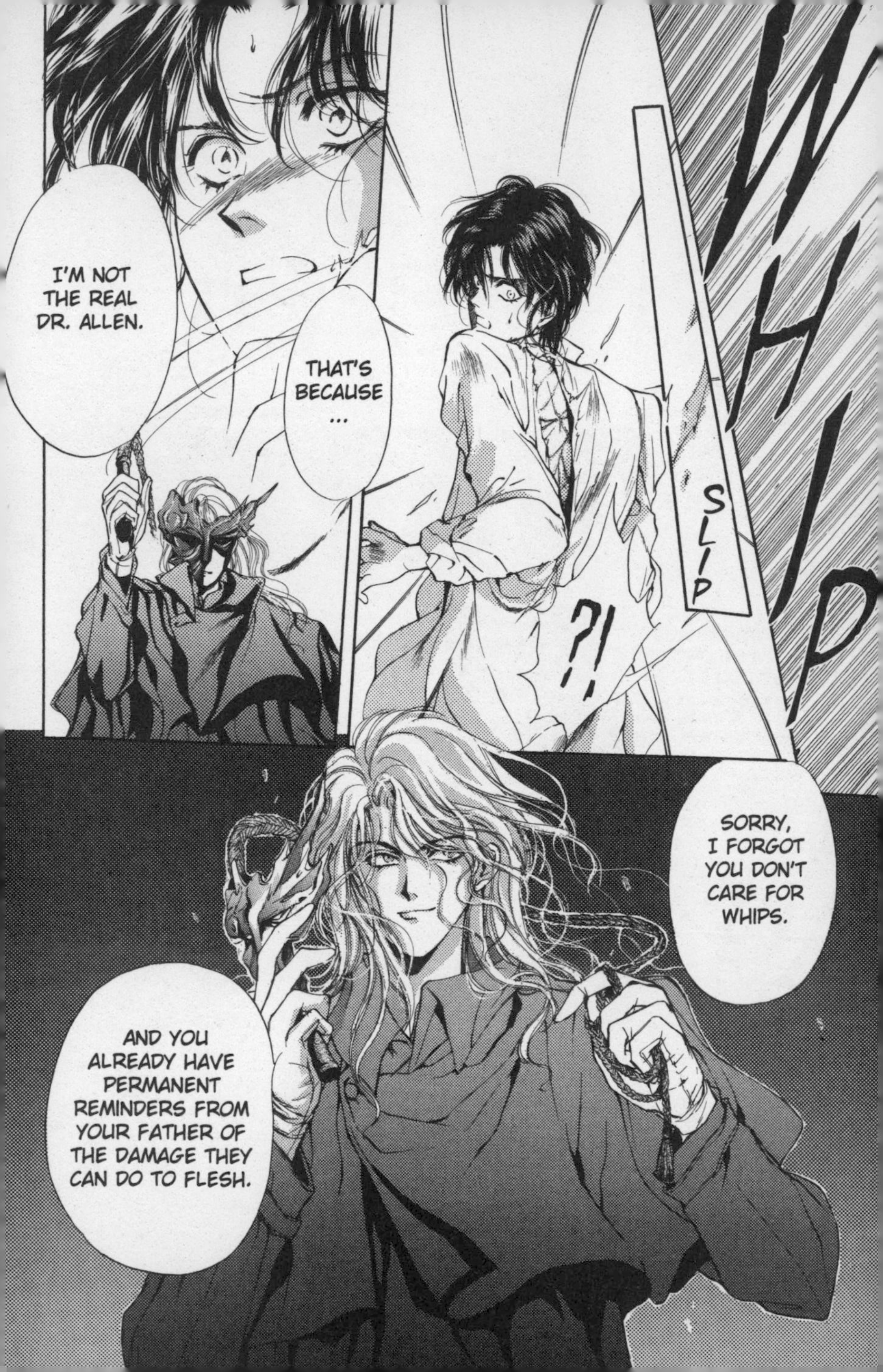
WHIP
SLIP
?!
I'M NOT THE REAL DR. ALLEN.
THAT'S BECAUSE ...
SORRY, I FORGOT YOU DON'T CARE FOR WHIPS.
AND YOU ALREADY HAVE PERMANENT REMINDERS FROM YOUR FATHER OF THE DAMAGE THEY CAN DO TO FLESH.

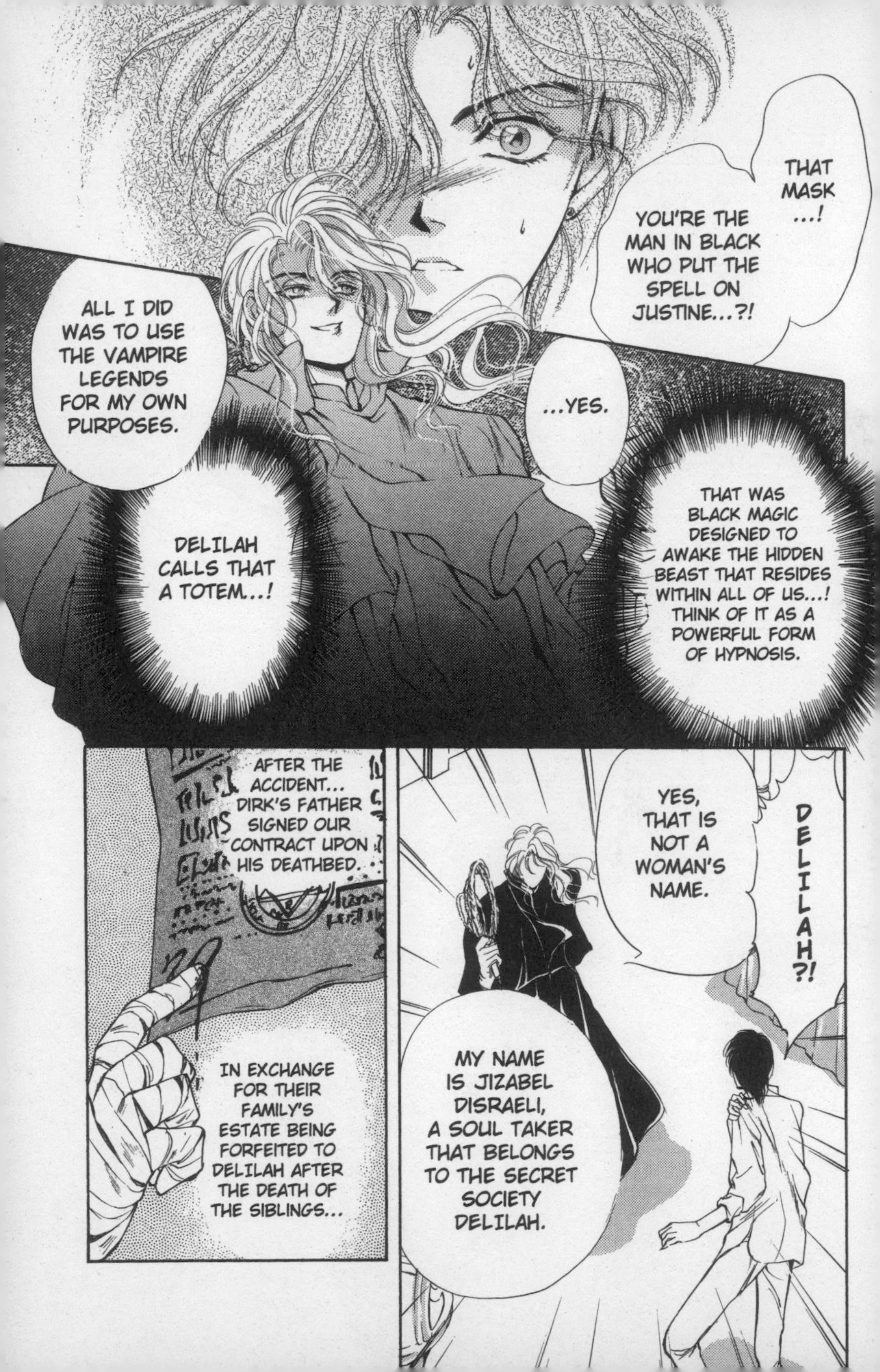
THAT MASK ...!
YOU'RE THE MAN IN BLACK WHO PUT THE SPELL ON JUSTINE...?!
...YES.
ALL I DID WAS TO USE THE VAMPIRE LEGENDS FOR MY OWN PURPOSES.
THAT WAS BLACK MAGIC DESIGNED TO AWAKE THE HIDDEN BEAST THAT RESIDES WITHIN ALL OF US...! THINK OF IT AS A POWERFUL FORM OF HYPNOSIS.
DELILAH CALLS THAT A TOTEM...!
DELILAH?!
YES, THAT IS NOT A WOMAN'S NAME.
MY NAME IS JIZABEL DISRAELI, A SOUL TAKER THAT BELONGS TO THE SECRET SOCIETY DELILAH.
AFTER THE ACCIDENT... DIRK'S FATHER SIGNED OUR CONTRACT UPON HIS DEATHBED.
IN EXCHANGE FOR THEIR FAMILY'S ESTATE BEING FORFEITED TO DELILAH AFTER THE DEATH OF THE SIBLINGS...

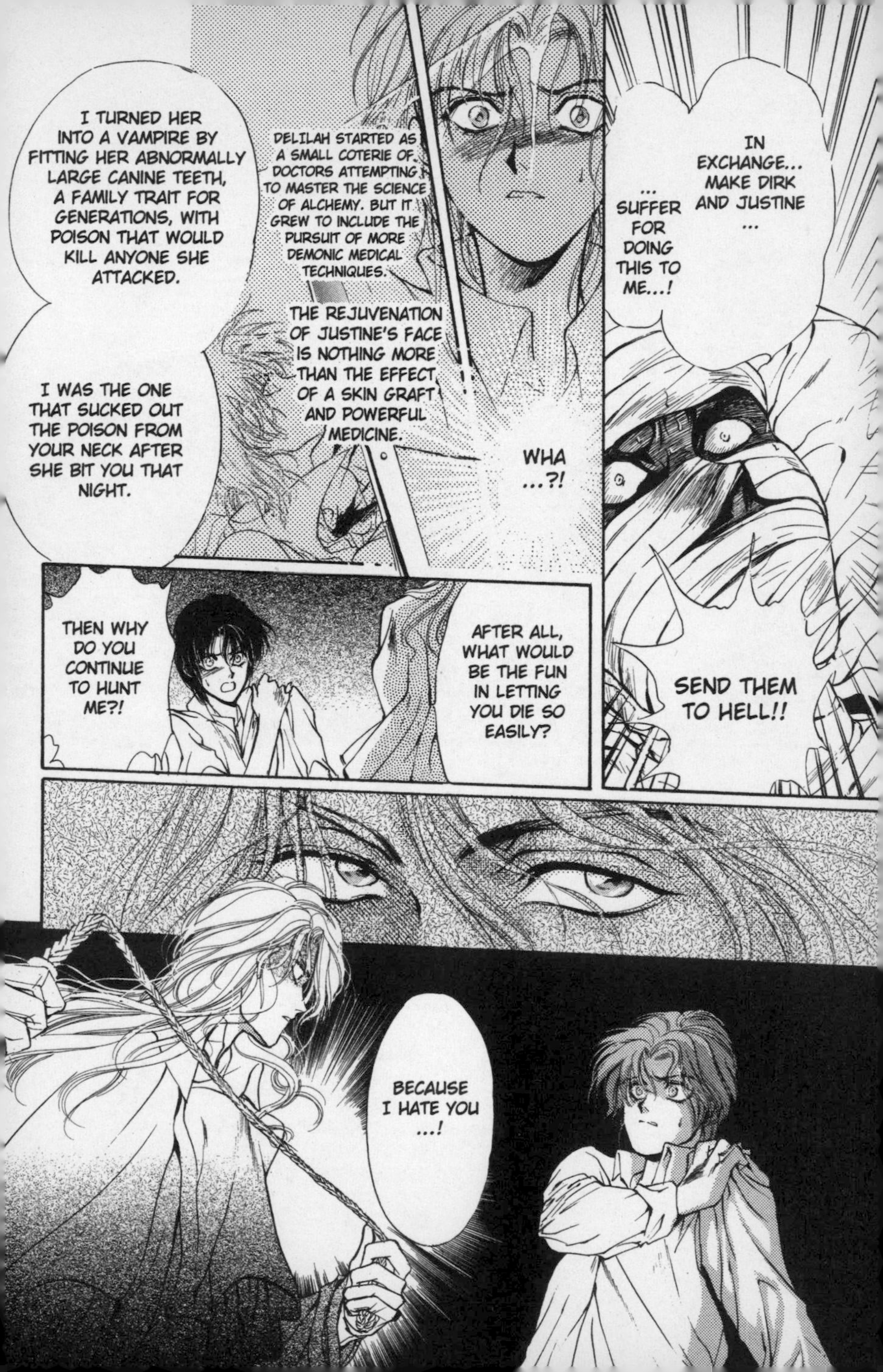
IN EXCHANGE... MAKE DIRK AND JUSTINE ...
... SUFFER FOR DOING THIS TO ME...!
SEND THEM TO HELL!!
DELILAH STARTED AS A SMALL COTERIE OF DOCTORS ATTEMPTING TO MASTER THE SCIENCE OF ALCHEMY. BUT IT GREW TO INCLUDE THE PURSUIT OF MORE DEMONIC MEDICAL TECHNIQUES.
THE REJUVENATION OF JUSTINE'S FACE IS NOTHING MORE THAN THE EFFECT OF A SKIN GRAFT AND POWERFUL MEDICINE.
WHA ...?!
I TURNED HER INTO A VAMPIRE BY FITTING HER ABNORMALLY LARGE CANINE TEETH, A FAMILY TRAIT FOR GENERATIONS, WITH POISON THAT WOULD KILL ANYONE SHE ATTACKED.
I WAS THE ONE THAT SUCKED OUT THE POISON FROM YOUR NECK AFTER SHE BIT YOU THAT NIGHT.
AFTER ALL, WHAT WOULD BE THE FUN IN LETTING YOU DIE SO EASILY?
THEN WHY DO YOU CONTINUE TO HUNT ME?!
BECAUSE I HATE YOU ...!

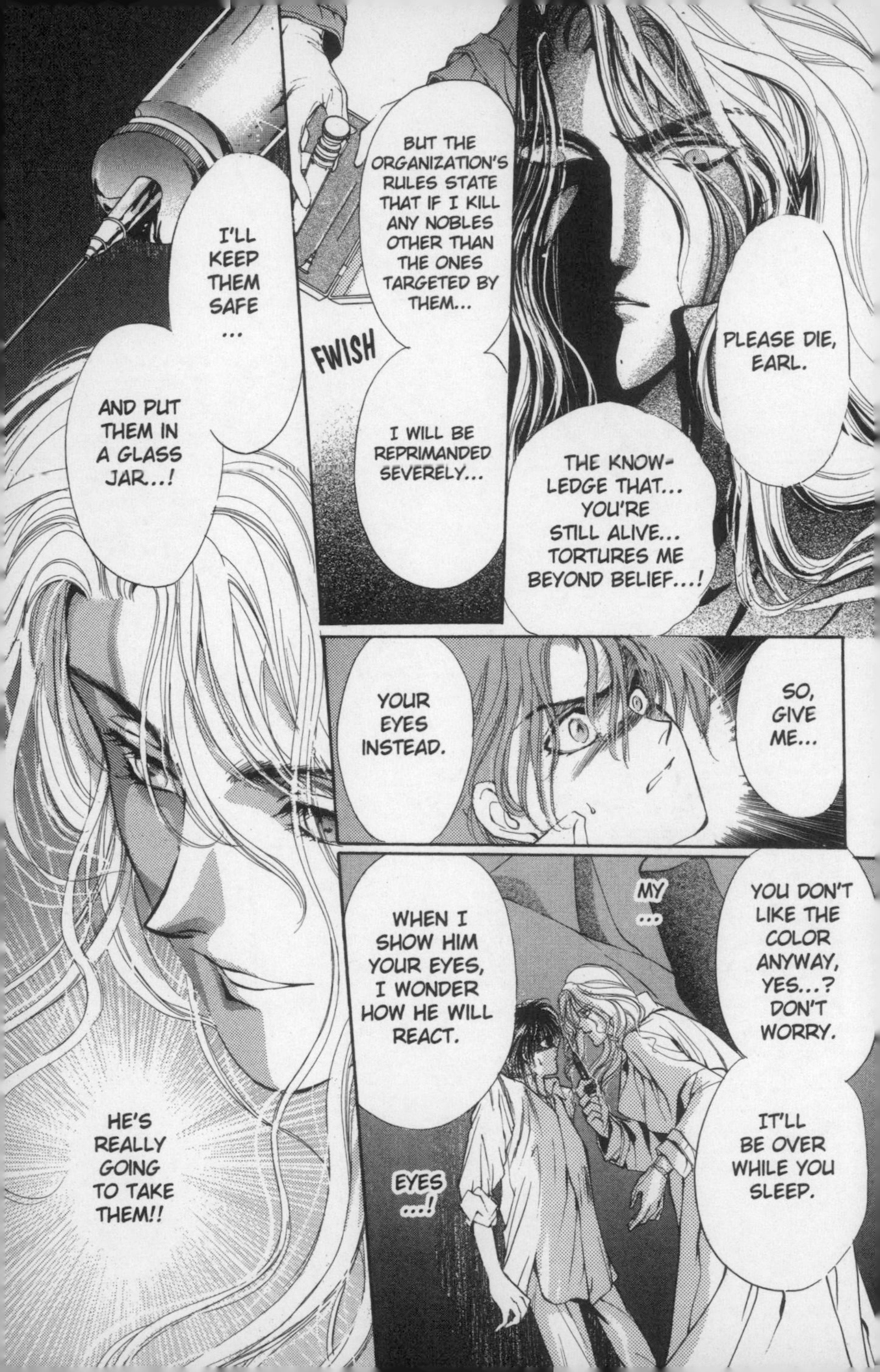
PLEASE DIE, EARL.
THE KNOWLEDGE THAT... YOU'RE STILL ALIVE... TORTURES ME BEYOND BELIEF...!
BUT THE ORGANIZATION'S RULES STATE THAT IF I KILL ANY NOBLES OTHER THAN THE ONES TARGETED BY THEM...
I WILL BE REPRIMANDED SEVERELY...
FWISH
SO, GIVE ME...
YOUR EYES INSTEAD.
YOU DON'T LIKE THE COLOR ANYWAY, YES...? DON'T WORRY.
MY ...
WHEN I SHOW HIM YOUR EYES, I WONDER HOW HE WILL REACT.
IT'LL BE OVER WHILE YOU SLEEP.
EYES ...!
I'LL KEEP THEM SAFE ...
AND PUT THEM IN A GLASS JAR...!
HE'S REALLY GOING TO TAKE THEM!!

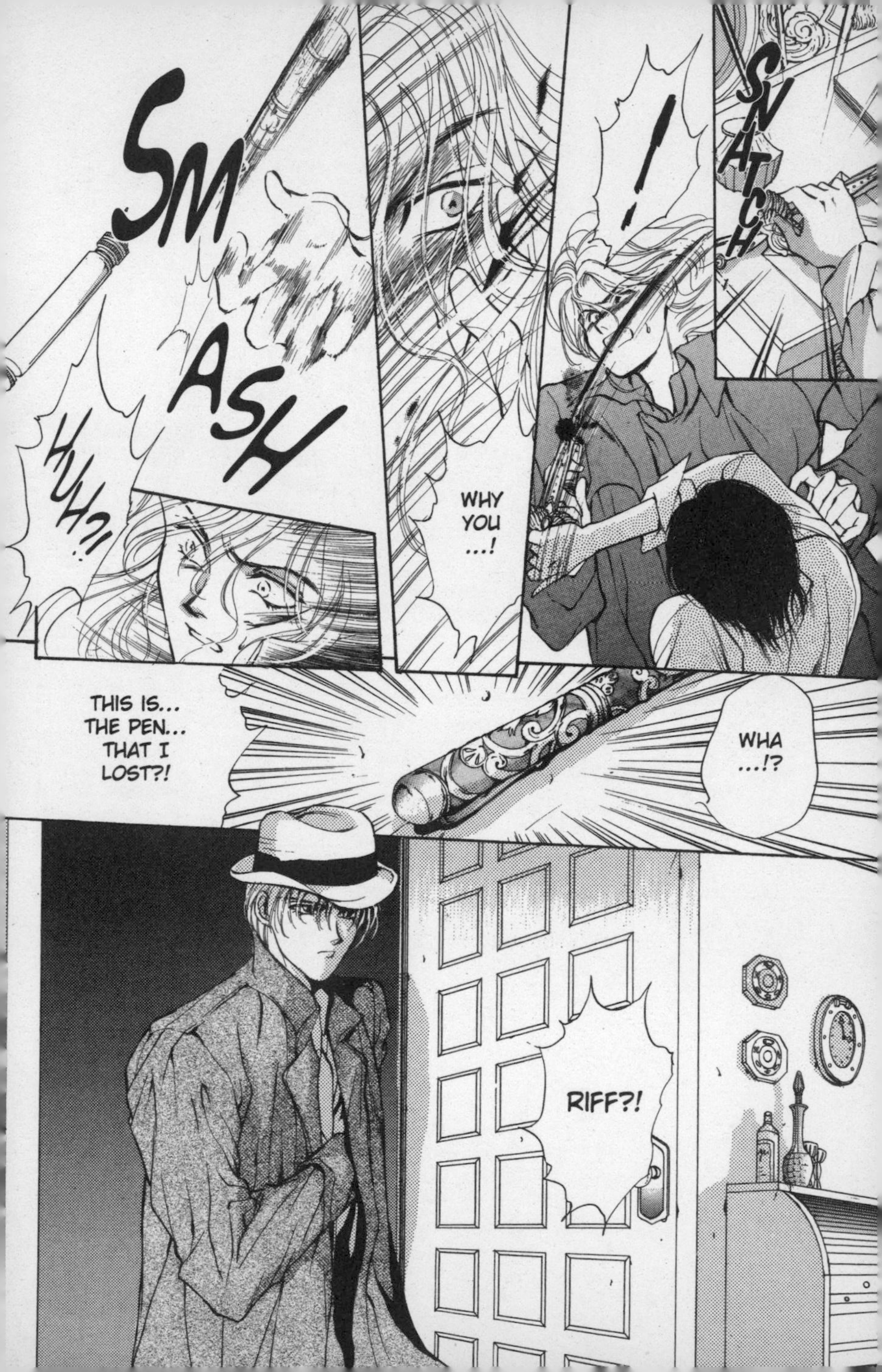
SNATCH
!!
WHY YOU ...!
SMASH
HUH?!
WHA ...!?
THIS IS... THE PEN... THAT I LOST?!
RIFF?!

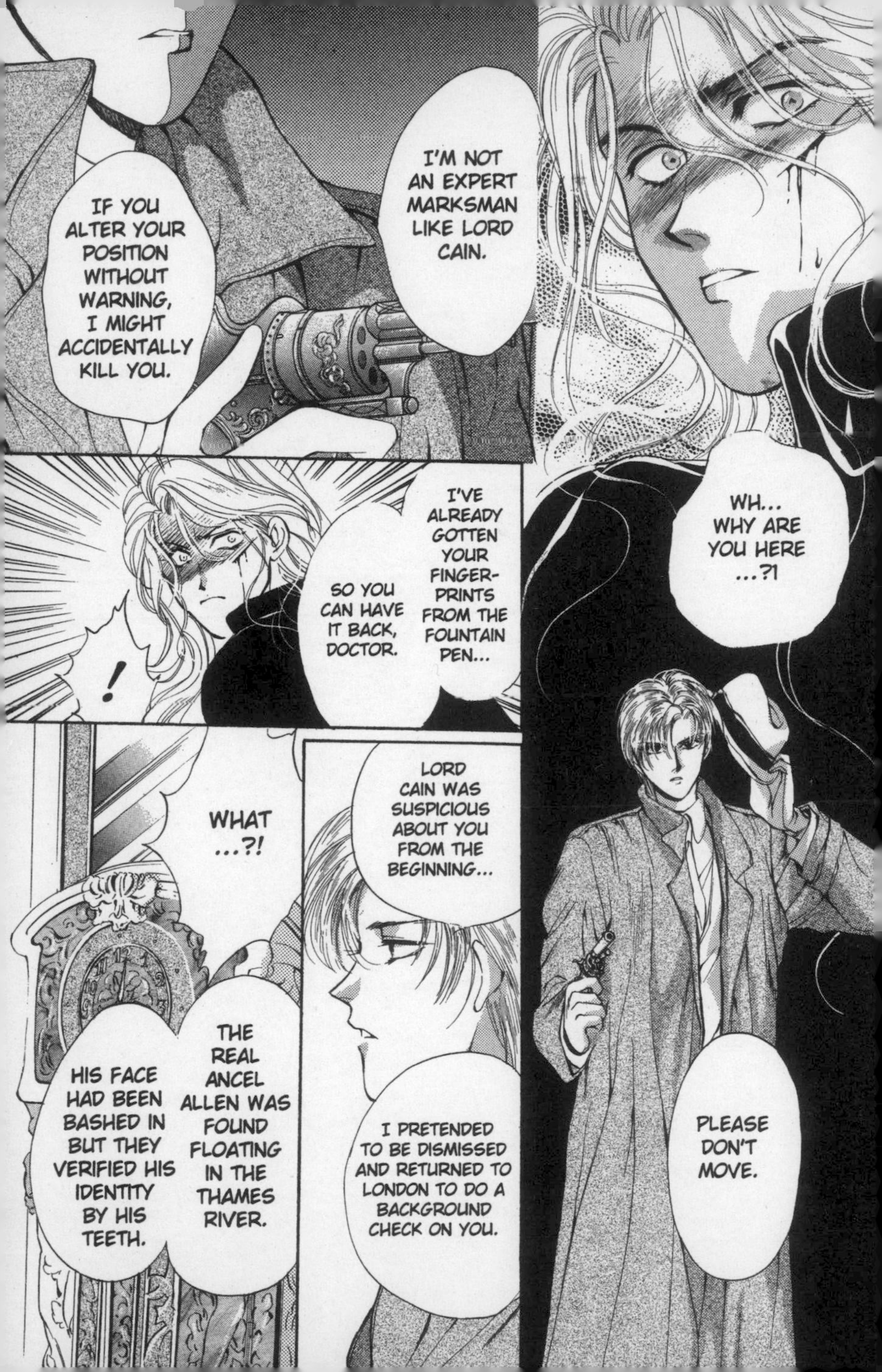

WH... WHY ARE YOU HERE ...?!
PLEASE DON'T MOVE.
I'M NOT AN EXPERT MARKSMAN LIKE LORD CAIN.
IF YOU ALTER YOUR POSITION WITHOUT WARNING, I MIGHT ACCIDENTALLY KILL YOU.
I'VE ALREADY GOTTEN YOUR FINGER-PRINTS FROM THE FOUNTAIN PEN...
SO YOU CAN HAVE IT BACK, DOCTOR.
!
LORD CAIN WAS SUSPICIOUS ABOUT YOU FROM THE BEGINNING...
I PRETENDED TO BE DISMISSED AND RETURNED TO LONDON TO DO A BACKGROUND CHECK ON YOU.
WHAT ...?!
THE REAL ANCEL ALLEN WAS FOUND FLOATING IN THE THAMES RIVER.
HIS FACE HAD BEEN BASHED IN BUT THEY VERIFIED HIS IDENTITY BY HIS TEETH.

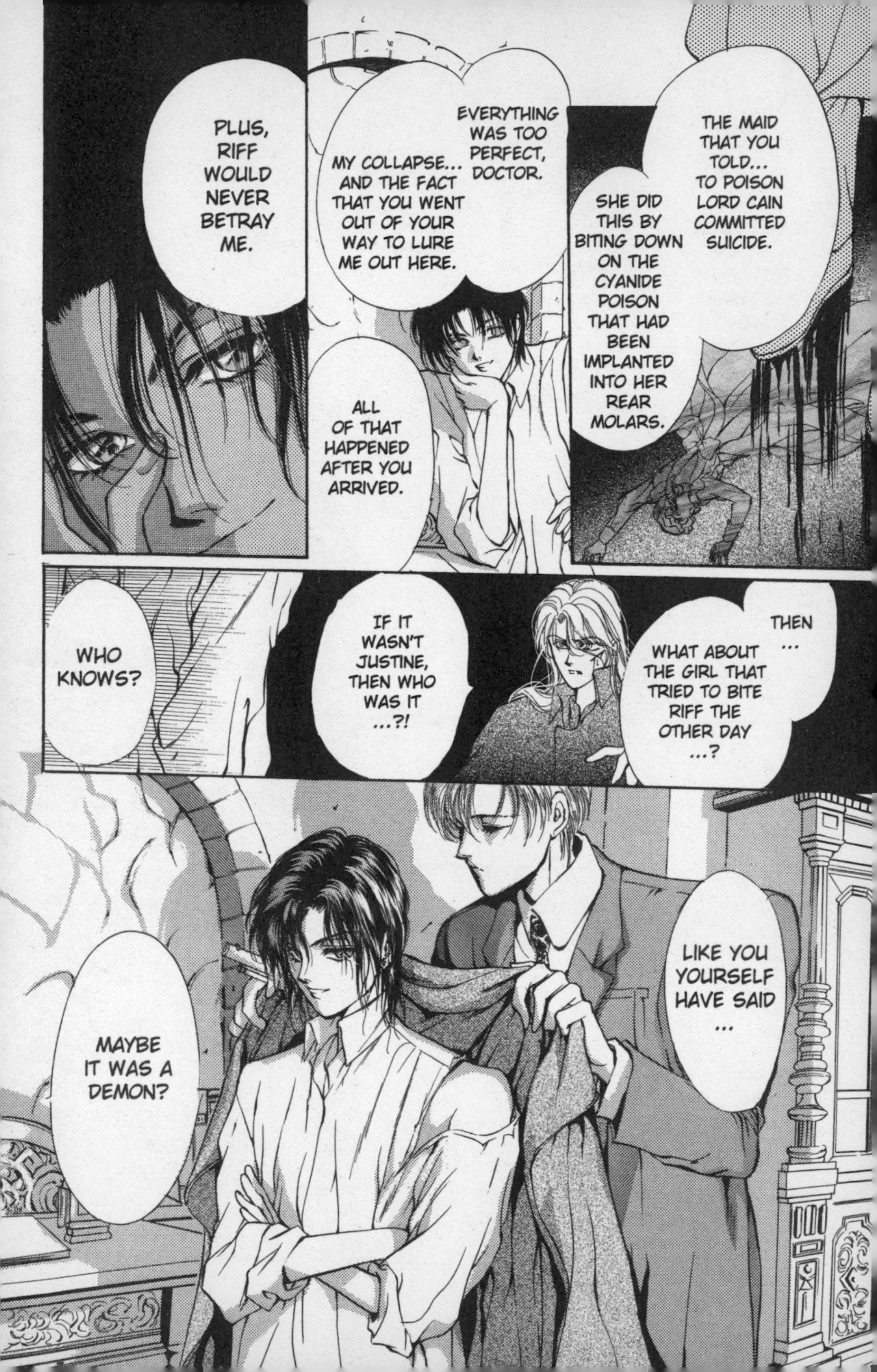
THE MAID THAT YOU TOLD... TO POISON LORD CAIN COMMITTED SUICIDE.
SHE DID THIS BY BITING DOWN ON THE CYANIDE POISON THAT HAD BEEN IMPLANTED INTO HER REAR MOLARS.
EVERYTHING WAS TOO PERFECT, DOCTOR.
MY COLLAPSE... AND THE FACT THAT YOU WENT OUT OF YOUR WAY TO LURE ME OUT HERE.
ALL OF THAT HAPPENED AFTER YOU ARRIVED.
PLUS, RIFF WOULD NEVER BETRAY ME.
THEN...
WHAT ABOUT THE GIRL THAT TRIED TO BITE RIFF THE OTHER DAY...?
IF IT WASN'T JUSTINE, THEN WHO WAS IT...?!
WHO KNOWS?
LIKE YOU YOURSELF HAVE SAID...
MAYBE IT WAS A DEMON?

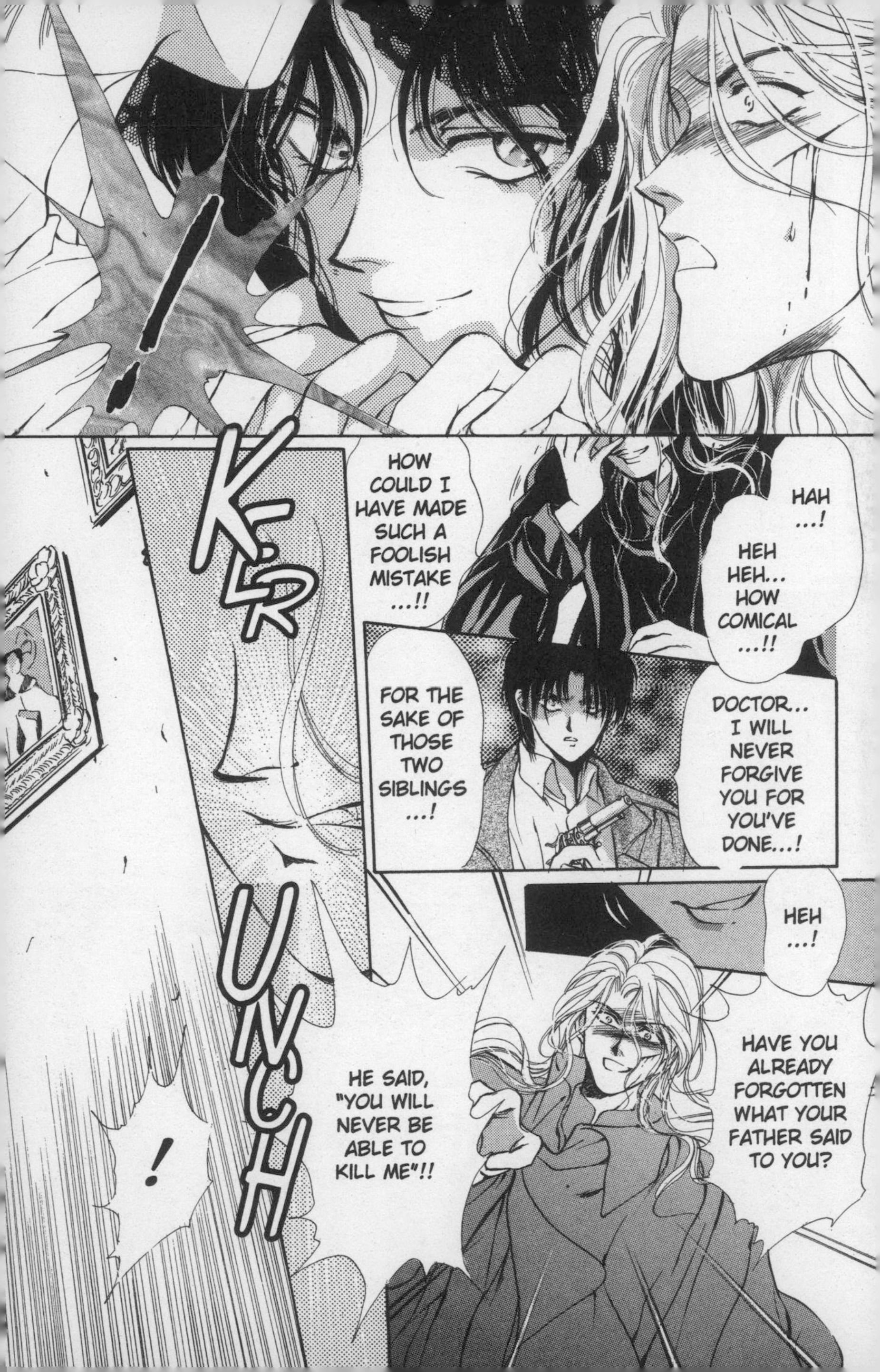
!
HAH ...!
HEH HEH... HOW COMICAL ...!!
HOW COULD I HAVE MADE SUCH A FOOLISH MISTAKE ...!!
DOCTOR... I WILL NEVER FORGIVE YOU FOR YOU'VE DONE...!
FOR THE SAKE OF THOSE TWO SIBLINGS ...!
HEH ...!
HAVE YOU ALREADY FORGOTTEN WHAT YOUR FATHER SAID TO YOU?
HE SAID, "YOU WILL NEVER BE ABLE TO KILL ME"!!
KLRUNCH
!

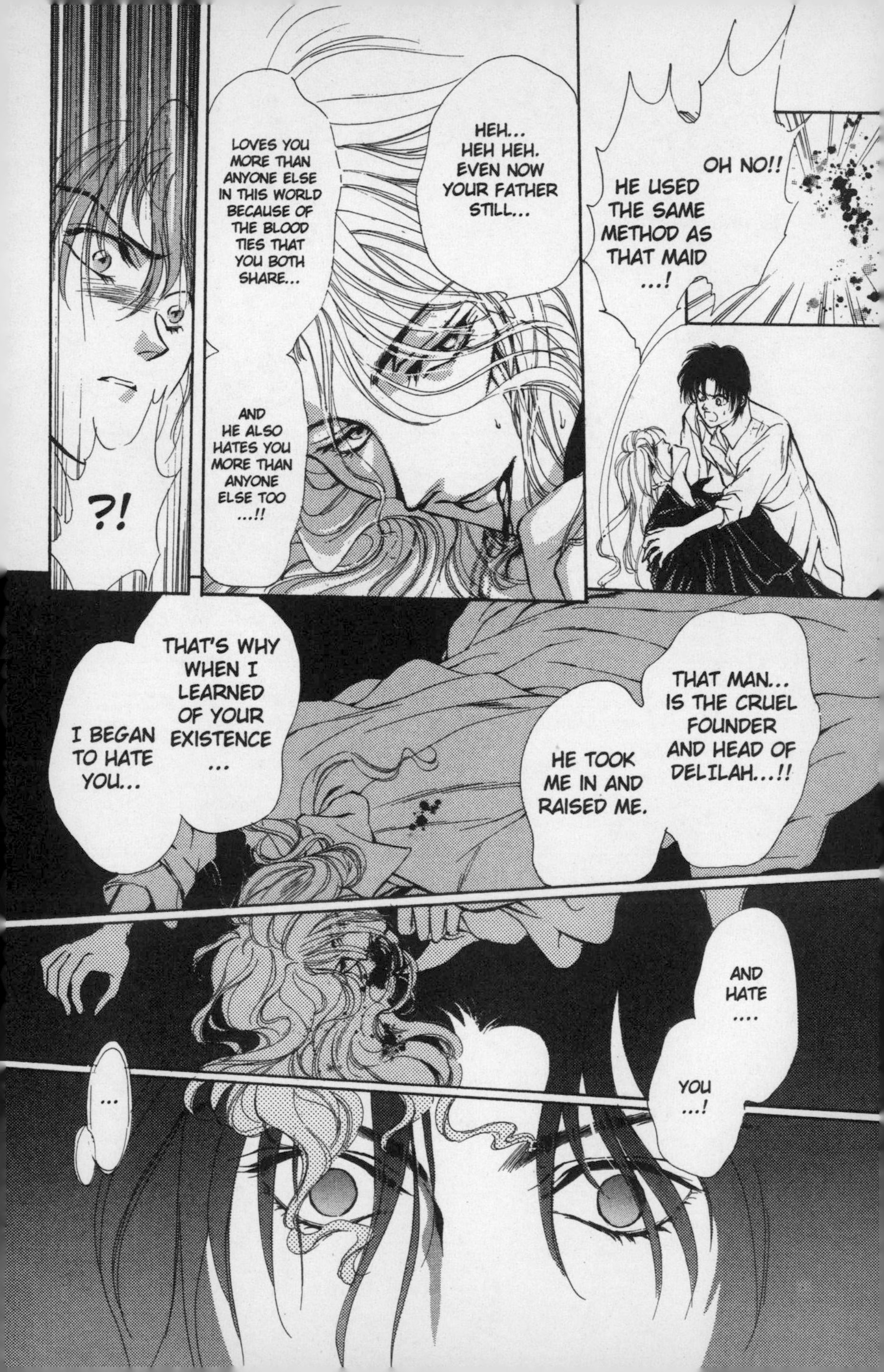
OH NO!!
HE USED THE SAME METHOD AS THAT MAID ...!
HEH... HEH HEH. EVEN NOW YOUR FATHER STILL...
LOVES YOU MORE THAN ANYONE ELSE IN THIS WORLD BECAUSE OF THE BLOOD TIES THAT YOU BOTH SHARE...
AND HE ALSO HATES YOU MORE THAN ANYONE ELSE TOO ...!!
?!
THAT MAN... IS THE CRUEL FOUNDER AND HEAD OF DELILAH...!!
HE TOOK ME IN AND RAISED ME.
THAT'S WHY WHEN I LEARNED OF YOUR EXISTENCE ...
I BEGAN TO HATE YOU...
AND HATE ....
YOU ...!
...

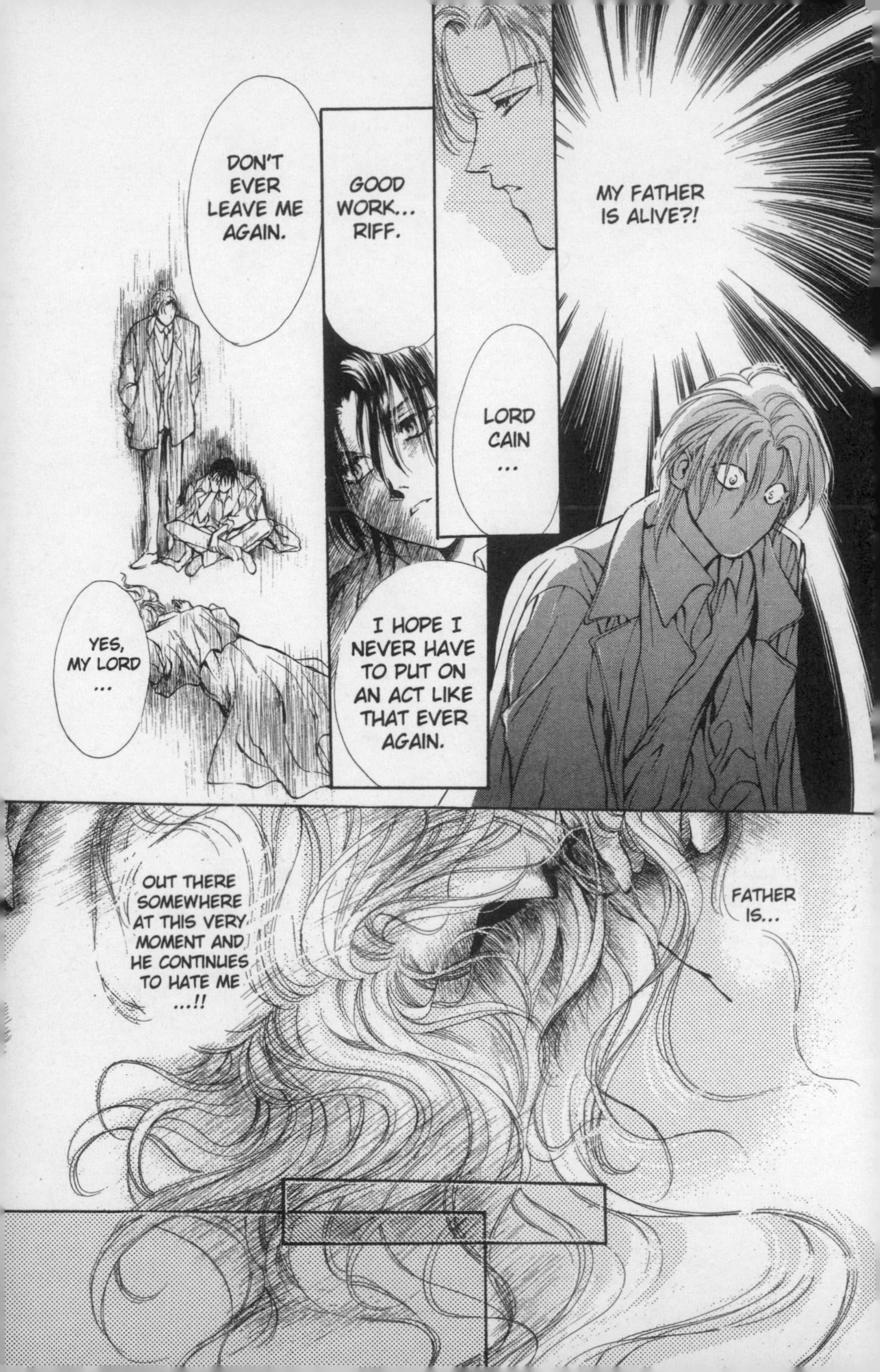
MY FATHER IS ALIVE?!
GOOD WORK... RIFF.
LORD CAIN ...
I HOPE I NEVER HAVE TO PUT ON AN ACT LIKE THAT EVER AGAIN.
DON'T EVER LEAVE ME AGAIN.
YES, MY LORD ...
FATHER IS...
OUT THERE SOMEWHERE AT THIS VERY MOMENT AND HE CONTINUES TO HATE ME ...!!

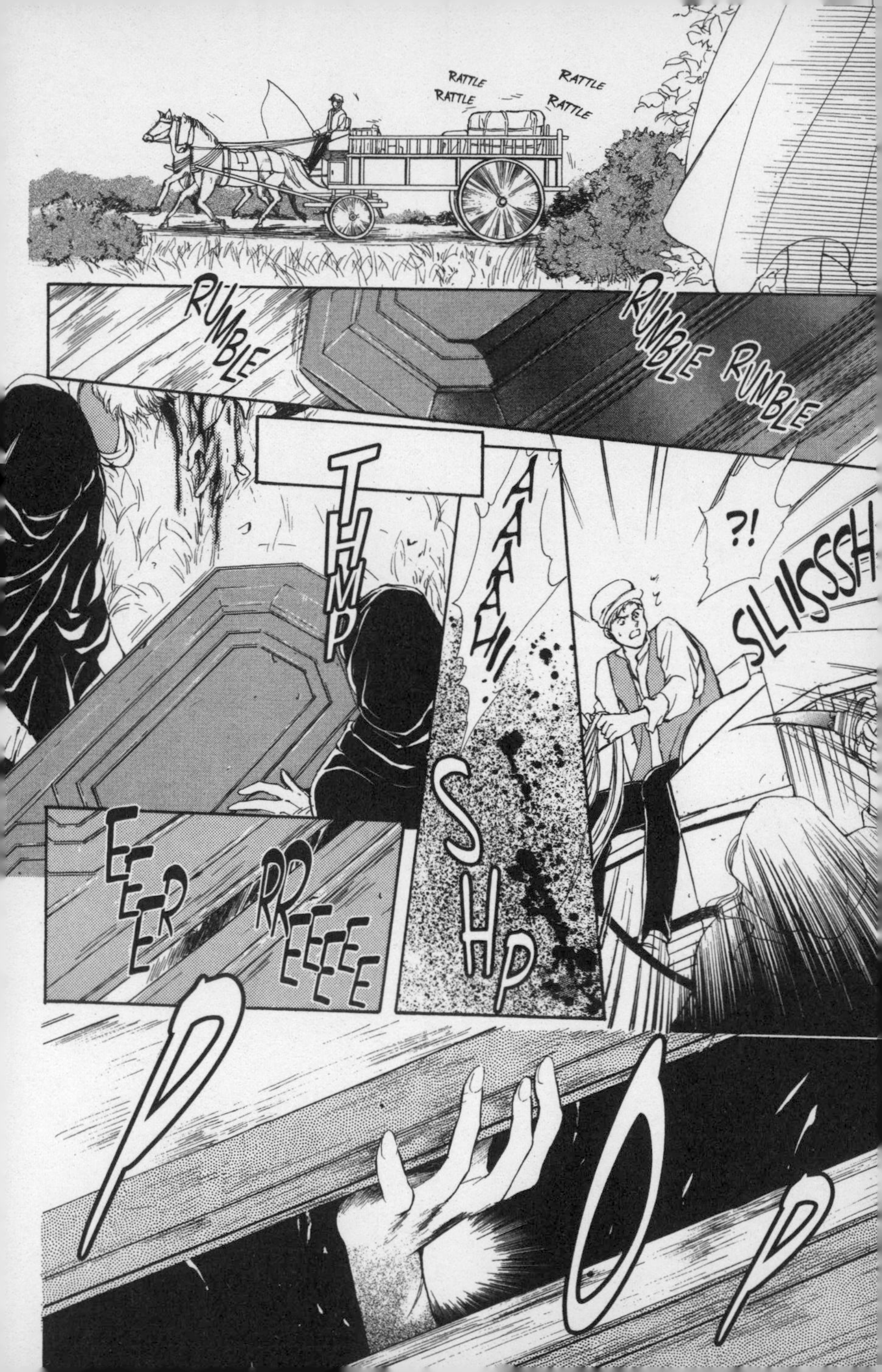
RATTLE
RATTLE
RATTLE
RATTLE
RUMBLE RUMBLE
RUMBLE
?!
SLIISSH
AAAAH!!
SHP
THUMP
EEEER RREEEEEE
POP

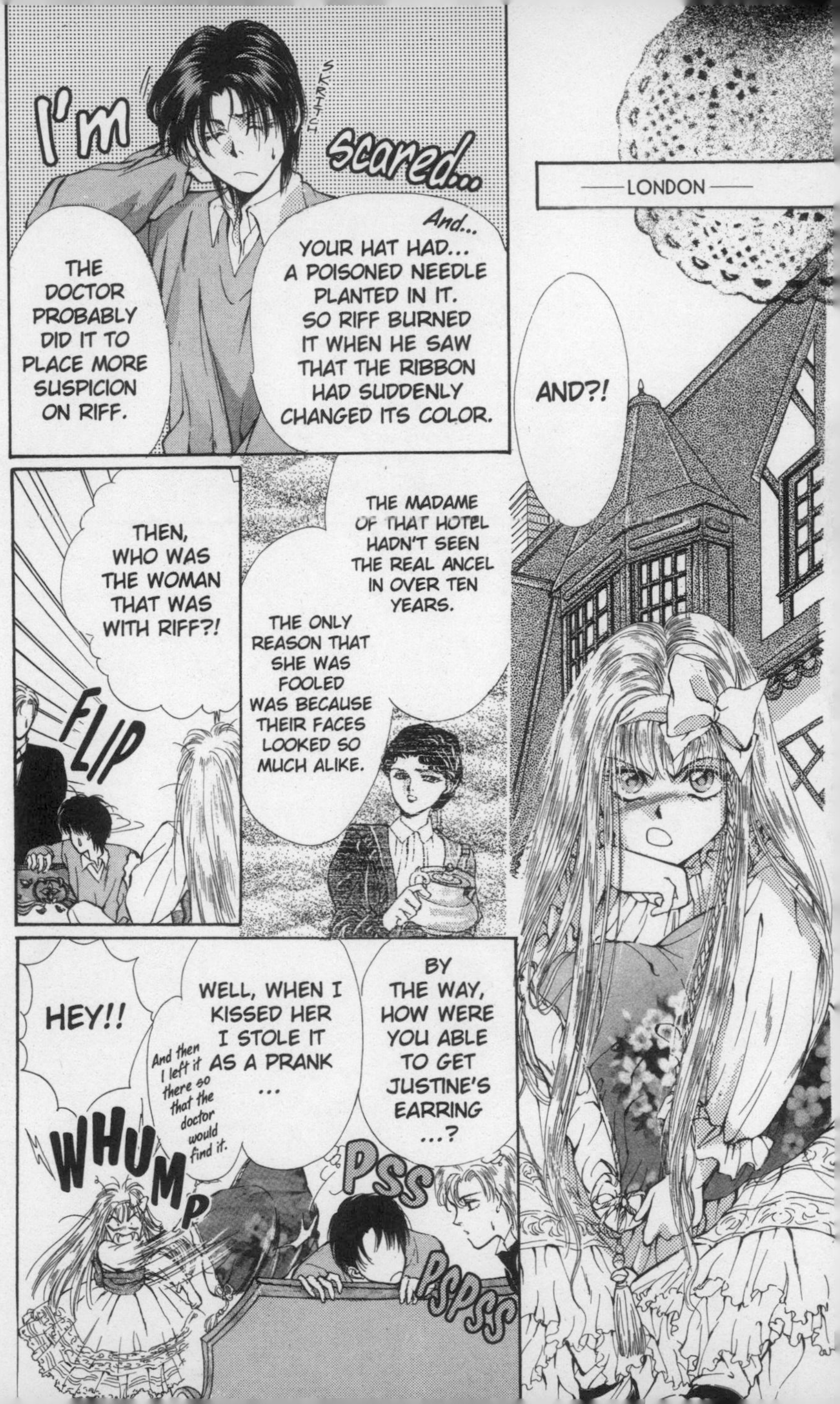
—LONDON—
AND?!
I'm scared...
SKRITCH
And...
YOUR HAT HAD... A POISONED NEEDLE PLANTED IN IT. SO RIFF BURNED IT WHEN HE SAW THAT THE RIBBON HAD SUDDENLY CHANGED ITS COLOR.
THE DOCTOR PROBABLY DID IT TO PLACE MORE SUSPICION ON RIFF.
THE MADAME OF THAT HOTEL HADN'T SEEN THE REAL ANCEL IN OVER TEN YEARS.
THE ONLY REASON THAT SHE WAS FOOLED WAS BECAUSE THEIR FACES LOOKED SO MUCH ALIKE.
THEN, WHO WAS THE WOMAN THAT WAS WITH RIFF?!
FLIP
BY THE WAY, HOW WERE YOU ABLE TO GET JUSTINE'S EARRING ...?
WELL, WHEN I KISSED HER I STOLE IT AS A PRANK ...
And then I left it there so that the doctor would find it.
HEY!!
PSS
PSPSS
WHUMP

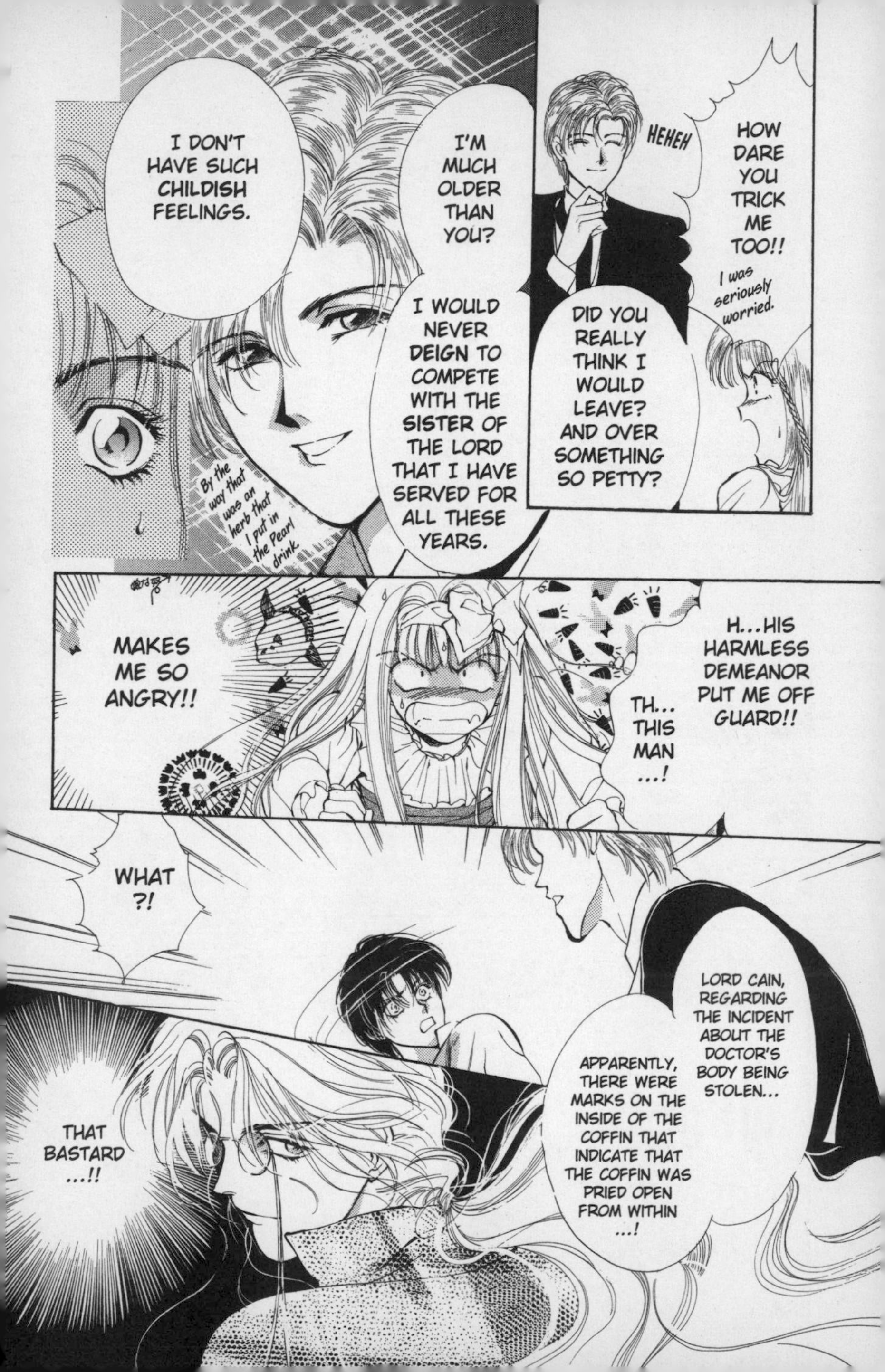
HOW DARE YOU TRICK ME TOO!!
HEHEH
I was seriously worried.
DID YOU REALLY THINK I WOULD LEAVE? AND OVER SOMETHING SO PETTY?
I'M MUCH OLDER THAN YOU?
I DON'T HAVE SUCH CHILDISH FEELINGS.
I WOULD NEVER DEIGN TO COMPETE WITH THE SISTER OF THE LORD THAT I HAVE SERVED FOR ALL THESE YEARS.
By the way that was an herb that I put in the Pearl drink.
H...HIS HARMLESS DEMEANOR PUT ME OFF GUARD!!
TH... THIS MAN ...!
MAKES ME SO ANGRY!!
LORD CAIN, REGARDING THE INCIDENT ABOUT THE DOCTOR'S BODY BEING STOLEN...
APPARENTLY, THERE WERE MARKS ON THE INSIDE OF THE COFFIN THAT INDICATE THAT THE COFFIN WAS PRIED OPEN FROM WITHIN ...!
WHAT ?!
THAT BASTARD ...!!

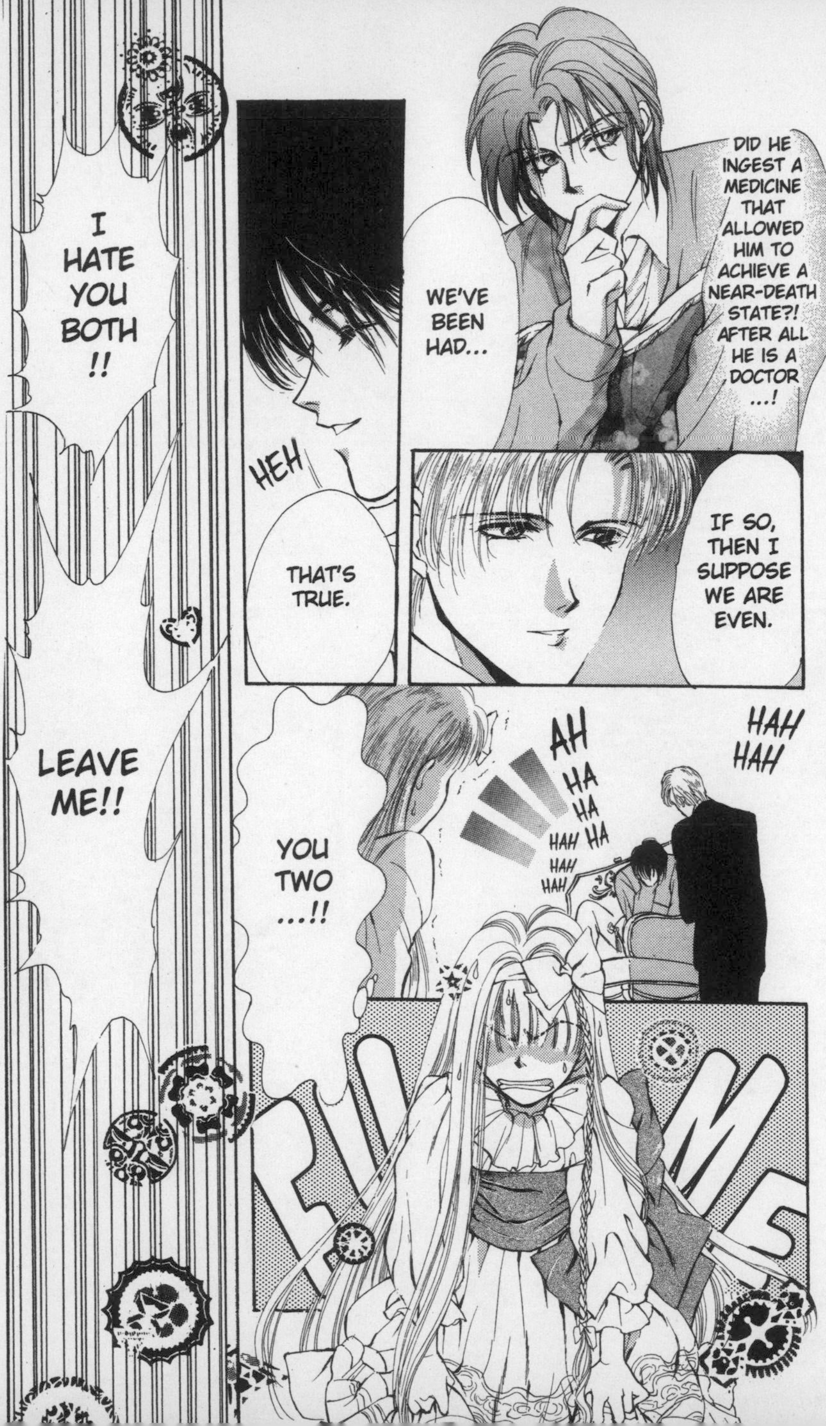
DID HE INGEST A MEDICINE THAT ALLOWED HIM TO ACHIEVE A NEAR-DEATH STATE?! AFTER ALL HE IS A DOCTOR ...!
WE'VE BEEN HAD...
IF SO, THEN I SUPPOSE WE ARE EVEN.
HEH
THAT'S TRUE.
HAH HAH
AH HA HA HA
HAH HAH HAH
YOU TWO ...!!
I HATE YOU BOTH !!
LEAVE ME!!

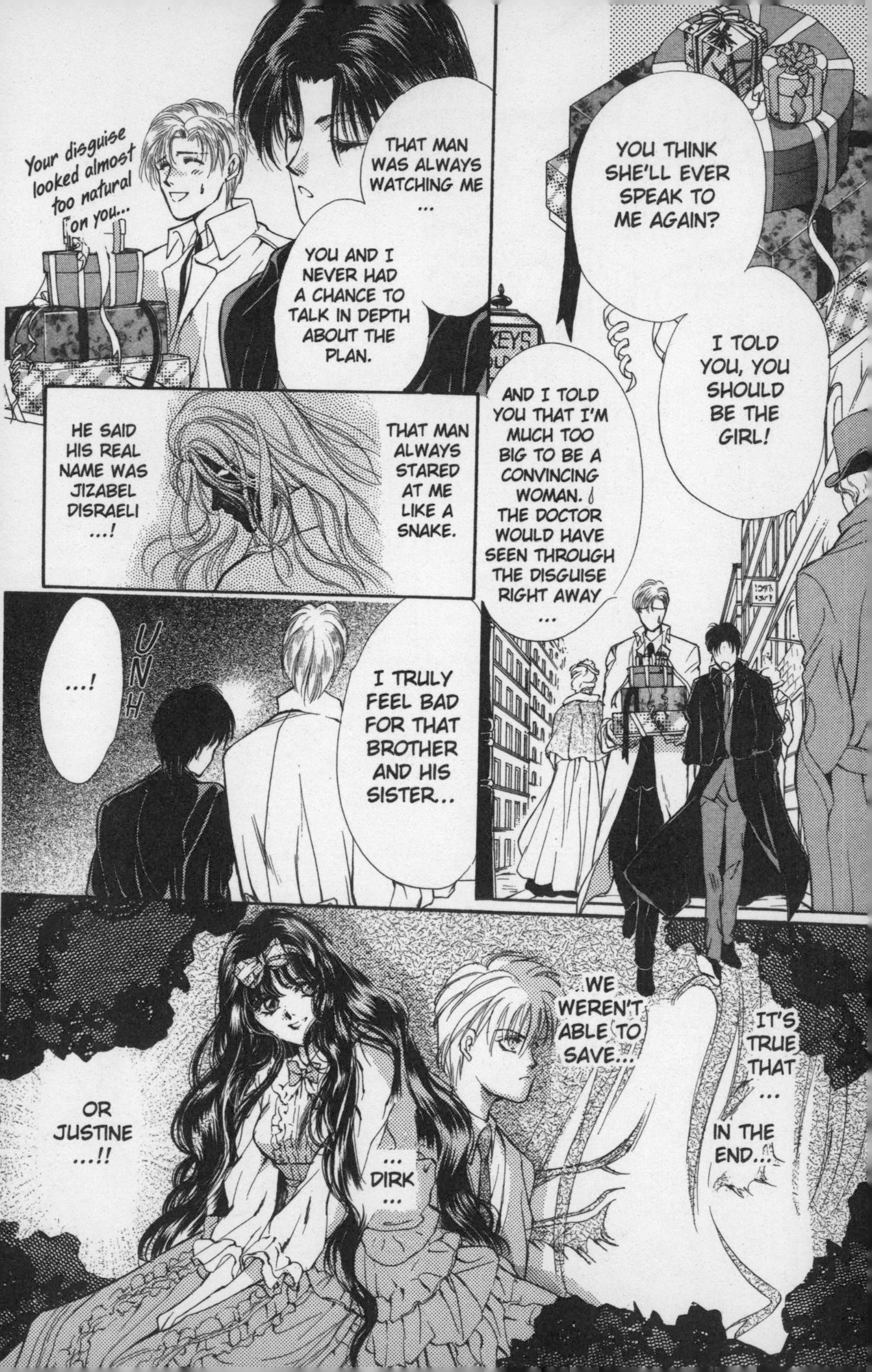
YOU THINK SHE'LL EVER SPEAK TO ME AGAIN?
I TOLD YOU, YOU SHOULD BE THE GIRL!
AND I TOLD YOU THAT I'M MUCH TOO BIG TO BE A CONVINCING WOMAN. THE DOCTOR WOULD HAVE SEEN THROUGH THE DISGUISE RIGHT AWAY ...
THAT MAN WAS ALWAYS WATCHING ME ...
YOU AND I NEVER HAD A CHANCE TO TALK IN DEPTH ABOUT THE PLAN.
Your disguise looked almost too natural on you...
THAT MAN ALWAYS STARED AT ME LIKE A SNAKE.
HE SAID HIS REAL NAME WAS JIZABEL DISRAELI ...!
I TRULY FEEL BAD FOR THAT BROTHER AND HIS SISTER...
UNH
...!
IT'S TRUE THAT ...
IN THE END...
WE WEREN'T ABLE TO SAVE...
... DIRK ...
OR JUSTINE ...!!

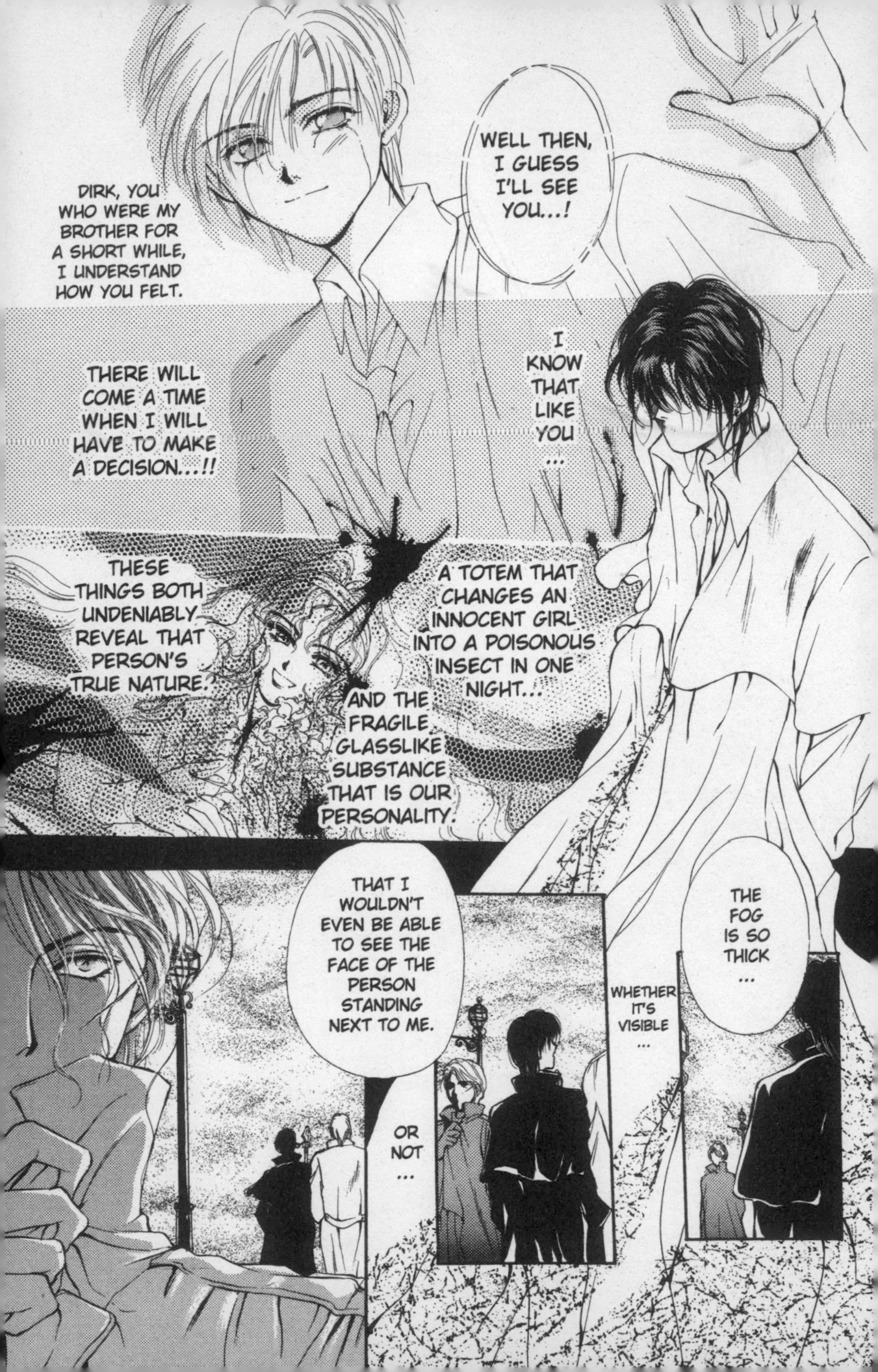
WELL THEN, I GUESS I'LL SEE YOU...!
DIRK, YOU WHO WERE MY BROTHER FOR A SHORT WHILE, I UNDERSTAND HOW YOU FELT.
I KNOW THAT LIKE YOU ...
THERE WILL COME A TIME WHEN I WILL HAVE TO MAKE A DECISION...!!
A TOTEM THAT CHANGES AN INNOCENT GIRL INTO A POISONOUS INSECT IN ONE NIGHT...
AND THE FRAGILE GLASSLIKE SUBSTANCE THAT IS OUR PERSONALITY.
THESE THINGS BOTH UNDENIABLY REVEAL THAT PERSON'S TRUE NATURE.
THE FOG IS SO THICK ...
WHETHER IT'S VISIBLE ...
THAT I WOULDN'T EVEN BE ABLE TO SEE THE FACE OF THE PERSON STANDING NEXT TO ME.
OR NOT ...

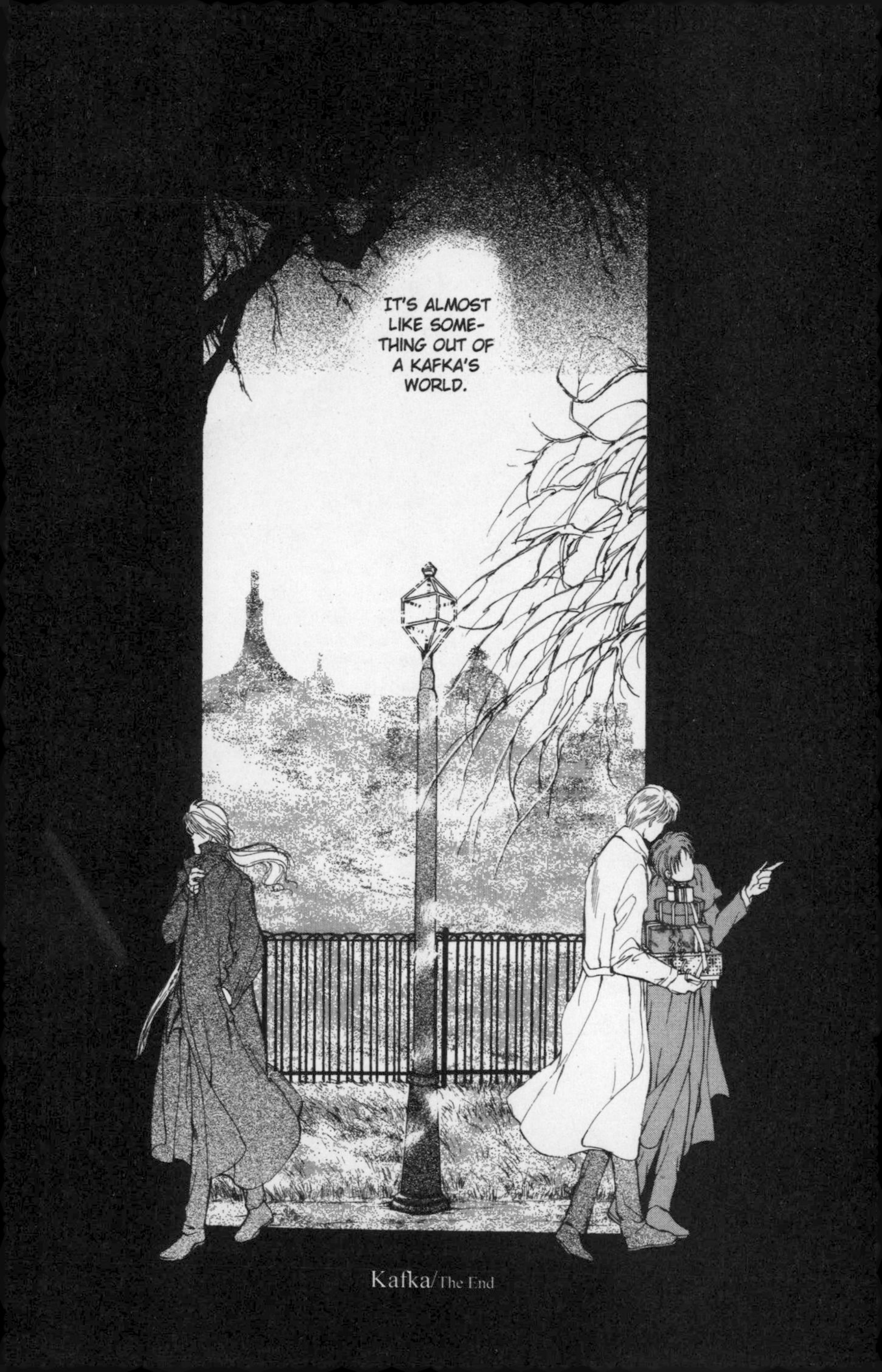
IT'S ALMOST LIKE SOME-THING OUT OF A KAFKA'S WORLD.

Kafka/The End

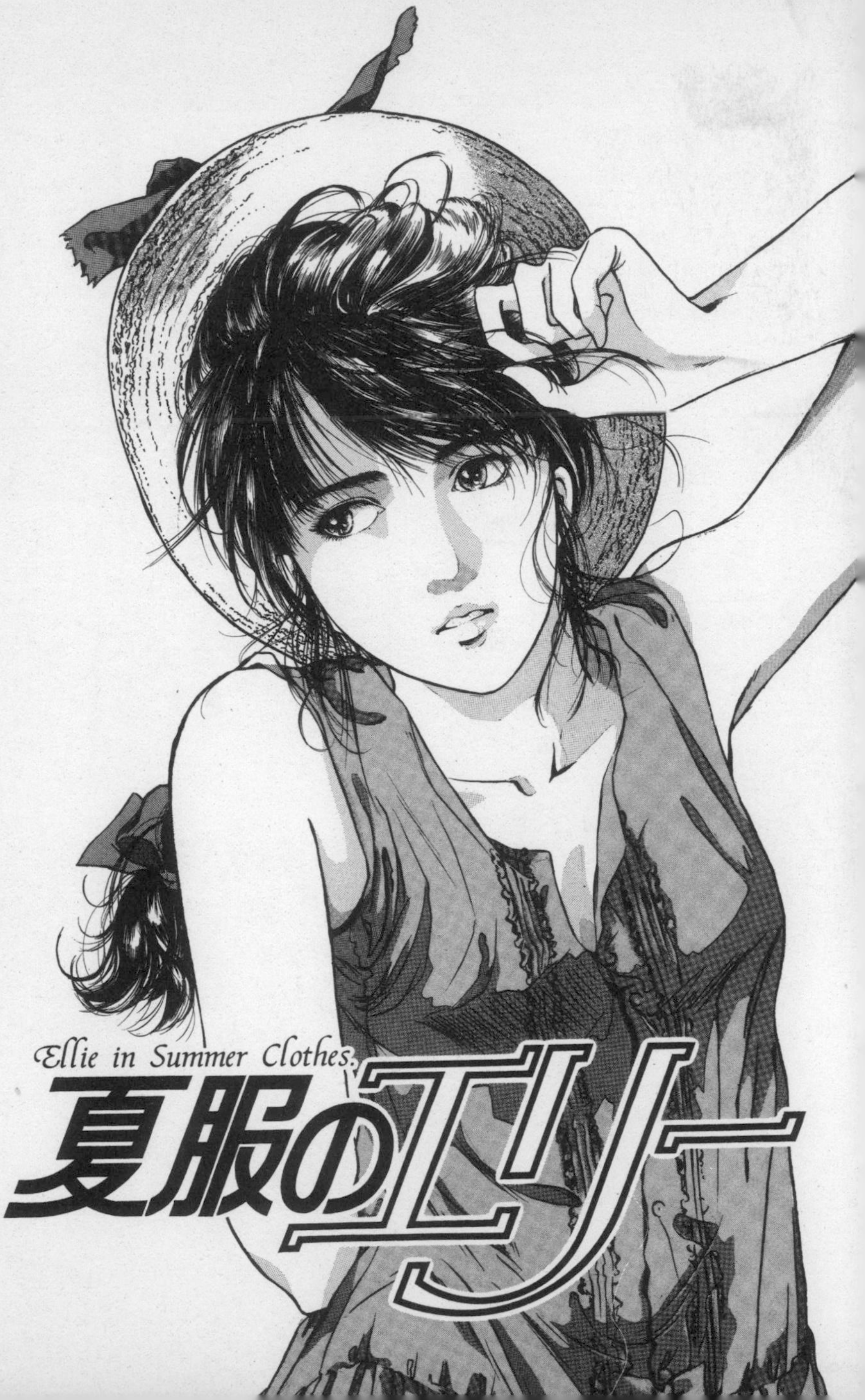
Ellie in Summer Clothes.
夏服のエリー

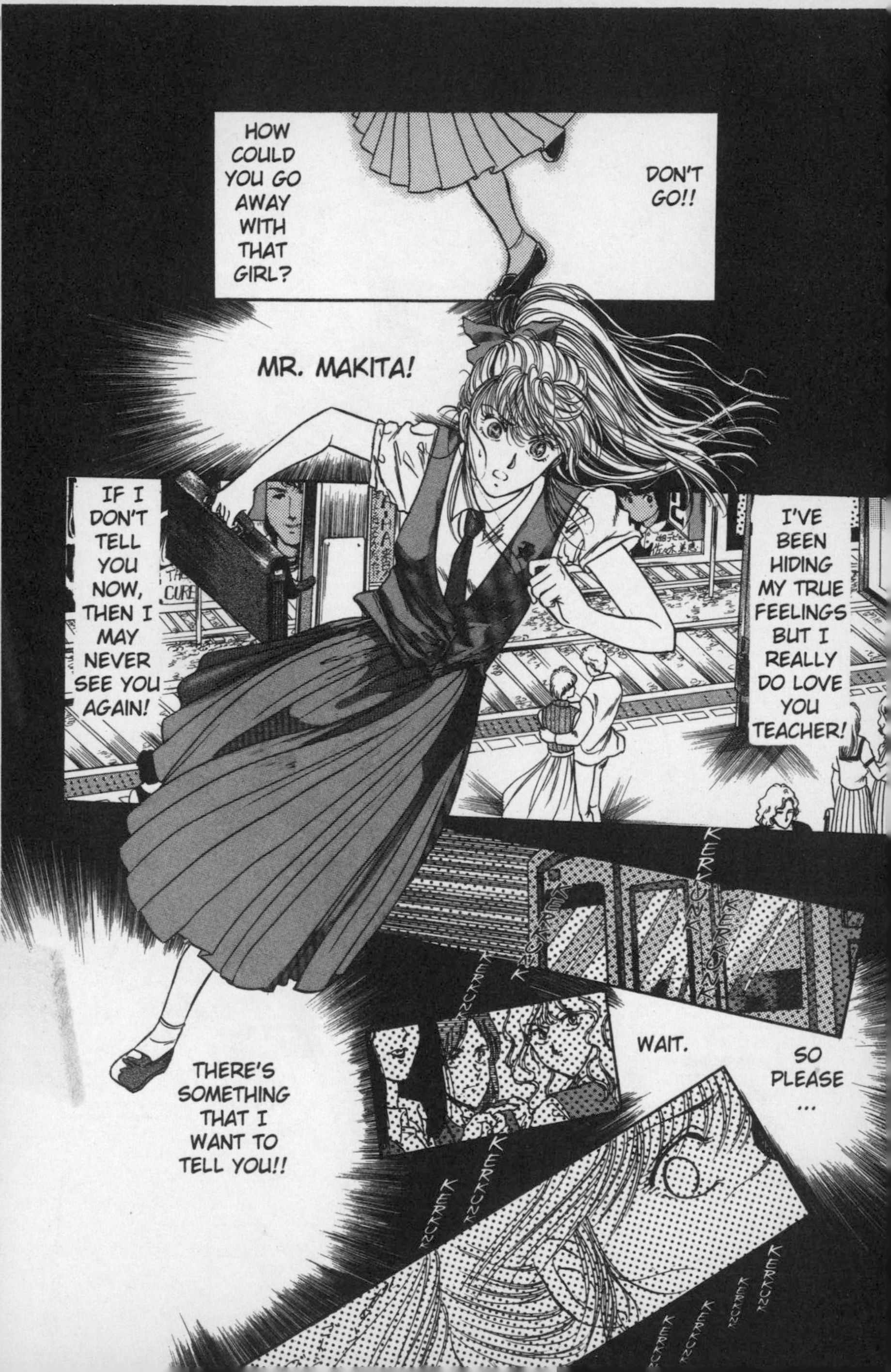
DON'T GO!!
HOW COULD YOU GO AWAY WITH THAT GIRL?
MR. MAKITA!
I'VE BEEN HIDING MY TRUE FEELINGS BUT I REALLY DO LOVE YOU TEACHER!
IF I DON'T TELL YOU NOW, THEN I MAY NEVER SEE YOU AGAIN!
KERKUNK
SO PLEASE ...
WAIT.
THERE'S SOMETHING THAT I WANT TO TELL YOU!!

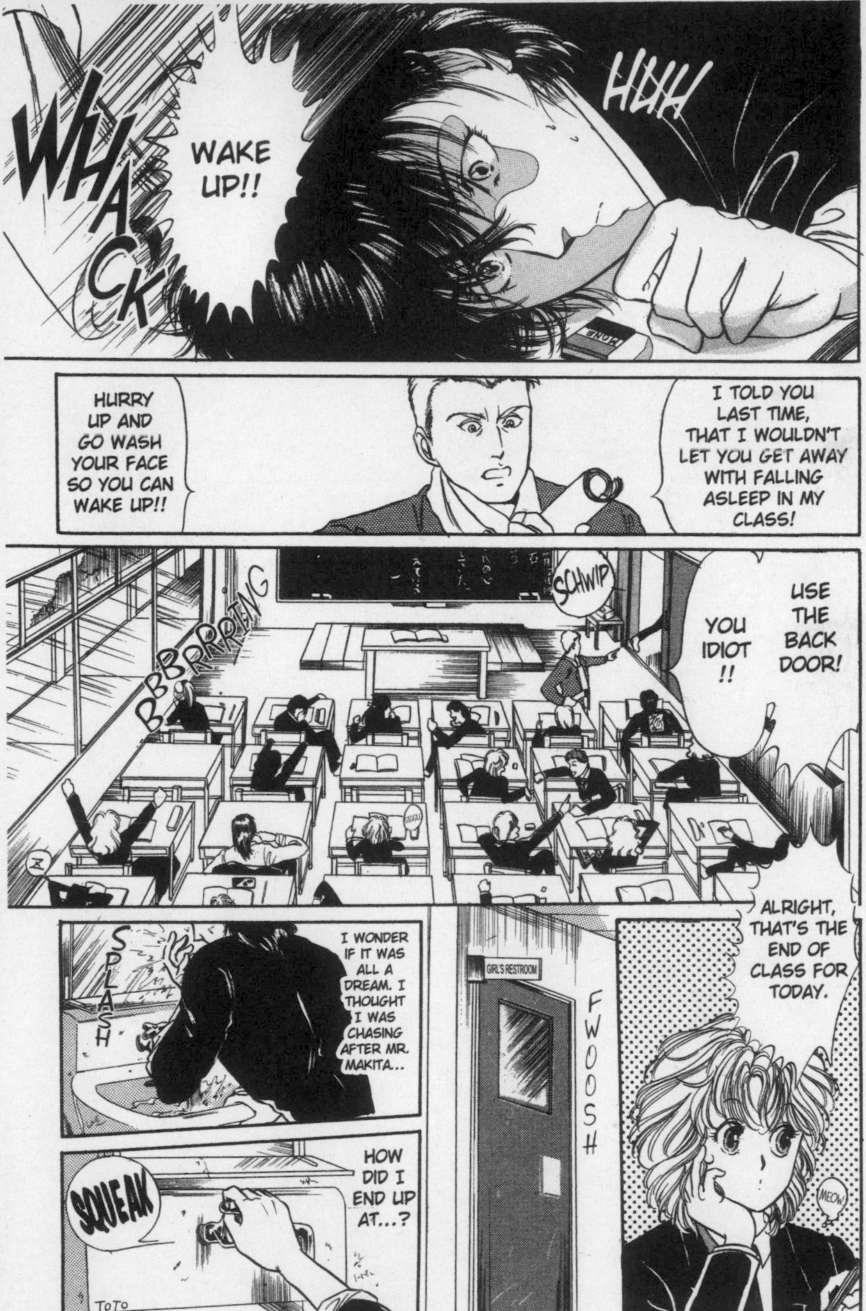
HUH
WAKE UP!!
WHACK
I TOLD YOU LAST TIME, THAT I WOULDN'T LET YOU GET AWAY WITH FALLING ASLEEP IN MY CLASS!
HURRY UP AND GO WASH YOUR FACE SO YOU CAN WAKE UP!!
USE THE BACK DOOR!
YOU IDIOT !!
SCHWIP
BBBRRRING
ALRIGHT, THAT'S THE END OF CLASS FOR TODAY.
MEOW
GIRL'S RESTROOM
FWOOSH
I WONDER IF IT WAS ALL A DREAM. I THOUGHT I WAS CHASING AFTER MR. MAKITA...
SPLASH
HOW DID I END UP AT...?
SQUEAK
TOTO

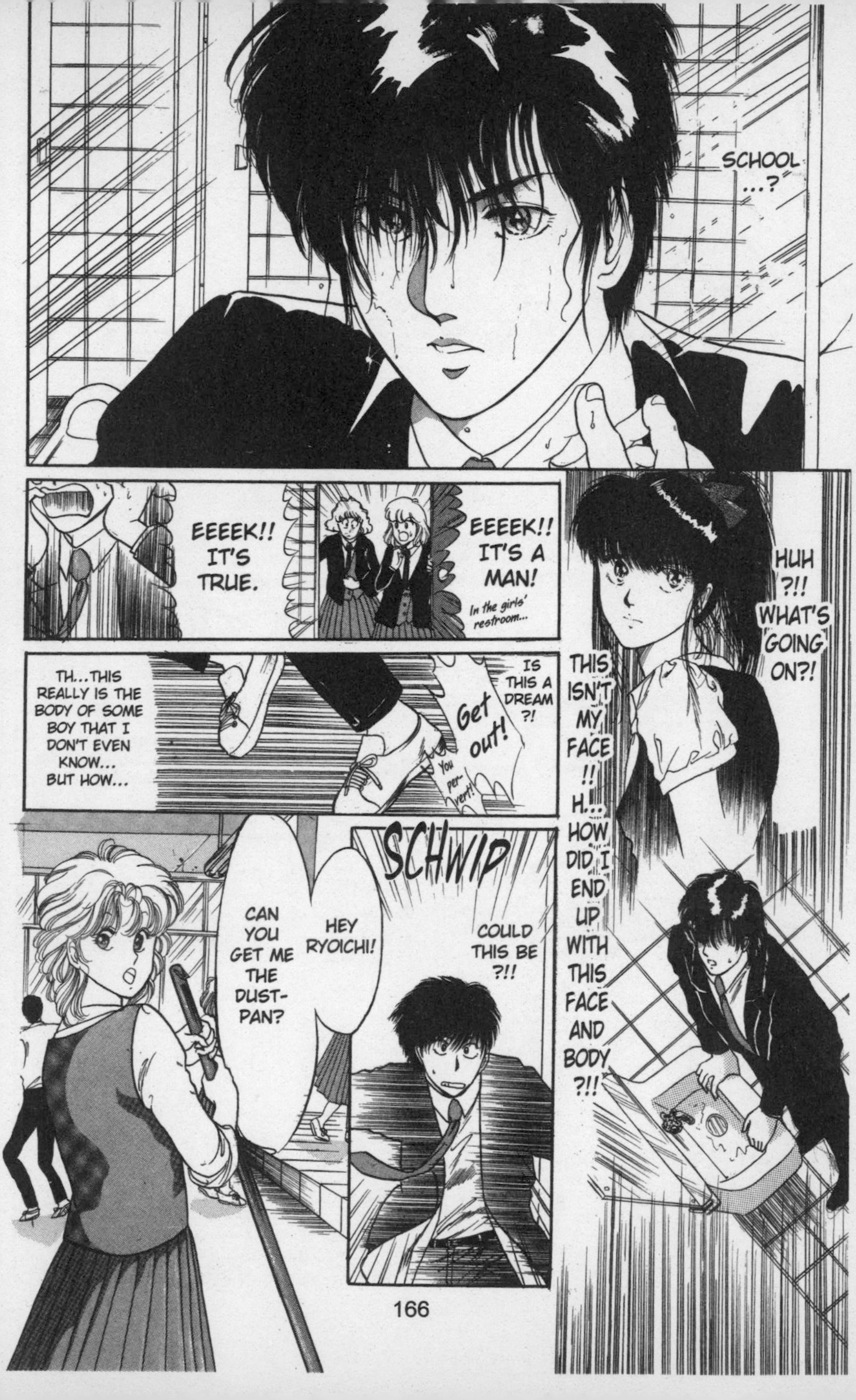
SCHOOL ...?
HUH ?!! WHAT'S GOING ON?!
THIS ISN'T MY FACE !! H... HOW DID I END UP WITH THIS FACE AND BODY ?!!
EEEEK!! IT'S A MAN!
In the girls' restroom...
EEEEK!! IT'S TRUE.
IS THIS A DREAM ?!
Get out!
You pervert!
TH...THIS REALLY IS THE BODY OF SOME BOY THAT I DON'T EVEN KNOW... BUT HOW...
SCHWIP
COULD THIS BE ?!!
HEY RYOICHI!
CAN YOU GET ME THE DUST-PAN?

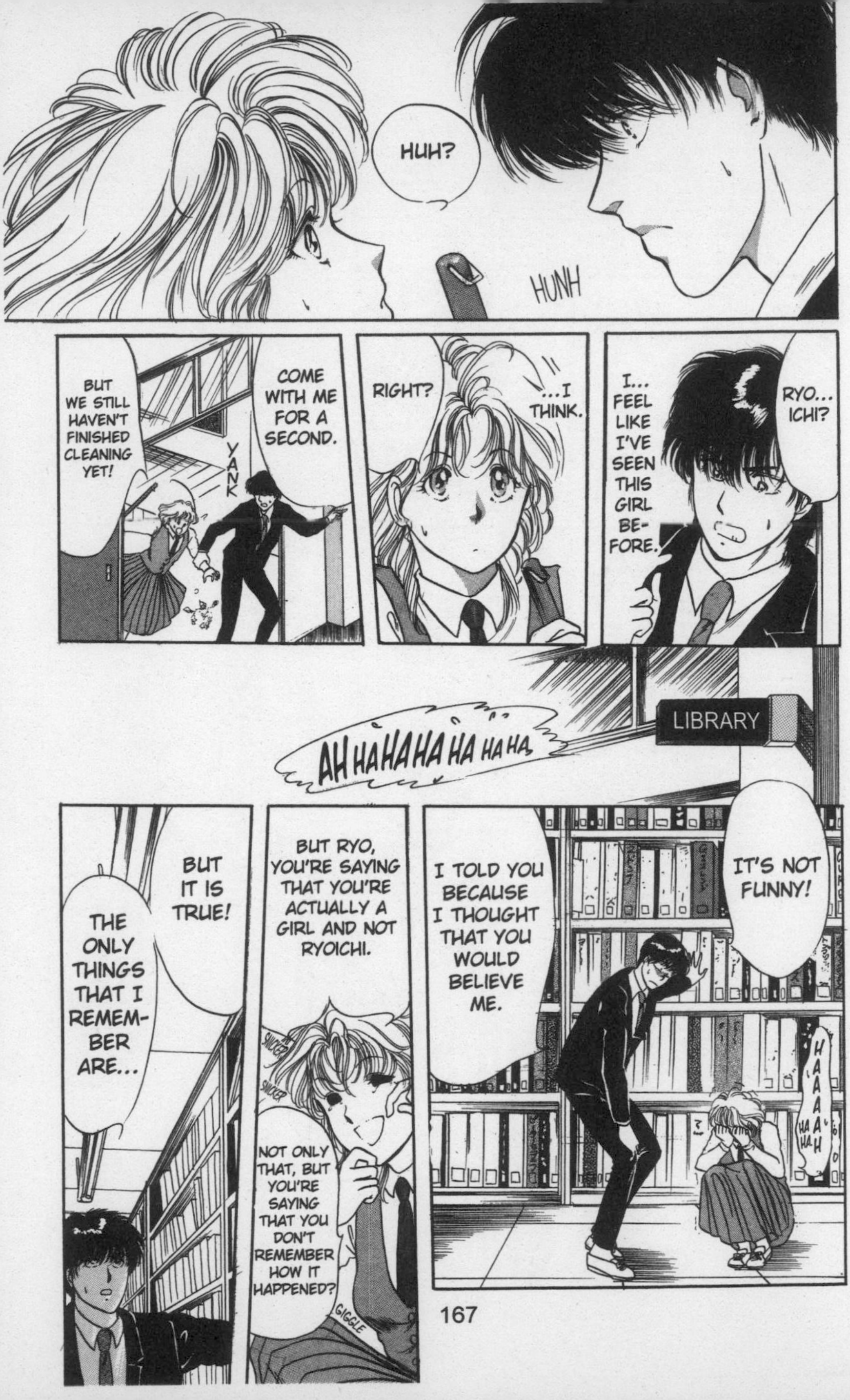
HUH?
HUNH
RYO... ICHI?
I... FEEL LIKE I'VE SEEN THIS GIRL BEFORE.
...I THINK.
RIGHT?
COME WITH ME FOR A SECOND.
YANK
BUT WE STILL HAVEN'T FINISHED CLEANING YET!
LIBRARY
AH HA HA HA HA HA HA
IT'S NOT FUNNY!
HAAAAH
HA HA
I TOLD YOU BECAUSE I THOUGHT THAT YOU WOULD BELIEVE ME.
BUT RYO, YOU'RE SAYING THAT YOU'RE ACTUALLY A GIRL AND NOT RYOICHI.
SNICKER
SNICKER
NOT ONLY THAT, BUT YOU'RE SAYING THAT YOU DON'T REMEMBER HOW IT HAPPENED?
GIGGLE
BUT IT IS TRUE!
THE ONLY THINGS THAT I REMEMBER ARE...

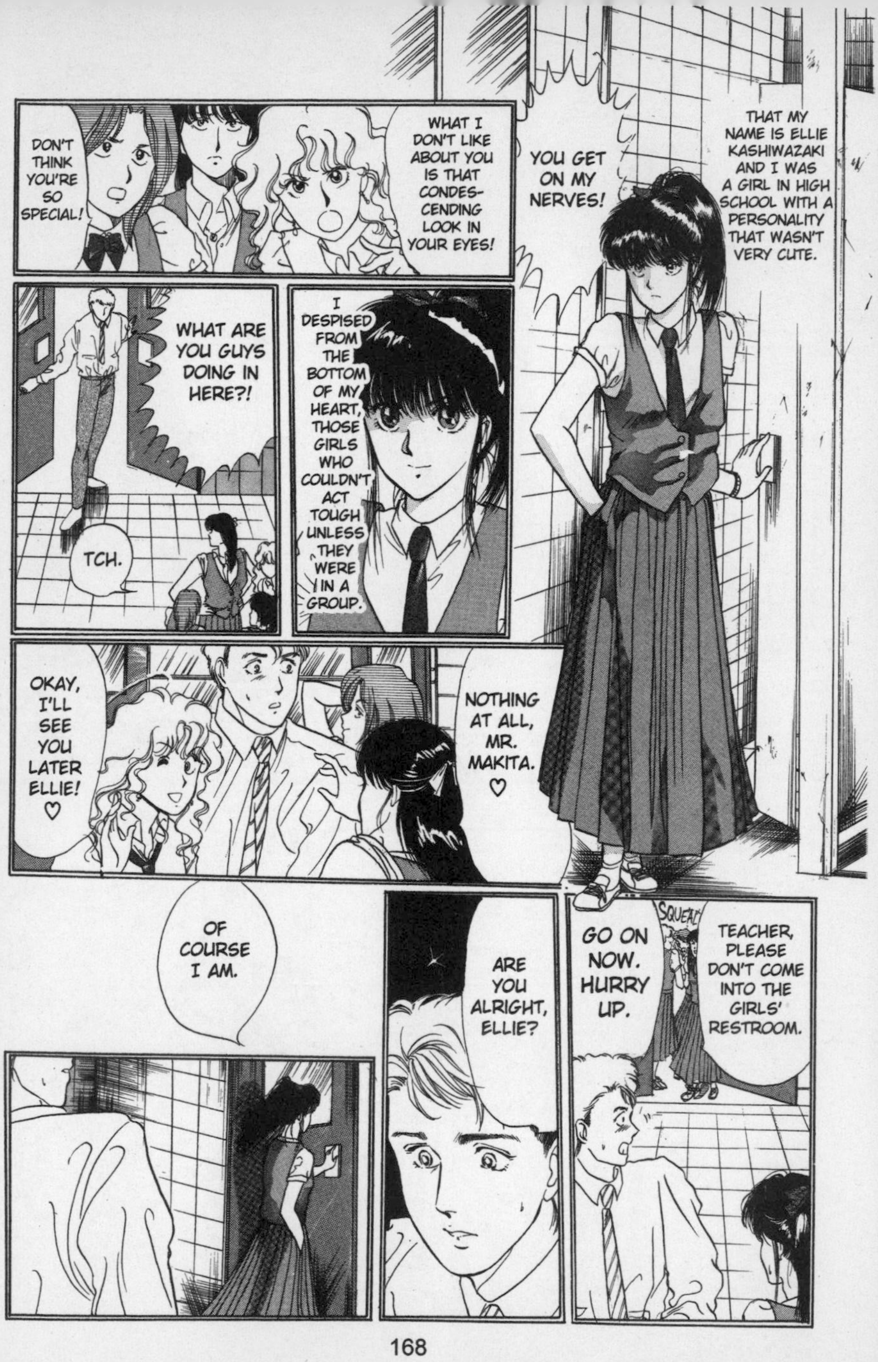
THAT MY NAME IS ELLIE KASHIWAZAKI AND I WAS A GIRL IN HIGH SCHOOL WITH A PERSONALITY THAT WASN'T VERY CUTE.
YOU GET ON MY NERVES!
WHAT I DON'T LIKE ABOUT YOU IS THAT CONDES-CENDING LOOK IN YOUR EYES!
DON'T THINK YOU'RE SO SPECIAL!
I DESPISED FROM THE BOTTOM OF MY HEART, THOSE GIRLS WHO COULDN'T ACT TOUGH UNLESS THEY WERE IN A GROUP.
WHAT ARE YOU GUYS DOING IN HERE?!
TCH.
NOTHING AT ALL, MR. MAKITA. ♡
OKAY, I'LL SEE YOU LATER ELLIE! ♡
TEACHER, PLEASE DON'T COME INTO THE GIRLS' RESTROOM.
SQUEAL
GO ON NOW. HURRY UP.
ARE YOU ALRIGHT, ELLIE?
OF COURSE I AM.

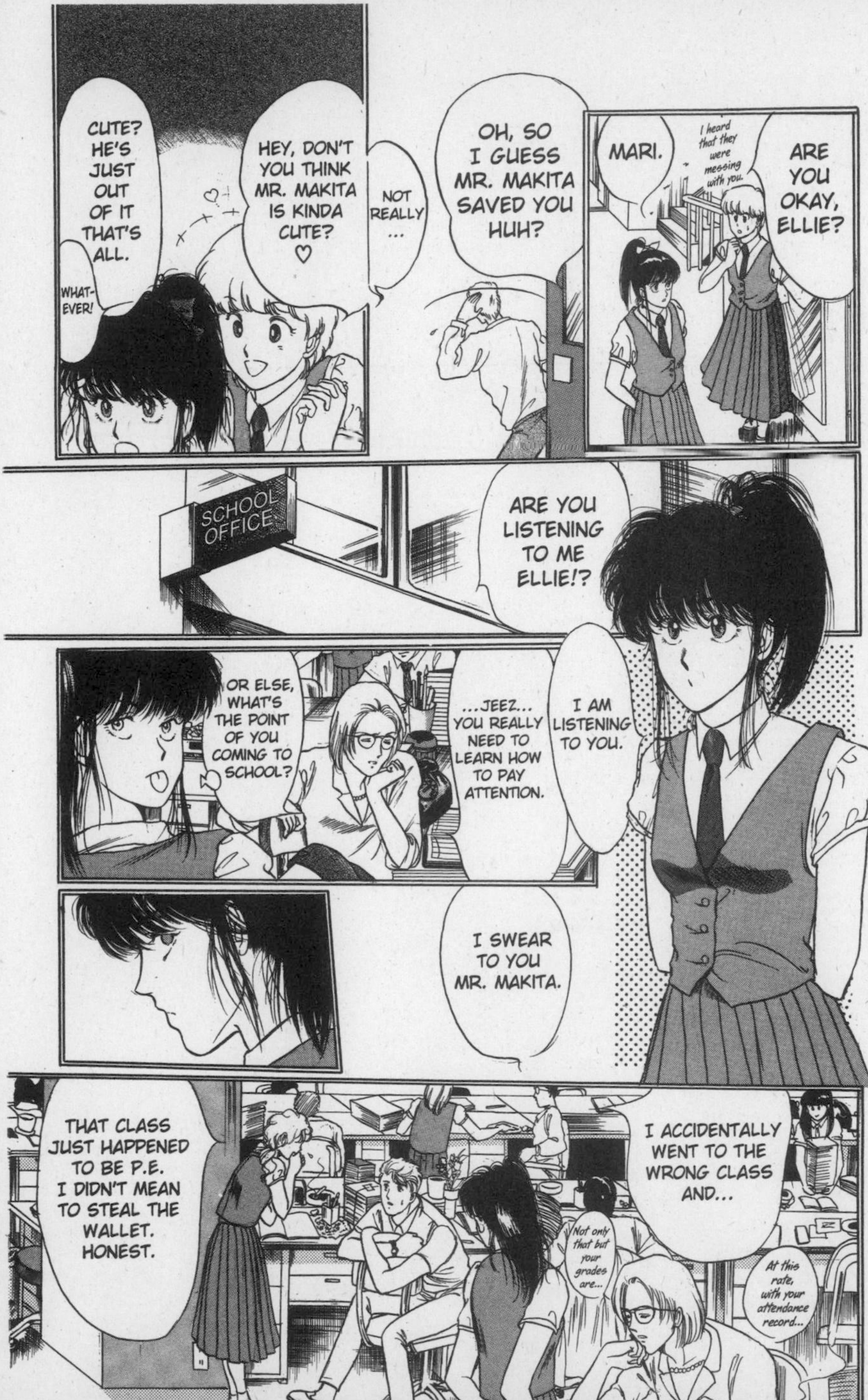
ARE YOU OKAY, ELLIE?
I heard that they were messing with you.
MARI.
OH, SO I GUESS MR. MAKITA SAVED YOU HUH?
HEY, DON'T YOU THINK MR. MAKITA IS KINDA CUTE? ♡
NOT REALLY ...
CUTE? HE'S JUST OUT OF IT THAT'S ALL.
WHAT-EVER!
ARE YOU LISTENING TO ME ELLIE!?
I AM LISTENING TO YOU.
I SWEAR TO YOU MR. MAKITA.
SCHOOL OFFICE
...JEEZ... YOU REALLY NEED TO LEARN HOW TO PAY ATTENTION.
OR ELSE, WHAT'S THE POINT OF YOU COMING TO SCHOOL?
I ACCIDENTALLY WENT TO THE WRONG CLASS AND...
At this rate, with your attendance record...
Not only that but your grades are...
THAT CLASS JUST HAPPENED TO BE P.E. I DIDN'T MEAN TO STEAL THE WALLET. HONEST.

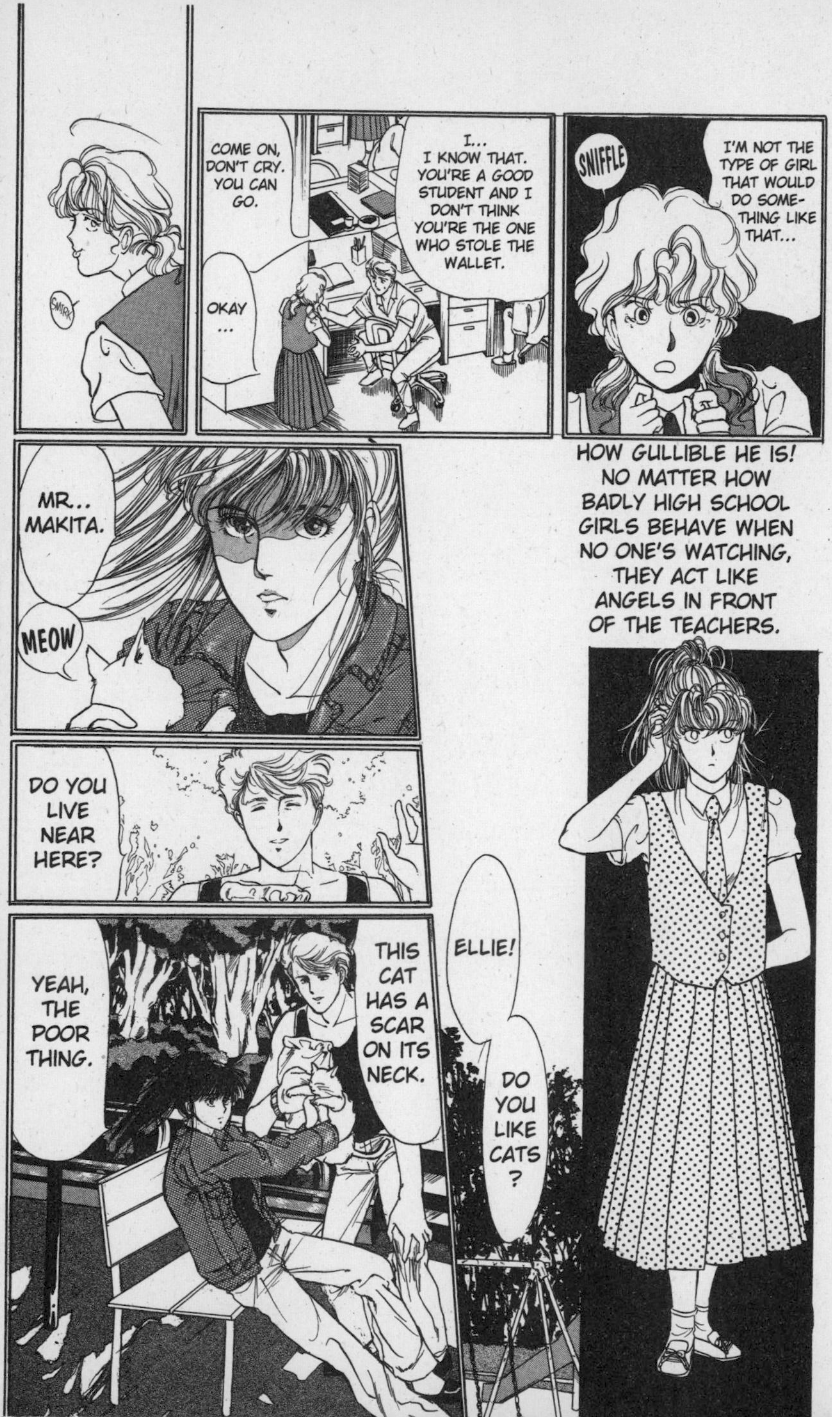
SNIFFLE
I'M NOT THE TYPE OF GIRL THAT WOULD DO SOMETHING LIKE THAT...
I... I KNOW THAT. YOU'RE A GOOD STUDENT AND I DON'T THINK YOU'RE THE ONE WHO STOLE THE WALLET.
COME ON, DON'T CRY. YOU CAN GO.
OKAY ...
SMIRK
HOW GULLIBLE HE IS! NO MATTER HOW BADLY HIGH SCHOOL GIRLS BEHAVE WHEN NO ONE'S WATCHING, THEY ACT LIKE ANGELS IN FRONT OF THE TEACHERS.
MR... MAKITA.
MEOW
DO YOU LIVE NEAR HERE?
ELLIE!
DO YOU LIKE CATS ?
THIS CAT HAS A SCAR ON ITS NECK.
YEAH, THE POOR THING.

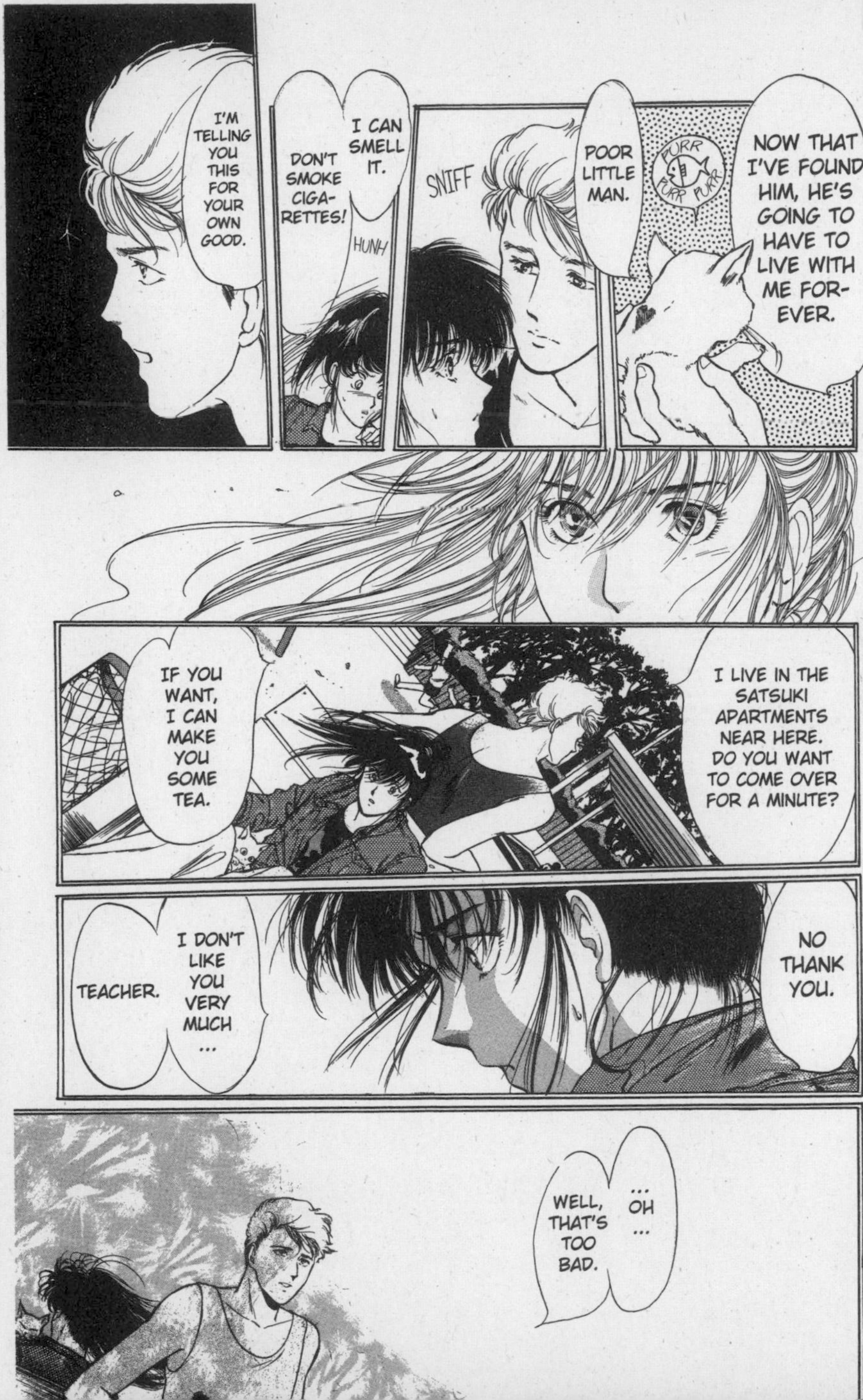
NOW THAT I'VE FOUND HIM, HE'S GOING TO HAVE TO LIVE WITH ME FOR-EVER.
PURR PURR PURR
POOR LITTLE MAN.
SNIFF
I CAN SMELL IT.
DON'T SMOKE CIGA-RETTES!
HUNH
I'M TELLING YOU THIS FOR YOUR OWN GOOD.
I LIVE IN THE SATSUKI APARTMENTS NEAR HERE. DO YOU WANT TO COME OVER FOR A MINUTE?
IF YOU WANT, I CAN MAKE YOU SOME TEA.
NO THANK YOU.
I DON'T LIKE YOU VERY MUCH ...
TEACHER.
... OH ...
WELL, THAT'S TOO BAD.

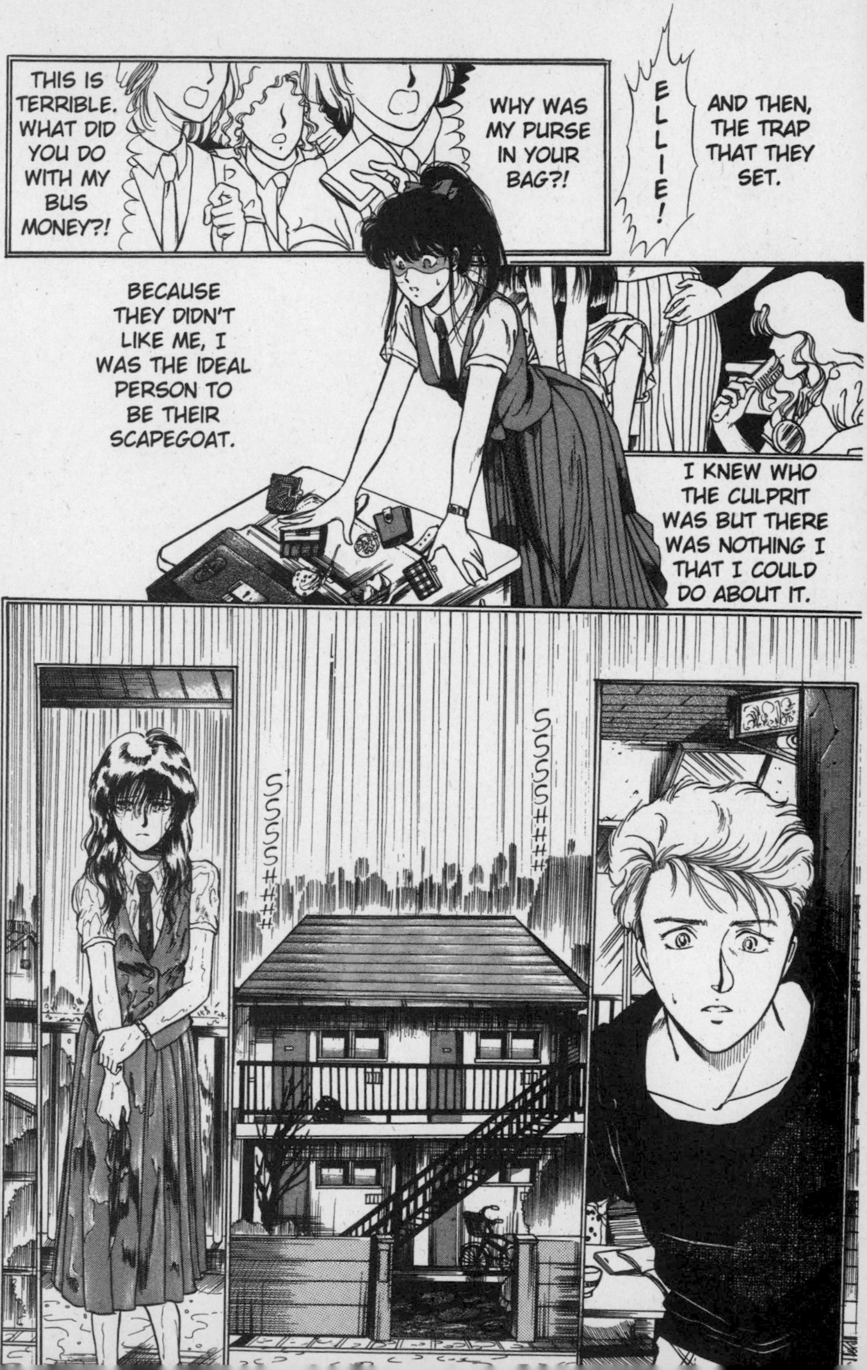
AND THEN, THE TRAP THAT THEY SET.
ELLIE!
WHY WAS MY PURSE IN YOUR BAG?!
THIS IS TERRIBLE. WHAT DID YOU DO WITH MY BUS MONEY?!
BECAUSE THEY DIDN'T LIKE ME, I WAS THE IDEAL PERSON TO BE THEIR SCAPEGOAT.
I KNEW WHO THE CULPRIT WAS BUT THERE WAS NOTHING I THAT I COULD DO ABOUT IT.
SSSSSHHHH
SSSSHHHH

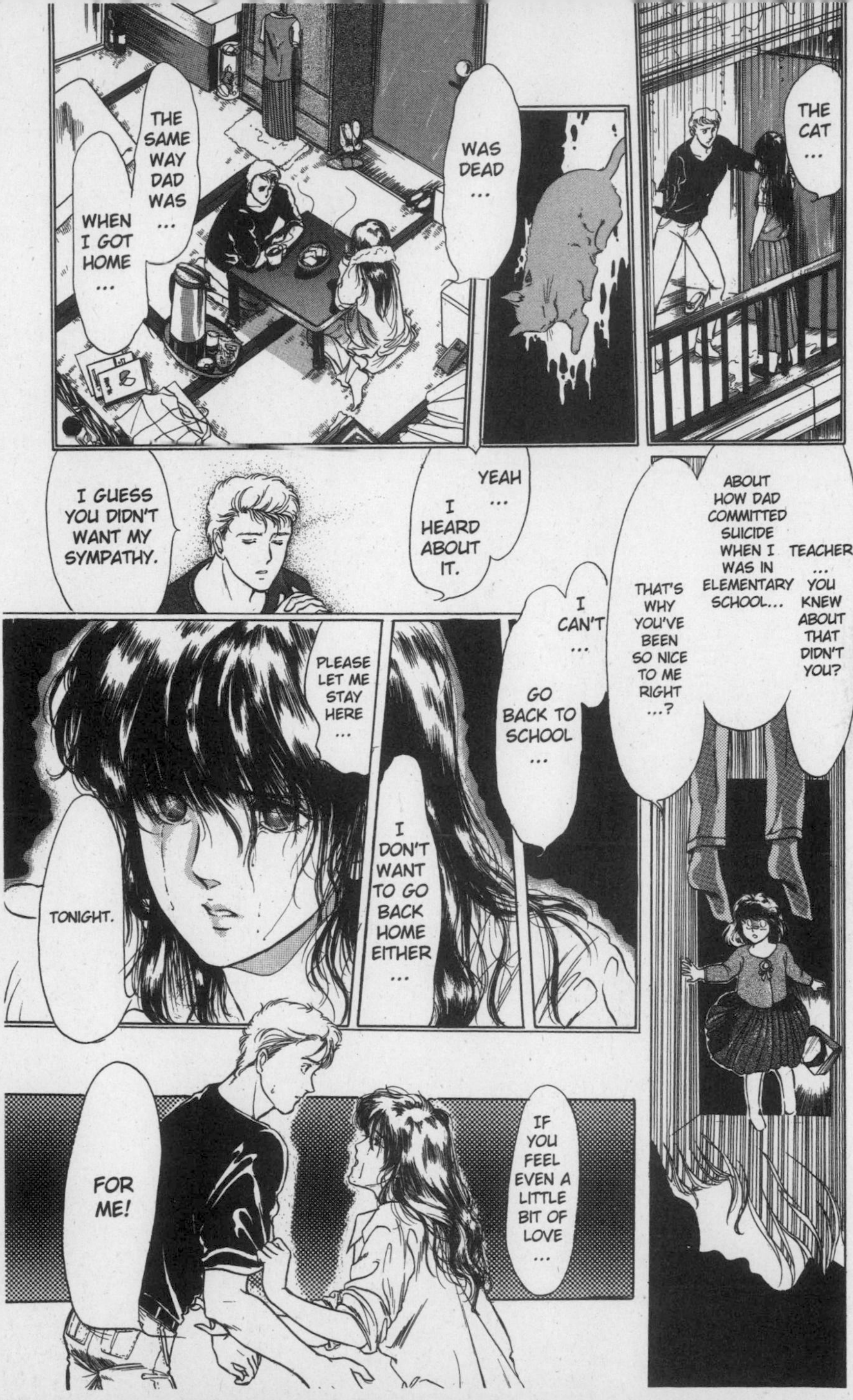
THE CAT ...
WAS DEAD ...
THE SAME WAY DAD WAS ...
WHEN I GOT HOME ...
TEACHER ... YOU KNEW ABOUT THAT DIDN'T YOU?
ABOUT HOW DAD COMMITTED SUICIDE WHEN I WAS IN ELEMENTARY SCHOOL...
THAT'S WHY YOU'VE BEEN SO NICE TO ME RIGHT ...?
YEAH ... I HEARD ABOUT IT.
I GUESS YOU DIDN'T WANT MY SYMPATHY.
I CAN'T ... GO BACK TO SCHOOL ...
I DON'T WANT TO GO BACK HOME EITHER ...
PLEASE LET ME STAY HERE ...
TONIGHT.
IF YOU FEEL EVEN A LITTLE BIT OF LOVE ...
FOR ME!

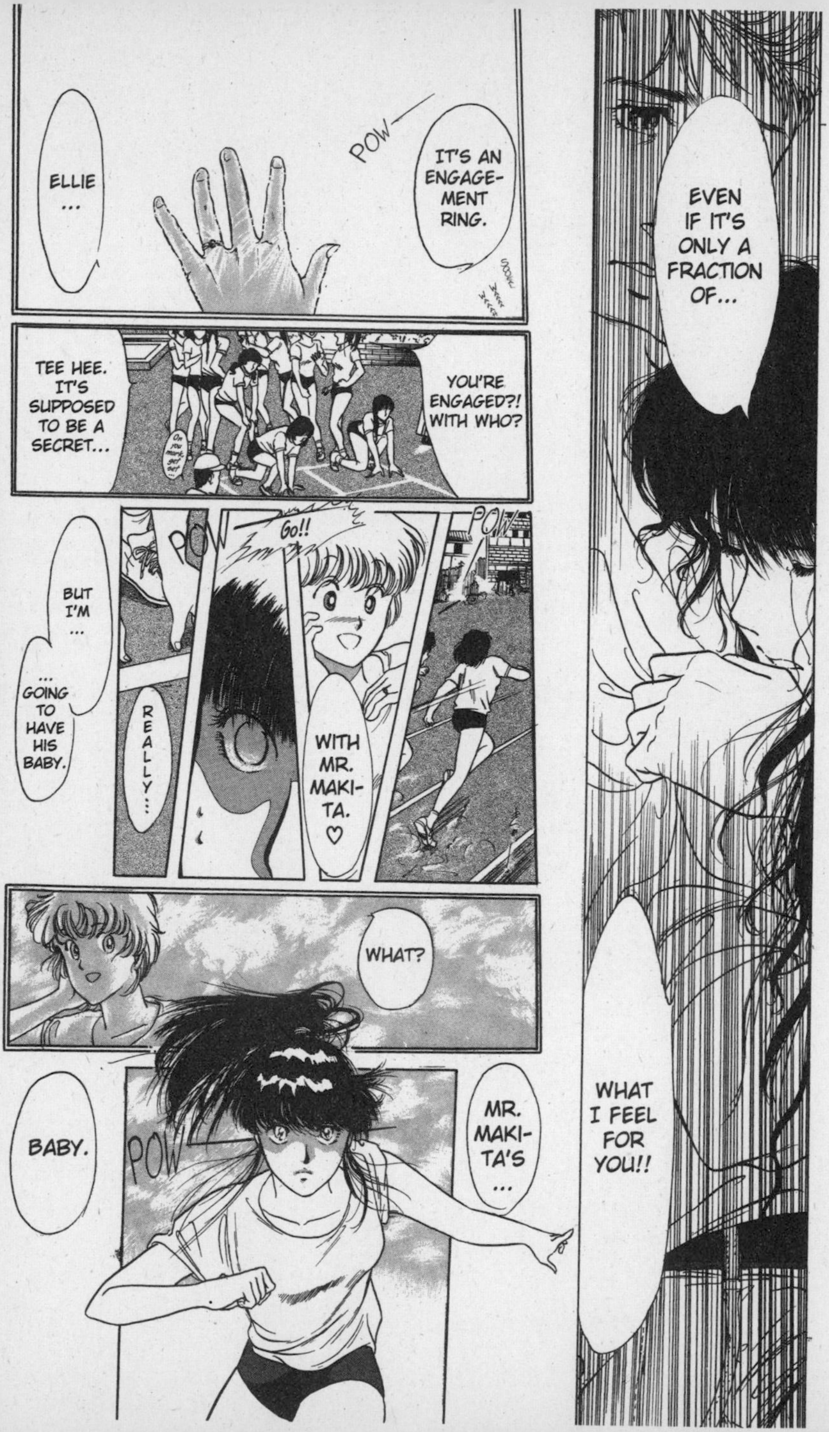
EVEN IF IT'S ONLY A FRACTION OF...
WHAT I FEEL FOR YOU!!
POW
IT'S AN ENGAGEMENT RING.
ELLIE ...
YOU'RE ENGAGED?! WITH WHO?
TEE HEE. IT'S SUPPOSED TO BE A SECRET...
POW
WITH MR. MAKITA. ♡
Go!!
REALLY...
POW
BUT I'M ...
... GOING TO HAVE HIS BABY.
WHAT?
MR. MAKITA'S ...
POW
BABY.

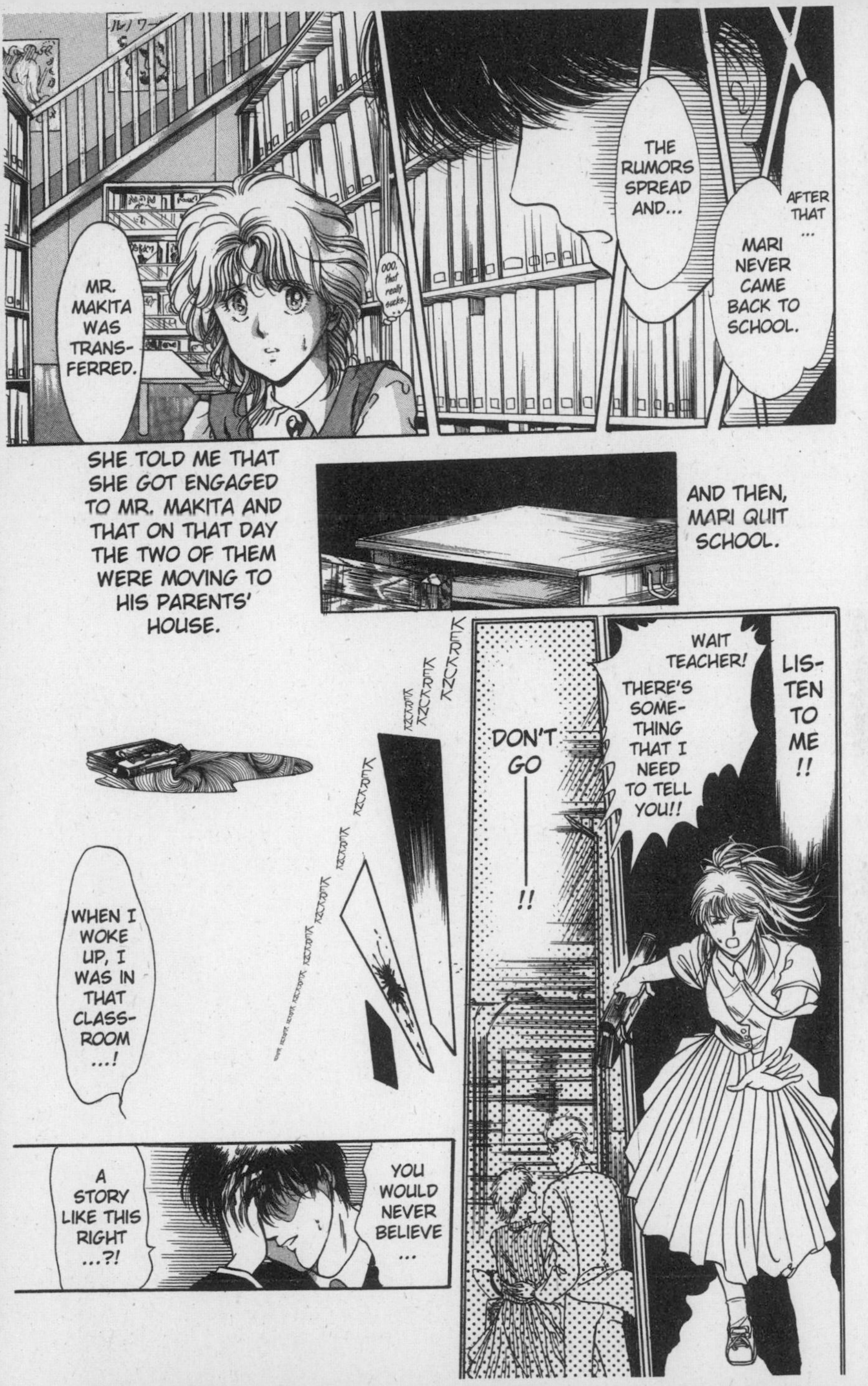
AFTER THAT ... MARI NEVER CAME BACK TO SCHOOL.
THE RUMORS SPREAD AND...
OOO, that really sucks...
MR. MAKITA WAS TRANS-FERRED.
AND THEN, MARI QUIT SCHOOL.
SHE TOLD ME THAT SHE GOT ENGAGED TO MR. MAKITA AND THAT ON THAT DAY THE TWO OF THEM WERE MOVING TO HIS PARENTS' HOUSE.
LIS-TEN TO ME!!
WAIT TEACHER!
THERE'S SOME-THING THAT I NEED TO TELL YOU!!
DON'T GO——!!
KERKUNK KERKUNK KERKUNK
KERKUNK KERKUNK KERKUNK KERKUNK KERKUNK
WHEN I WOKE UP, I WAS IN THAT CLASS-ROOM ...!
YOU WOULD NEVER BELIEVE ...
A STORY LIKE THIS RIGHT ...?!

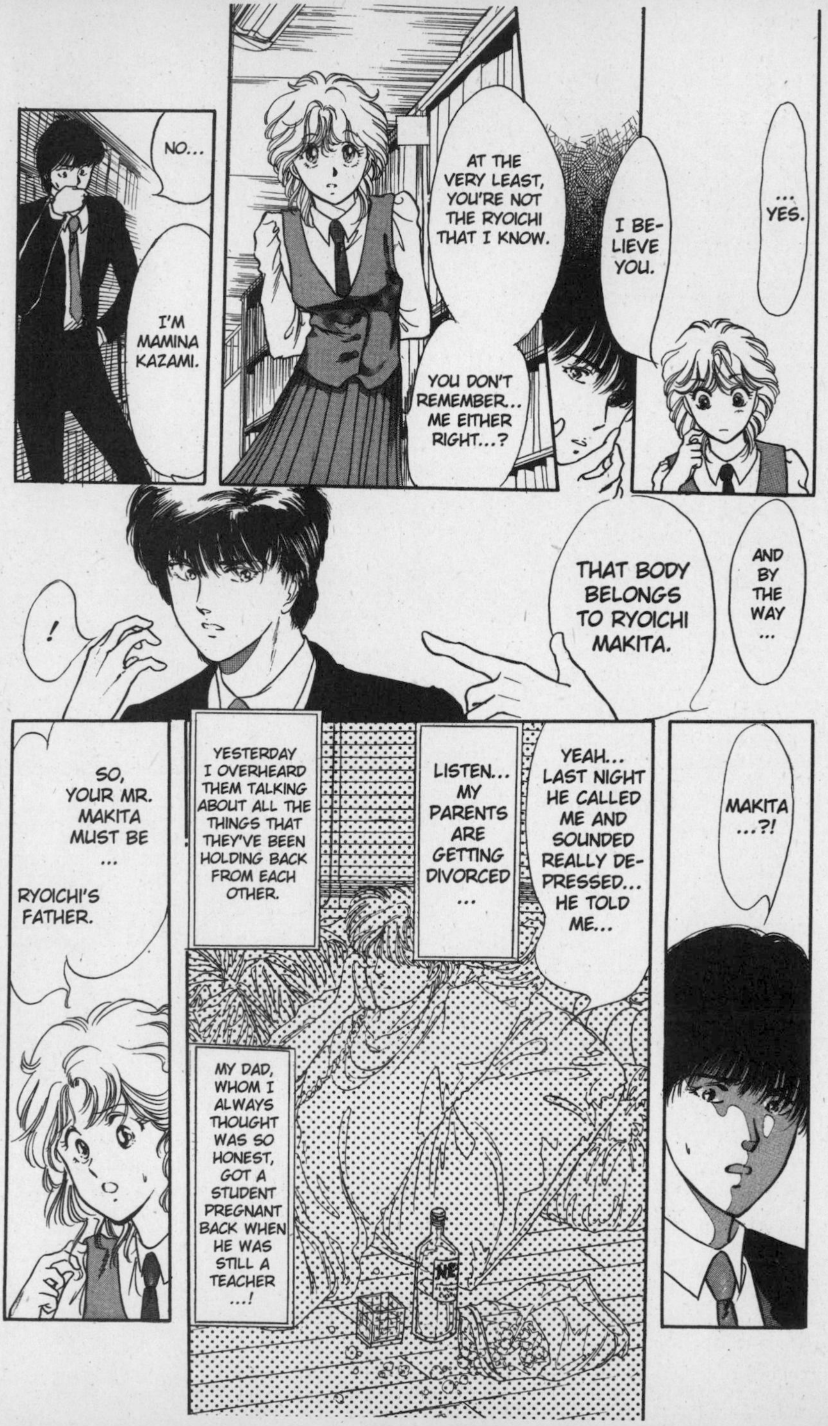
... YES.
I BE-LIEVE YOU.
AT THE VERY LEAST, YOU'RE NOT THE RYOICHI THAT I KNOW.
YOU DON'T REMEMBER... ME EITHER RIGHT...?
NO...
I'M MAMINA KAZAMI.
AND BY THE WAY ...
THAT BODY BELONGS TO RYOICHI MAKITA.
!
MAKITA ...?!
YEAH... LAST NIGHT HE CALLED ME AND SOUNDED REALLY DE-PRESSED... HE TOLD ME...
LISTEN... MY PARENTS ARE GETTING DIVORCED ...
YESTERDAY I OVERHEARD THEM TALKING ABOUT ALL THE THINGS THAT THEY'VE BEEN HOLDING BACK FROM EACH OTHER.
MY DAD, WHOM I ALWAYS THOUGHT WAS SO HONEST, GOT A STUDENT PREGNANT BACK WHEN HE WAS STILL A TEACHER ...!
SO, YOUR MR. MAKITA MUST BE ...
RYOICHI'S FATHER.

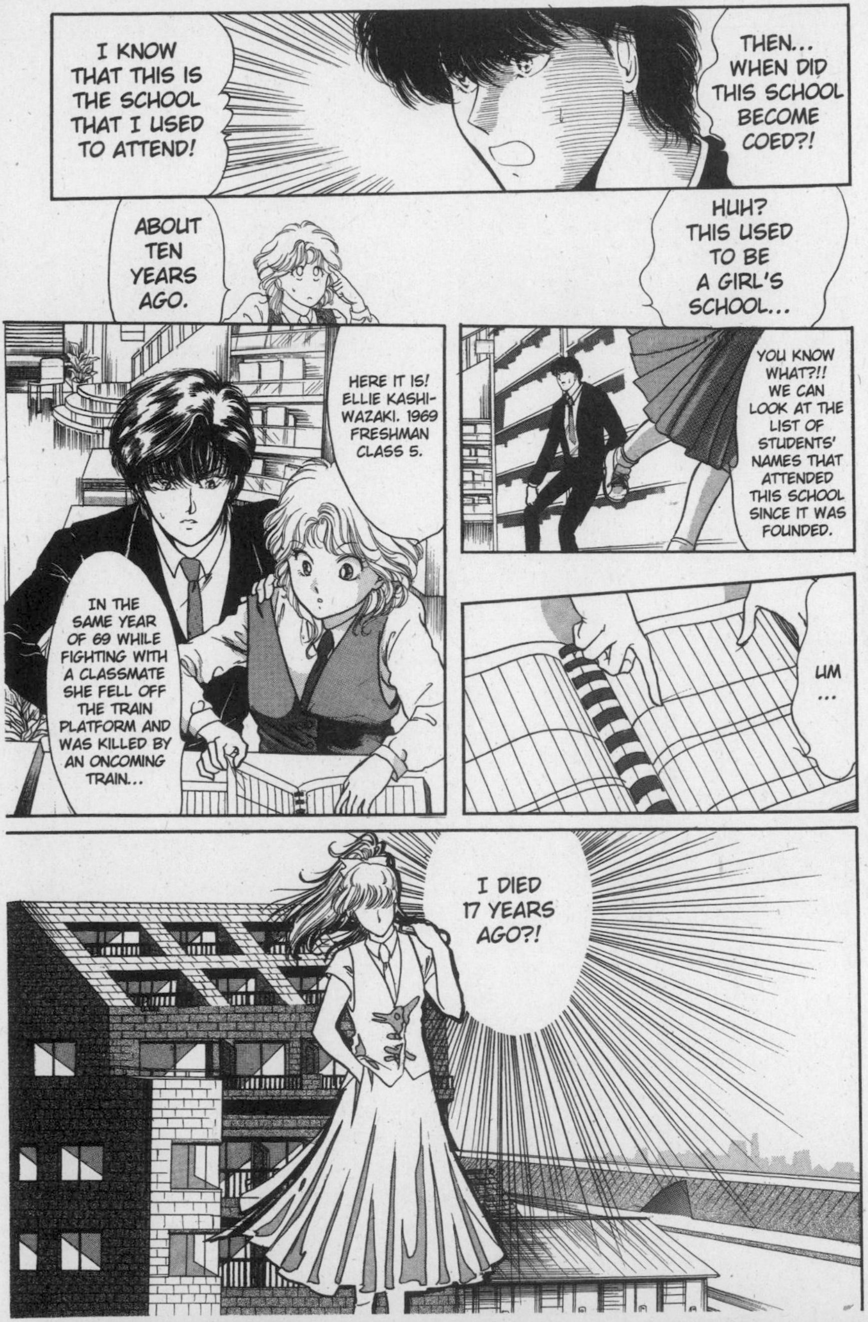
THEN... WHEN DID THIS SCHOOL BECOME COED?!
I KNOW THAT THIS IS THE SCHOOL THAT I USED TO ATTEND!
HUH? THIS USED TO BE A GIRL'S SCHOOL...
ABOUT TEN YEARS AGO.
YOU KNOW WHAT?!! WE CAN LOOK AT THE LIST OF STUDENTS' NAMES THAT ATTENDED THIS SCHOOL SINCE IT WAS FOUNDED.
UM ...
HERE IT IS! ELLIE KASHI-WAZAKI. 1969 FRESHMAN CLASS 5.
IN THE SAME YEAR OF 69 WHILE FIGHTING WITH A CLASSMATE SHE FELL OFF THE TRAIN PLATFORM AND WAS KILLED BY AN ONCOMING TRAIN...
I DIED 17 YEARS AGO?!

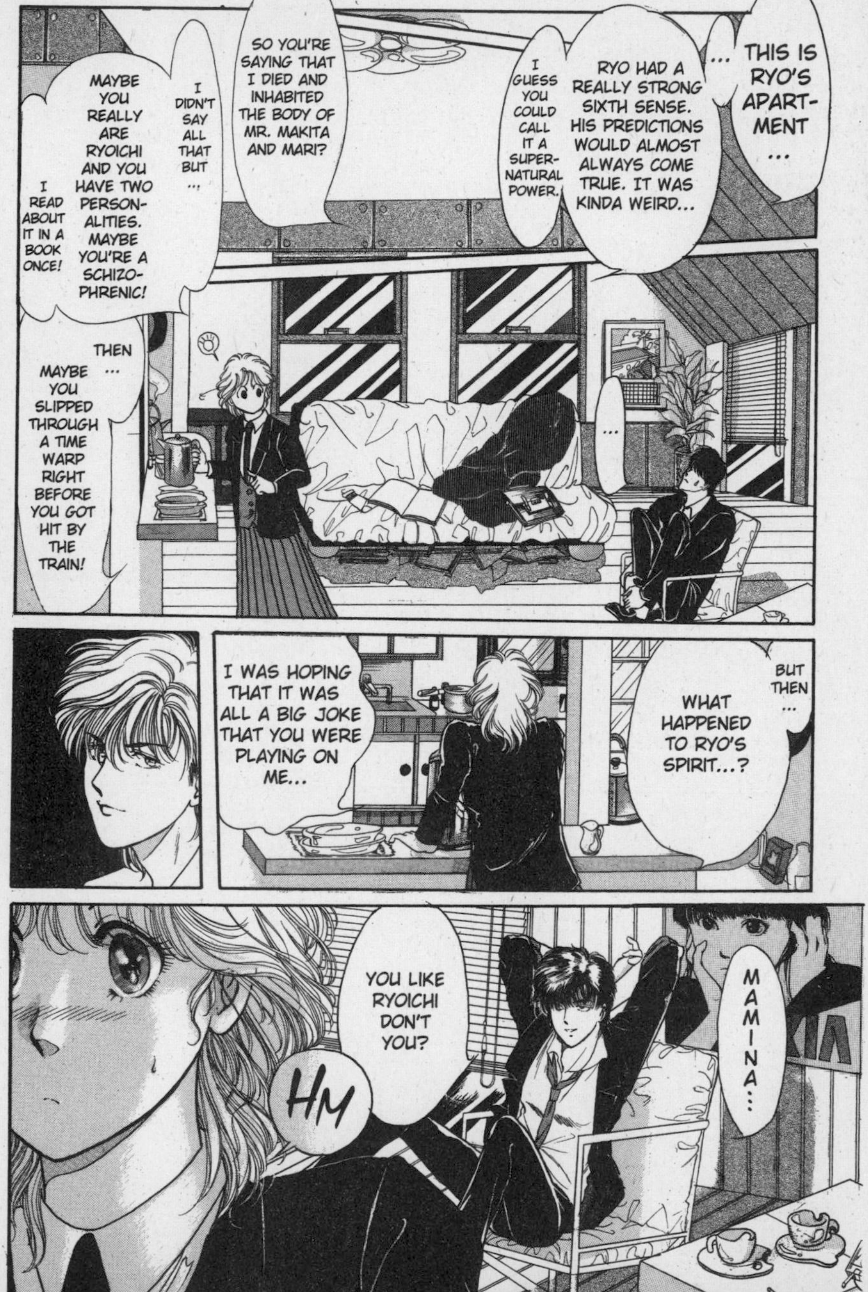
... THIS IS RYO'S APARTMENT ...
RYO HAD A REALLY STRONG SIXTH SENSE. HIS PREDICTIONS WOULD ALMOST ALWAYS COME TRUE. IT WAS KINDA WEIRD...
I GUESS YOU COULD CALL IT A SUPERNATURAL POWER.
SO YOU'RE SAYING THAT I DIED AND INHABITED THE BODY OF MR. MAKITA AND MARI?
I DIDN'T SAY ALL THAT BUT ...
MAYBE YOU REALLY ARE RYOICHI AND YOU HAVE TWO PERSONALITIES. MAYBE YOU'RE A SCHIZOPHRENIC!
I READ ABOUT IT IN A BOOK ONCE!
...
THEN ...
MAYBE YOU SLIPPED THROUGH A TIME WARP RIGHT BEFORE YOU GOT HIT BY THE TRAIN!
BUT THEN ...
WHAT HAPPENED TO RYO'S SPIRIT...?
I WAS HOPING THAT IT WAS ALL A BIG JOKE THAT YOU WERE PLAYING ON ME...
MAMINA...
YOU LIKE RYOICHI DON'T YOU?
HM

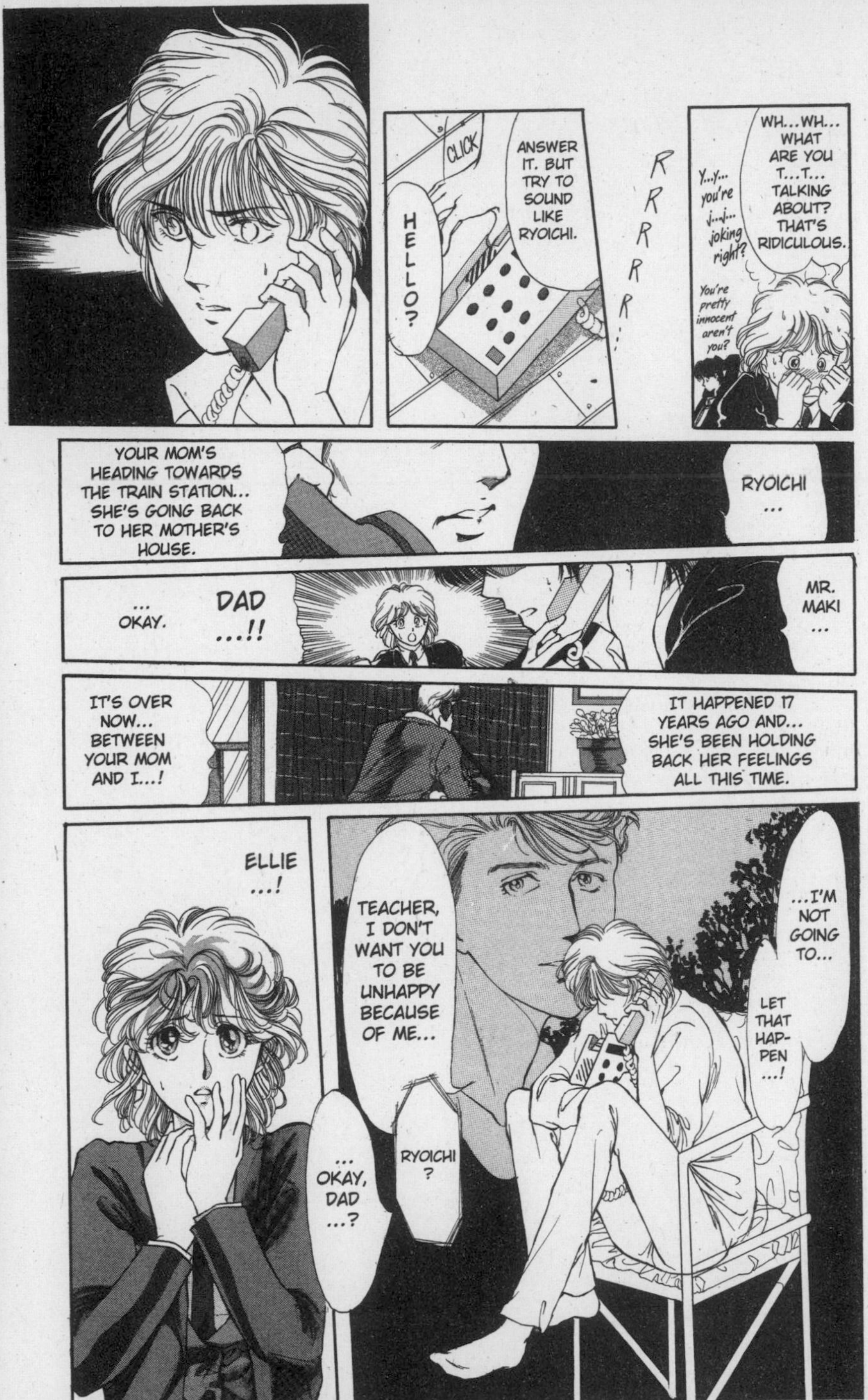
WH...WH... WHAT ARE YOU T...T... TALKING ABOUT? THAT'S RIDICULOUS.
Y...y... you're j...j... joking right?
You're pretty innocent aren't you?
RRRRR
ANSWER IT. BUT TRY TO SOUND LIKE RYOICHI.
CLICK
HELLO?
RYOICHI ...
YOUR MOM'S HEADING TOWARDS THE TRAIN STATION... SHE'S GOING BACK TO HER MOTHER'S HOUSE.
MR. MAKI ...
DAD ...!!
... OKAY.
IT HAPPENED 17 YEARS AGO AND... SHE'S BEEN HOLDING BACK HER FEELINGS ALL THIS TIME.
IT'S OVER NOW... BETWEEN YOUR MOM AND I...!
...I'M NOT GOING TO...
LET THAT HAP-PEN ...!
TEACHER, I DON'T WANT YOU TO BE UNHAPPY BECAUSE OF ME...
RYOICHI ?
... OKAY, DAD ...?
ELLIE ...!

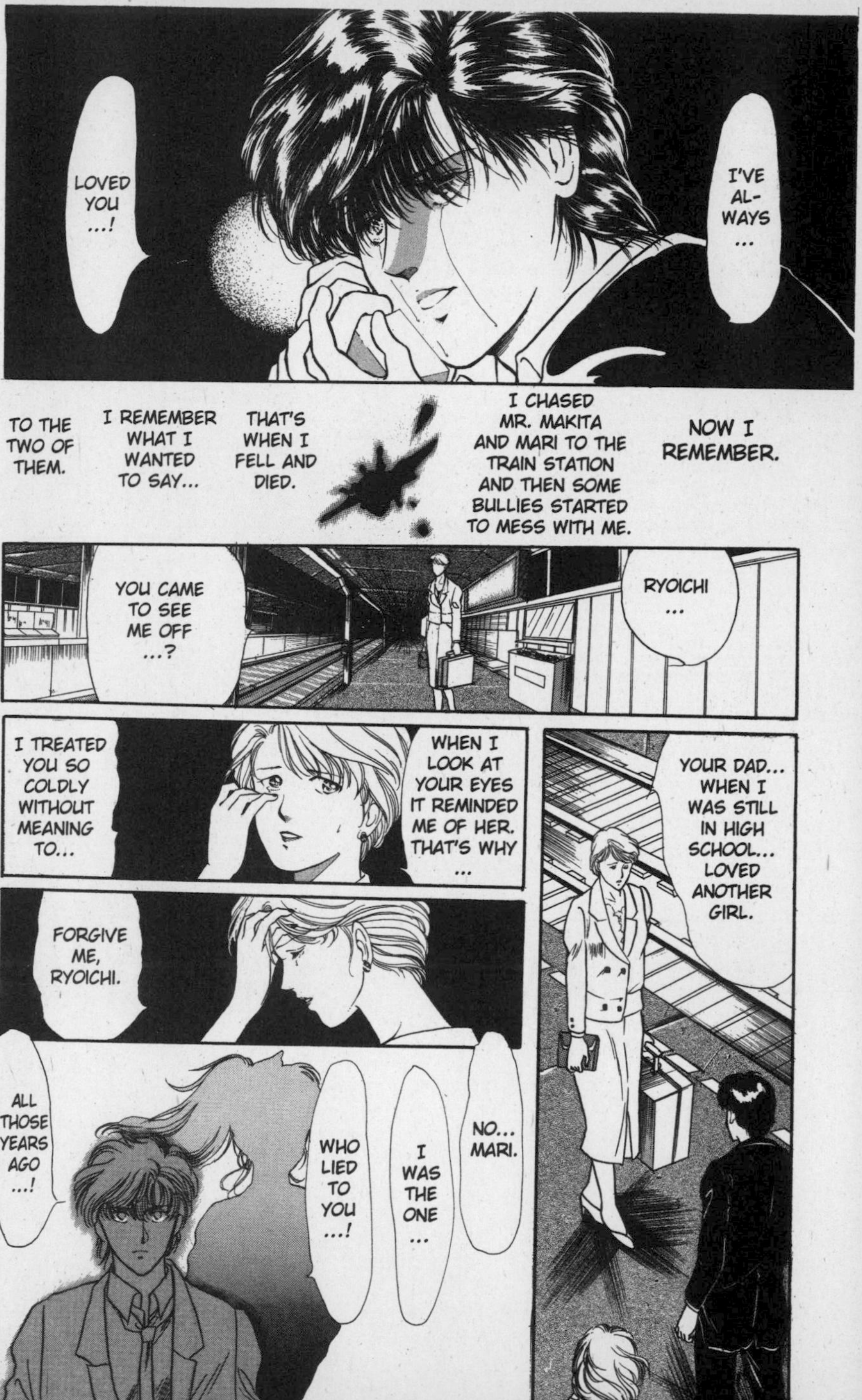
I'VE AL-WAYS ...
LOVED YOU ...!
NOW I REMEMBER.
I CHASED MR. MAKITA AND MARI TO THE TRAIN STATION AND THEN SOME BULLIES STARTED TO MESS WITH ME.
THAT'S WHEN I FELL AND DIED.
I REMEMBER WHAT I WANTED TO SAY...
TO THE TWO OF THEM.
RYOICHI ...
YOU CAME TO SEE ME OFF ...?
YOUR DAD... WHEN I WAS STILL IN HIGH SCHOOL... LOVED ANOTHER GIRL.
WHEN I LOOK AT YOUR EYES IT REMINDED ME OF HER. THAT'S WHY ...
I TREATED YOU SO COLDLY WITHOUT MEANING TO...
FORGIVE ME, RYOICHI.
NO... MARI.
I WAS THE ONE ...
WHO LIED TO YOU ...!
ALL THOSE YEARS AGO ...!

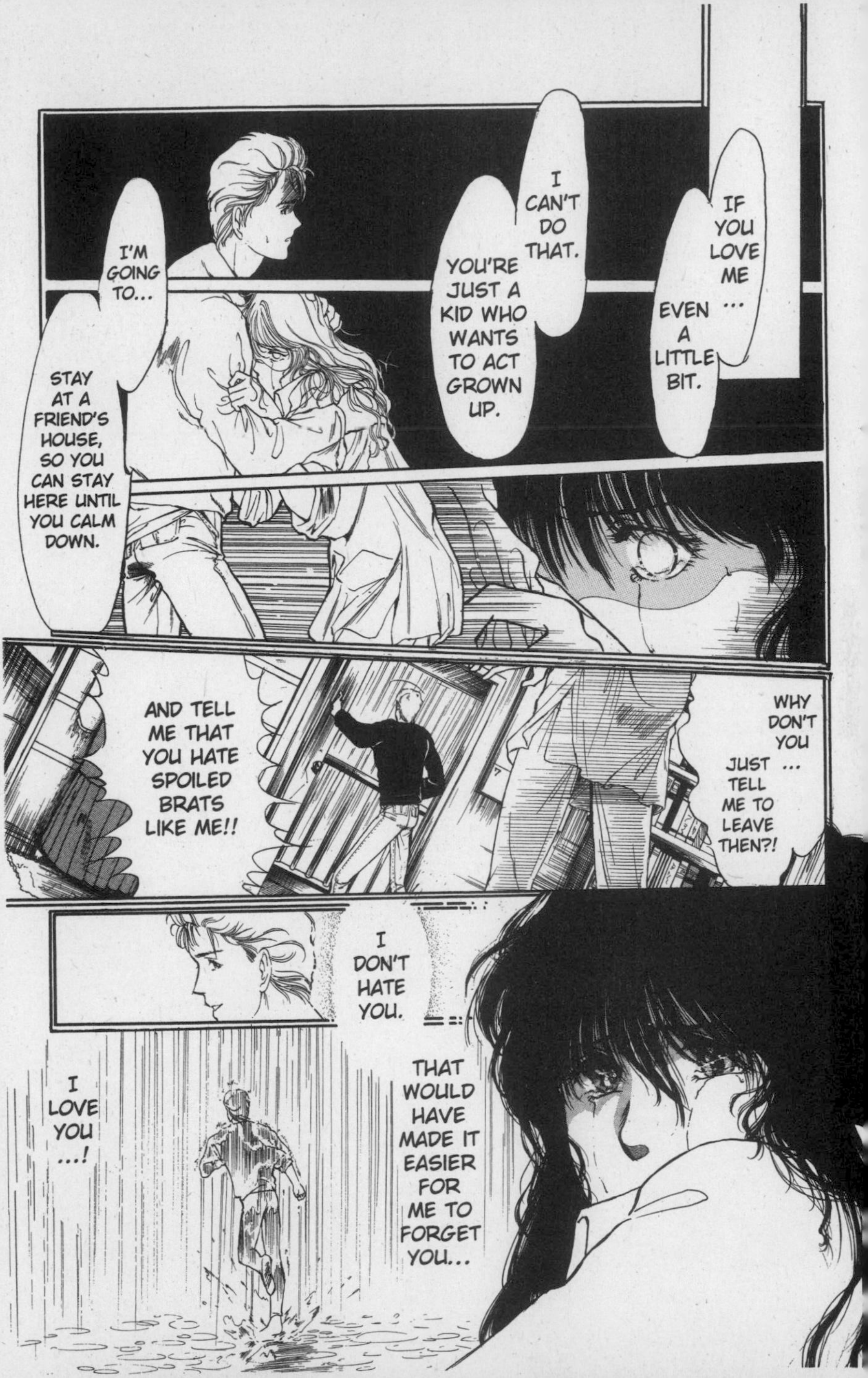
IF YOU LOVE ME ... EVEN A LITTLE BIT.
I CAN'T DO THAT.
YOU'RE JUST A KID WHO WANTS TO ACT GROWN UP.
I'M GOING TO...
STAY AT A FRIEND'S HOUSE, SO YOU CAN STAY HERE UNTIL YOU CALM DOWN.
WHY DON'T YOU JUST ... TELL ME TO LEAVE THEN?!
AND TELL ME THAT YOU HATE SPOILED BRATS LIKE ME!!
I DON'T HATE YOU.
THAT WOULD HAVE MADE IT EASIER FOR ME TO FORGET YOU...
I LOVE YOU ...!

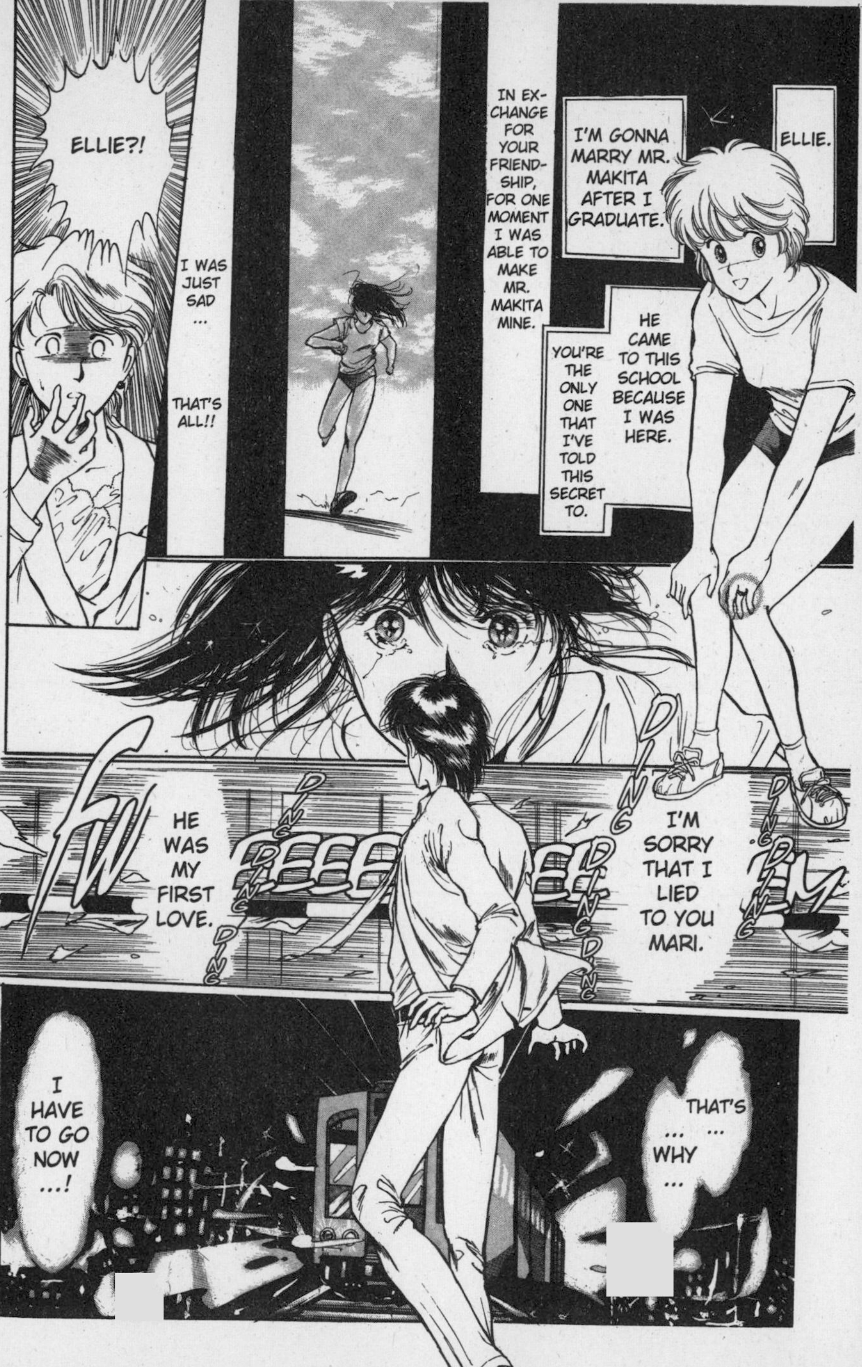
ELLIE.
I'M GONNA MARRY MR. MAKITA AFTER I GRADUATE.
HE CAME TO THIS SCHOOL BECAUSE I WAS HERE.
YOU'RE THE ONLY ONE THAT I'VE TOLD THIS SECRET TO.
IN EXCHANGE FOR YOUR FRIENDSHIP, FOR ONE MOMENT I WAS ABLE TO MAKE MR. MAKITA MINE.
I WAS JUST SAD ...
THAT'S ALL!!
ELLIE?!
DING DING
I'M SORRY THAT I LIED TO YOU MARI.
DING DING DING
FWEEEEEEEEEM
DING DING DING
HE WAS MY FIRST LOVE.
FW
THAT'S ... WHY ...
I HAVE TO GO NOW ...!

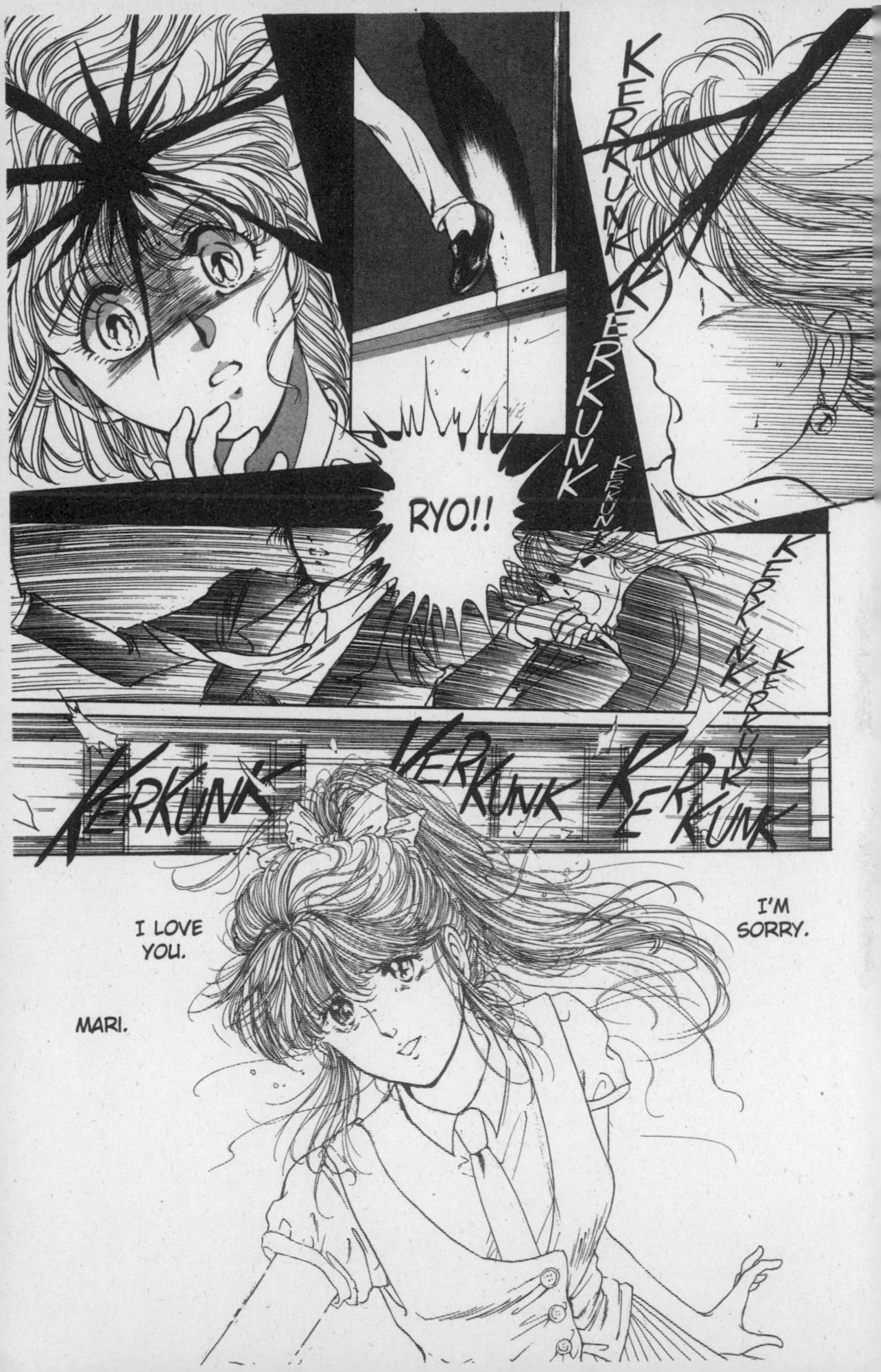
KERKUNK
KERKUNK
KERKUNK
RYO!!
KERKUNK
KERKUNK
KERKUNK
KERKUNK
KERKUNK
KERKUNK
I'M SORRY.
I LOVE YOU.
MARI.

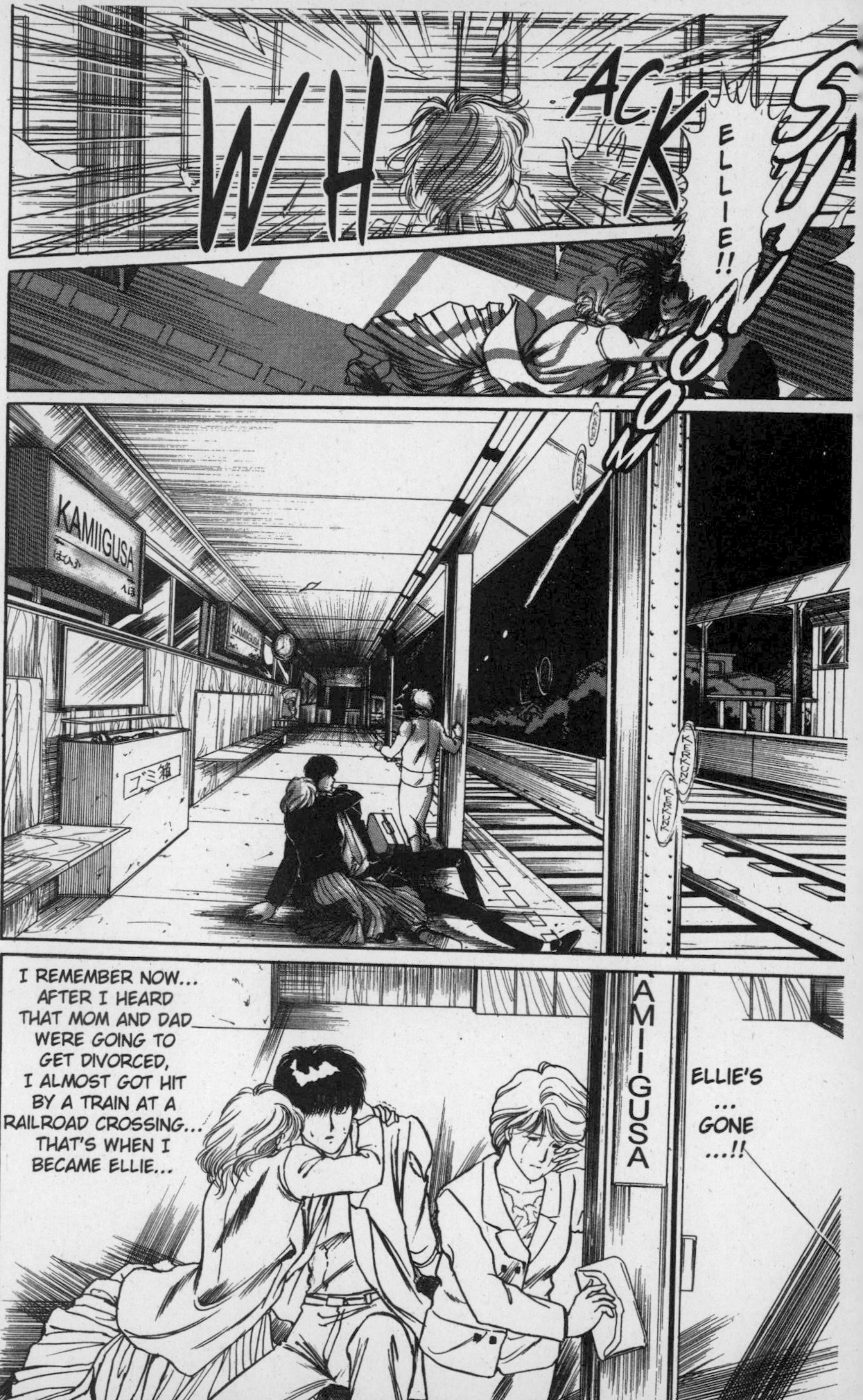
WHACK
ELLIE!!
SWOOOM
KAMIIGUSA
ゴミ箱
KERUN
KERUN
ELLIE'S ... GONE ...!!
I REMEMBER NOW... AFTER I HEARD THAT MOM AND DAD WERE GOING TO GET DIVORCED, I ALMOST GOT HIT BY A TRAIN AT A RAILROAD CROSSING... THAT'S WHEN I BECAME ELLIE...
KAMIIGUSA

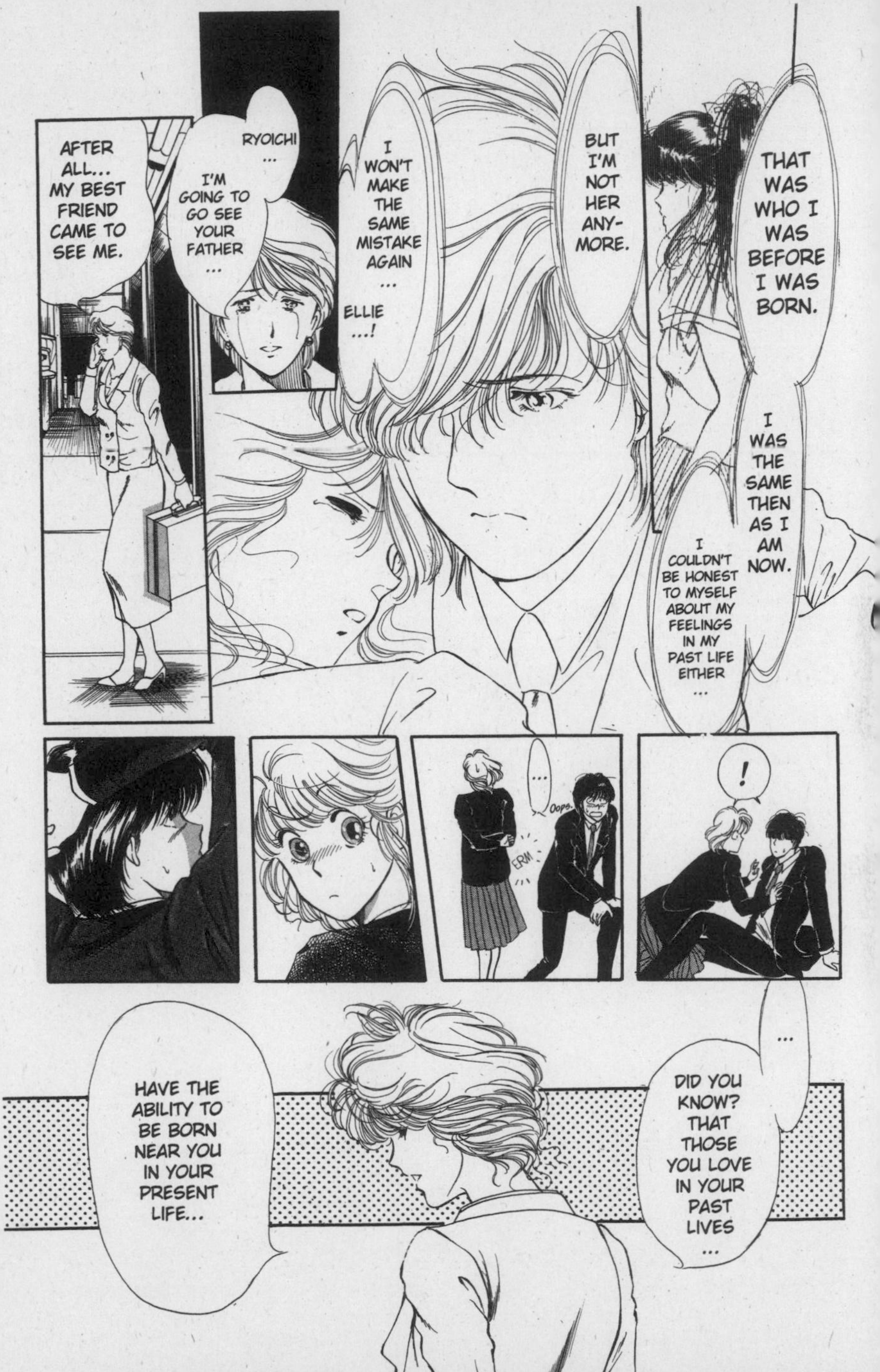
THAT WAS WHO I WAS BEFORE I WAS BORN.
I WAS THE SAME THEN AS I AM NOW.
I COULDN'T BE HONEST TO MYSELF ABOUT MY FEELINGS IN MY PAST LIFE EITHER...
BUT I'M NOT HER ANYMORE.
I WON'T MAKE THE SAME MISTAKE AGAIN...
ELLIE...!
RYOICHI...
I'M GOING TO GO SEE YOUR FATHER...
AFTER ALL... MY BEST FRIEND CAME TO SEE ME.
!
...
Oops.
ERM
...
DID YOU KNOW? THAT THOSE YOU LOVE IN YOUR PAST LIVES...
HAVE THE ABILITY TO BE BORN NEAR YOU IN YOUR PRESENT LIFE...

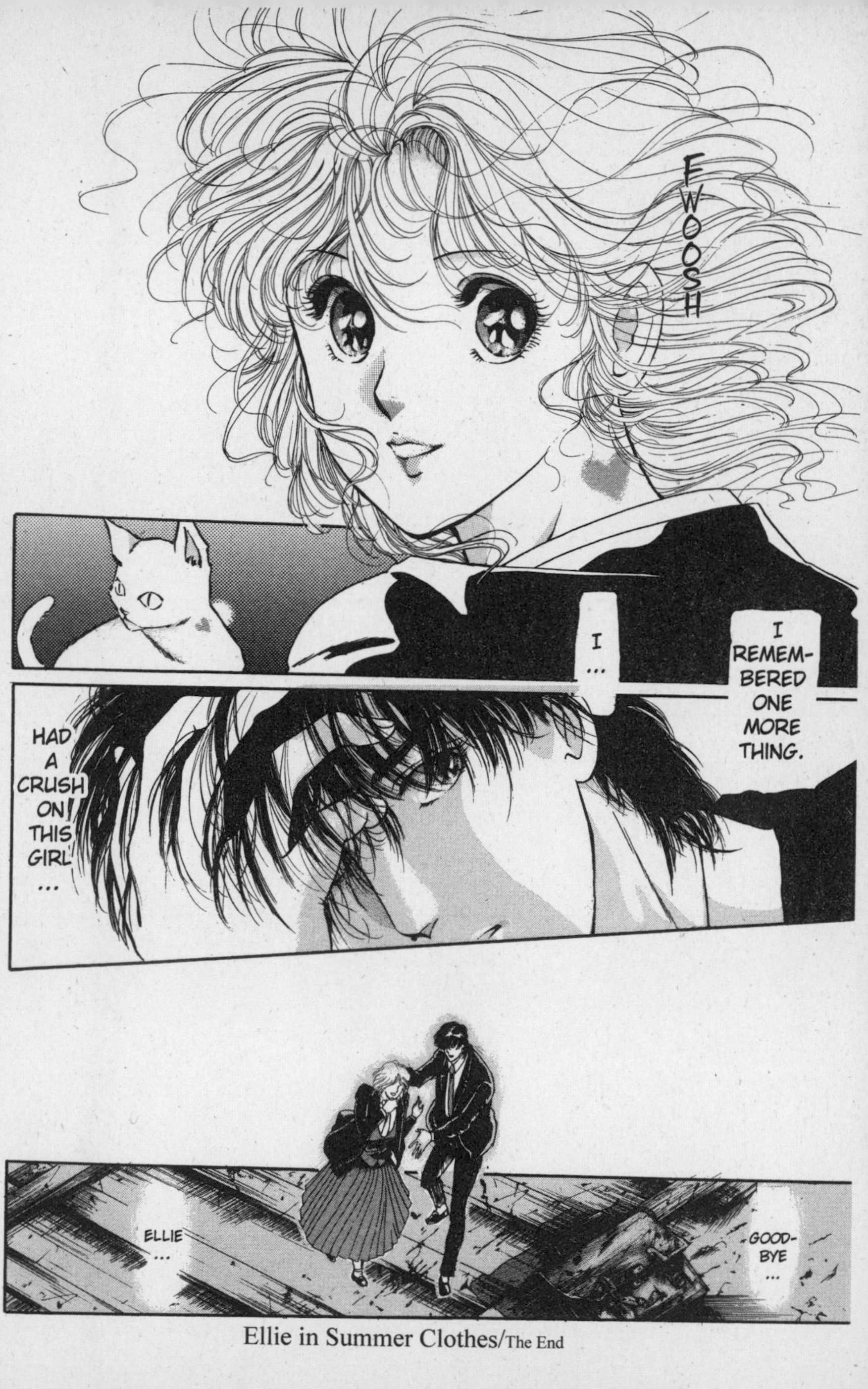
FWOOSH
I REMEMBERED ONE MORE THING.
I ...
HAD A CRUSH ON THIS GIRL ...
GOOD-BYE ...
ELLIE ...

Ellie in Summer Clothes/The End

POSTSCRIPT

The mystery of Riff.

The young manservant's secrets. If you're not interested you should skip it because it's kind of boring. '

Why does the hat look so bad on him in story 5?!(Hey) In the same story 5 why does he use such flowery language towards a young girl?! And why is his nickname, Mr. Sato?!...Who cares?' Well then, allow me to explain. (By the way in Kafka he should be called Mr. Toshio but somehow Mr. Sato seemed more appropriate...) Most likely, the average reader will not know what I'm talking about. Except for the people that are in this line of business...Some people came really close to giving me the right answer but..'' please just keep it a secret.' It's an inside joke so...It's really not big a deal though. And that childish attitude that he has with Mary...I was kind of undecided about that because I thought it might make him unlikable. But it turns out there was absolutely no reason to worry. (Everyone was nice.) It's true that his personality has changed a little bit since the beginning but he was just having a little fun by teasing Mary, that's all. It would have been scary if he'd been serious.

I received some letters that asked me, "When Riff left, how did Cain get by on his own?" Also, "He should be able to dress himself and tie his own shoelaces anyway." Well, Cain does know how to do those things by himself. But it's a form of communication between the two of them because they've been together so long that they're almost like father and child. That's also the time that they talk about things that are unrelated to work. Plus the English social hierarchy was so strict back then that some servants said that they preferred condescending masters. Lately, Riff is almost like Cain's mother...is what I've been thinking. Cain used to cry on Riff when he was young so he gets nostalgic when he smells the scent of Riff's crisp white shirt... That's why he still kind of acts like a kid around him. And Riff is the oldest of his siblings and he lost his younger brother so... Huh.? What am I saying?'

Now that I think about it, I received a letter regarding the subject of English butlers. Here's a little excerpt. "A butler is employed by aristocrats and nobles to run the affairs of their households. They live in servant's quarters within their master's household. Because they are required to consider their master's family to be more important than their own, this profession is more suited to bachelors." Is what they said. I see. But the next part gets more interesting. "Traditionally 50% of butlers are homosexual." If they do get married, then they live in a separate section of the house with their family." A...are you serious?! Close to half of them are...? That's scary. But until 1967, it was illegal to be homosexual in England. (Why do I know about that?) Traditionally huh...? That's England for you. Also, "It was forbidden for the master and his servants to have a relationship." Well, I'm sure that was true. Or else how would anyone get any work done? Thank you for this interesting letter.
I wrote a lot this time. I wonder if anybody's reading it.

I don't know what I was thinking when I did this illustration. It looks good on him though.

By the way...after "Kafka" there's a piece called "Ellie in Summer Clothes"... Which is actually my debut piece. Oh man. It looks so terrible. What the hell is this?!... Is probably what you thought right? Right? Right? Well you're right. I was against including it in this volume until the very end. But...we didn't have enough pages to fill the book so... Oh man I am so embarrassed!! Why am I dashing the hopes of all the people out there who want to become shojo manga artists? By the way, I wrote that when I was still in my teens... Whoa. This is a dream...! Forget about it! I never wanted to see it again if I could've helped it... My manager claims that he can "see in it the origin of my present style." Whatever... Looking at work I've done in the past is never easy... I wonder if they're going to put out some more. I really hope not.

I saw something really interesting the recently...;
I saw a f...fanzine of The Earl Cain Series.
Wow, that's always been a dream of mine from way back. I never knew anyone would take the time to parody my work.♡ Well they might not publish anymore volumes. If...one of you finds a copy please write to me and tell me what it's like. (Better yet please send me a copy if you can...!) Regardless of the content, it's OK with me.♡ I want to see it even if it is a little bit naughty... Oh I've left it to the last page but there was a request for my profile so here it is
Well then, see ya next time.♡

Born: December 18th. Sign: Sagittarius.
Blood type: B Sex: Female I think...
Personality: Quick to be interested in something and then quick to get bored with it. HP and MP 0. Things I like: ZABADAK, Nintendo, Rupert Graves, lace(frilly ones), cats, movies, cheesecake, dollhouses, coffee, long naps, the moon, salmon pink tulips, babies' breath, Alice In Wonderland, and tragic love.

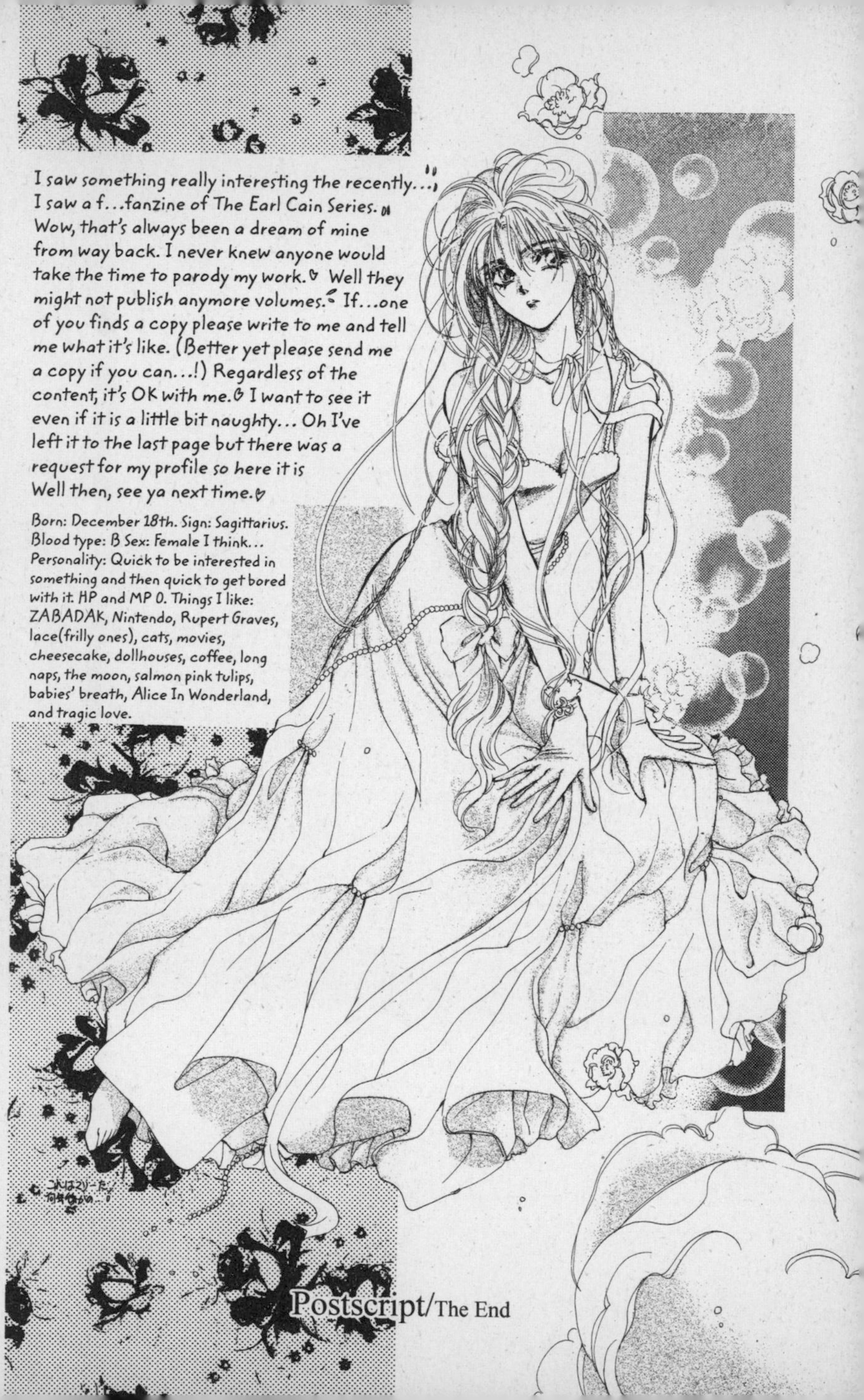

Postscript/The End

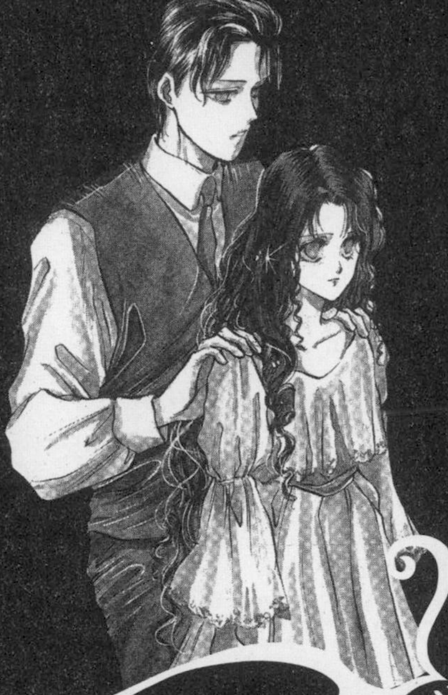

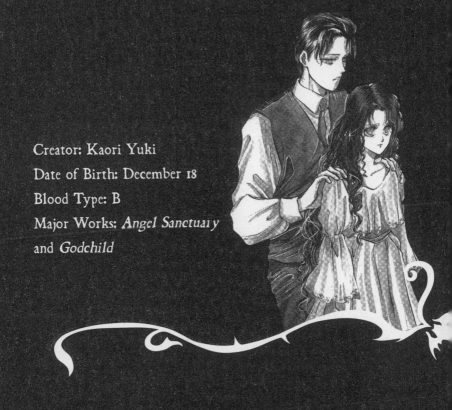

Creator: Kaori Yuki

Date of Birth: December 18

Blood Type: B

Major Works: *Angel Sanctuary* and *Godchild*

Kaori Yuki was born in Tokyo and started drawing at a very early age. Following her debut work *Natsufuku no Erie* (Ellie in Summer Clothes) in the Japanese magazine *Bessatsu Hana to Yume* (1987), she wrote a compelling series of short stories: *Zankoku na Douwatachi* (Cruel Fairy Tales), *Neji* (Screw), and *Sareki Ôkoku* (Gravel Kingdom).

As proven by her best-selling series *Angel Sanctuary* and *Godchild*, her celebrated body of work has etched an indelible mark on the gothic comics genre. She likes mysteries and British films, and is a fan of the movie *Dead Poets Society* and the show *Twin Peaks*.

THE CAIN SAGA, vol. 3
The Shojo Beat Manga Edition

STORY & ART BY KAORI YUKI

Translation/Akira Watanabe
Touch-up Art & Lettering/James Gaubatz
Design/Izumi Evers
Editor/Joel Enos

Managing Editor/Megan Bates
Editorial Director/Elizabeth Kawasaki
VP & Editor in Chief/Yumi Hoashi
Sr. Director of Acquisitions/Rika Inouye
Sr. VP of Marketing/Liza Coppola
Exec. VP of Sales & Marketing/John Easum
Publisher/Hyoe Narita

Printed in Canada

Published by VIZ Media, LLC
P.O. Box 77010
San Francisco, CA 94107

Shojo Beat Manga Edition
10 9 8 7 6 5 4 3 2 1
First printing, February 2007

PARENTAL ADVISORY
THE CAIN SAGA is rated M for Mature and is recommended for mature readers.
Contains graphic violence and adult themes.

store.viz.com

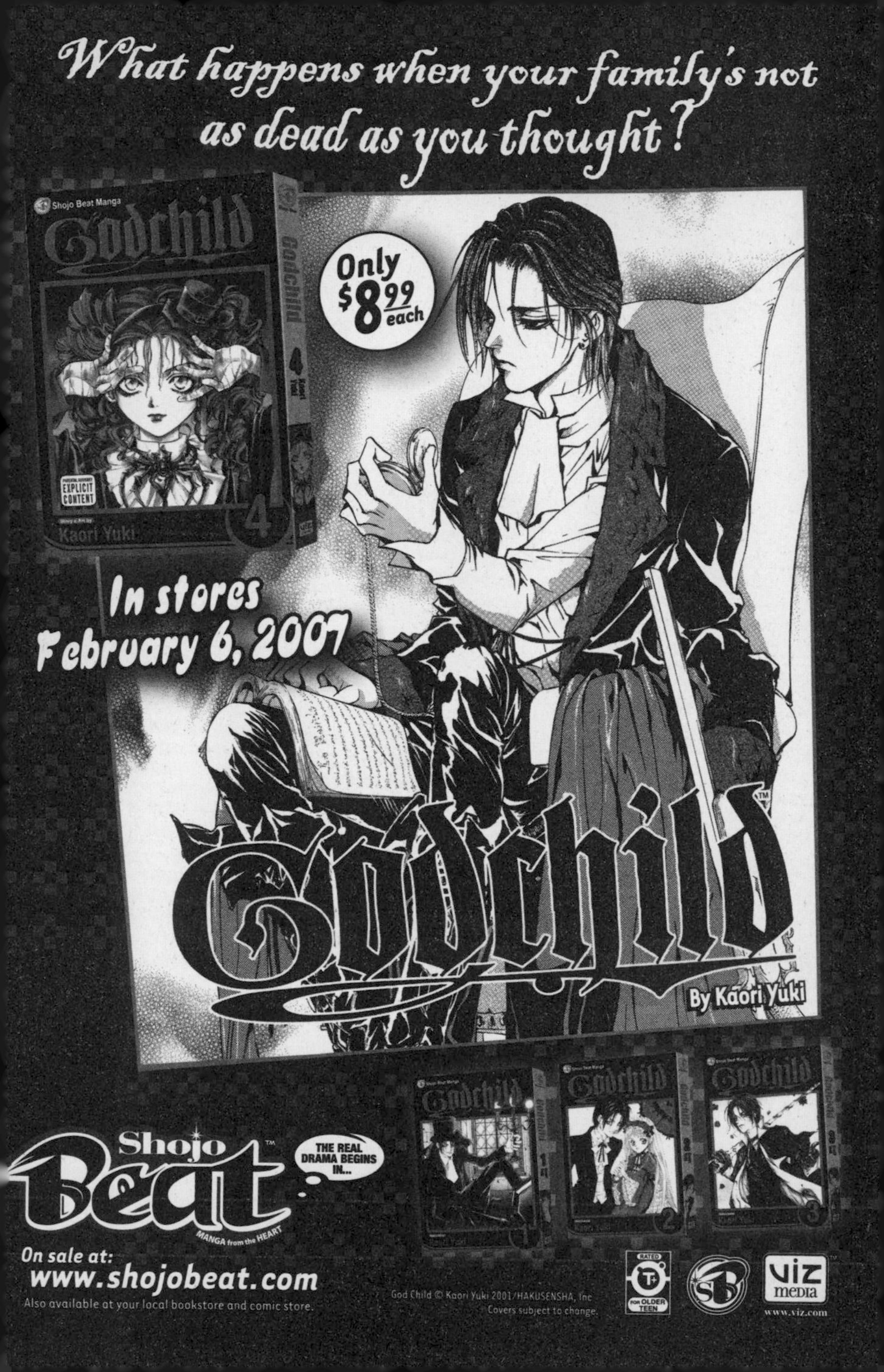
What happens when your family's not as dead as you thought?
Only $8.99 each
In stores February 6, 2007
Godchild
By Kaori Yuki
Shojo Beat
MANGA from the HEART
THE REAL DRAMA BEGINS IN...
On sale at:
www.shojobeat.com
Also available at your local bookstore and comic store.
God Child © Kaori Yuki 2001/HAKUSENSHA, Inc
Covers subject to change.
RATED T+ FOR OLDER TEEN
viz media
www.viz.com

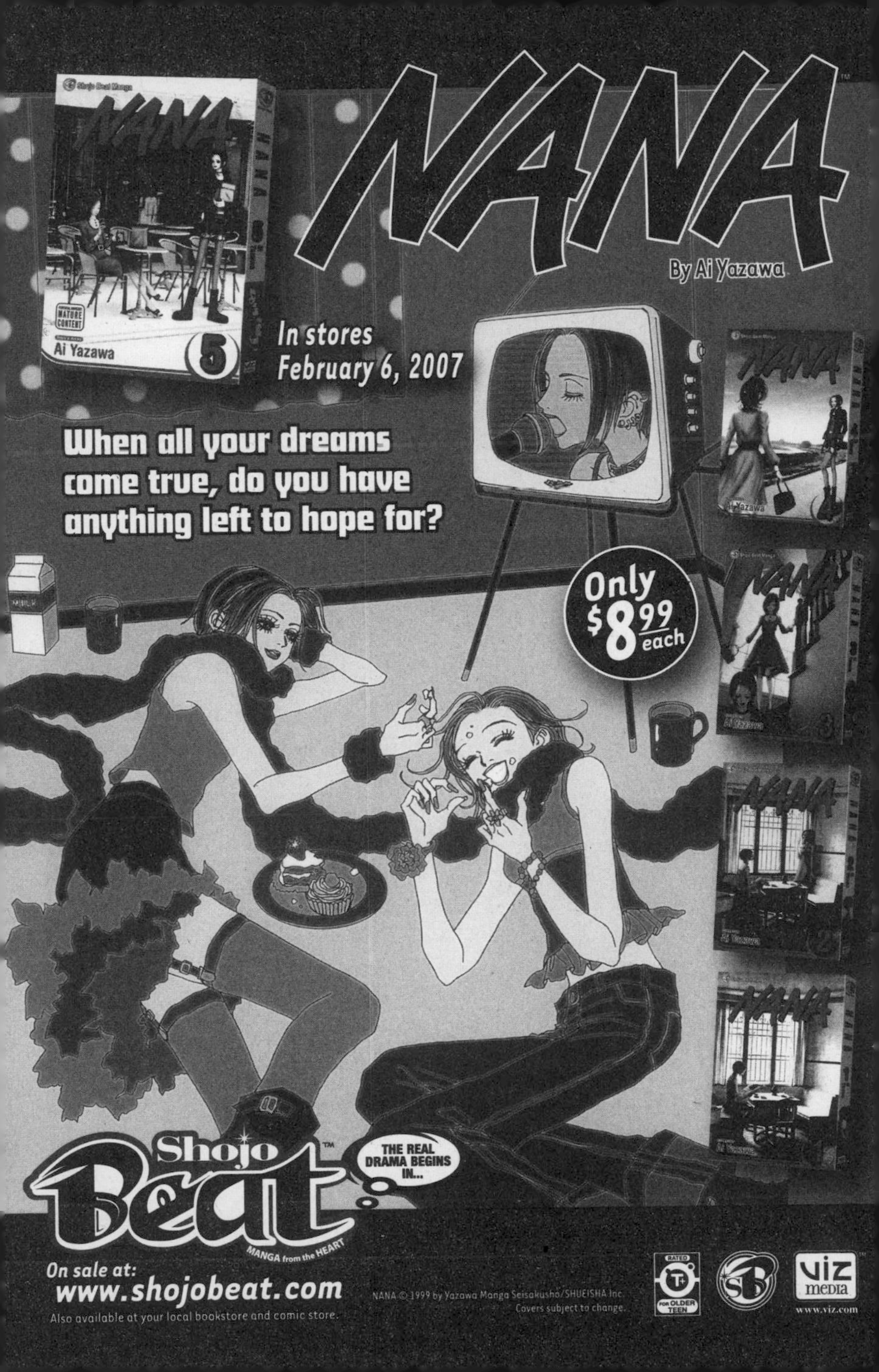
NANA™
By Ai Yazawa
In stores February 6, 2007
When all your dreams come true, do you have anything left to hope for?
Only $8.99 each
Shojo Beat™
MANGA from the HEART
THE REAL DRAMA BEGINS IN...
On sale at:
www.shojobeat.com
Also available at your local bookstore and comic store.
NANA © 1999 by Yazawa Manga Seisakusho/SHUEISHA Inc.
Covers subject to change.
RATED T+ FOR OLDER TEEN
viz media
www.viz.com

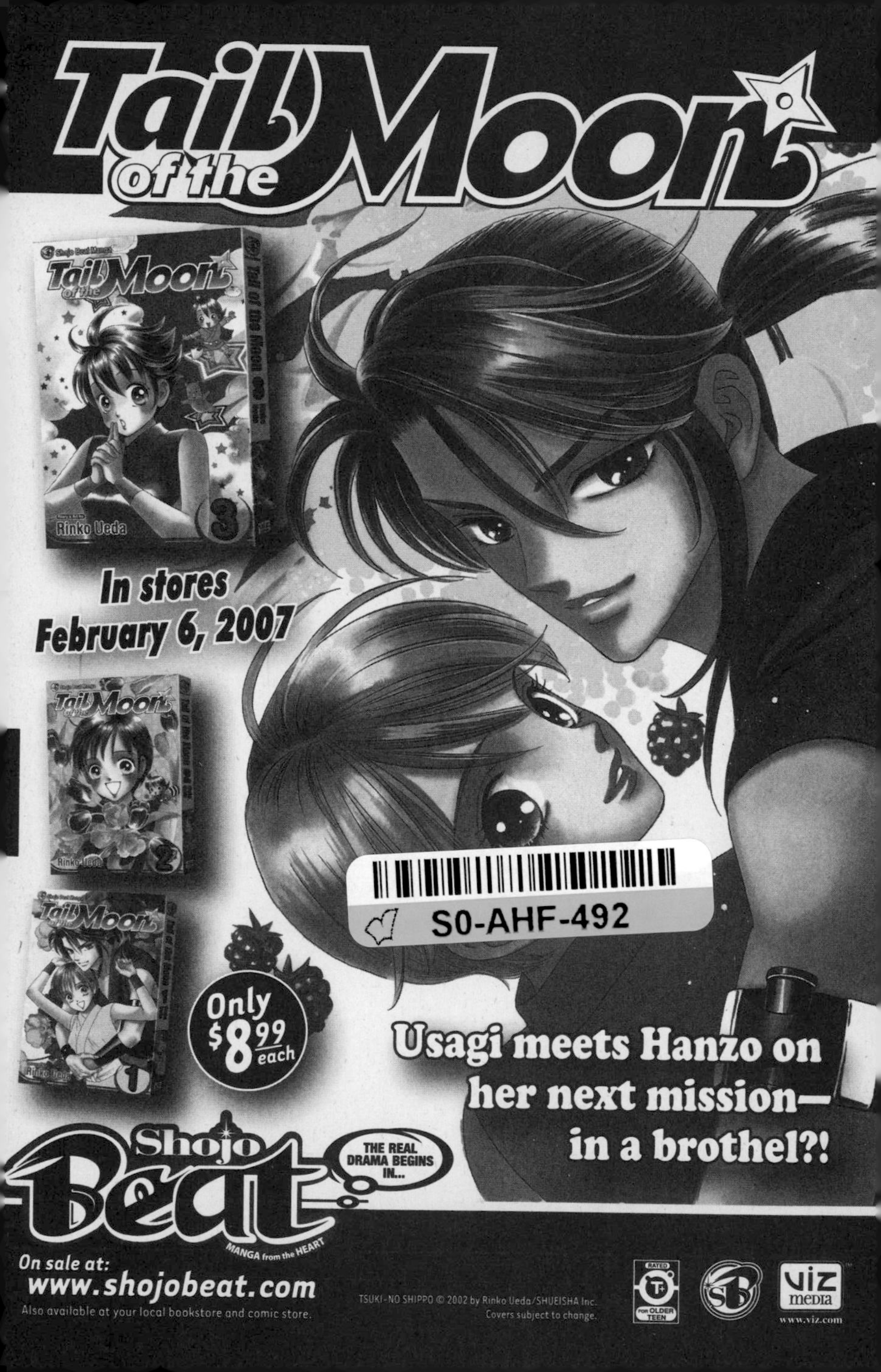

Tail of the Moon
Tail of the Moon 3
Rinko Ueda
In stores February 6, 2007
Tail of the Moon 2
Rinko Ueda
Tail of the Moon 1
Rinko Ueda
Only $8.99 each
S0-AHF-492
Usagi meets Hanzo on her next mission—in a brothel?!
Shojo Beat
THE REAL DRAMA BEGINS IN...
MANGA from the HEART
On sale at:
www.shojobeat.com
Also available at your local bookstore and comic store.
TSUKI-NO SHIPPO © 2002 by Rinko Ueda/SHUEISHA Inc.
Covers subject to change.
RATED T+ FOR OLDER TEEN
viz media
www.viz.com